WRITTEN BY
MARK SABLE

ART BY
ROBBI RODRIGUEZ

GREY TONES
NICK FILARDI

LETTERS & DESIGN
KRISTYN FERRETTI

LOGO
FONOGRAFIKS

CHAPTER

1

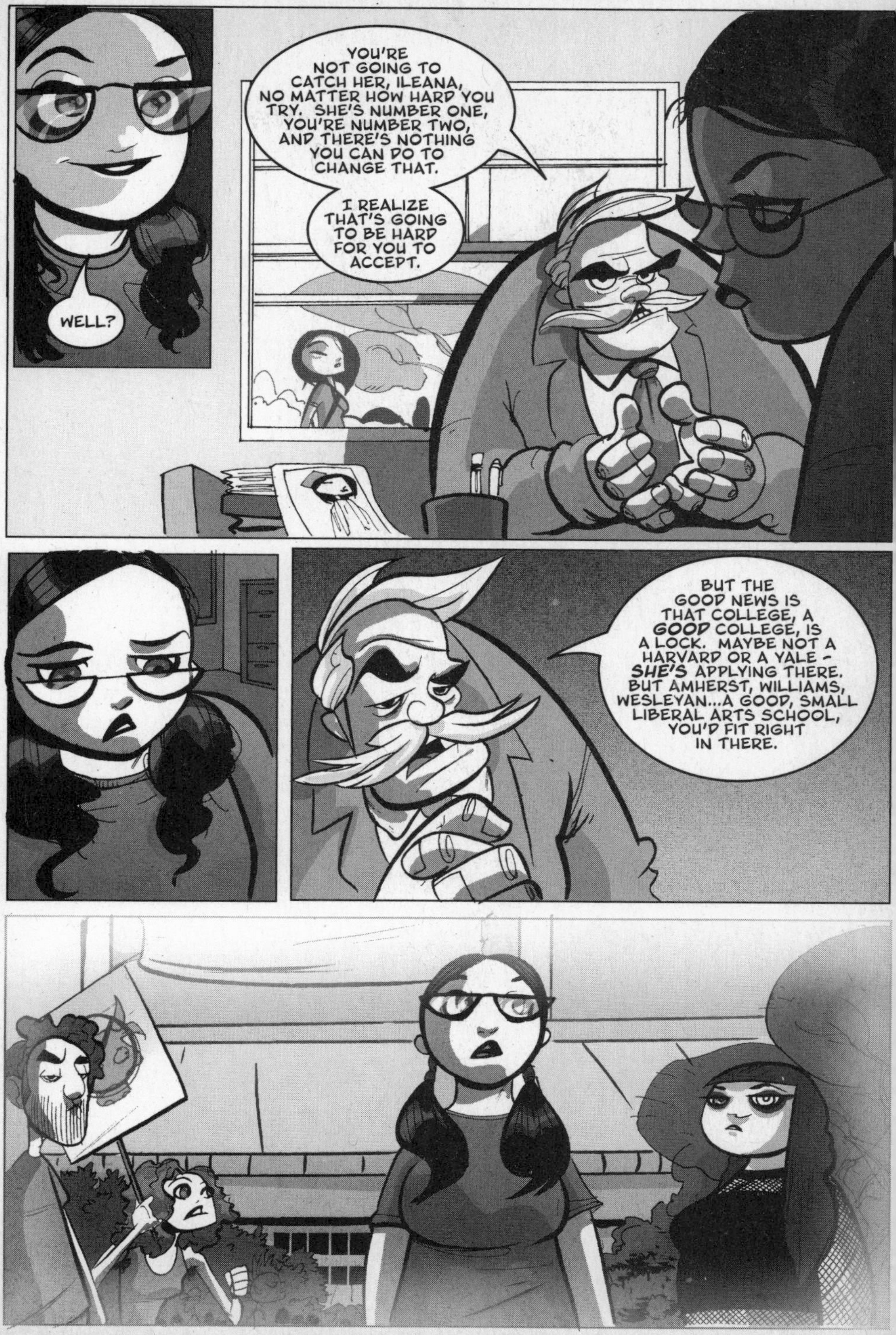
WELL?
YOU'RE NOT GOING TO CATCH HER, ILEANA, NO MATTER HOW HARD YOU TRY. SHE'S NUMBER ONE, YOU'RE NUMBER TWO, AND THERE'S NOTHING YOU CAN DO TO CHANGE THAT.
I REALIZE THAT'S GOING TO BE HARD FOR YOU TO ACCEPT.
BUT THE GOOD NEWS IS THAT COLLEGE, A GOOD COLLEGE, IS A LOCK. MAYBE NOT A HARVARD OR A YALE - SHE'S APPLYING THERE. BUT AMHERST, WILLIAMS, WESLEYAN...A GOOD, SMALL LIBERAL ARTS SCHOOL, YOU'D FIT RIGHT IN THERE.

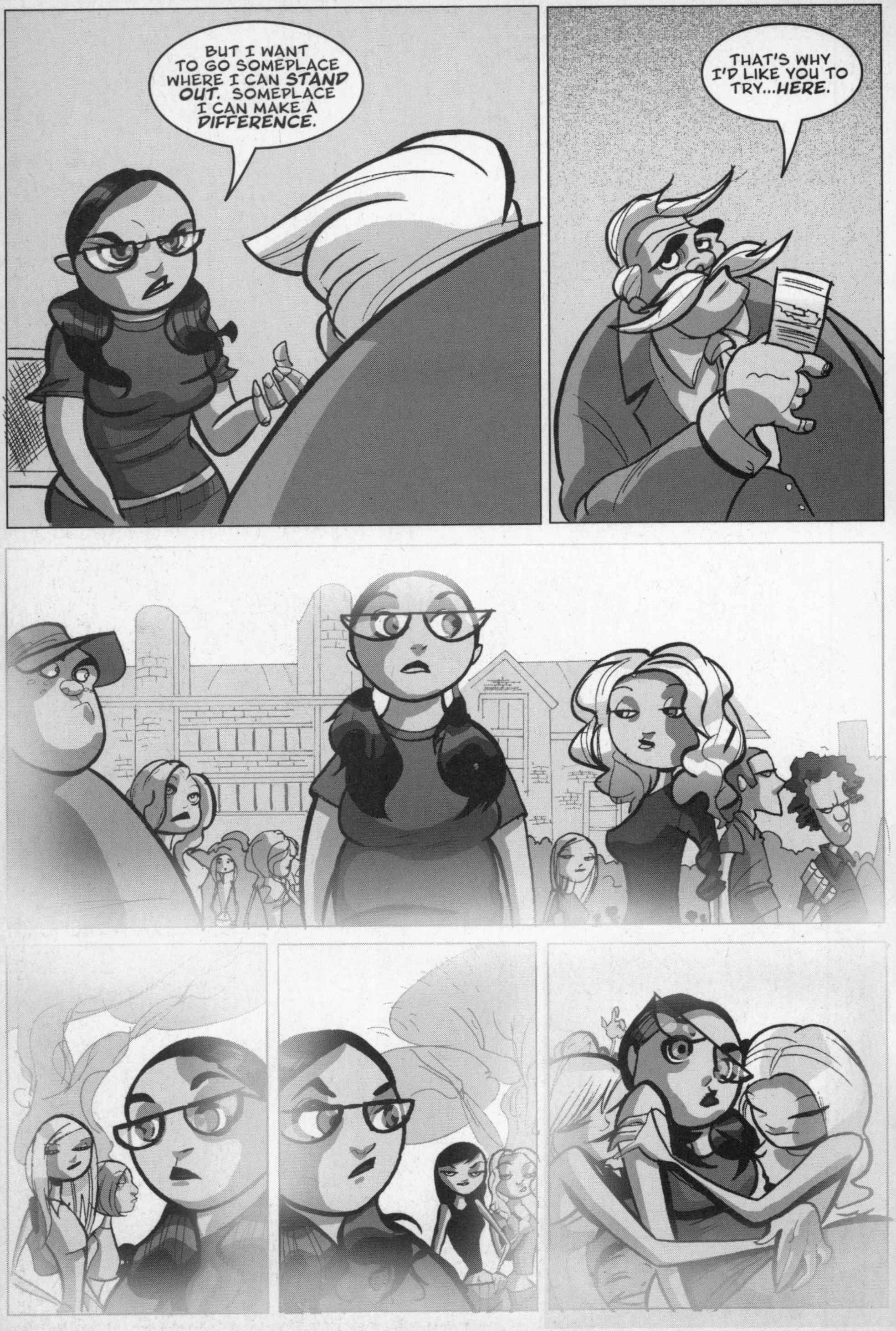
BUT I WANT TO GO SOMEPLACE WHERE I CAN STAND OUT. SOMEPLACE I CAN MAKE A DIFFERENCE.
THAT'S WHY I'D LIKE YOU TO TRY...HERE.

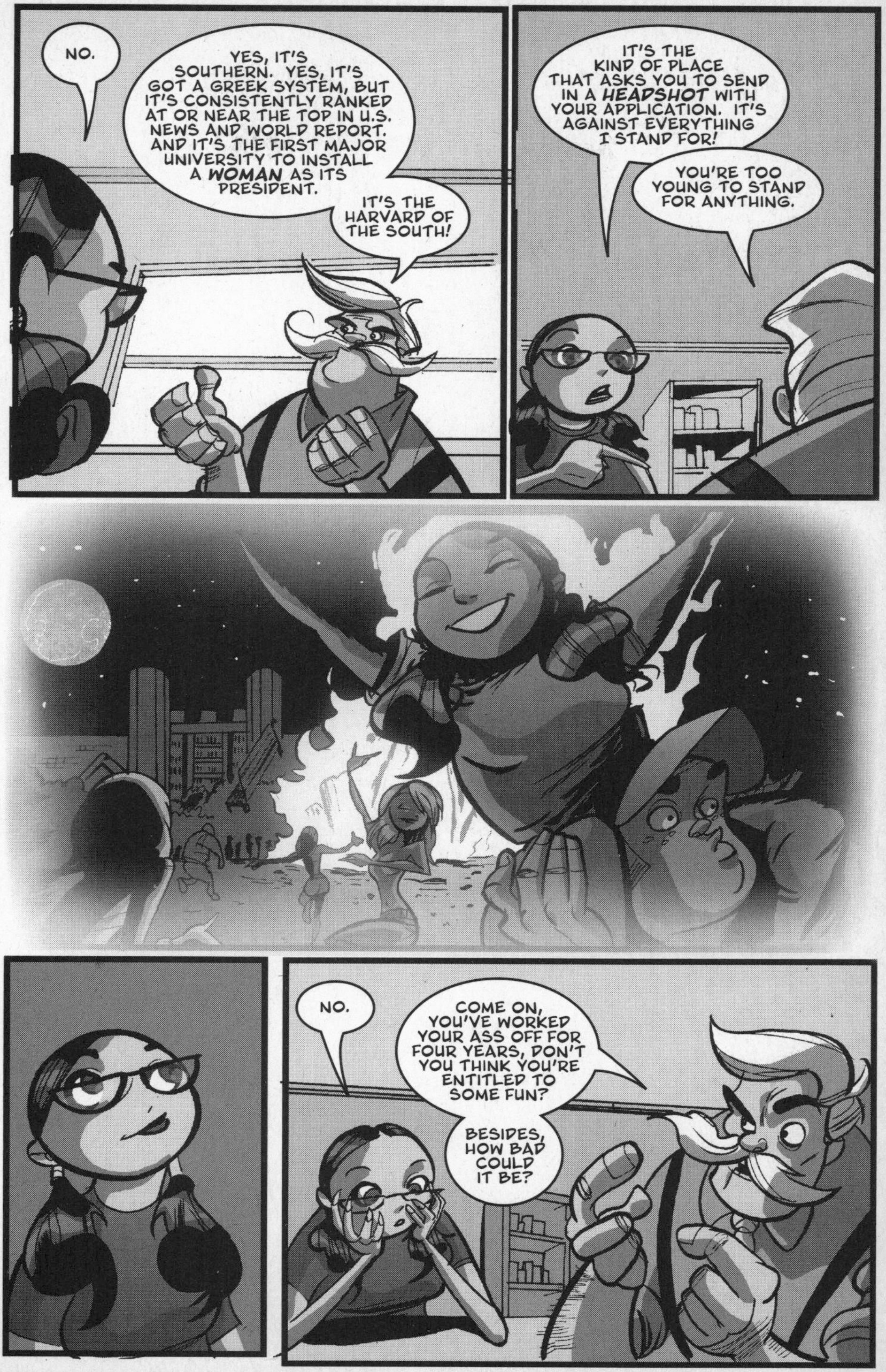
NO.
YES, IT'S SOUTHERN. YES, IT'S GOT A GREEK SYSTEM, BUT IT'S CONSISTENTLY RANKED AT OR NEAR THE TOP IN U.S. NEWS AND WORLD REPORT. AND IT'S THE FIRST MAJOR UNIVERSITY TO INSTALL A **WOMAN** AS ITS PRESIDENT.
IT'S THE HARVARD OF THE SOUTH!
IT'S THE KIND OF PLACE THAT ASKS YOU TO SEND IN A **HEADSHOT** WITH YOUR APPLICATION. IT'S AGAINST EVERYTHING I STAND FOR!
YOU'RE TOO YOUNG TO STAND FOR ANYTHING.
NO.
COME ON, YOU'VE WORKED YOUR ASS OFF FOR FOUR YEARS, DON'T YOU THINK YOU'RE ENTITLED TO SOME FUN?
BESIDES, HOW BAD COULD IT BE?

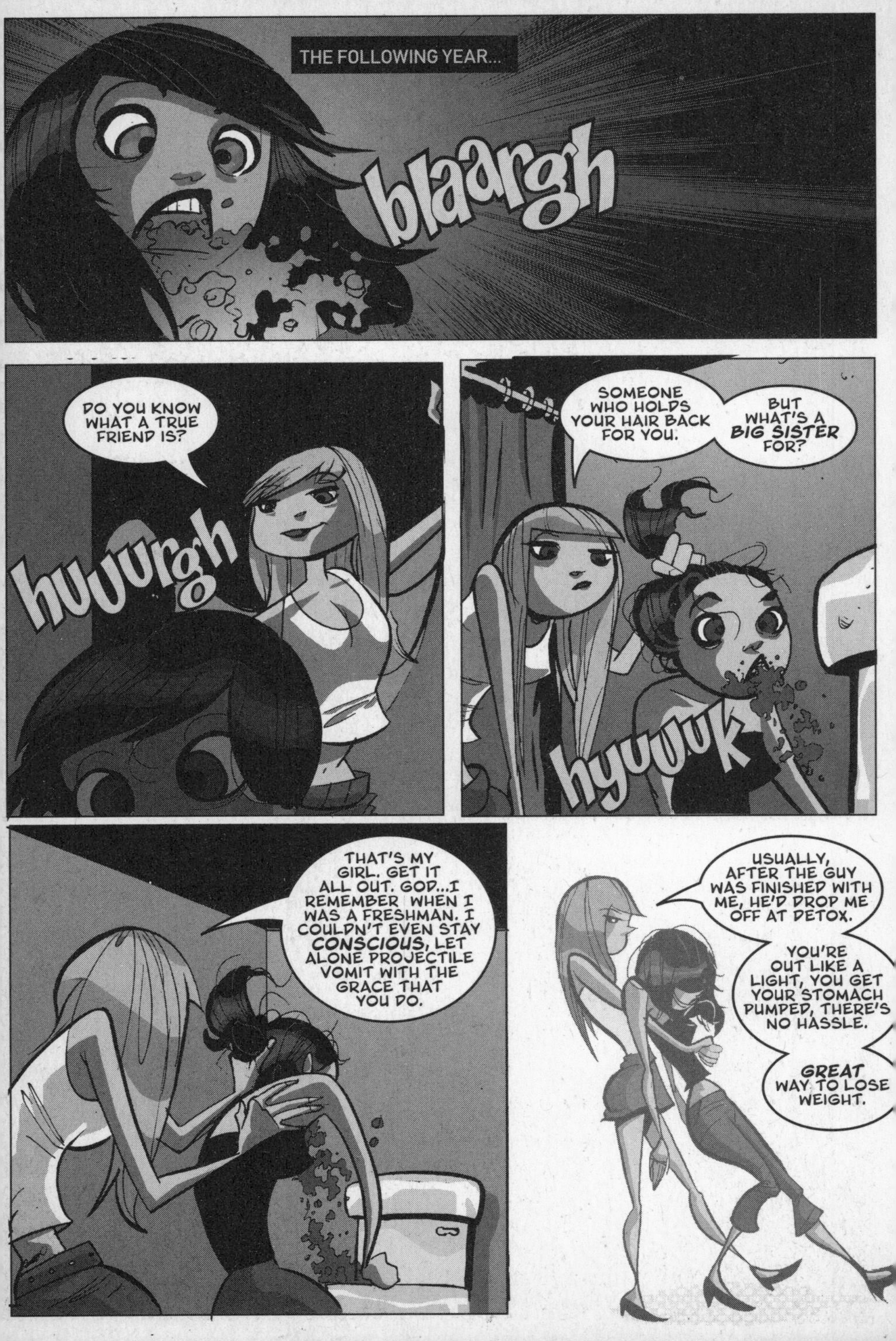
THE FOLLOWING YEAR...
blaargh
DO YOU KNOW WHAT A TRUE FRIEND IS?
huuurgh
SOMEONE WHO HOLDS YOUR HAIR BACK FOR YOU.
BUT WHAT'S A BIG SISTER FOR?
hyuuuk
THAT'S MY GIRL. GET IT ALL OUT. GOD...I REMEMBER WHEN I WAS A FRESHMAN. I COULDN'T EVEN STAY CONSCIOUS, LET ALONE PROJECTILE VOMIT WITH THE GRACE THAT YOU DO.
USUALLY, AFTER THE GUY WAS FINISHED WITH ME, HE'D DROP ME OFF AT DETOX.
YOU'RE OUT LIKE A LIGHT, YOU GET YOUR STOMACH PUMPED, THERE'S NO HASSLE.
GREAT WAY TO LOSE WEIGHT.

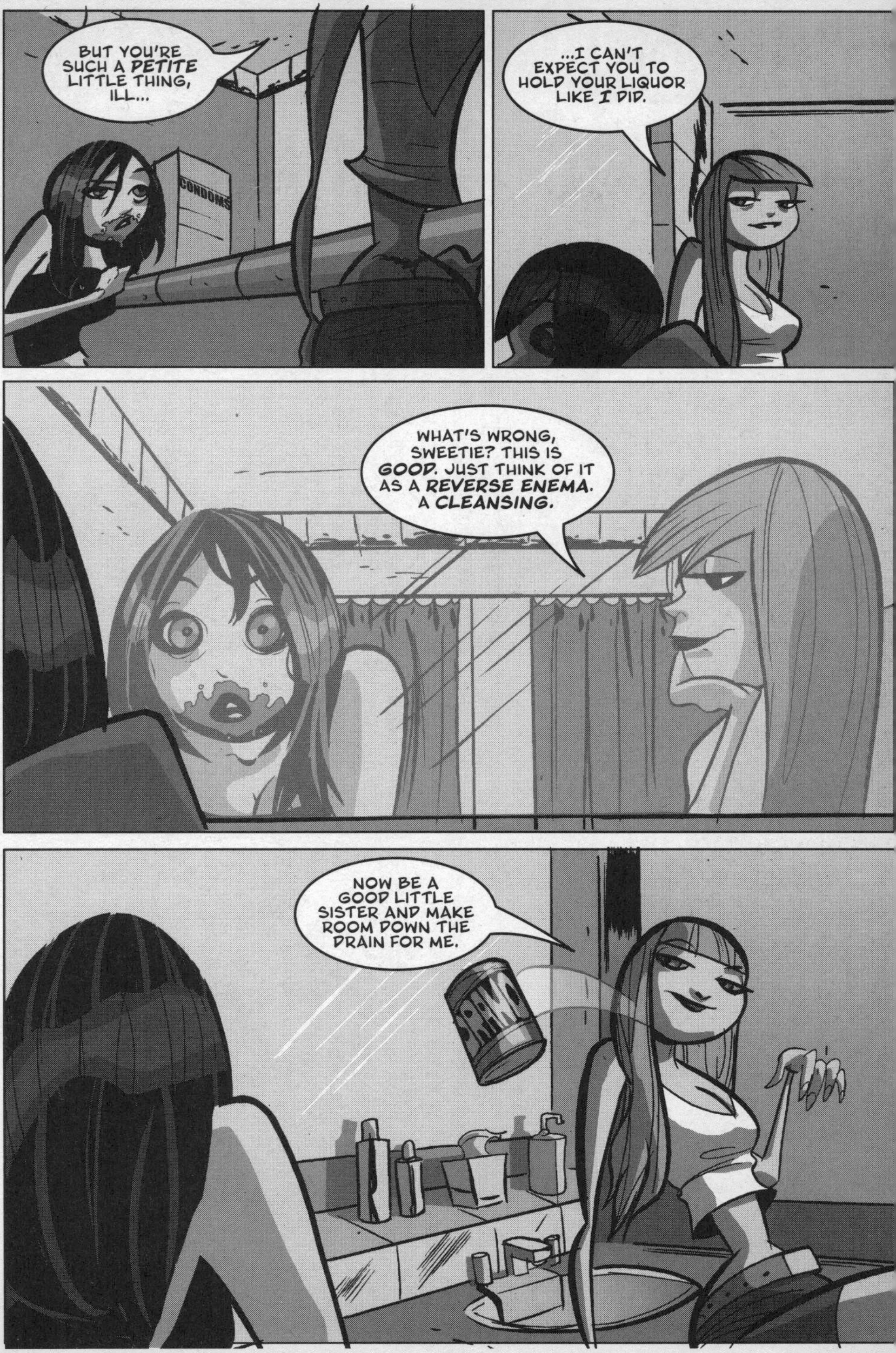
BUT YOU'RE SUCH A *PETITE* LITTLE THING, ILL...
CONDOMS
...I CAN'T EXPECT YOU TO HOLD YOUR LIQUOR LIKE *I* DID.
WHAT'S WRONG, SWEETIE? THIS IS **GOOD**. JUST THINK OF IT AS A ***REVERSE ENEMA***. A **CLEANSING**.
NOW BE A GOOD LITTLE SISTER AND MAKE ROOM DOWN THE DRAIN FOR ME.

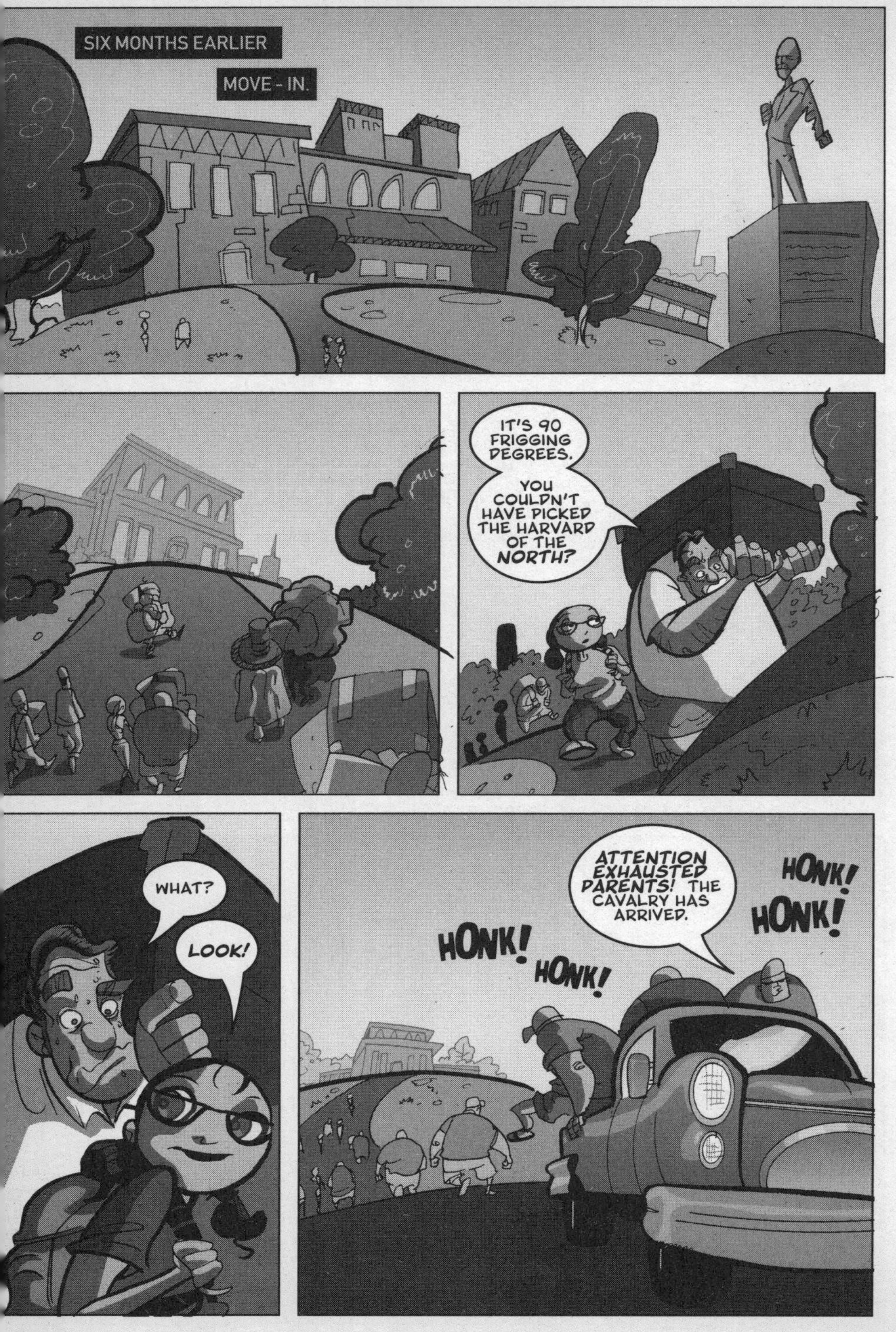

SIX MONTHS EARLIER
MOVE - IN.
IT'S 90 FRIGGING DEGREES.
YOU COULDN'T HAVE PICKED THE HARVARD OF THE NORTH?
WHAT?
LOOK!
ATTENTION EXHAUSTED PARENTS! THE CAVALRY HAS ARRIVED.
HONK! HONK!
HONK! HONK!

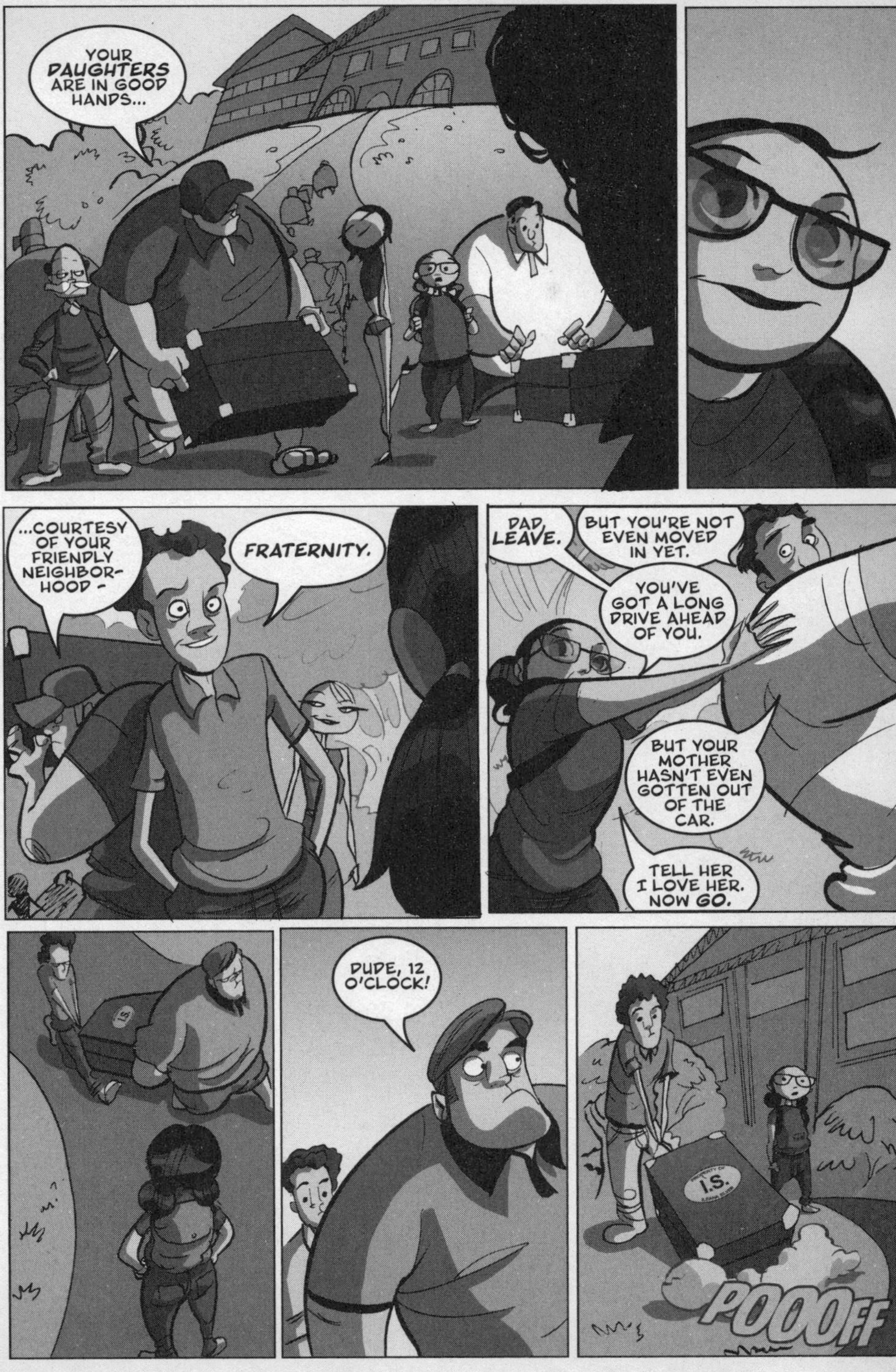
YOUR DAUGHTERS ARE IN GOOD HANDS...
...COURTESY OF YOUR FRIENDLY NEIGHBOR-HOOD -
FRATERNITY.
DAD, LEAVE.
BUT YOU'RE NOT EVEN MOVED IN YET.
YOU'VE GOT A LONG DRIVE AHEAD OF YOU.
BUT YOUR MOTHER HASN'T EVEN GOTTEN OUT OF THE CAR.
TELL HER I LOVE HER. NOW GO.
I.S.
DUDE, 12 O'CLOCK!
I.S.
POOOFF

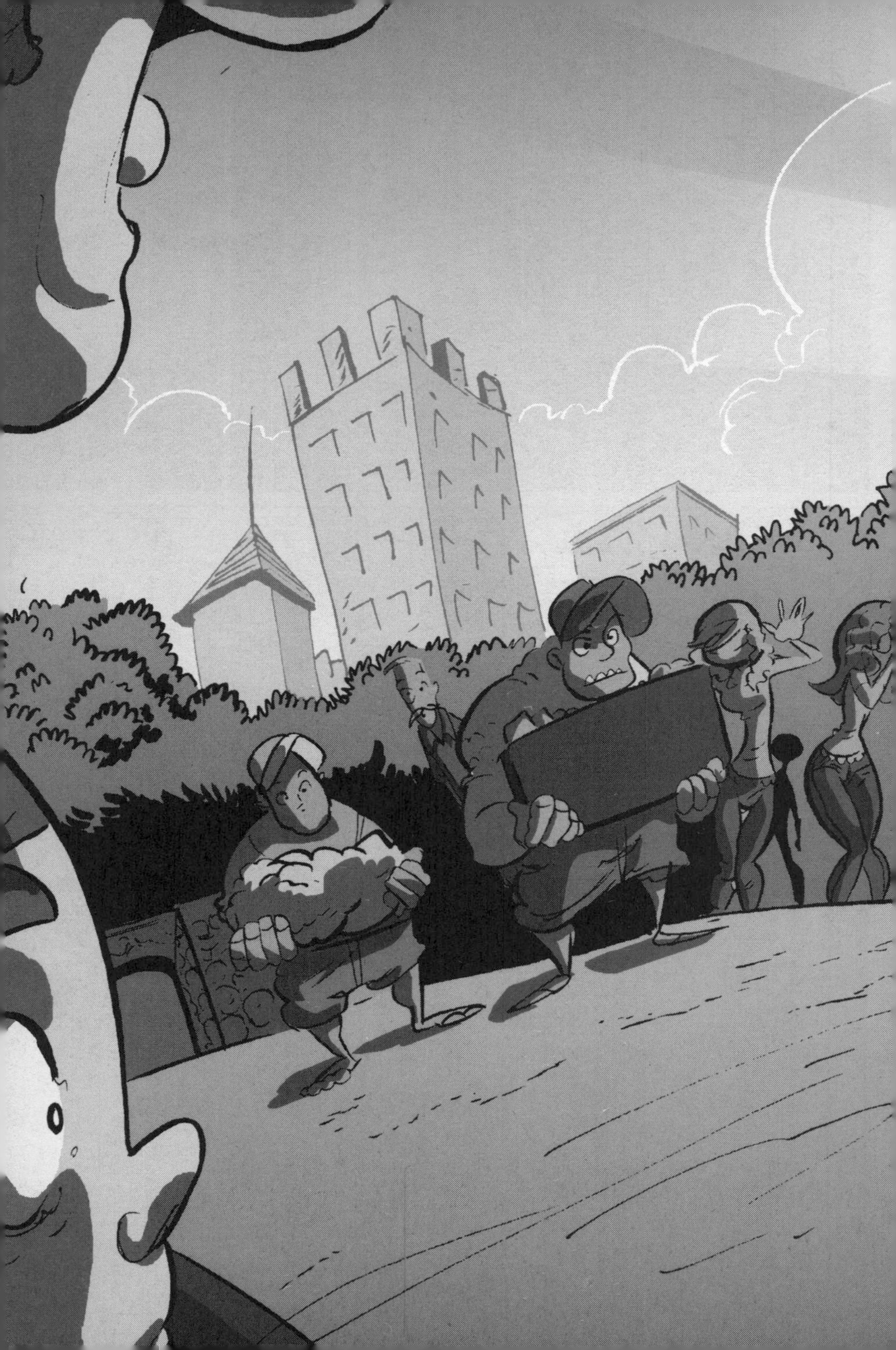

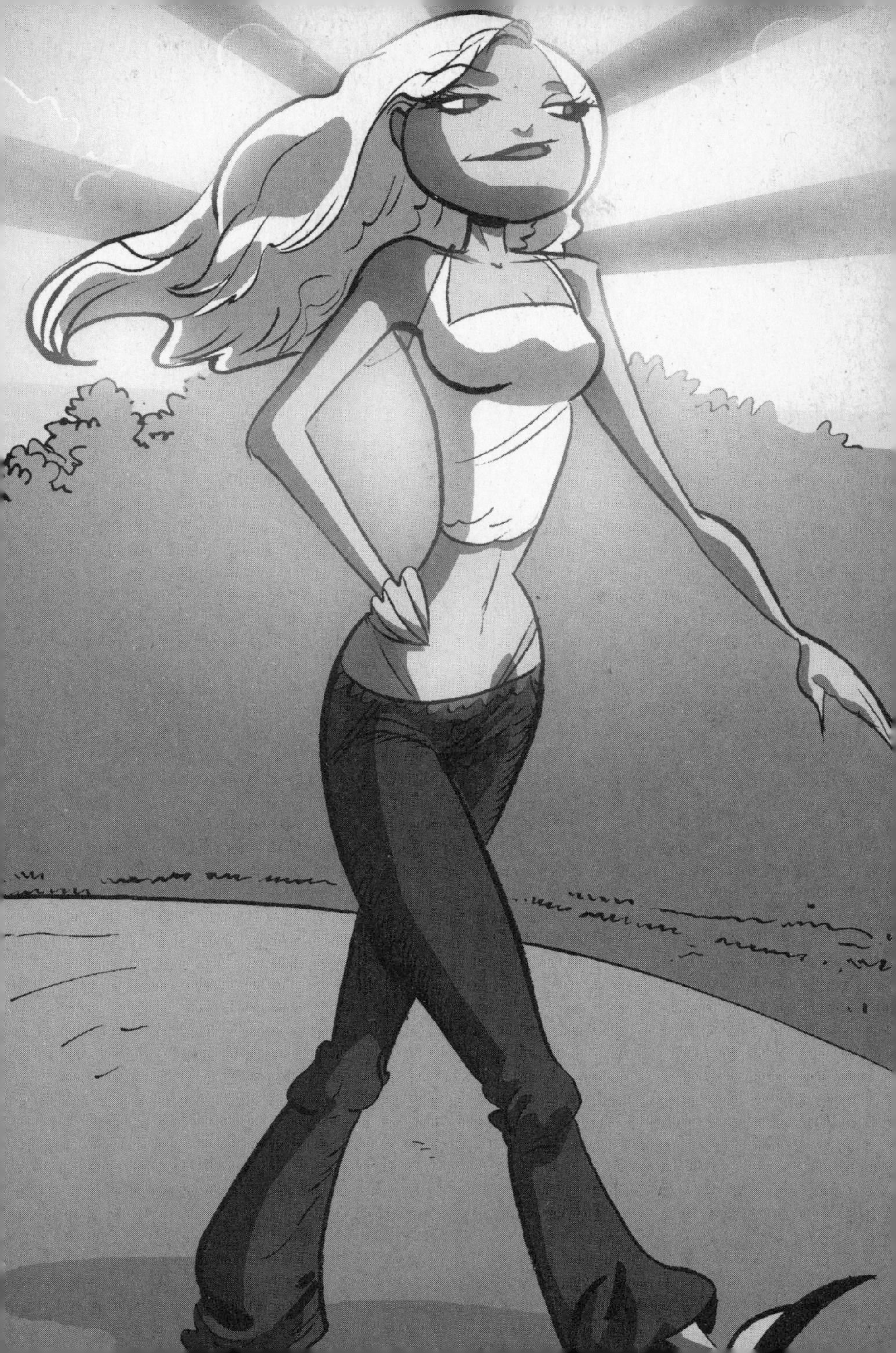

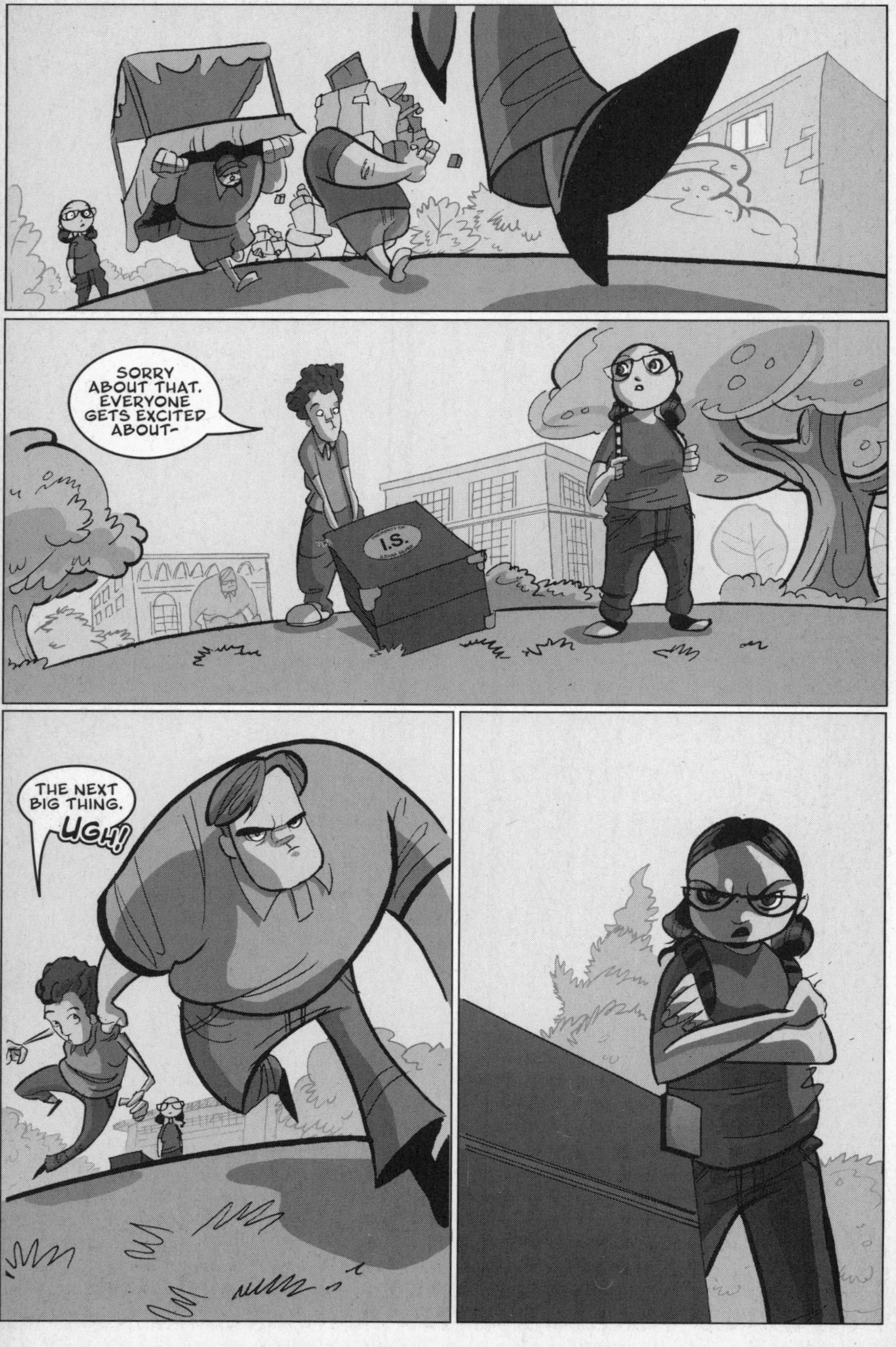
SORRY ABOUT THAT. EVERYONE GETS EXCITED ABOUT-
I.S.
THE NEXT BIG THING.
UGH!

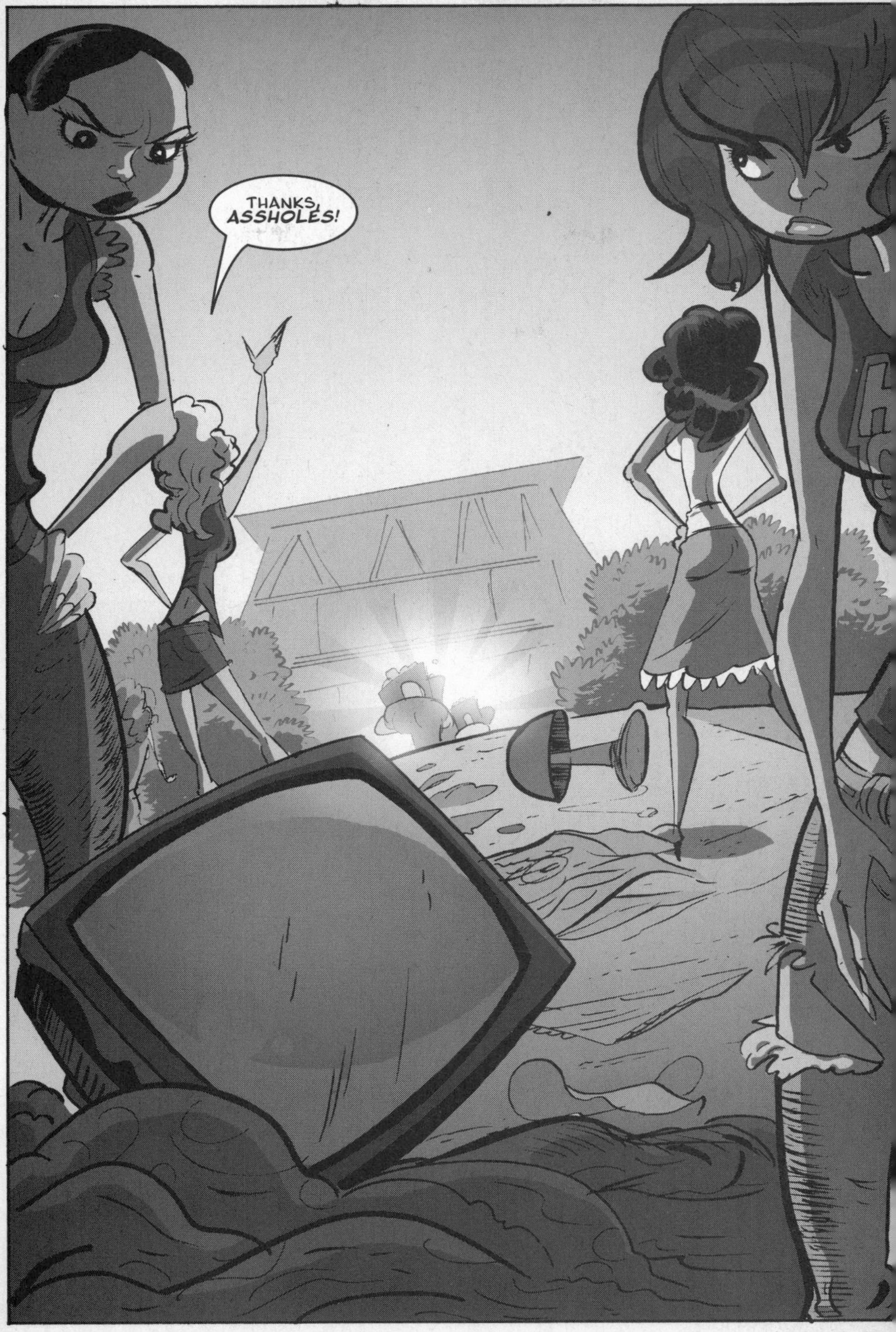
THANKS, ASSHOLES!

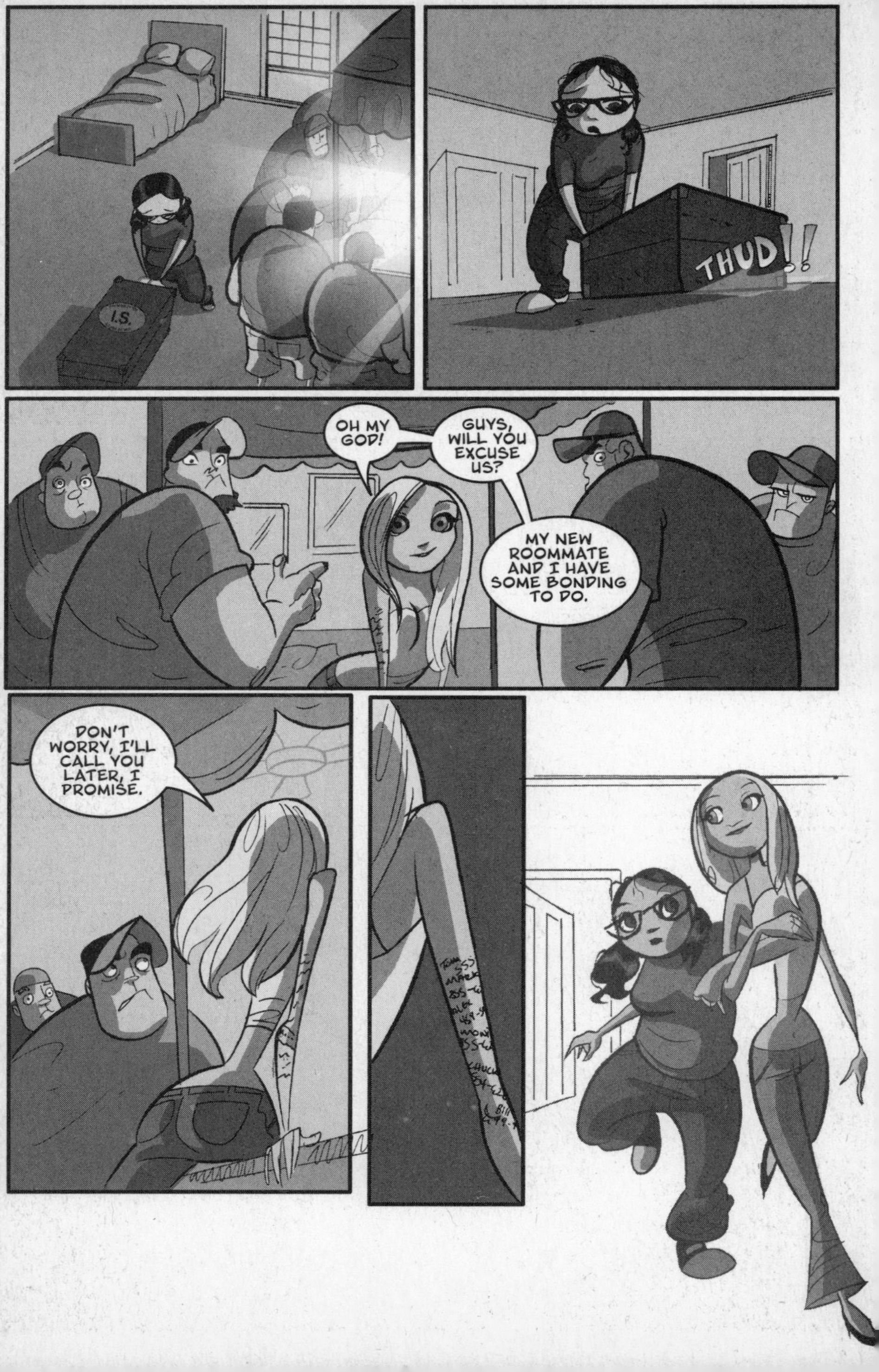
THUD!!
OH MY GOD!
GUYS, WILL YOU EXCUSE US?
MY NEW ROOMMATE AND I HAVE SOME BONDING TO DO.
DON'T WORRY, I'LL CALL YOU LATER, I PROMISE.

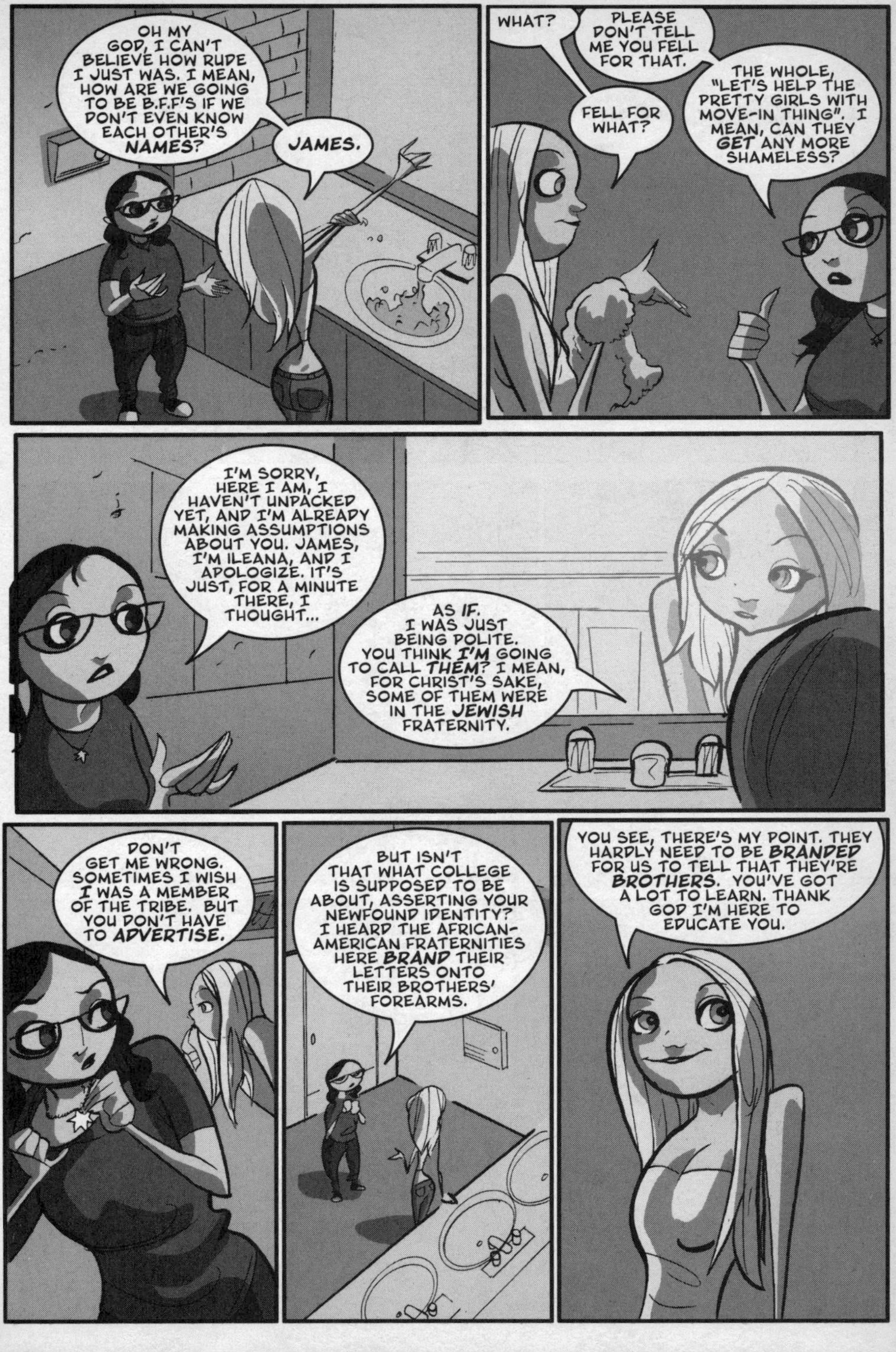
OH MY GOD, I CAN'T BELIEVE HOW RUDE I JUST WAS. I MEAN, HOW ARE WE GOING TO BE B.F.F'S IF WE DON'T EVEN KNOW EACH OTHER'S NAMES?
JAMES.
WHAT?
PLEASE DON'T TELL ME YOU FELL FOR THAT.
FELL FOR WHAT?
THE WHOLE, "LET'S HELP THE PRETTY GIRLS WITH MOVE-IN THING". I MEAN, CAN THEY GET ANY MORE SHAMELESS?
I'M SORRY, HERE I AM, I HAVEN'T UNPACKED YET, AND I'M ALREADY MAKING ASSUMPTIONS ABOUT YOU. JAMES, I'M ILEANA, AND I APOLOGIZE. IT'S JUST, FOR A MINUTE THERE, I THOUGHT...
AS IF. I WAS JUST BEING POLITE. YOU THINK I'M GOING TO CALL THEM? I MEAN, FOR CHRIST'S SAKE, SOME OF THEM WERE IN THE JEWISH FRATERNITY.
DON'T GET ME WRONG. SOMETIMES I WISH I WAS A MEMBER OF THE TRIBE. BUT YOU DON'T HAVE TO ADVERTISE.
BUT ISN'T THAT WHAT COLLEGE IS SUPPOSED TO BE ABOUT, ASSERTING YOUR NEWFOUND IDENTITY? I HEARD THE AFRICAN-AMERICAN FRATERNITIES HERE BRAND THEIR LETTERS ONTO THEIR BROTHERS' FOREARMS.
YOU SEE, THERE'S MY POINT. THEY HARDLY NEED TO BE BRANDED FOR US TO TELL THAT THEY'RE BROTHERS. YOU'VE GOT A LOT TO LEARN. THANK GOD I'M HERE TO EDUCATE YOU.

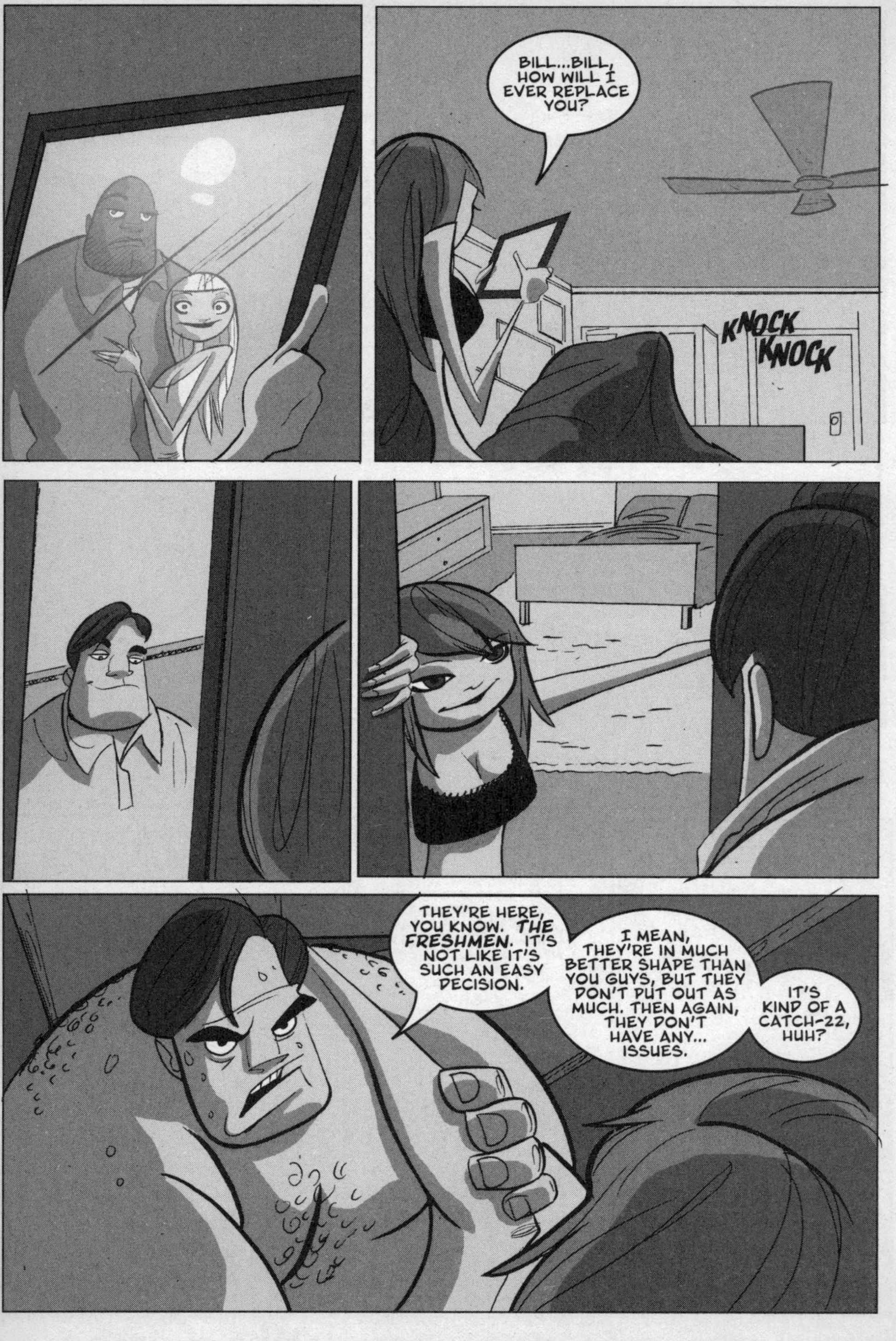
BILL...BILL, HOW WILL I EVER REPLACE YOU?
KNOCK KNOCK
THEY'RE HERE, YOU KNOW. *THE FRESHMEN.* IT'S NOT LIKE IT'S SUCH AN EASY DECISION.
I MEAN, THEY'RE IN MUCH BETTER SHAPE THAN YOU GUYS, BUT THEY DON'T PUT OUT AS MUCH. THEN AGAIN, THEY DON'T HAVE ANY... ISSUES.
IT'S KIND OF A CATCH-22, HUH?

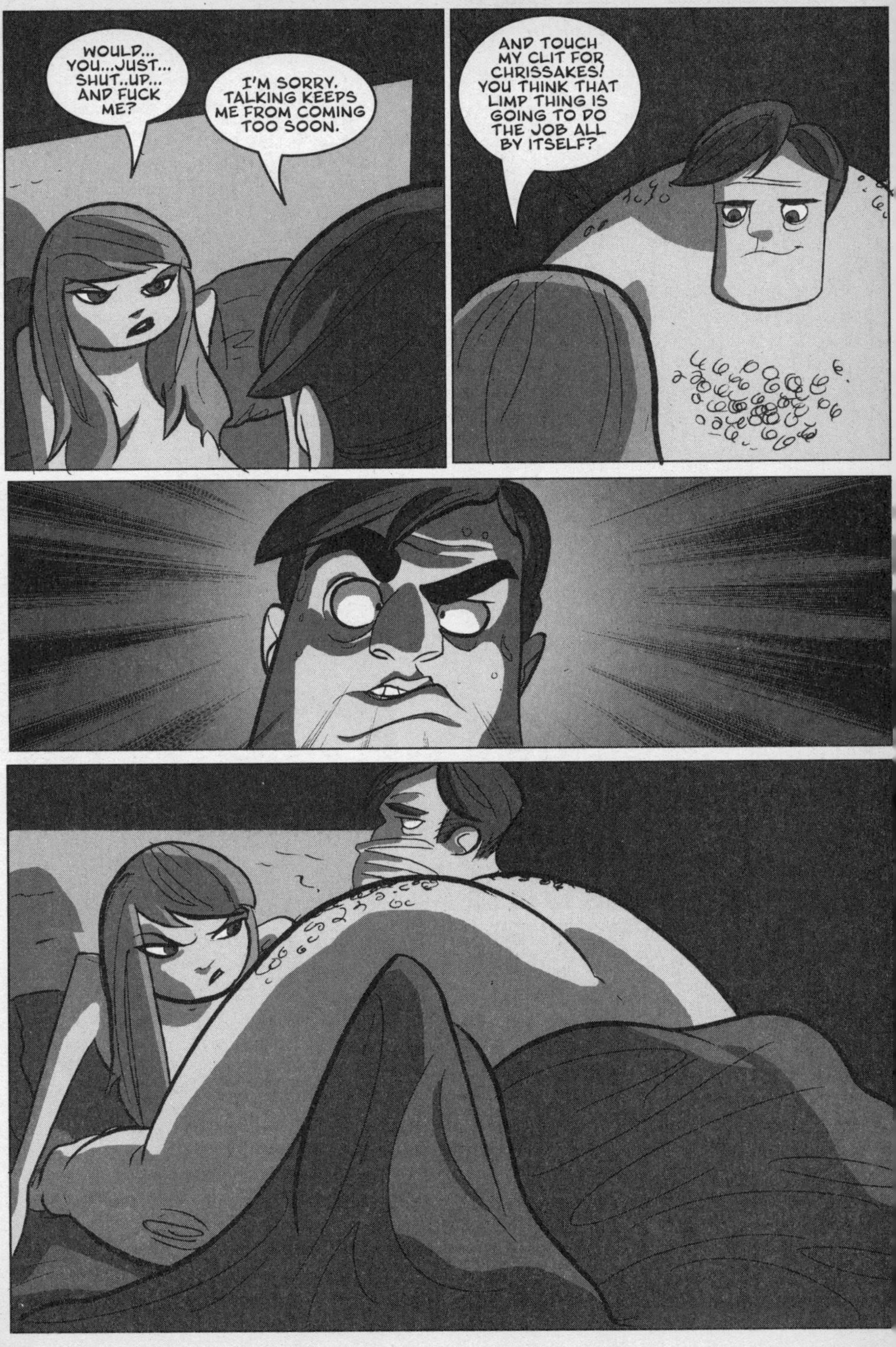
WOULD... YOU...JUST... SHUT..UP... AND FUCK ME?
I'M SORRY. TALKING KEEPS ME FROM COMING TOO SOON.
AND TOUCH MY CLIT FOR CHRISSAKES! YOU THINK THAT LIMP THING IS GOING TO DO THE JOB ALL BY ITSELF?

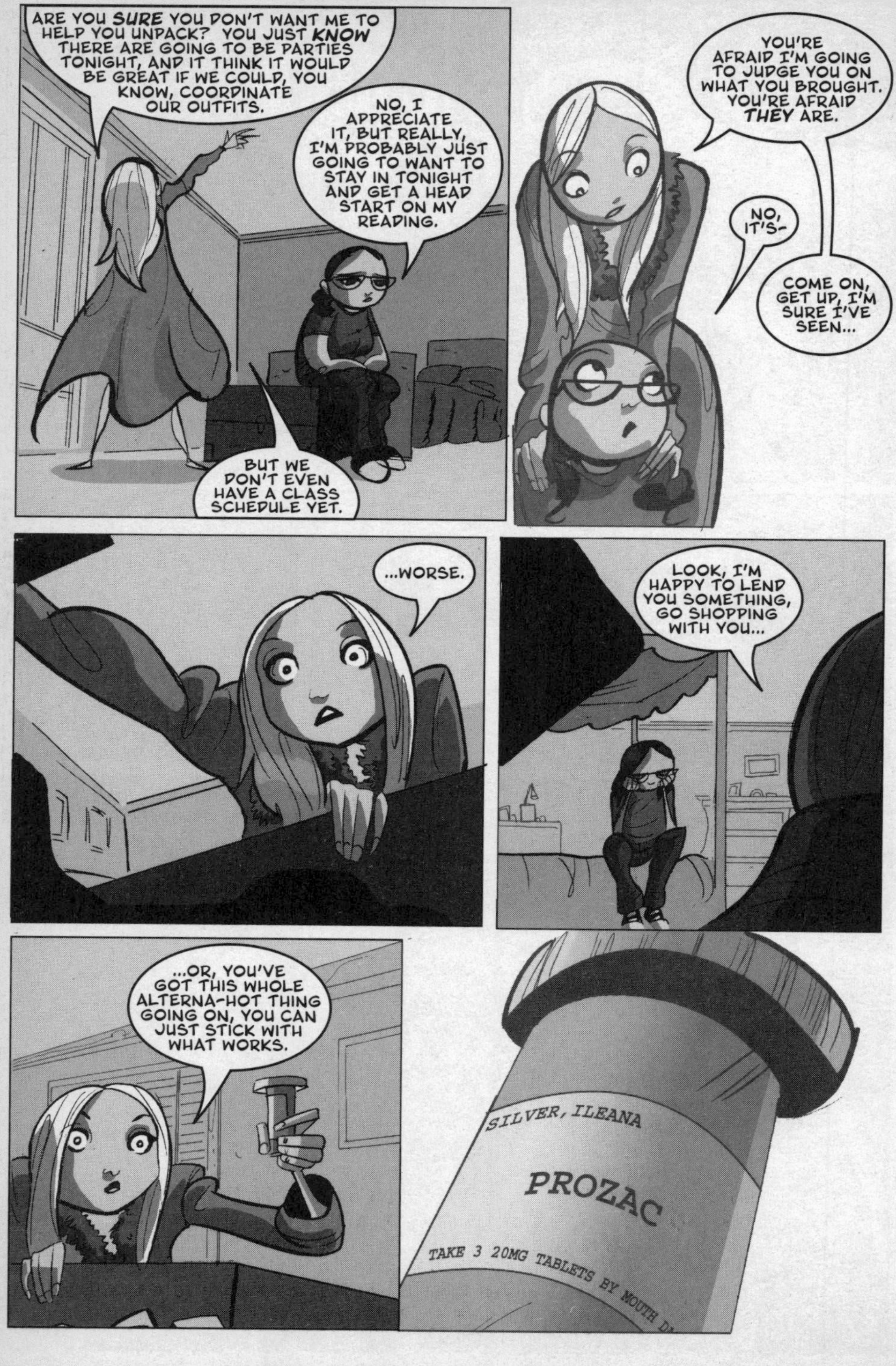
ARE YOU SURE YOU DON'T WANT ME TO HELP YOU UNPACK? YOU JUST KNOW THERE ARE GOING TO BE PARTIES TONIGHT, AND IT THINK IT WOULD BE GREAT IF WE COULD, YOU KNOW, COORDINATE OUR OUTFITS.
NO, I APPRECIATE IT, BUT REALLY, I'M PROBABLY JUST GOING TO WANT TO STAY IN TONIGHT AND GET A HEAD START ON MY READING.
BUT WE DON'T EVEN HAVE A CLASS SCHEDULE YET.
YOU'RE AFRAID I'M GOING TO JUDGE YOU ON WHAT YOU BROUGHT. YOU'RE AFRAID THEY ARE.
NO, IT'S-
COME ON, GET UP, I'M SURE I'VE SEEN...
...WORSE.
LOOK, I'M HAPPY TO LEND YOU SOMETHING, GO SHOPPING WITH YOU...
...OR, YOU'VE GOT THIS WHOLE ALTERNA-HOT THING GOING ON, YOU CAN JUST STICK WITH WHAT WORKS.
SILVER, ILEANA
PROZAC
TAKE 3 20MG TABLETS BY MOUTH

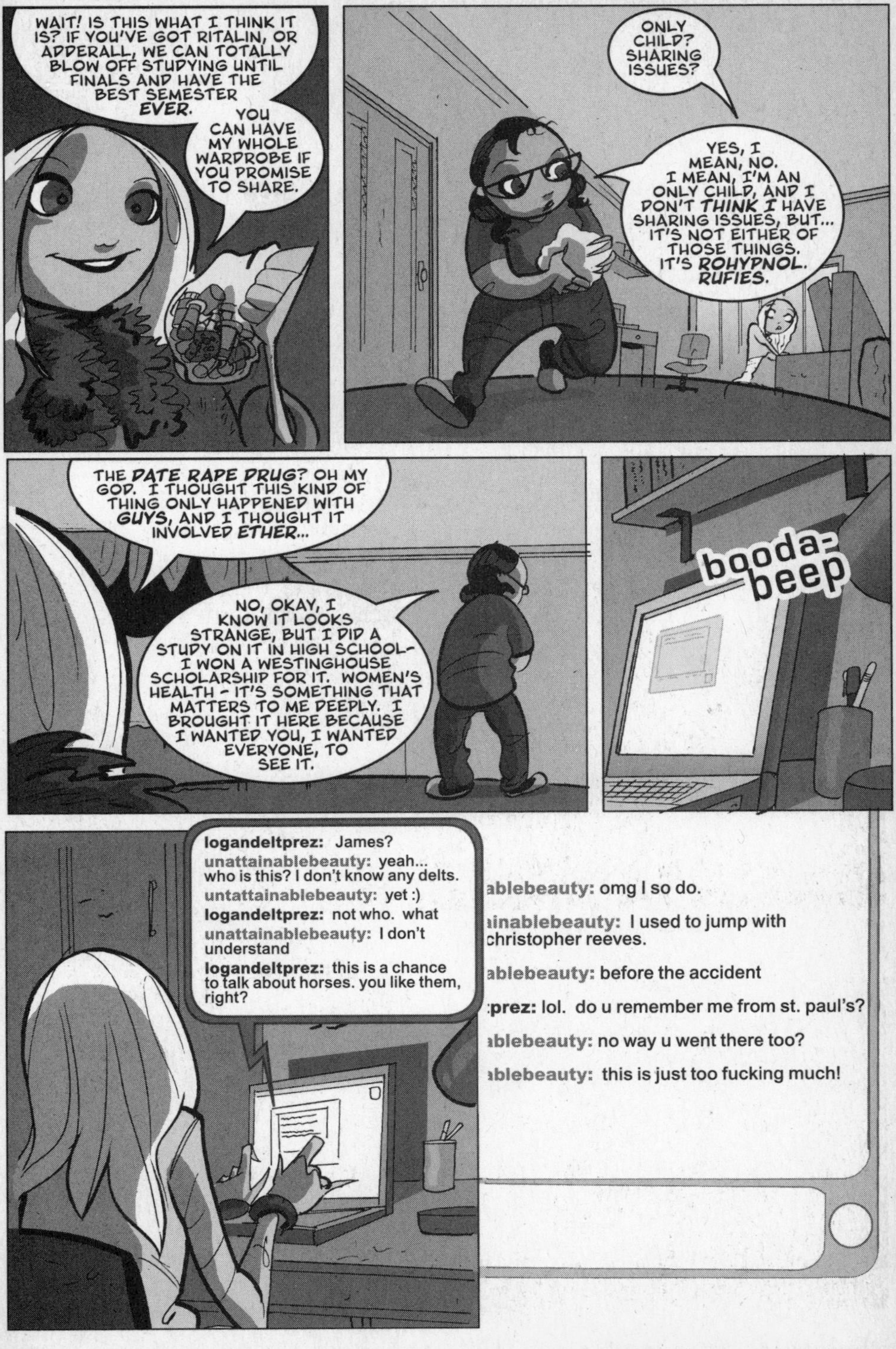
WAIT! IS THIS WHAT I THINK IT IS? IF YOU'VE GOT RITALIN, OR ADDERALL, WE CAN TOTALLY BLOW OFF STUDYING UNTIL FINALS AND HAVE THE BEST SEMESTER EVER.
YOU CAN HAVE MY WHOLE WARDROBE IF YOU PROMISE TO SHARE.
ONLY CHILD? SHARING ISSUES?
YES, I MEAN, NO. I MEAN, I'M AN ONLY CHILD, AND I DON'T THINK I HAVE SHARING ISSUES, BUT... IT'S NOT EITHER OF THOSE THINGS. IT'S ROHYPNOL. RUFIES.
THE DATE RAPE DRUG? OH MY GOD. I THOUGHT THIS KIND OF THING ONLY HAPPENED WITH GUYS, AND I THOUGHT IT INVOLVED ETHER...
NO, OKAY, I KNOW IT LOOKS STRANGE, BUT I DID A STUDY ON IT IN HIGH SCHOOL- I WON A WESTINGHOUSE SCHOLARSHIP FOR IT. WOMEN'S HEALTH - IT'S SOMETHING THAT MATTERS TO ME DEEPLY. I BROUGHT IT HERE BECAUSE I WANTED YOU, I WANTED EVERYONE, TO SEE IT.
booda-beep
logandeltprez: James?
unattainablebeauty: yeah... who is this? I don't know any delts.
untattainablebeauty: yet :)
logandeltprez: not who. what
unattainablebeauty: I don't understand
logandeltprez: this is a chance to talk about horses. you like them, right?
ablebeauty: omg I so do.
ainablebeauty: I used to jump with christopher reeves.
ablebeauty: before the accident
prez: lol. do u remember me from st. paul's?
ablebeauty: no way u went there too?
ablebeauty: this is just too fucking much!

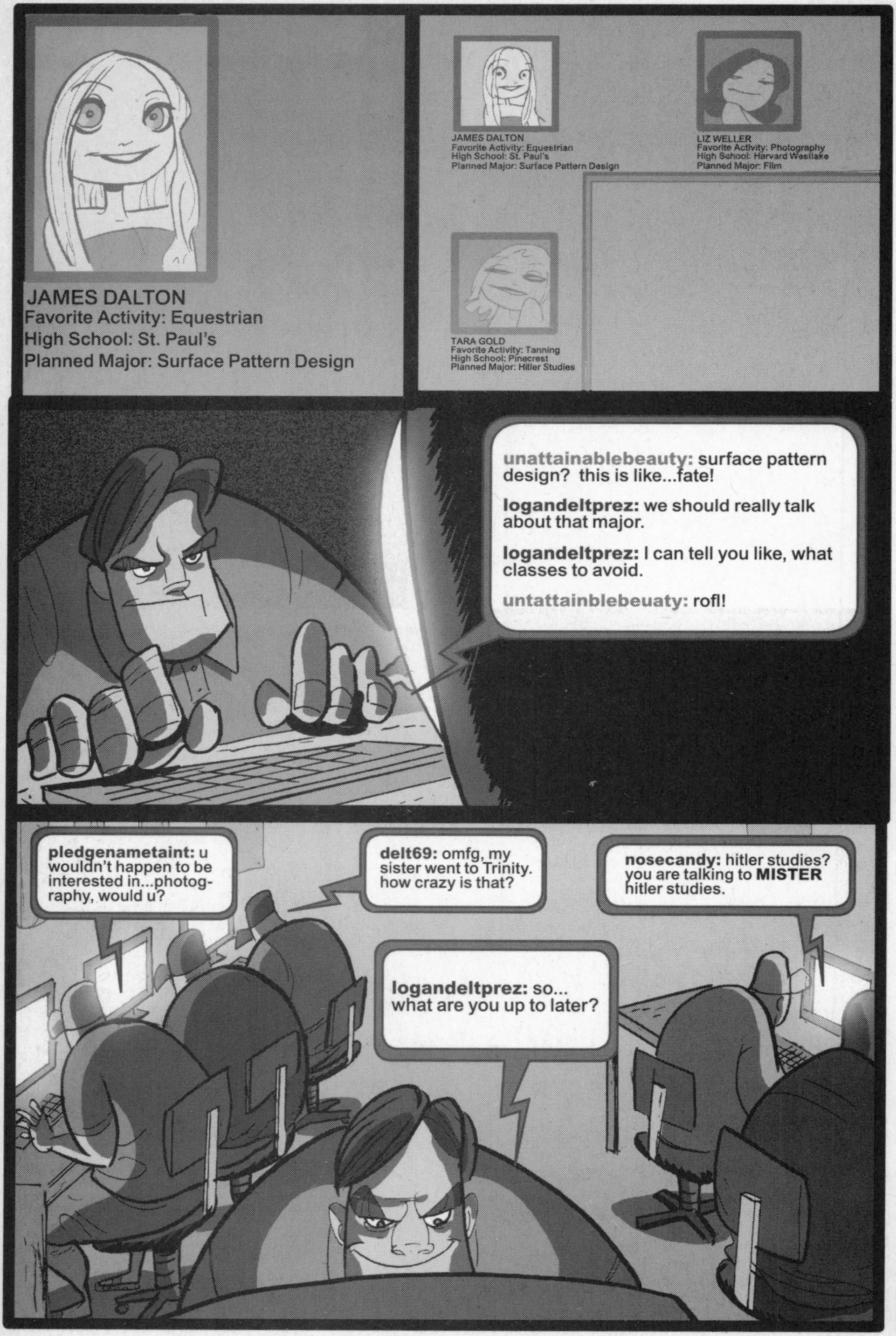
JAMES DALTON
Favorite Activity: Equestrian
High School: St. Paul's
Planned Major: Surface Pattern Design
JAMES DALTON
Favorite Activity: Equestrian
High School: St. Paul's
Planned Major: Surface Pattern Design
LIZ WELLER
Favorite Activity: Photography
High School: Harvard Westlake
Planned Major: Film
TARA GOLD
Favorite Activity: Tanning
High School: Pinecrest
Planned Major: Hitler Studies
unattainablebeauty: surface pattern design? this is like...fate!
logandeltprez: we should really talk about that major.
logandeltprez: I can tell you like, what classes to avoid.
untattainblebeuaty: rofl!
pledgenametaint: u wouldn't happen to be interested in...photog-raphy, would u?
delt69: omfg, my sister went to Trinity. how crazy is that?
nosecandy: hitler studies? you are talking to MISTER hitler studies.
logandeltprez: so... what are you up to later?

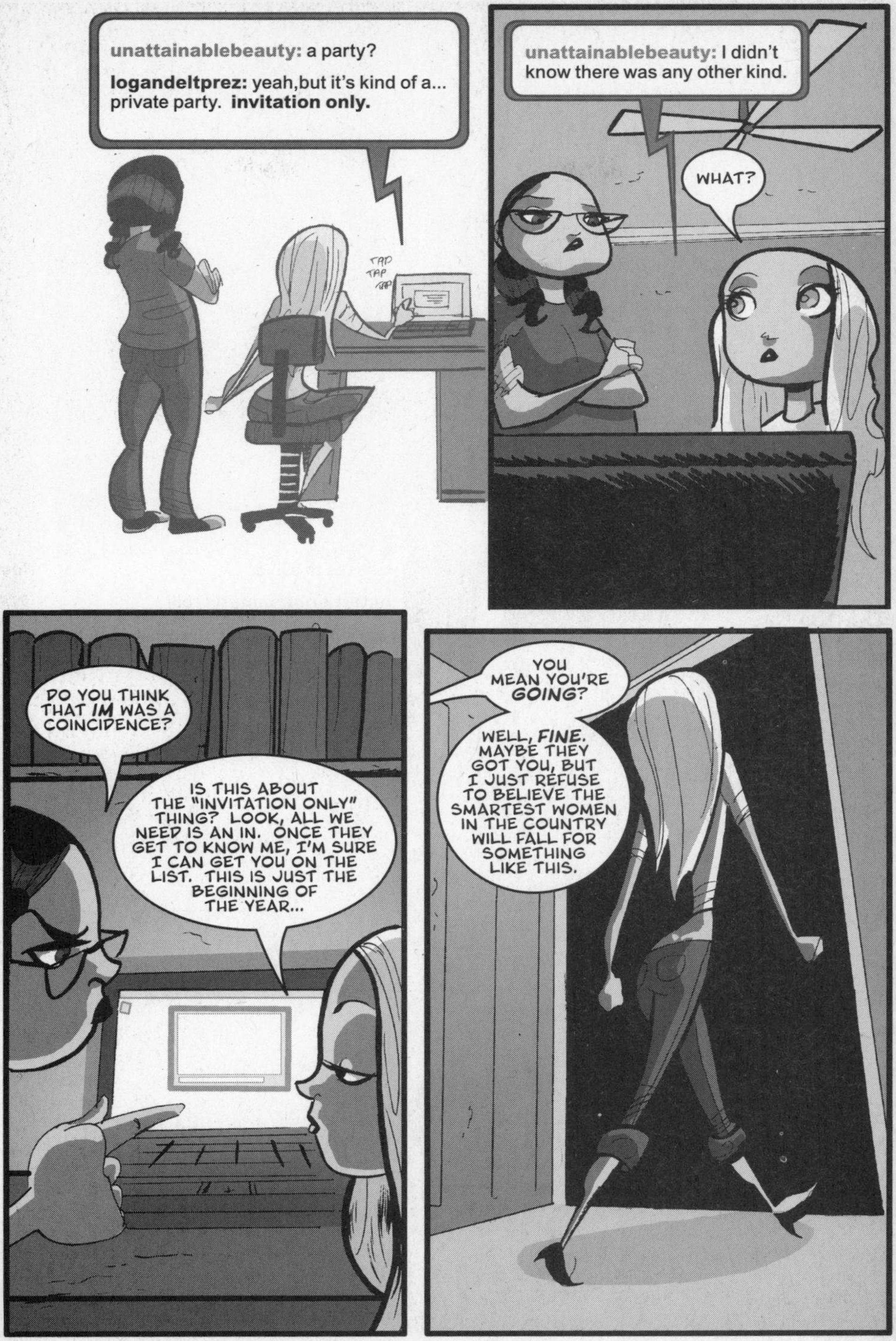
unattainablebeauty: a party?
logandeltprez: yeah,but it's kind of a... private party. invitation only.
TAP TAP TAP
unattainablebeauty: I didn't know there was any other kind.
WHAT?
DO YOU THINK THAT IM WAS A COINCIDENCE?
IS THIS ABOUT THE "INVITATION ONLY" THING? LOOK, ALL WE NEED IS AN IN. ONCE THEY GET TO KNOW ME, I'M SURE I CAN GET YOU ON THE LIST. THIS IS JUST THE BEGINNING OF THE YEAR...
YOU MEAN YOU'RE GOING?
WELL, FINE. MAYBE THEY GOT YOU, BUT I JUST REFUSE TO BELIEVE THE SMARTEST WOMEN IN THE COUNTRY WILL FALL FOR SOMETHING LIKE THIS.

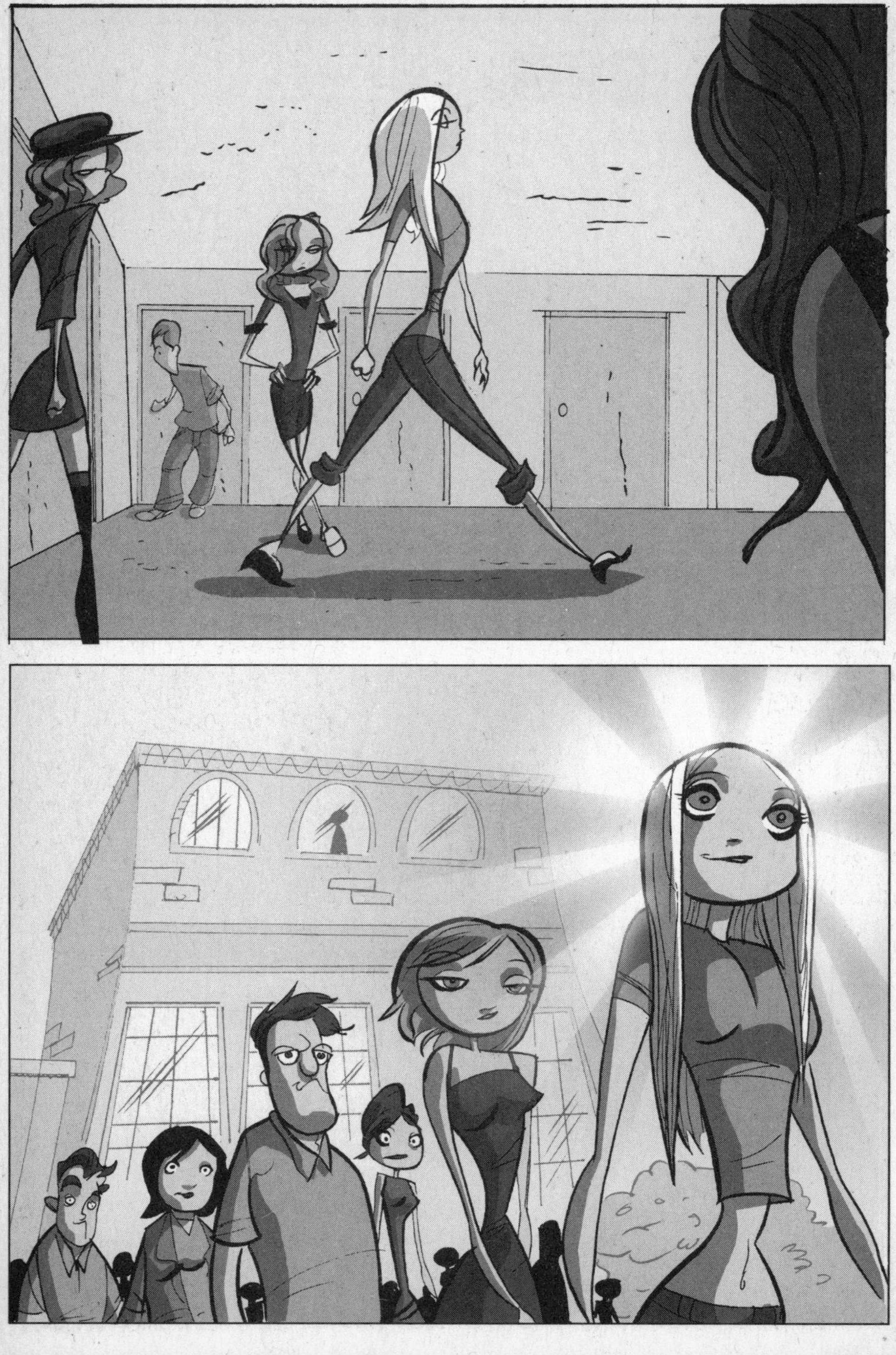

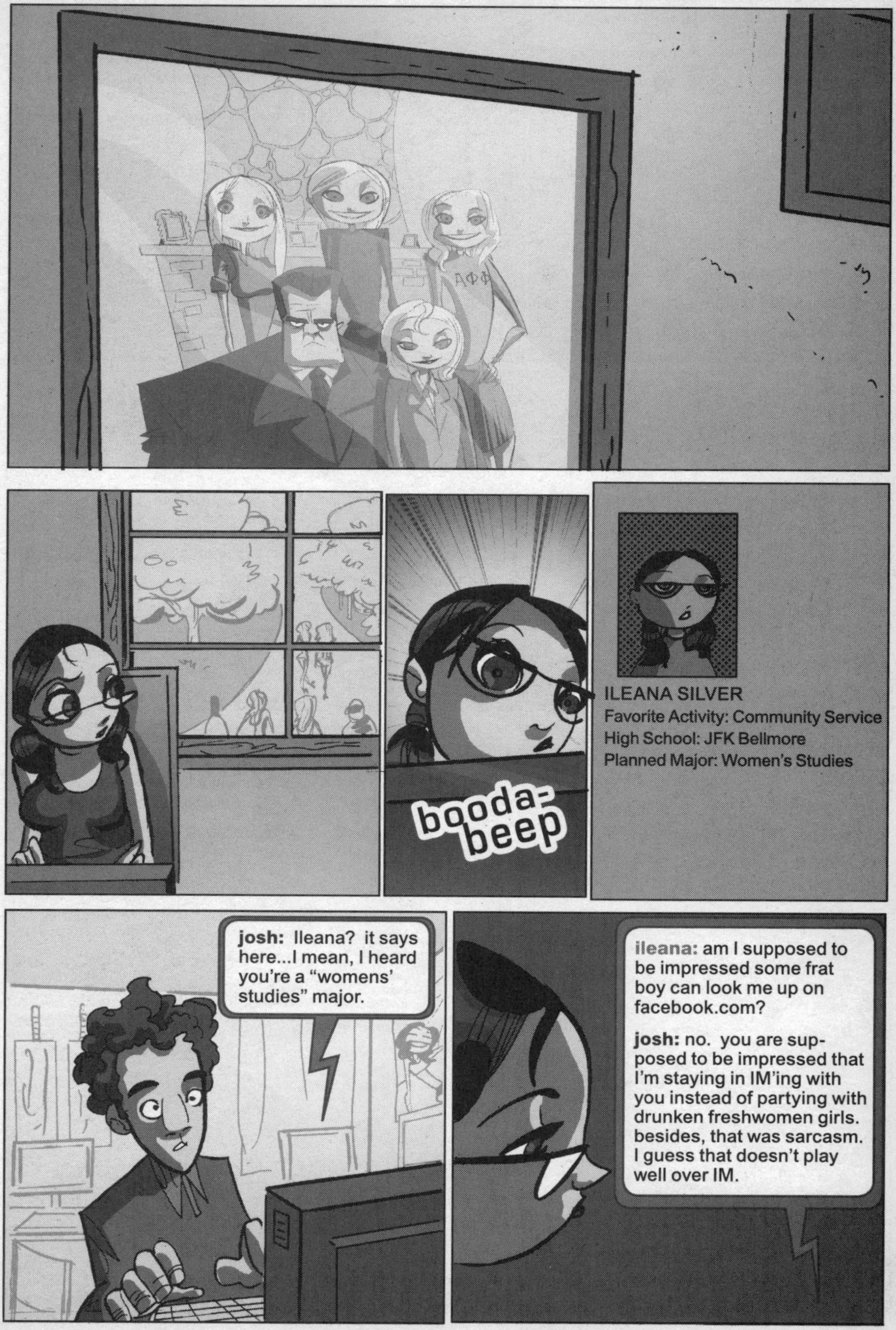
ΑΦΦ
ILEANA SILVER
Favorite Activity: Community Service
High School: JFK Bellmore
Planned Major: Women's Studies
booda-beep
josh: Ileana? it says here...I mean, I heard you're a "womens' studies" major.
ileana: am I supposed to be impressed some frat boy can look me up on facebook.com?
josh: no. you are supposed to be impressed that I'm staying in IM'ing with you instead of partying with drunken freshwomen girls. besides, that was sarcasm. I guess that doesn't play well over IM.

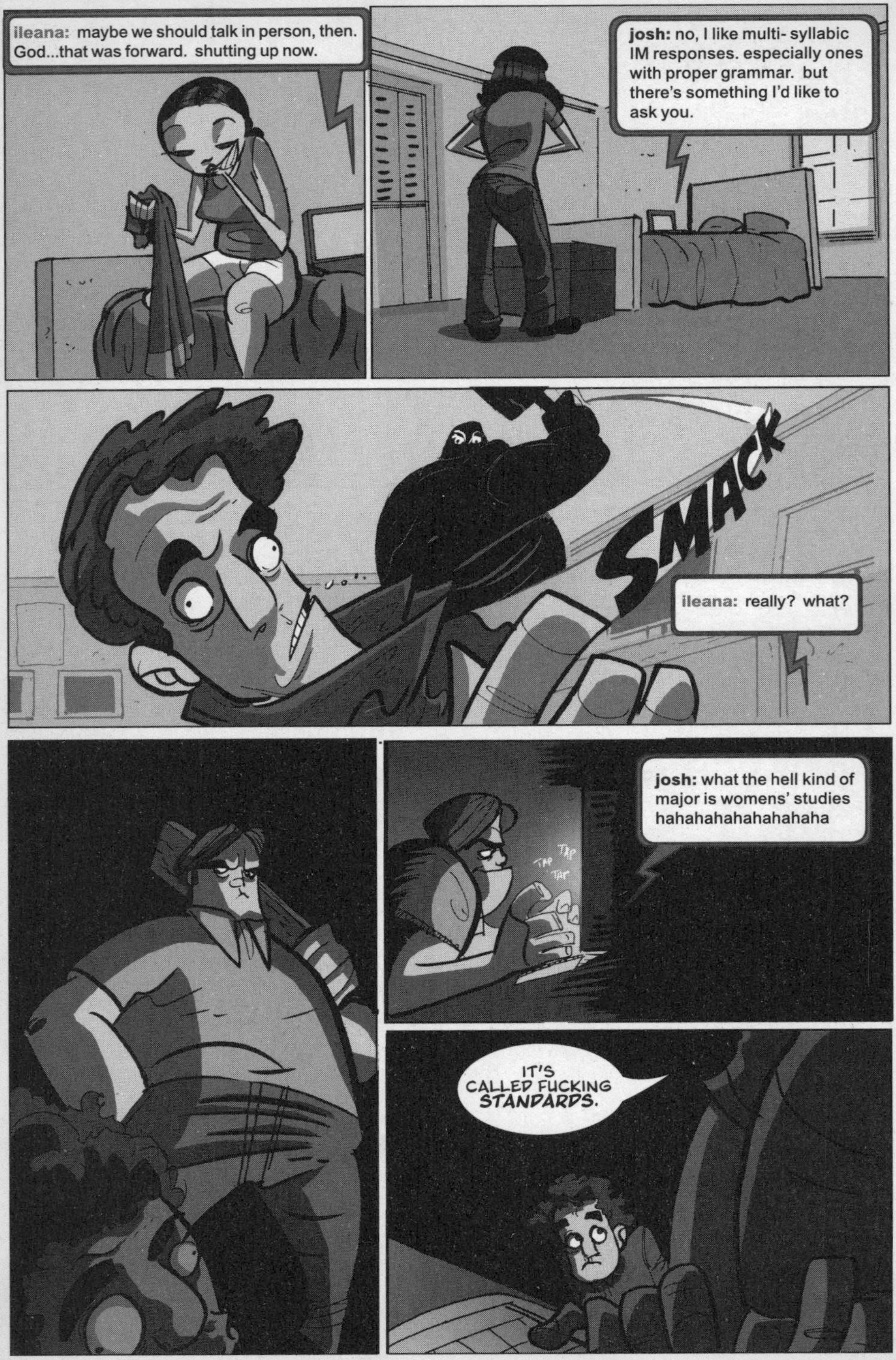
ileana: maybe we should talk in person, then. God...that was forward. shutting up now.
josh: no, I like multi- syllabic IM responses. especially ones with proper grammar. but there's something I'd like to ask you.
SMACK
ileana: really? what?
josh: what the hell kind of major is womens' studies hahahahahahahahaha
TAP TAP TAP TAP
IT'S CALLED FUCKING STANDARDS.

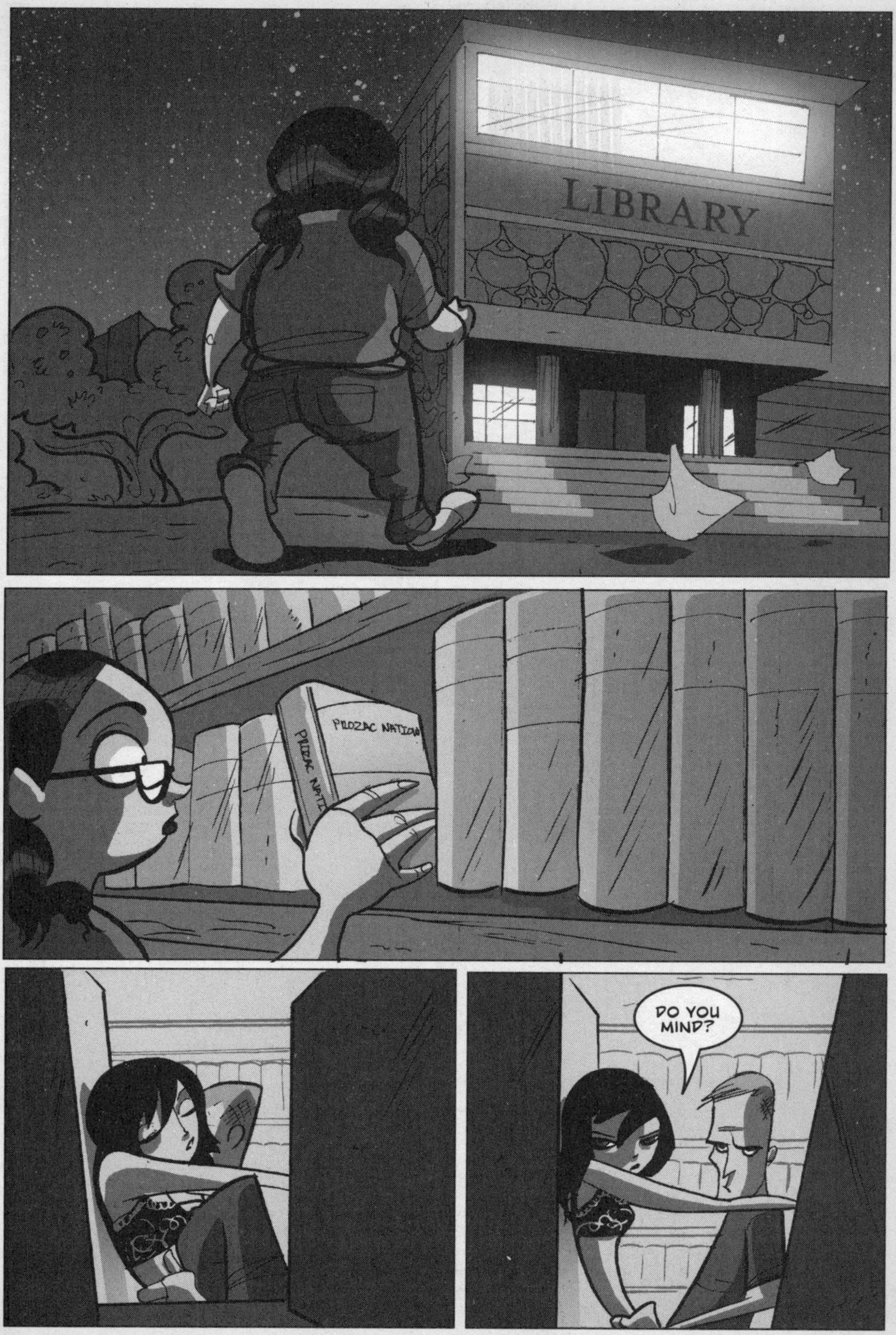
LIBRARY
PROZAC NATION
PROZAC NATI
DO YOU MIND?

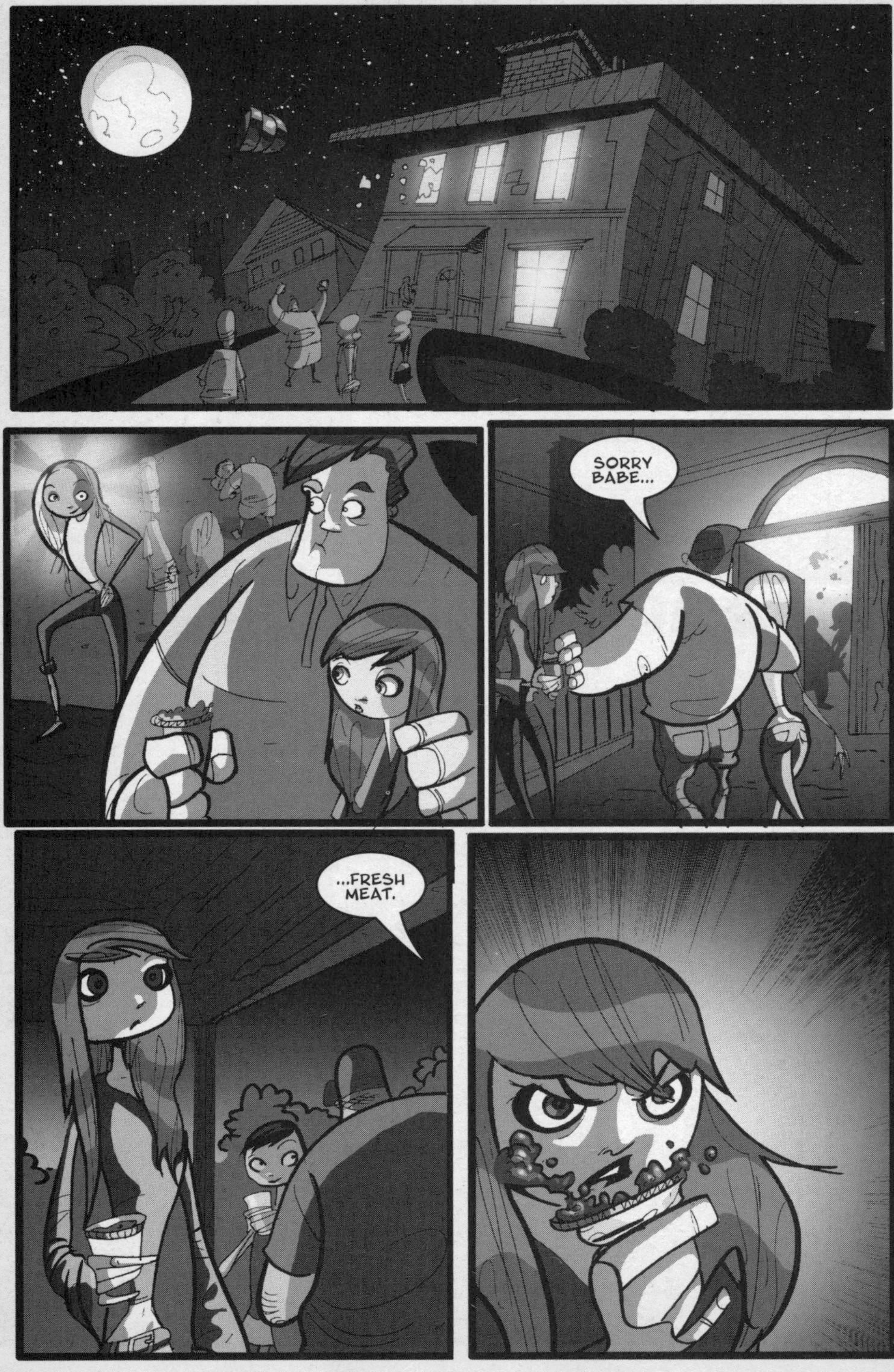
SORRY BABE...
...FRESH MEAT.

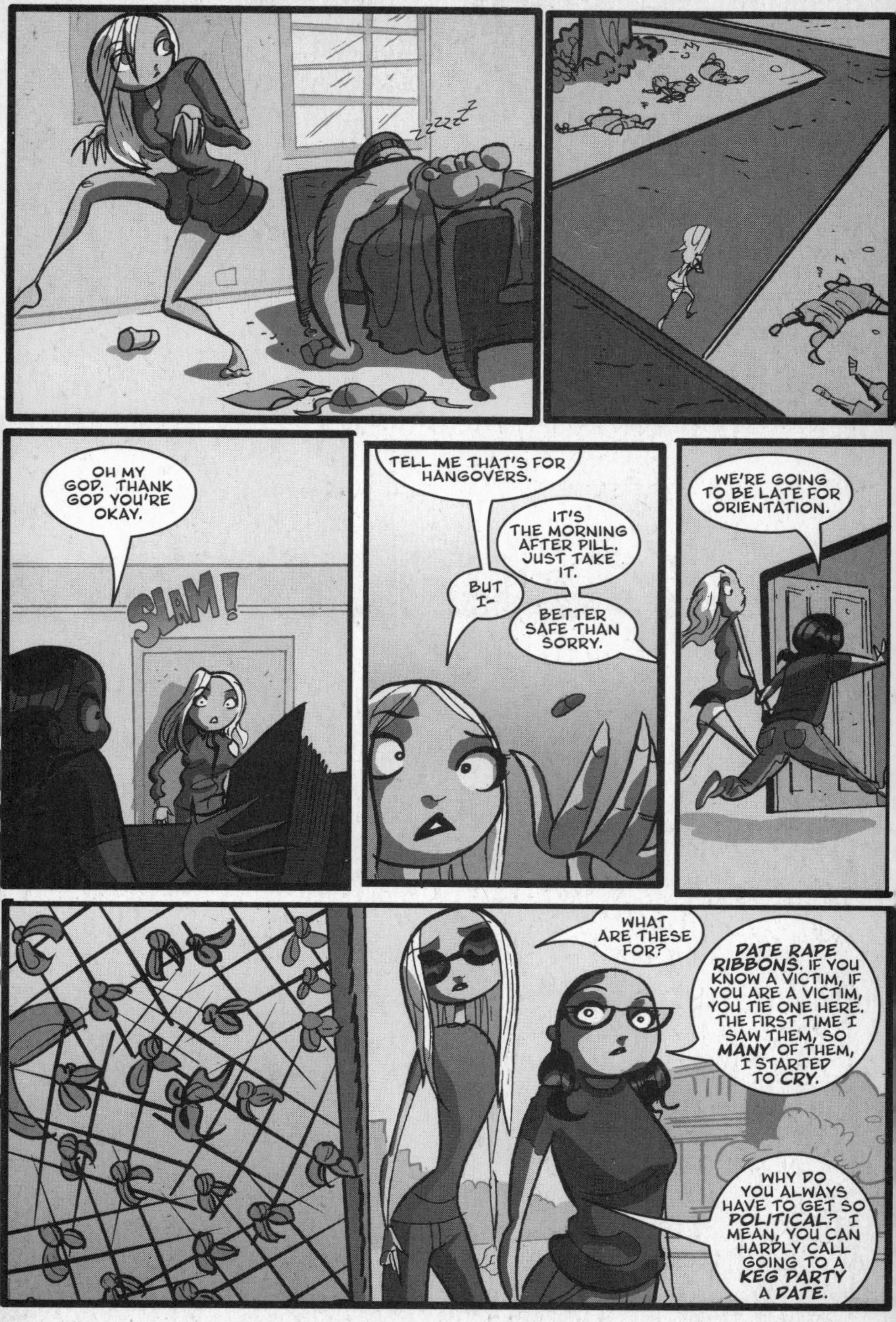
Z Z Z Z Z Z Z
OH MY GOD. THANK GOD YOU'RE OKAY.
SLAM!
TELL ME THAT'S FOR HANGOVERS.
IT'S THE MORNING AFTER PILL. JUST TAKE IT.
BUT I-
BETTER SAFE THAN SORRY.
WE'RE GOING TO BE LATE FOR ORIENTATION.
WHAT ARE THESE FOR?
DATE RAPE RIBBONS. IF YOU KNOW A VICTIM, IF YOU ARE A VICTIM, YOU TIE ONE HERE. THE FIRST TIME I SAW THEM, SO MANY OF THEM, I STARTED TO CRY.
WHY DO YOU ALWAYS HAVE TO GET SO POLITICAL? I MEAN, YOU CAN HARDLY CALL GOING TO A KEG PARTY A DATE.

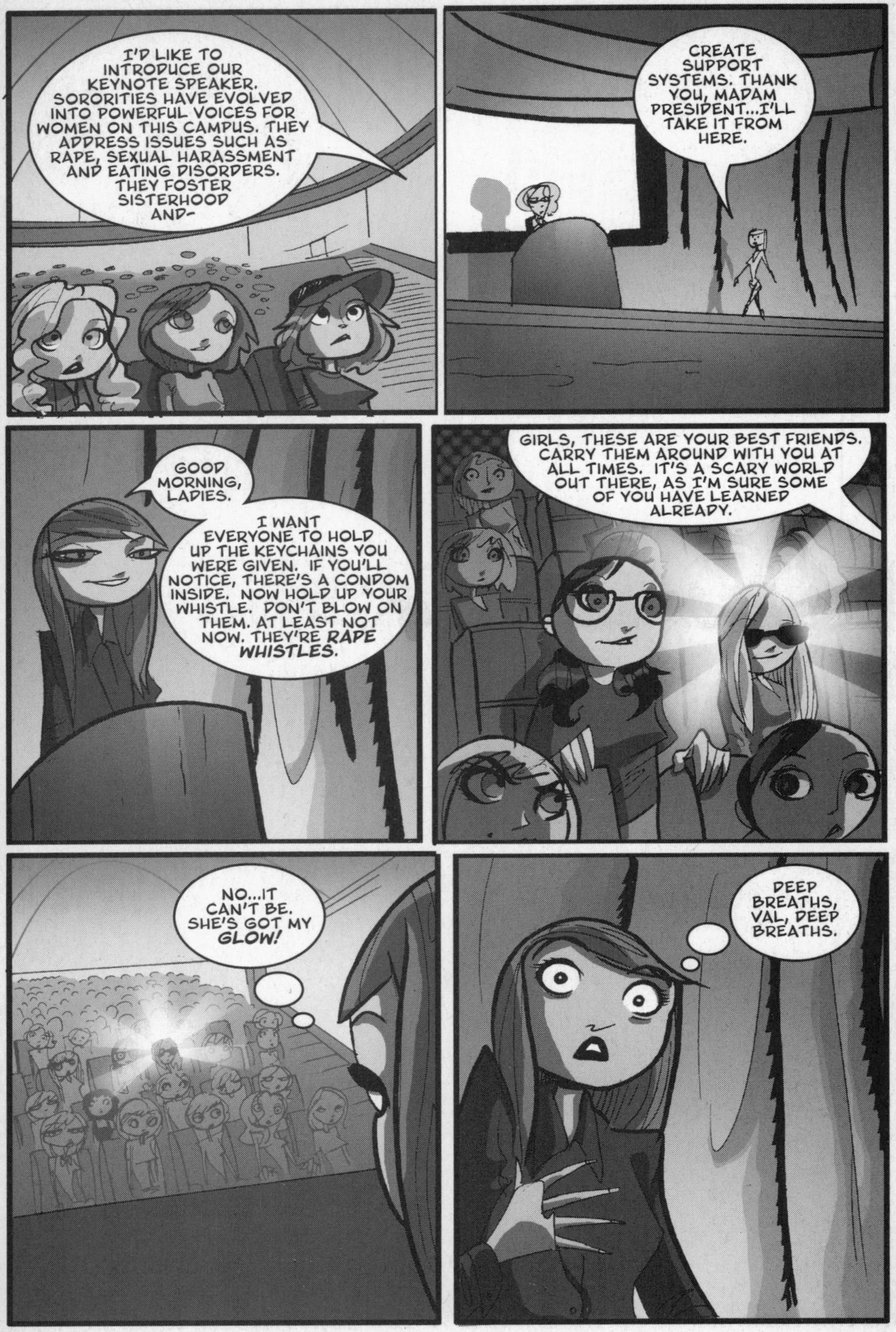
I'D LIKE TO INTRODUCE OUR KEYNOTE SPEAKER. SORORITIES HAVE EVOLVED INTO POWERFUL VOICES FOR WOMEN ON THIS CAMPUS. THEY ADDRESS ISSUES SUCH AS RAPE, SEXUAL HARASSMENT AND EATING DISORDERS. THEY FOSTER SISTERHOOD AND-
CREATE SUPPORT SYSTEMS. THANK YOU, MADAM PRESIDENT...I'LL TAKE IT FROM HERE.
GOOD MORNING, LADIES.
I WANT EVERYONE TO HOLD UP THE KEYCHAINS YOU WERE GIVEN. IF YOU'LL NOTICE, THERE'S A CONDOM INSIDE. NOW HOLD UP YOUR WHISTLE. DON'T BLOW ON THEM. AT LEAST NOT NOW. THEY'RE *RAPE WHISTLES*.
GIRLS, THESE ARE YOUR BEST FRIENDS. CARRY THEM AROUND WITH YOU AT ALL TIMES. IT'S A SCARY WORLD OUT THERE, AS I'M SURE SOME OF YOU HAVE LEARNED ALREADY.
NO...IT CAN'T BE. SHE'S GOT MY *GLOW!*
DEEP BREATHS, VAL, DEEP BREATHS.

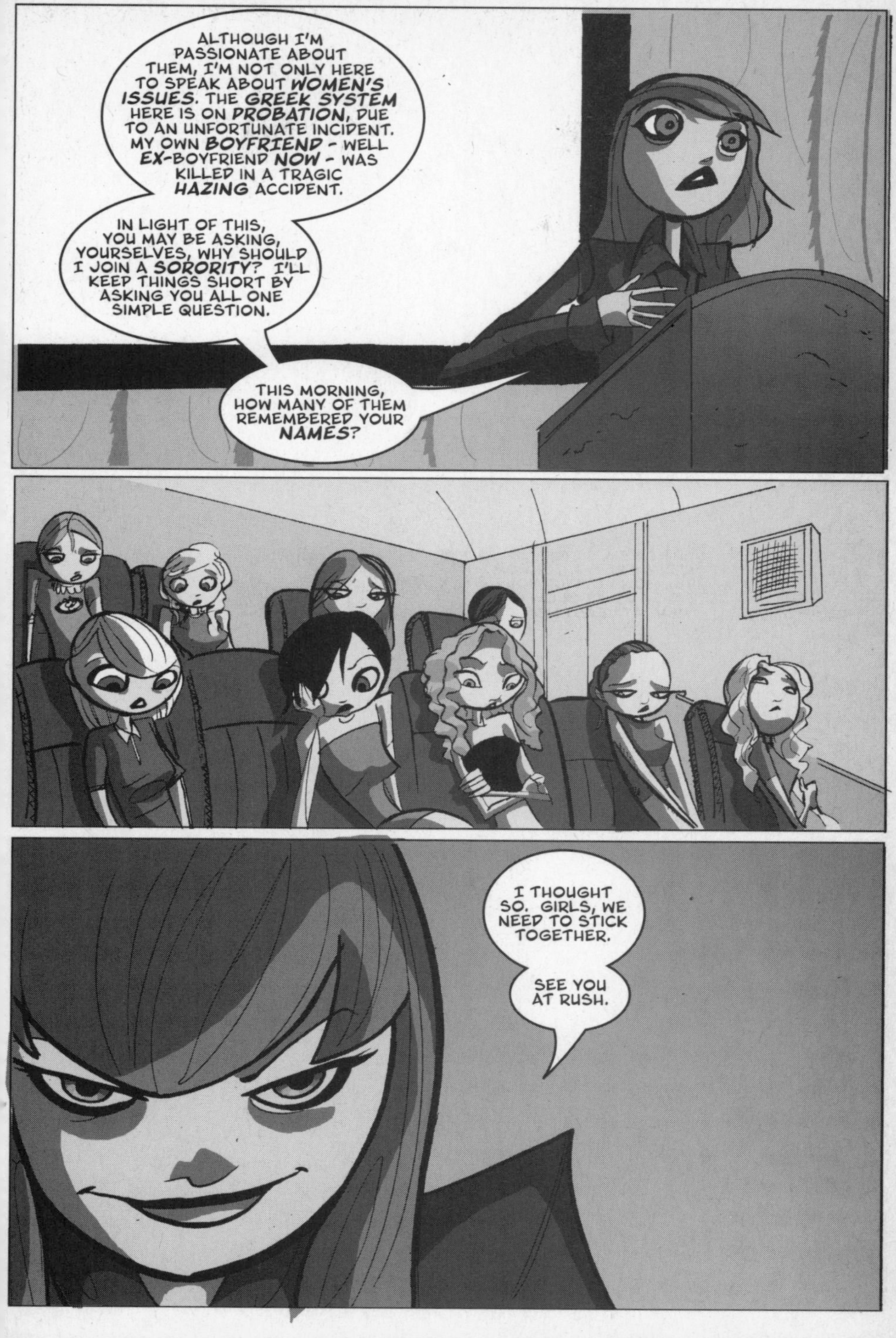
ALTHOUGH I'M PASSIONATE ABOUT THEM, I'M NOT ONLY HERE TO SPEAK ABOUT WOMEN'S ISSUES. THE GREEK SYSTEM HERE IS ON PROBATION, DUE TO AN UNFORTUNATE INCIDENT. MY OWN BOYFRIEND - WELL EX-BOYFRIEND NOW - WAS KILLED IN A TRAGIC HAZING ACCIDENT.
IN LIGHT OF THIS, YOU MAY BE ASKING, YOURSELVES, WHY SHOULD I JOIN A SORORITY? I'LL KEEP THINGS SHORT BY ASKING YOU ALL ONE SIMPLE QUESTION.
THIS MORNING, HOW MANY OF THEM REMEMBERED YOUR NAMES?
I THOUGHT SO. GIRLS, WE NEED TO STICK TOGETHER.
SEE YOU AT RUSH.

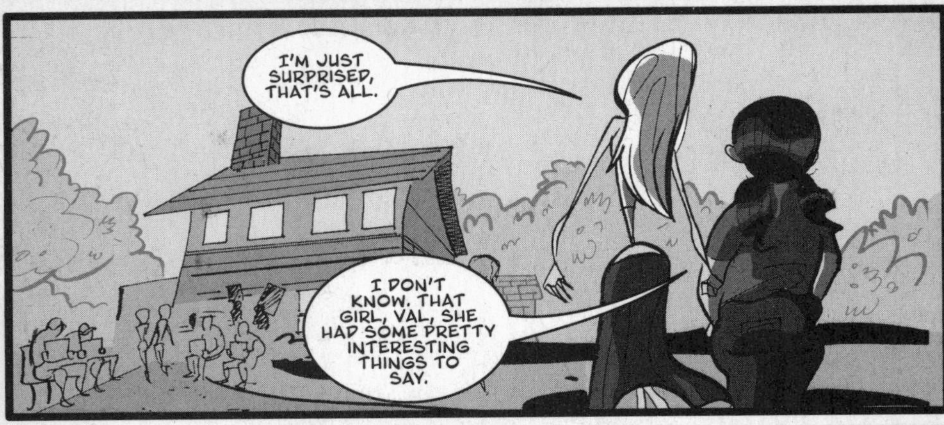
I'M JUST SURPRISED, THAT'S ALL.
I DON'T KNOW. THAT GIRL, VAL, SHE HAD SOME PRETTY INTERESTING THINGS TO SAY.

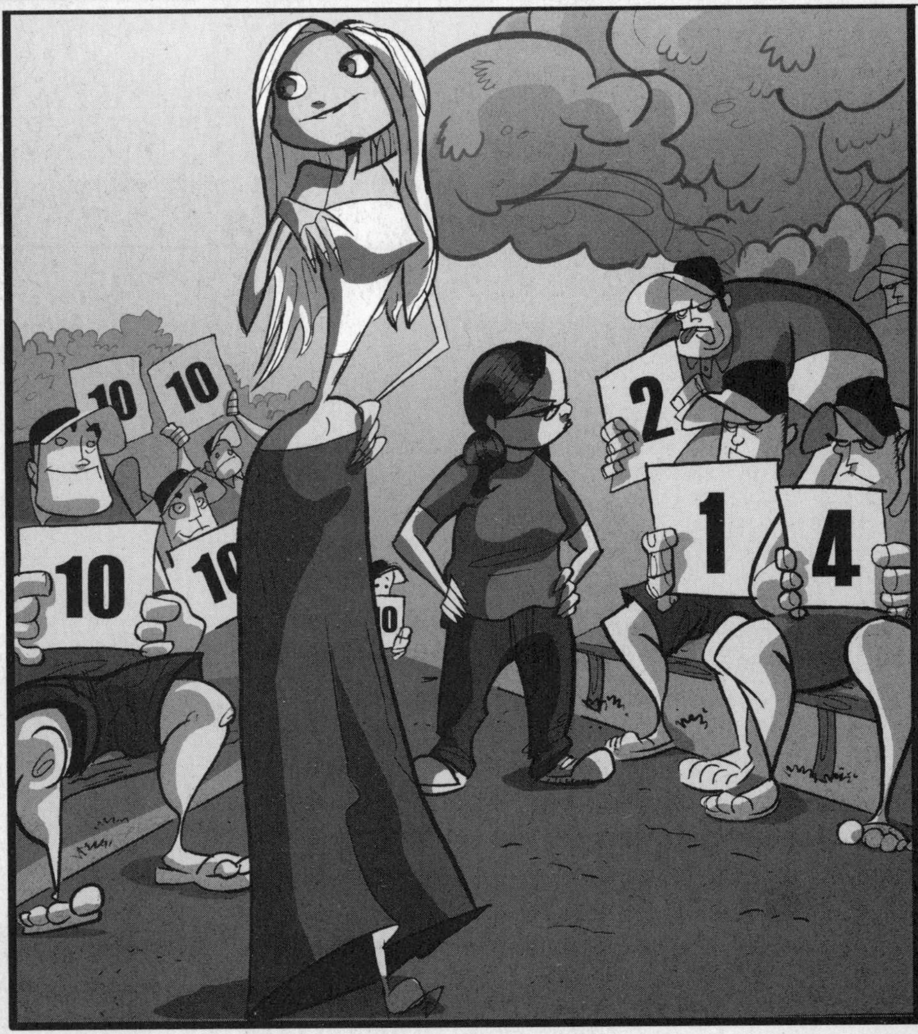
10
10
10
10
2
1
4

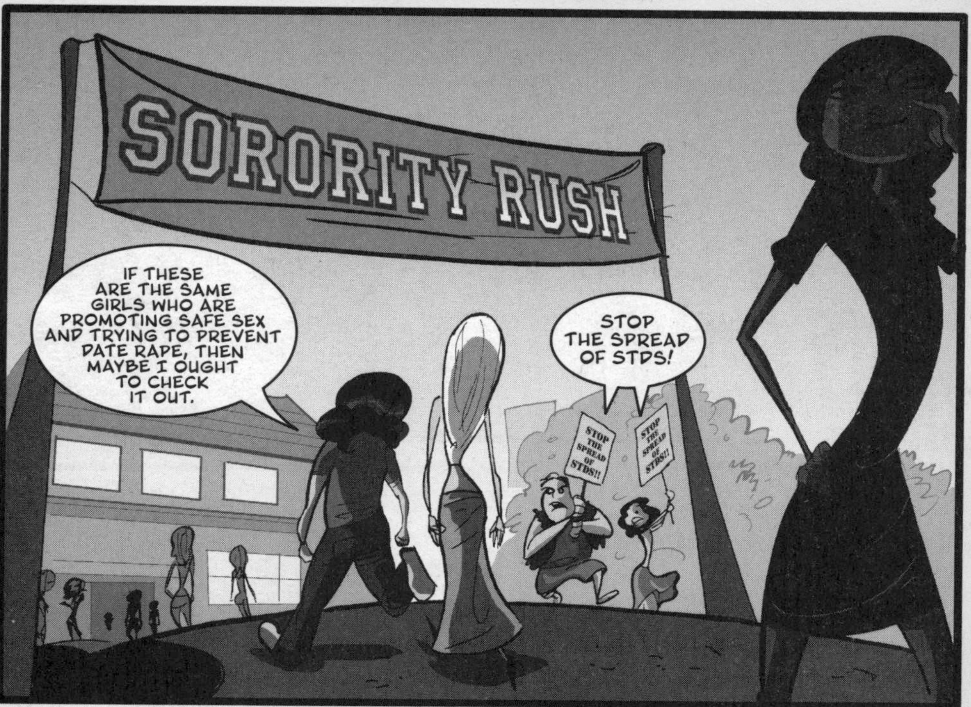
SORORITY RUSH
IF THESE ARE THE SAME GIRLS WHO ARE PROMOTING SAFE SEX AND TRYING TO PREVENT DATE RAPE, THEN MAYBE I OUGHT TO CHECK IT OUT.
STOP THE SPREAD OF STDS!
STOP THE SPREAD OF STDS!!
STOP THE SPREAD OF STDS!!

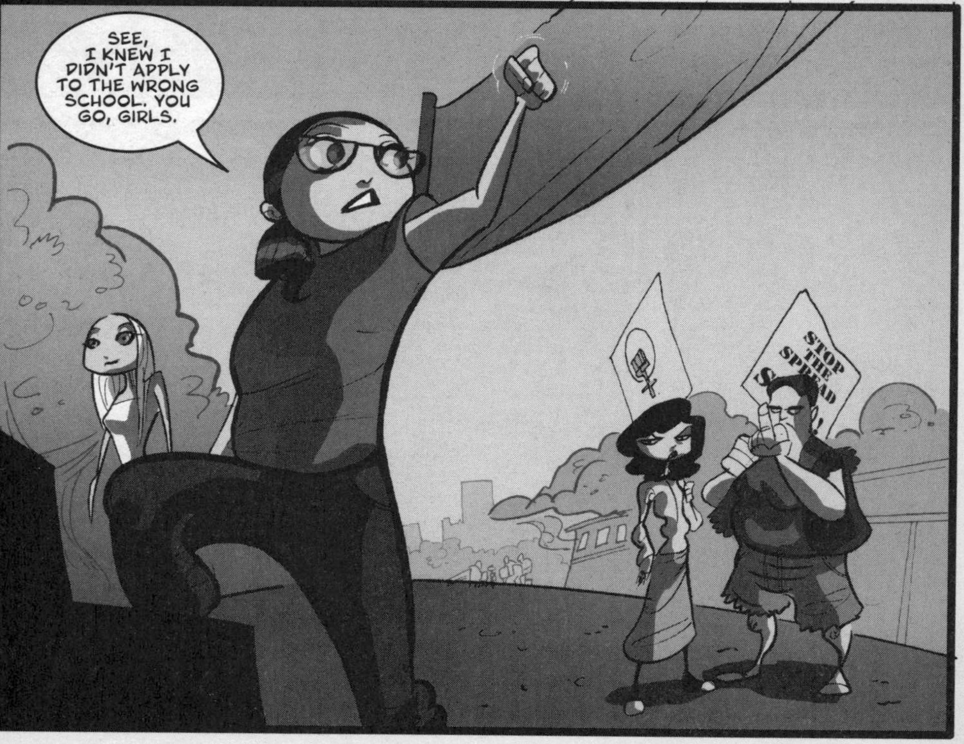
SEE, I KNEW I DIDN'T APPLY TO THE WRONG SCHOOL. YOU GO, GIRLS.
STOP THE SPREAD

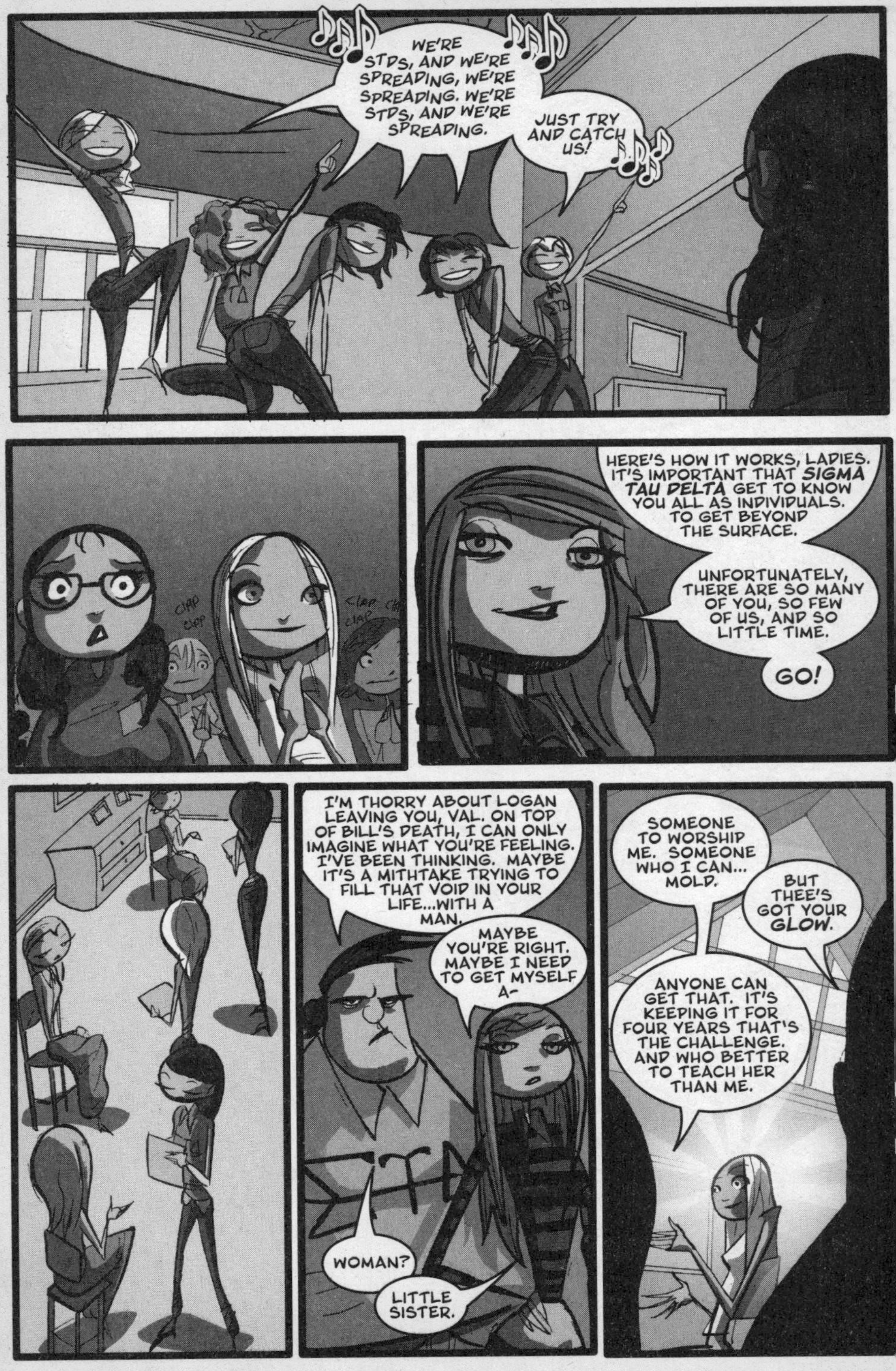
WE'RE STDS, AND WE'RE SPREADING, WE'RE SPREADING. WE'RE STDS, AND WE'RE SPREADING.
JUST TRY AND CATCH US!
HERE'S HOW IT WORKS, LADIES. IT'S IMPORTANT THAT SIGMA TAU DELTA GET TO KNOW YOU ALL AS INDIVIDUALS. TO GET BEYOND THE SURFACE.
UNFORTUNATELY, THERE ARE SO MANY OF YOU, SO FEW OF US, AND SO LITTLE TIME.
GO!
I'M THORRY ABOUT LOGAN LEAVING YOU, VAL. ON TOP OF BILL'S DEATH, I CAN ONLY IMAGINE WHAT YOU'RE FEELING. I'VE BEEN THINKING. MAYBE IT'S A MITHTAKE TRYING TO FILL THAT VOID IN YOUR LIFE...WITH A MAN.
MAYBE YOU'RE RIGHT. MAYBE I NEED TO GET MYSELF A-
WOMAN?
LITTLE SISTER.
SOMEONE TO WORSHIP ME. SOMEONE WHO I CAN... MOLD.
BUT THEE'S GOT YOUR GLOW.
ANYONE CAN GET THAT. IT'S KEEPING IT FOR FOUR YEARS THAT'S THE CHALLENGE. AND WHO BETTER TO TEACH HER THAN ME.

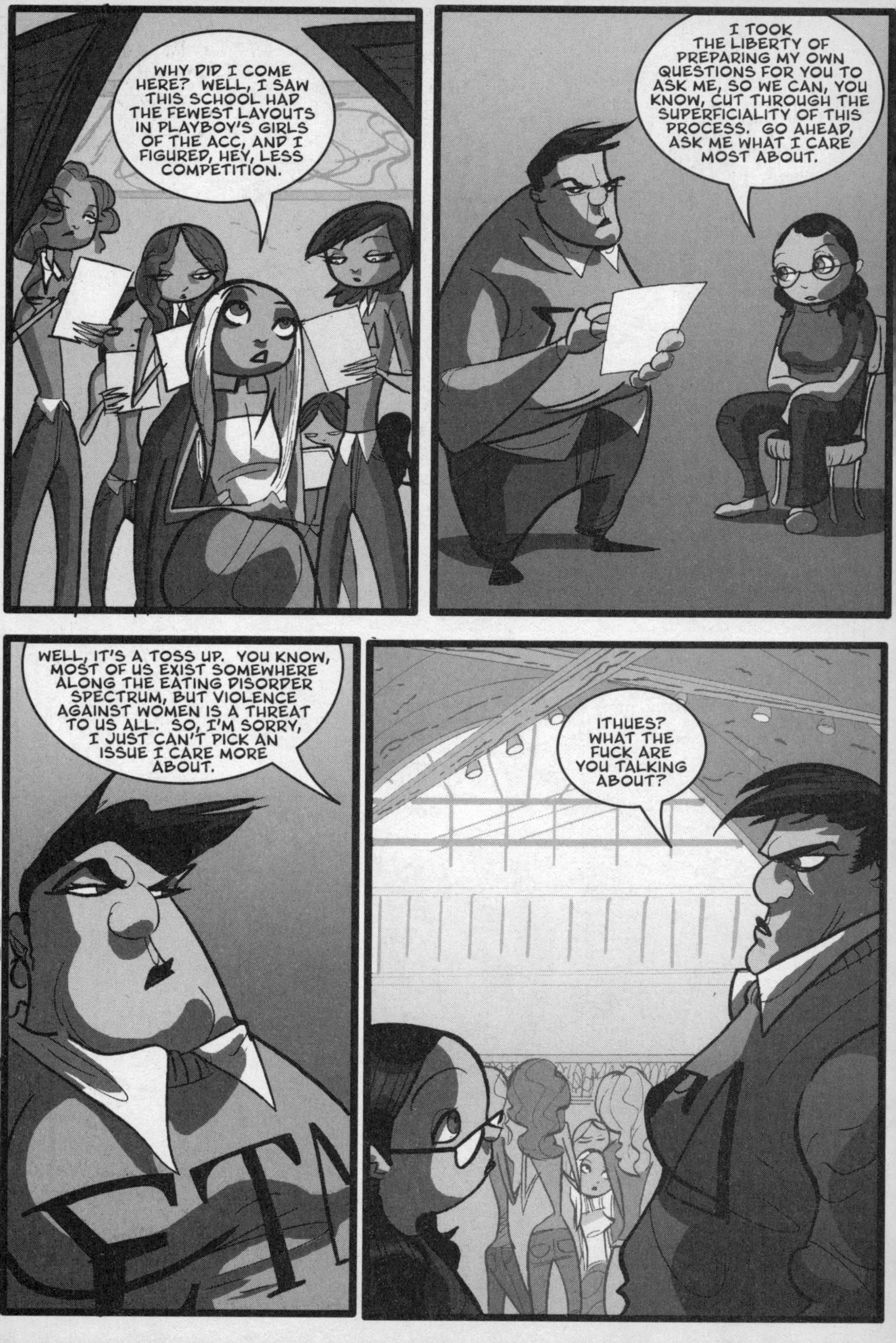
WHY DID I COME HERE? WELL, I SAW THIS SCHOOL HAD THE FEWEST LAYOUTS IN PLAYBOY'S GIRLS OF THE ACC, AND I FIGURED, HEY, LESS COMPETITION.
I TOOK THE LIBERTY OF PREPARING MY OWN QUESTIONS FOR YOU TO ASK ME, SO WE CAN, YOU KNOW, CUT THROUGH THE SUPERFICIALITY OF THIS PROCESS. GO AHEAD, ASK ME WHAT I CARE MOST ABOUT.
WELL, IT'S A TOSS UP. YOU KNOW, MOST OF US EXIST SOMEWHERE ALONG THE EATING DISORDER SPECTRUM, BUT VIOLENCE AGAINST WOMEN IS A THREAT TO US ALL. SO, I'M SORRY, I JUST CAN'T PICK AN ISSUE I CARE MORE ABOUT.
ITHUES? WHAT THE FUCK ARE YOU TALKING ABOUT?

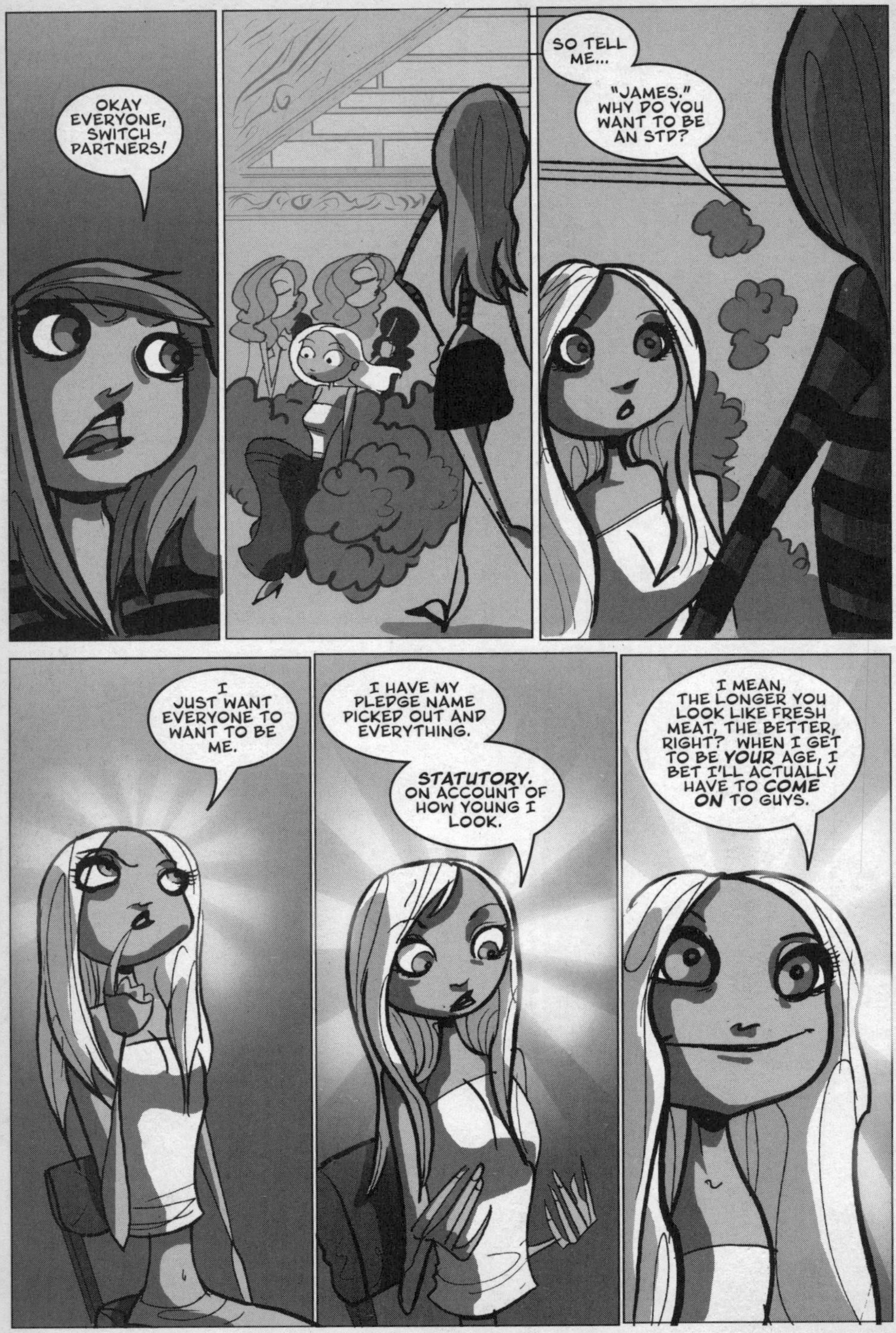
OKAY EVERYONE, SWITCH PARTNERS!
SO TELL ME...
"JAMES." WHY DO YOU WANT TO BE AN STD?
I JUST WANT EVERYONE TO WANT TO BE ME.
I HAVE MY PLEDGE NAME PICKED OUT AND EVERYTHING.
STATUTORY. ON ACCOUNT OF HOW YOUNG I LOOK.
I MEAN, THE LONGER YOU LOOK LIKE FRESH MEAT, THE BETTER, RIGHT? WHEN I GET TO BE YOUR AGE, I BET I'LL ACTUALLY HAVE TO COME ON TO GUYS.

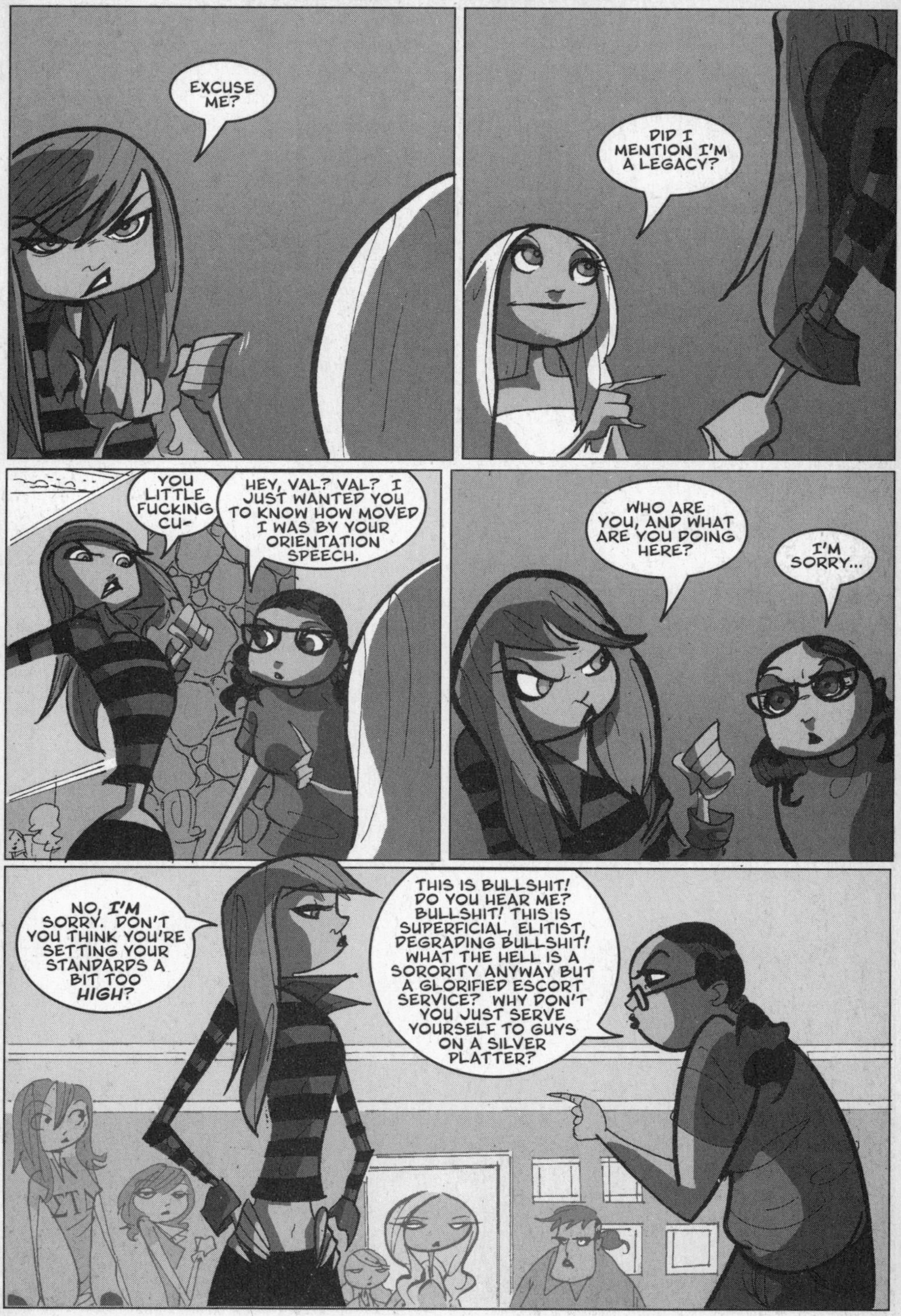
EXCUSE ME?
DID I MENTION I'M A LEGACY?
YOU LITTLE FUCKING CU-
HEY, VAL? VAL? I JUST WANTED YOU TO KNOW HOW MOVED I WAS BY YOUR ORIENTATION SPEECH.
WHO ARE YOU, AND WHAT ARE YOU DOING HERE?
I'M SORRY...
NO, *I'M* SORRY. DON'T YOU THINK YOU'RE SETTING YOUR STANDARDS A BIT TOO *HIGH*?
THIS IS BULLSHIT! DO YOU HEAR ME? BULLSHIT! THIS IS SUPERFICIAL, ELITIST, DEGRADING BULLSHIT! WHAT THE HELL IS A SORORITY ANYWAY BUT A GLORIFIED ESCORT SERVICE? WHY DON'T YOU JUST SERVE YOURSELF TO GUYS ON A SILVER PLATTER?

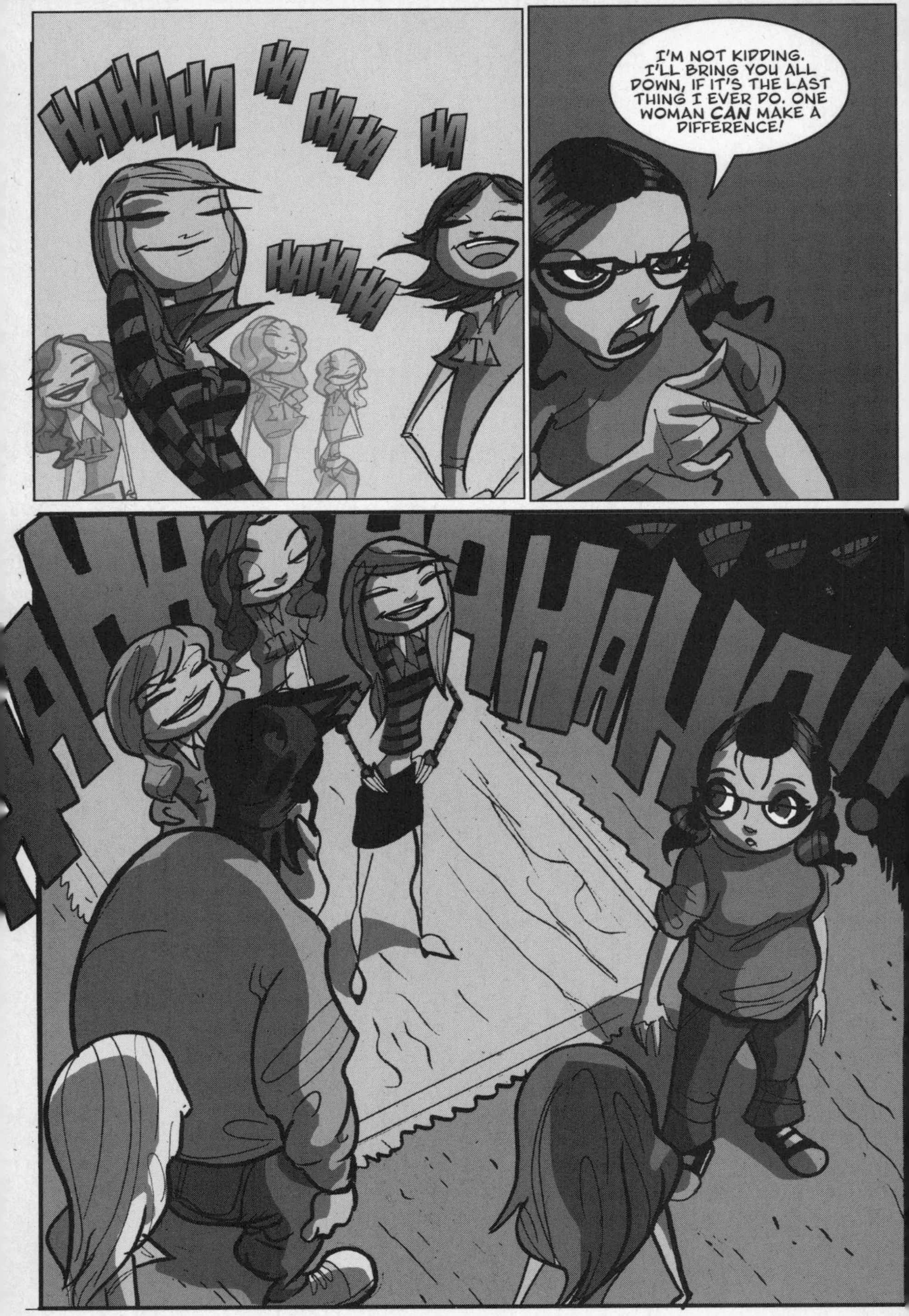
HAHAHA
HA
HAHA
HA
HAHAHA
I'M NOT KIDDING. I'LL BRING YOU ALL DOWN, IF IT'S THE LAST THING I EVER DO. ONE WOMAN **CAN** MAKE A DIFFERENCE!

CHAPTER

2

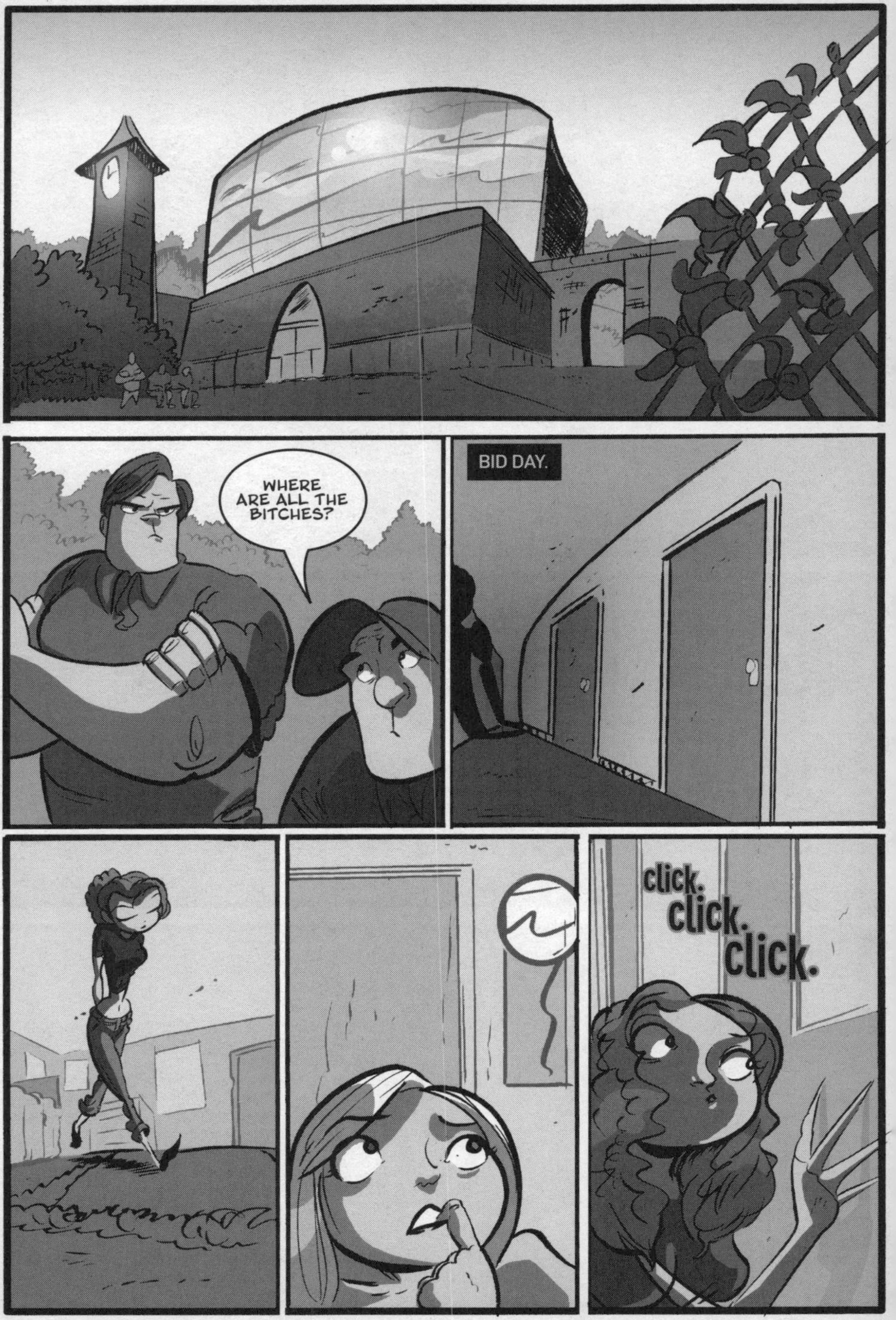
WHERE ARE ALL THE BITCHES?
BID DAY.
click.
click.
click.

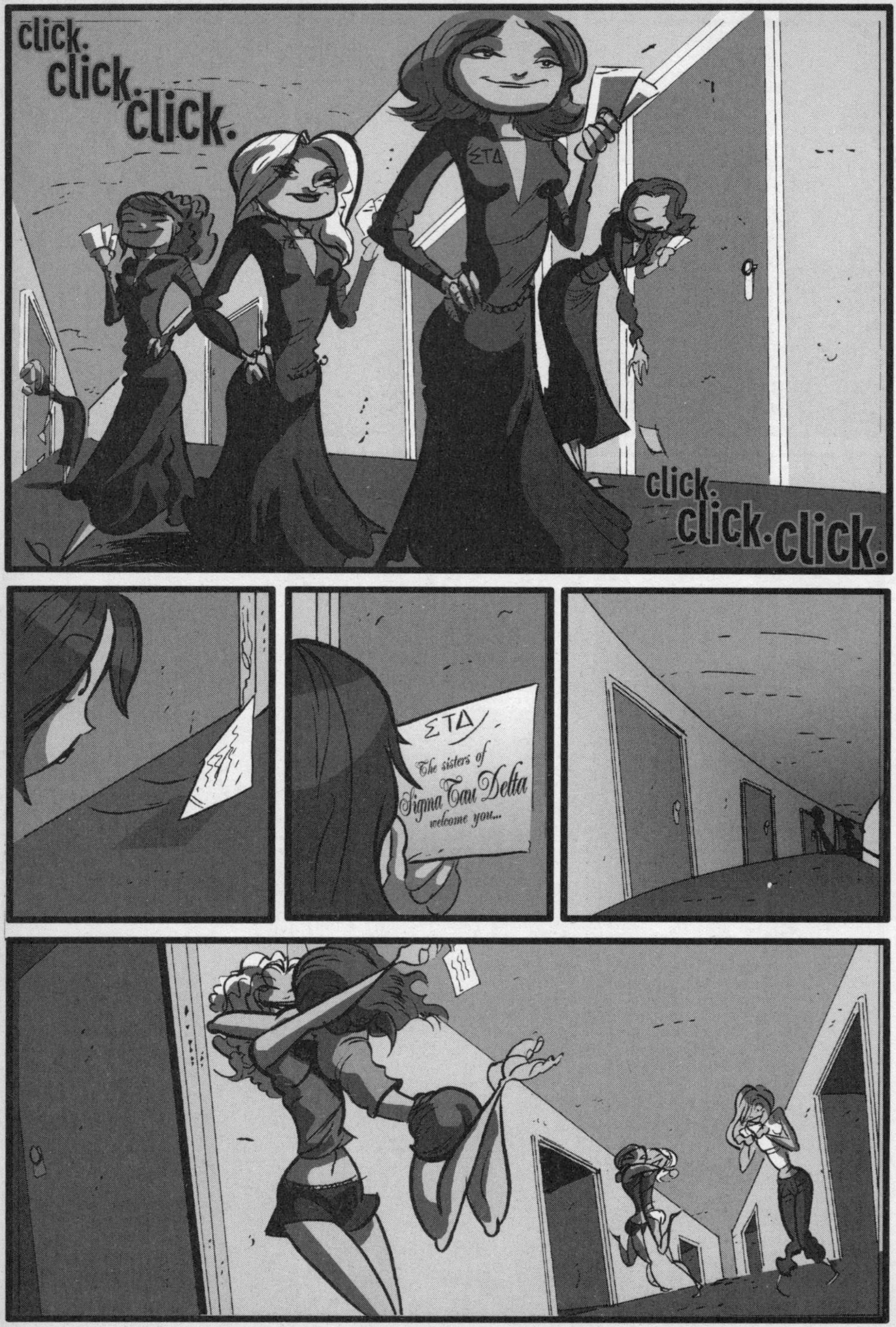

click.
click.
click.
click.
click.
click.
ΣΤΔ
The sisters of
Sigma Tau Delta
welcome you...

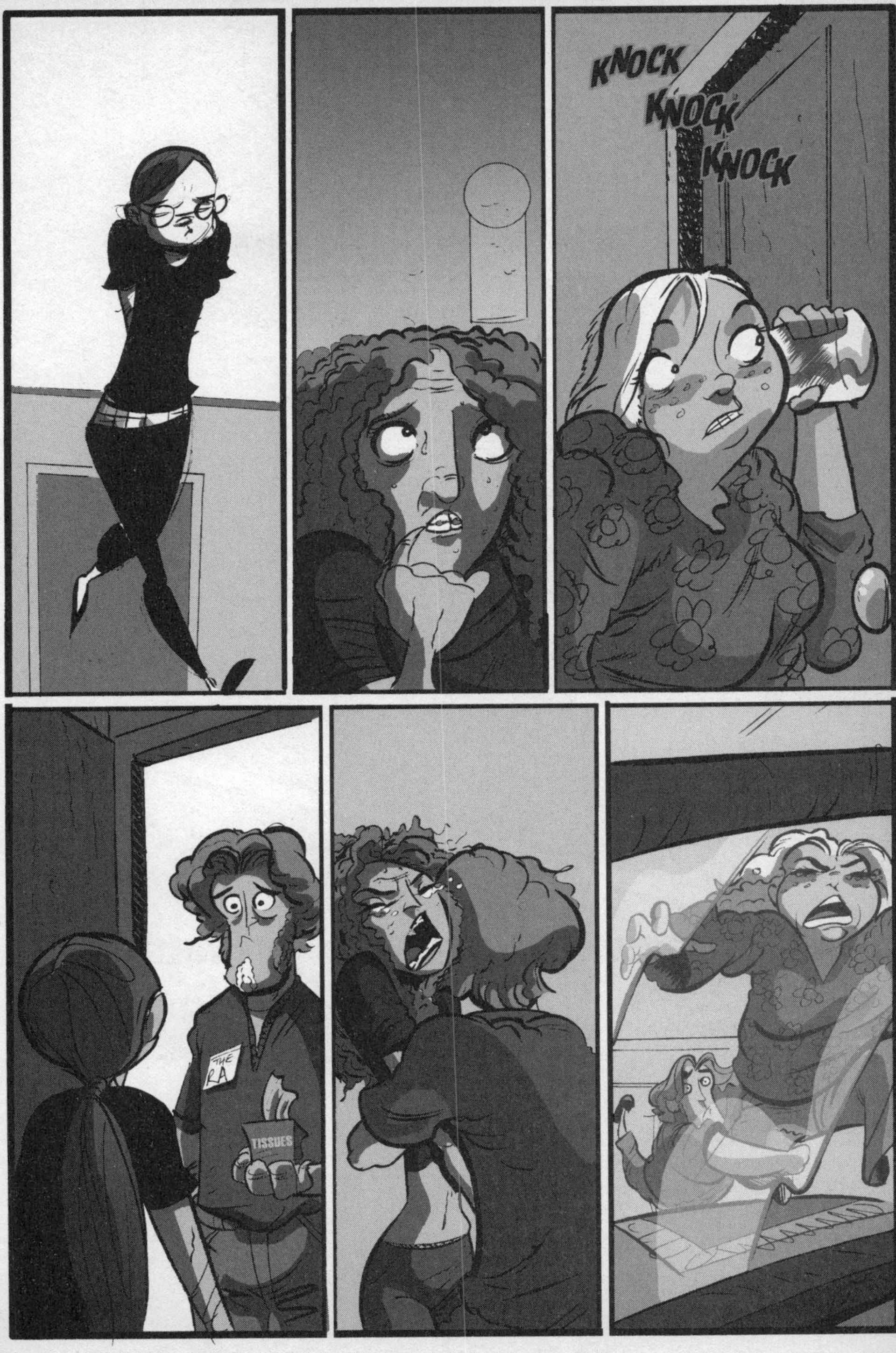
KNOCK
KNOCK
KNOCK
THE RA
TISSUES

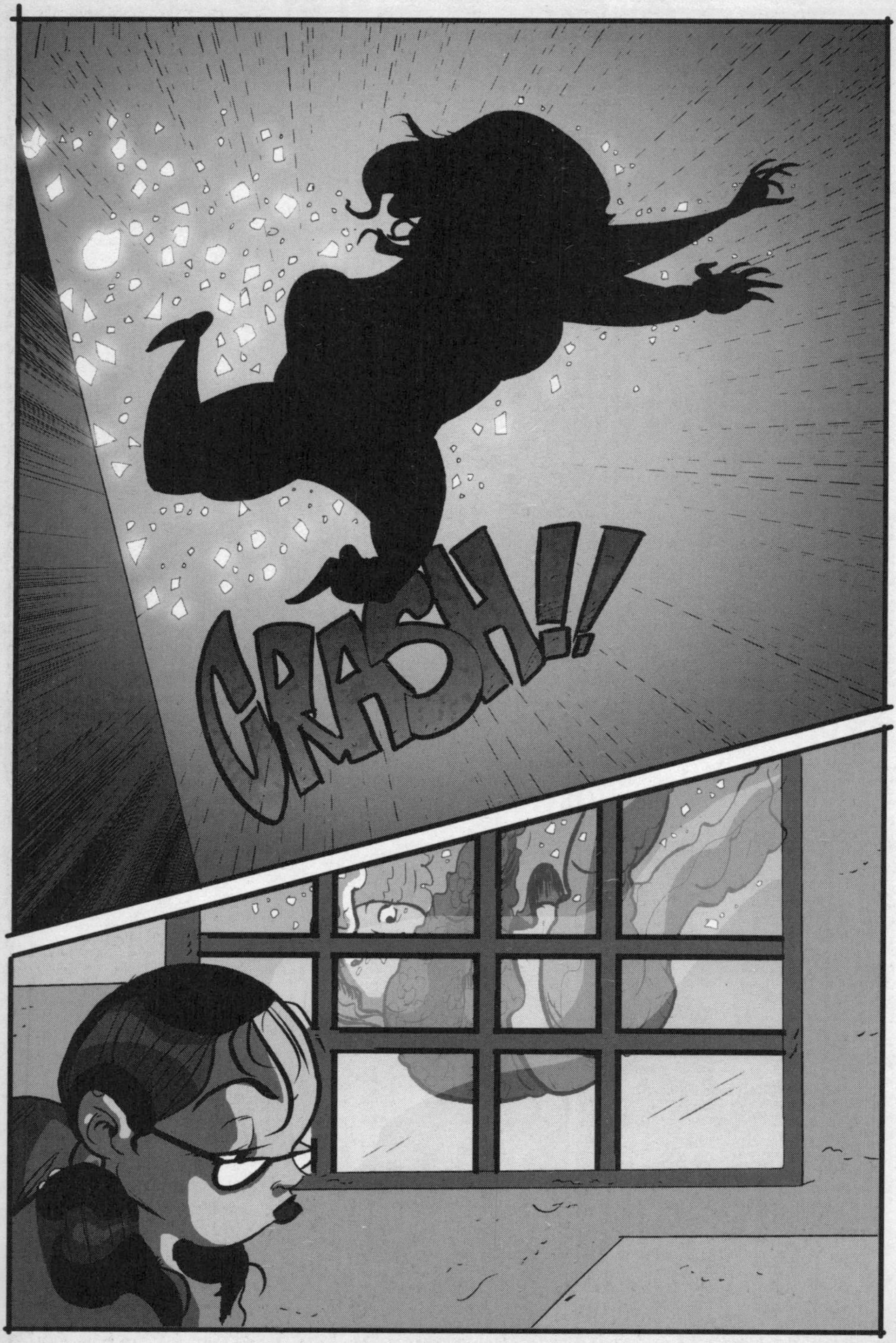
CRASH!!!

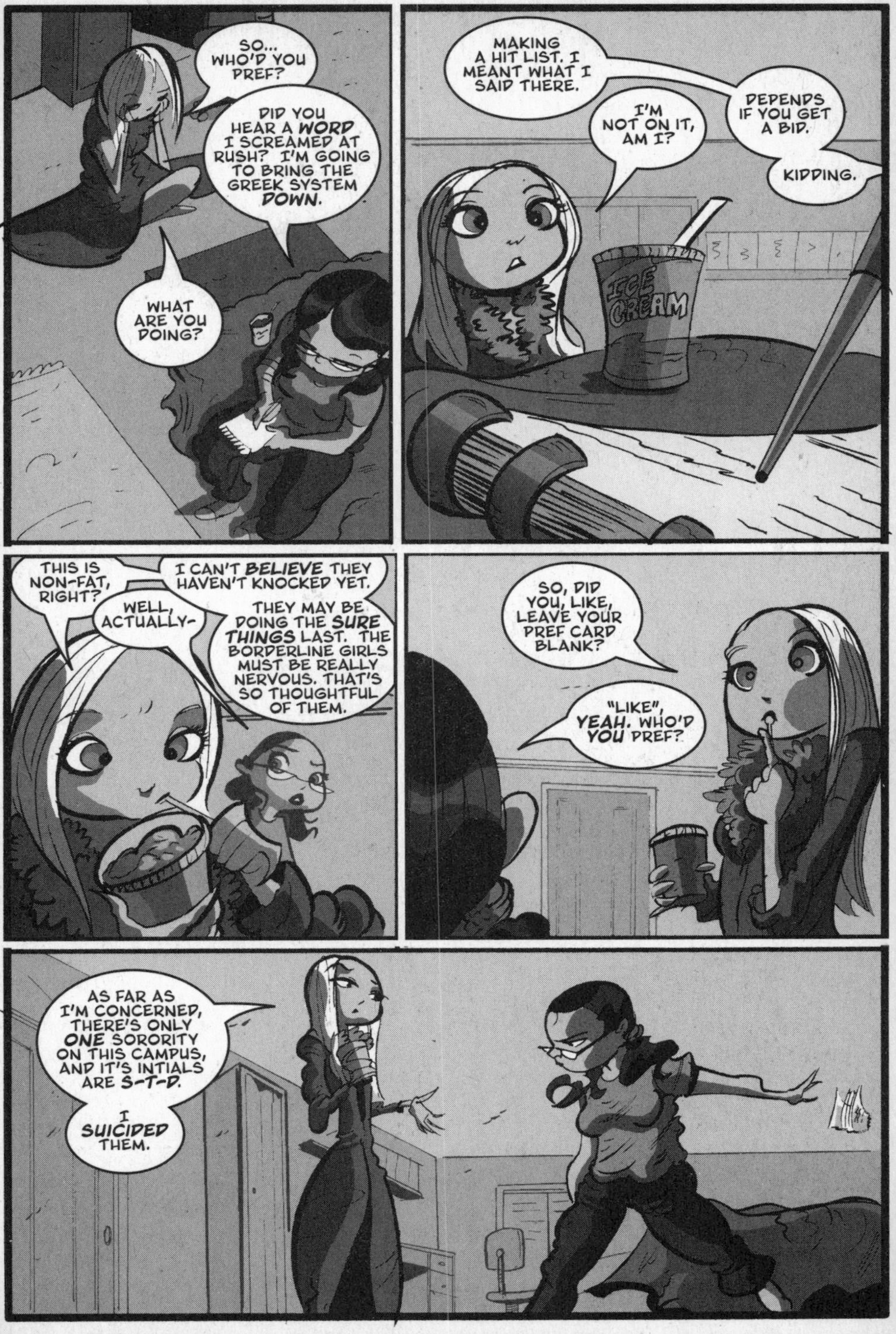

SO... WHO'D YOU PREF?
DID YOU HEAR A **WORD** I SCREAMED AT RUSH? I'M GOING TO BRING THE GREEK SYSTEM **DOWN**.
WHAT ARE YOU DOING?
MAKING A HIT LIST. I MEANT WHAT I SAID THERE.
I'M NOT ON IT, AM I?
DEPENDS IF YOU GET A BID.
KIDDING.
ICE CREAM
THIS IS NON-FAT, RIGHT?
I CAN'T **BELIEVE** THEY HAVEN'T KNOCKED YET.
WELL, ACTUALLY-
THEY MAY BE DOING THE **SURE THINGS** LAST. THE BORDERLINE GIRLS MUST BE REALLY NERVOUS. THAT'S SO THOUGHTFUL OF THEM.
SO, DID YOU, LIKE, LEAVE YOUR PREF CARD BLANK?
"LIKE", **YEAH.** WHO'D **YOU** PREF?
AS FAR AS I'M CONCERNED, THERE'S ONLY **ONE** SORORITY ON THIS CAMPUS, AND IT'S INTIALS ARE **S-T-D.**
I **SUICIDED** THEM.

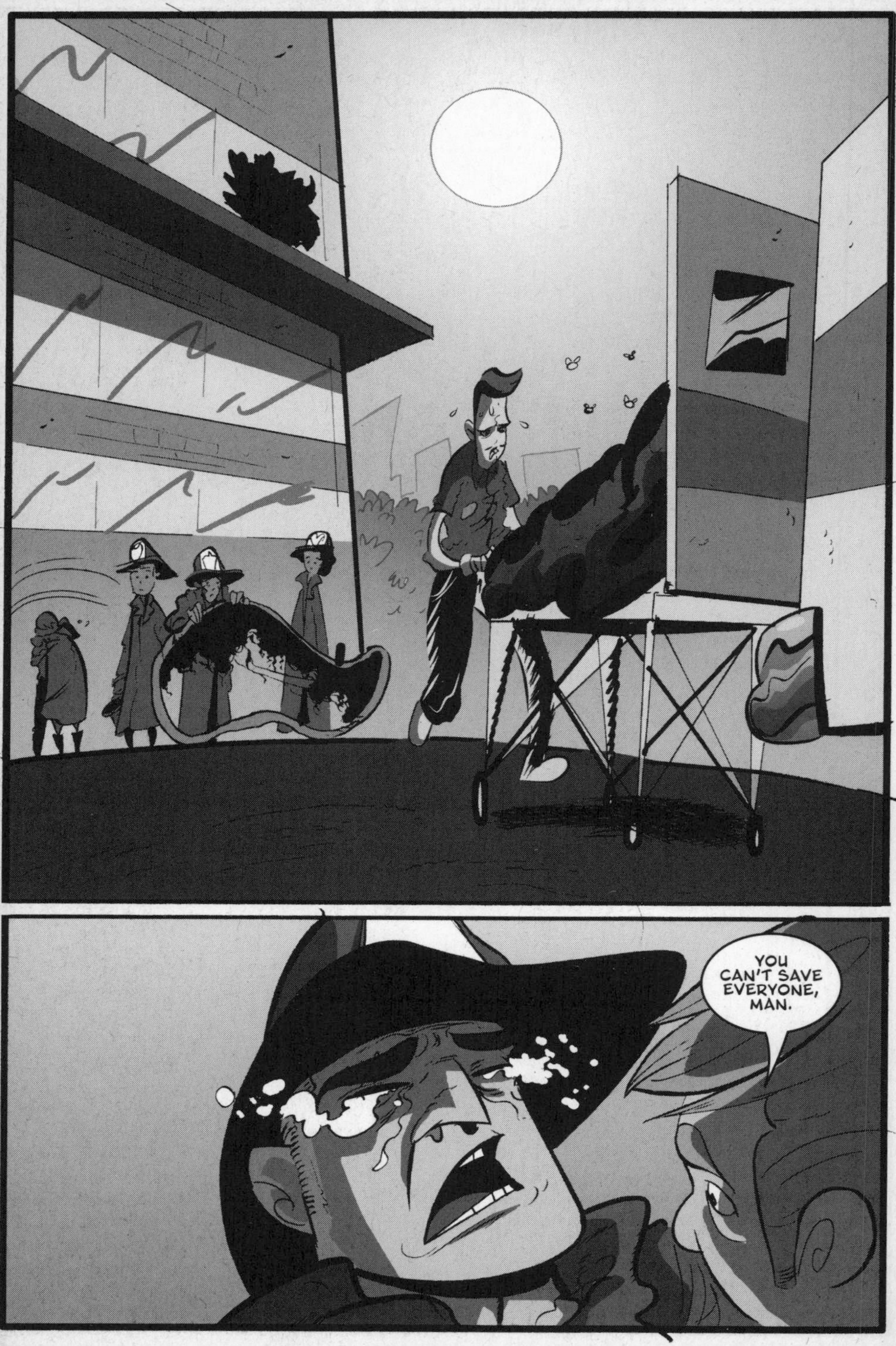
YOU CAN'T SAVE EVERYONE, MAN.

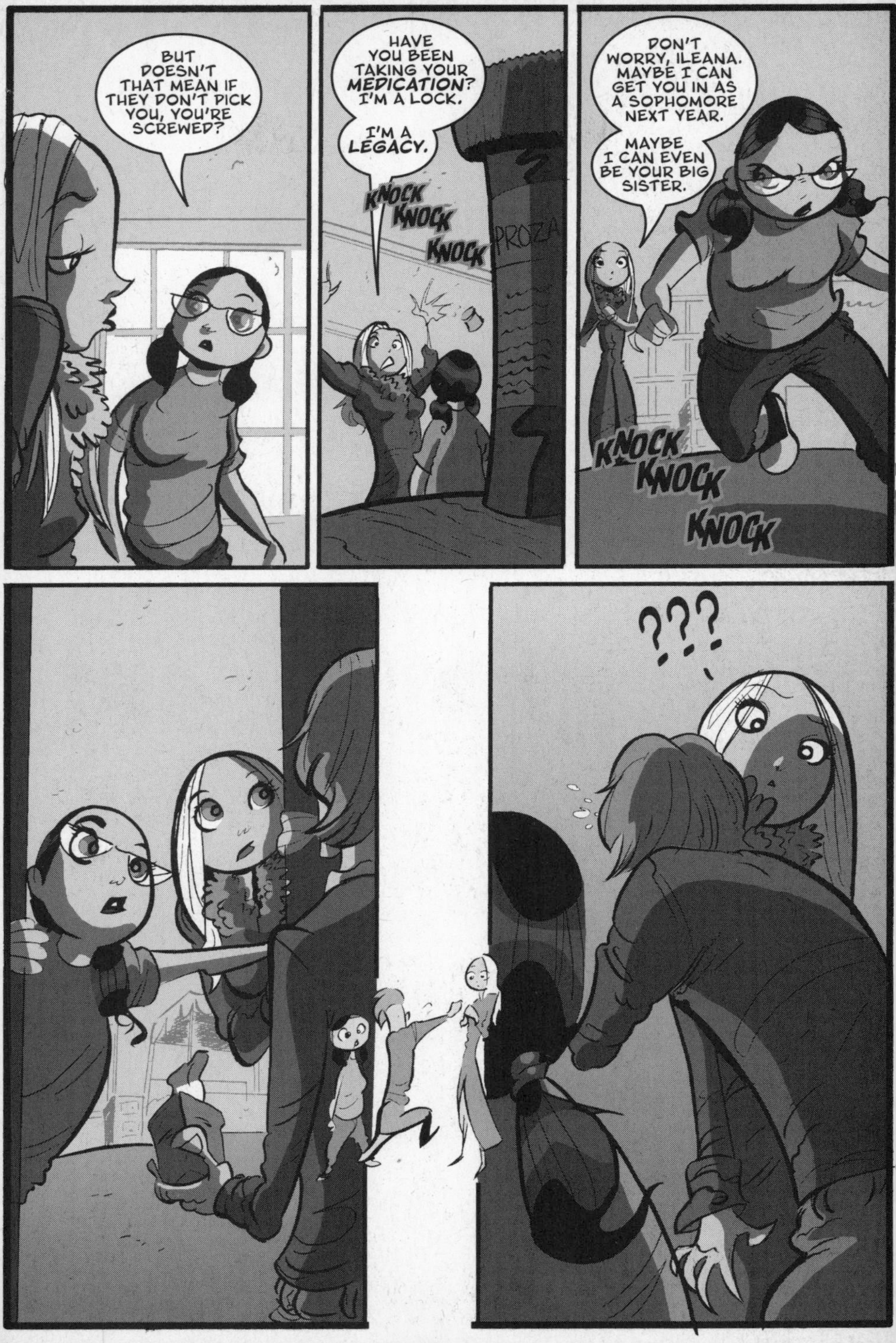
BUT DOESN'T THAT MEAN IF THEY DON'T PICK YOU, YOU'RE SCREWED?
HAVE YOU BEEN TAKING YOUR MEDICATION? I'M A LOCK.
I'M A LEGACY.
KNOCK KNOCK KNOCK
PROZA
DON'T WORRY, ILEANA. MAYBE I CAN GET YOU IN AS A SOPHOMORE NEXT YEAR.
MAYBE I CAN EVEN BE YOUR BIG SISTER.
KNOCK KNOCK KNOCK
???

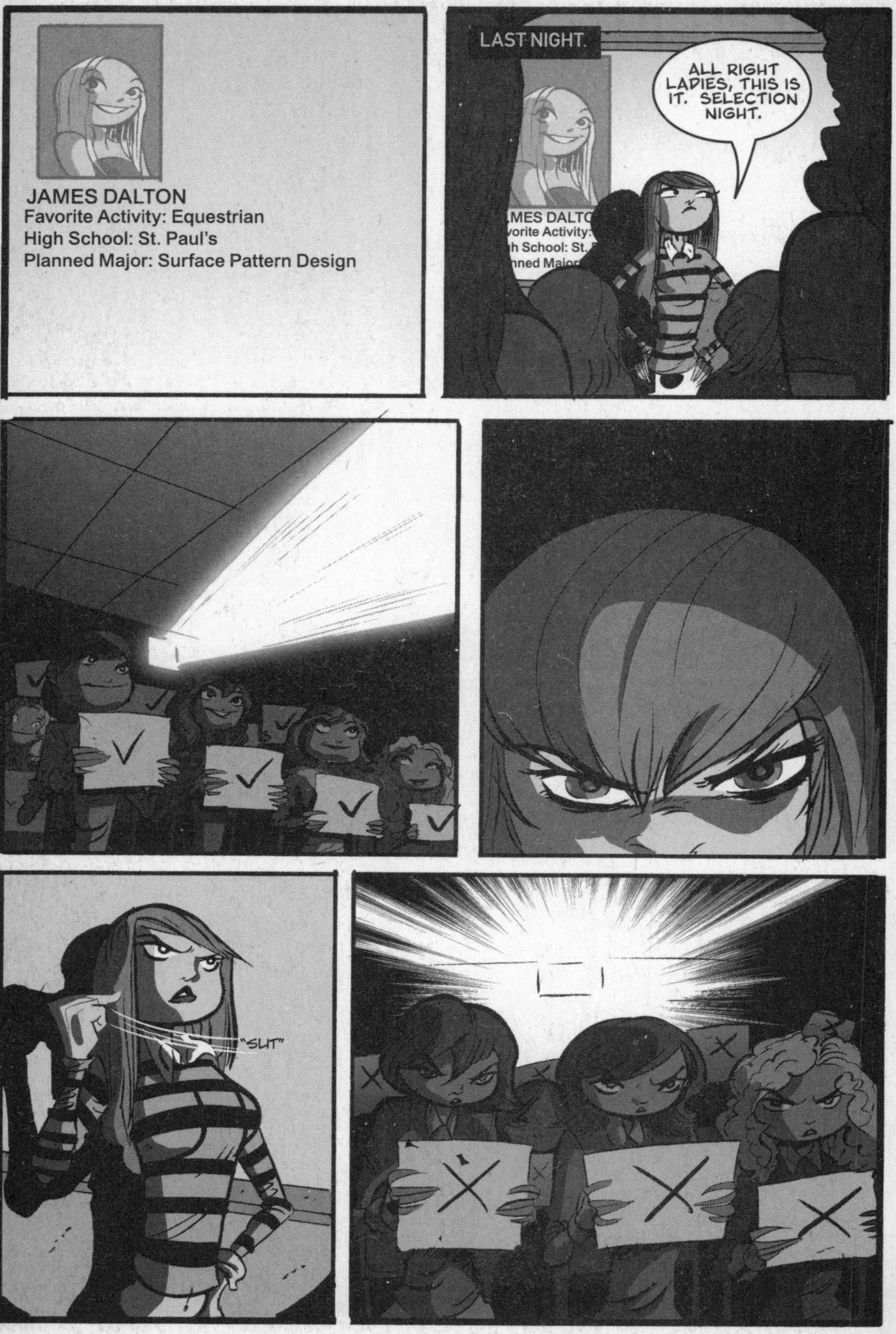
JAMES DALTON
Favorite Activity: Equestrian
High School: St. Paul's
Planned Major: Surface Pattern Design
LAST NIGHT.
ALL RIGHT LADIES, THIS IS IT. SELECTION NIGHT.
"SLUT"

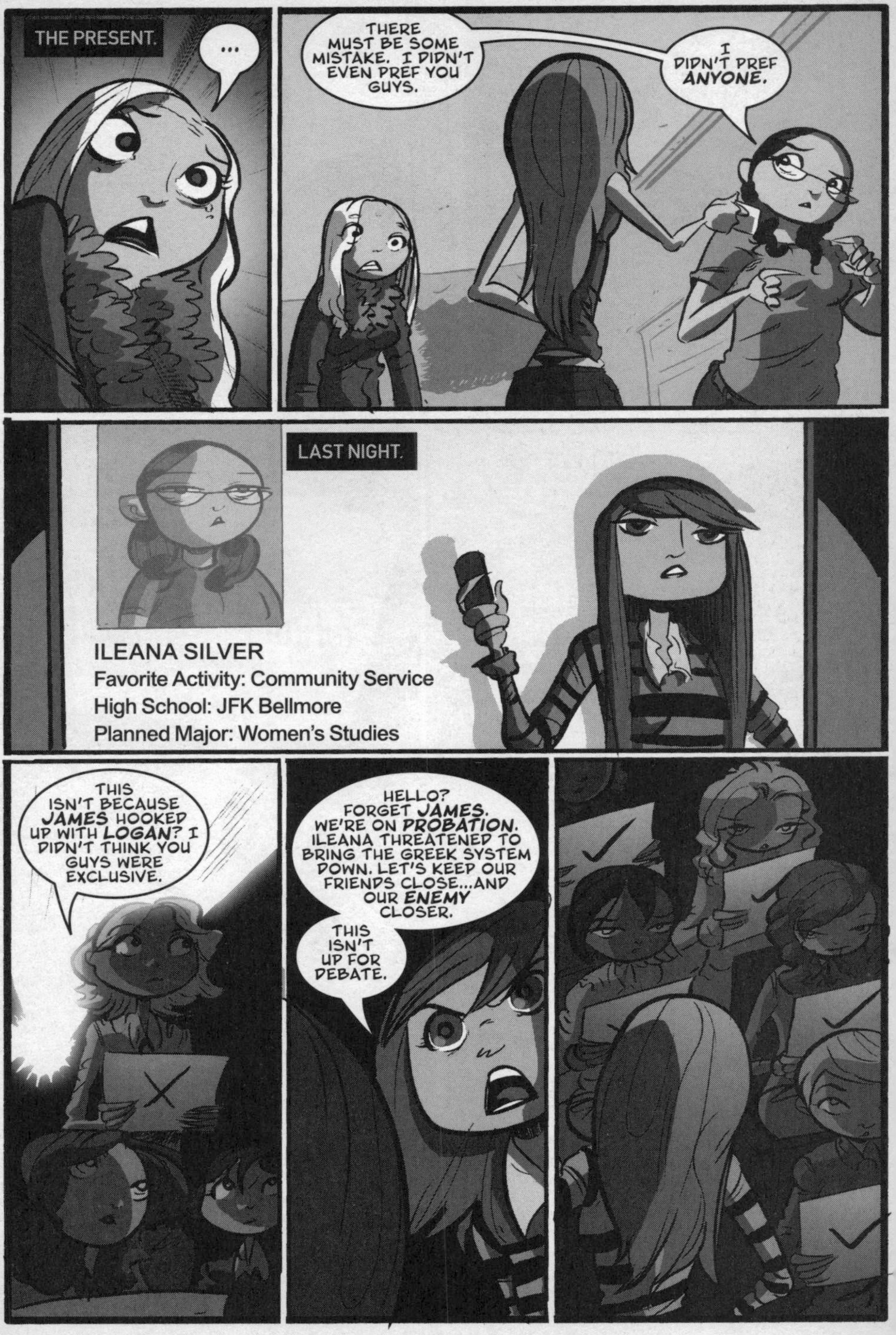
THE PRESENT.
...
THERE MUST BE SOME MISTAKE. I DIDN'T EVEN PREF YOU GUYS.
I DIDN'T PREF ANYONE.
LAST NIGHT.
ILEANA SILVER
Favorite Activity: Community Service
High School: JFK Bellmore
Planned Major: Women's Studies
THIS ISN'T BECAUSE JAMES HOOKED UP WITH LOGAN? I DIDN'T THINK YOU GUYS WERE EXCLUSIVE.
HELLO? FORGET JAMES. WE'RE ON PROBATION. ILEANA THREATENED TO BRING THE GREEK SYSTEM DOWN. LET'S KEEP OUR FRIENDS CLOSE...AND OUR ENEMY CLOSER.
THIS ISN'T UP FOR DEBATE.

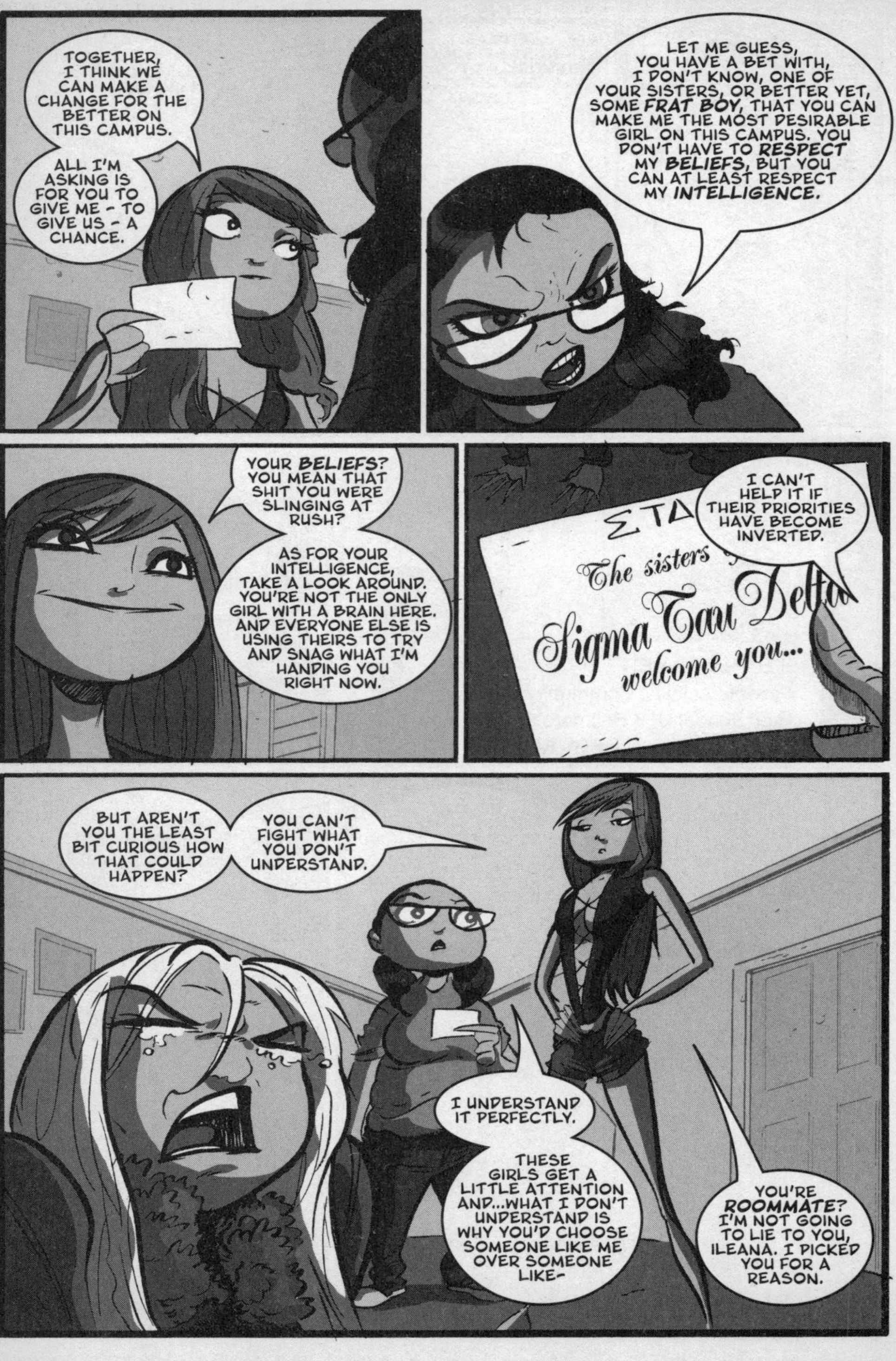
TOGETHER, I THINK WE CAN MAKE A CHANGE FOR THE BETTER ON THIS CAMPUS.
ALL I'M ASKING IS FOR YOU TO GIVE ME - TO GIVE US - A CHANCE.
LET ME GUESS, YOU HAVE A BET WITH, I DON'T KNOW, ONE OF YOUR SISTERS, OR BETTER YET, SOME FRAT BOY, THAT YOU CAN MAKE ME THE MOST DESIRABLE GIRL ON THIS CAMPUS. YOU DON'T HAVE TO RESPECT MY BELIEFS, BUT YOU CAN AT LEAST RESPECT MY INTELLIGENCE.
YOUR BELIEFS? YOU MEAN THAT SHIT YOU WERE SLINGING AT RUSH?
AS FOR YOUR INTELLIGENCE, TAKE A LOOK AROUND. YOU'RE NOT THE ONLY GIRL WITH A BRAIN HERE. AND EVERYONE ELSE IS USING THEIRS TO TRY AND SNAG WHAT I'M HANDING YOU RIGHT NOW.
ΣΤΔ
The sisters
Sigma Tau Delta
welcome you...
I CAN'T HELP IT IF THEIR PRIORITIES HAVE BECOME INVERTED.
BUT AREN'T YOU THE LEAST BIT CURIOUS HOW THAT COULD HAPPEN?
YOU CAN'T FIGHT WHAT YOU DON'T UNDERSTAND.
I UNDERSTAND IT PERFECTLY.
THESE GIRLS GET A LITTLE ATTENTION AND...WHAT I DON'T UNDERSTAND IS WHY YOU'D CHOOSE SOMEONE LIKE ME OVER SOMEONE LIKE-
YOU'RE ROOMMATE? I'M NOT GOING TO LIE TO YOU, ILEANA. I PICKED YOU FOR A REASON.

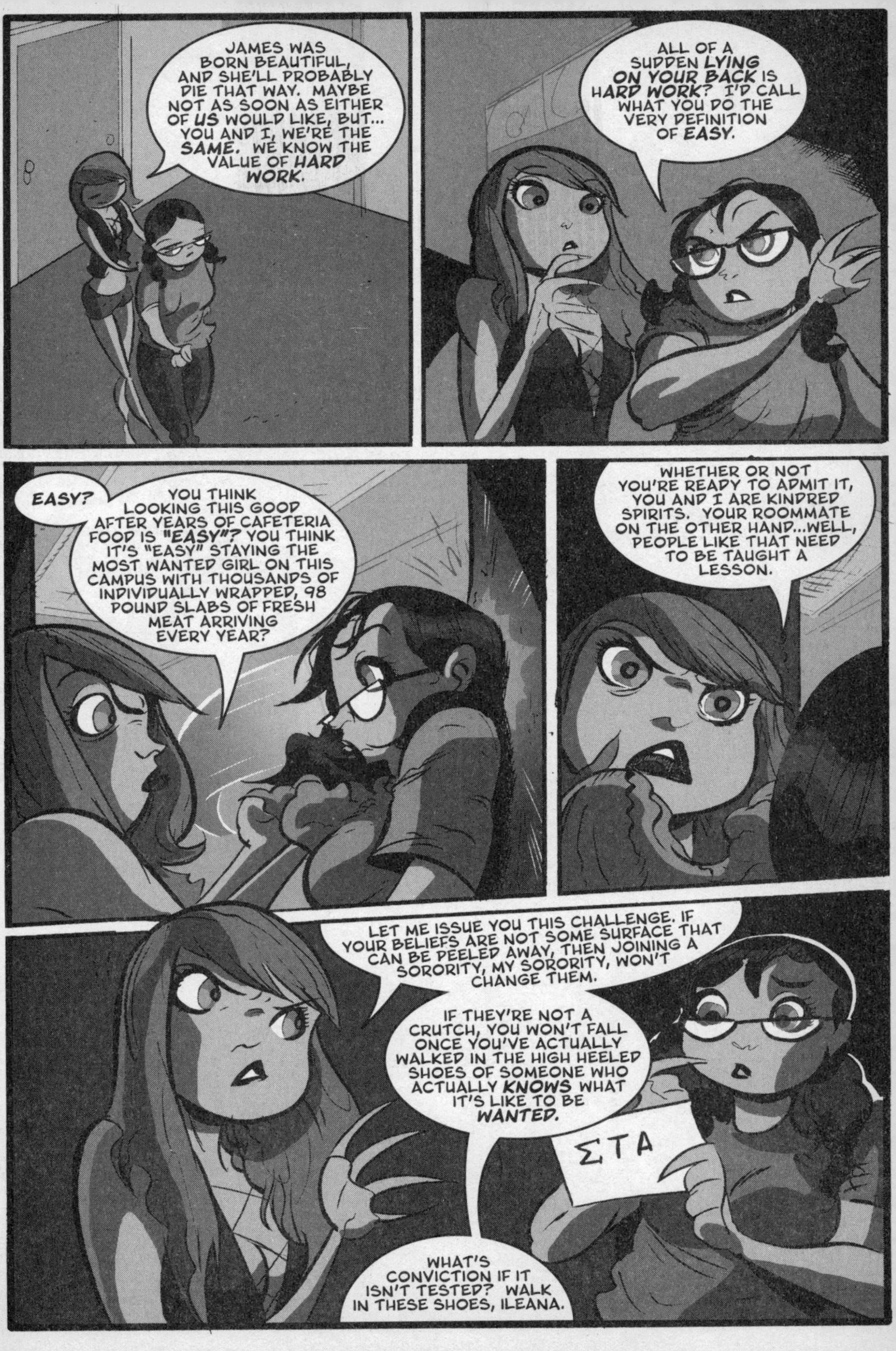
JAMES WAS BORN BEAUTIFUL, AND SHE'LL PROBABLY DIE THAT WAY. MAYBE NOT AS SOON AS EITHER OF US WOULD LIKE, BUT... YOU AND I, WE'RE THE SAME. WE KNOW THE VALUE OF HARD WORK.
ALL OF A SUDDEN LYING ON YOUR BACK IS HARD WORK? I'D CALL WHAT YOU DO THE VERY DEFINITION OF EASY.
EASY?
YOU THINK LOOKING THIS GOOD AFTER YEARS OF CAFETERIA FOOD IS "EASY"? YOU THINK IT'S "EASY" STAYING THE MOST WANTED GIRL ON THIS CAMPUS WITH THOUSANDS OF INDIVIDUALLY WRAPPED, 98 POUND SLABS OF FRESH MEAT ARRIVING EVERY YEAR?
WHETHER OR NOT YOU'RE READY TO ADMIT IT, YOU AND I ARE KINDRED SPIRITS. YOUR ROOMMATE ON THE OTHER HAND...WELL, PEOPLE LIKE THAT NEED TO BE TAUGHT A LESSON.
LET ME ISSUE YOU THIS CHALLENGE. IF YOUR BELIEFS ARE NOT SOME SURFACE THAT CAN BE PEELED AWAY, THEN JOINING A SORORITY, MY SORORITY, WON'T CHANGE THEM.
IF THEY'RE NOT A CRUTCH, YOU WON'T FALL ONCE YOU'VE ACTUALLY WALKED IN THE HIGH HEELED SHOES OF SOMEONE WHO ACTUALLY KNOWS WHAT IT'S LIKE TO BE WANTED.
ΣΤΑ
WHAT'S CONVICTION IF IT ISN'T TESTED? WALK IN THESE SHOES, ILEANA.

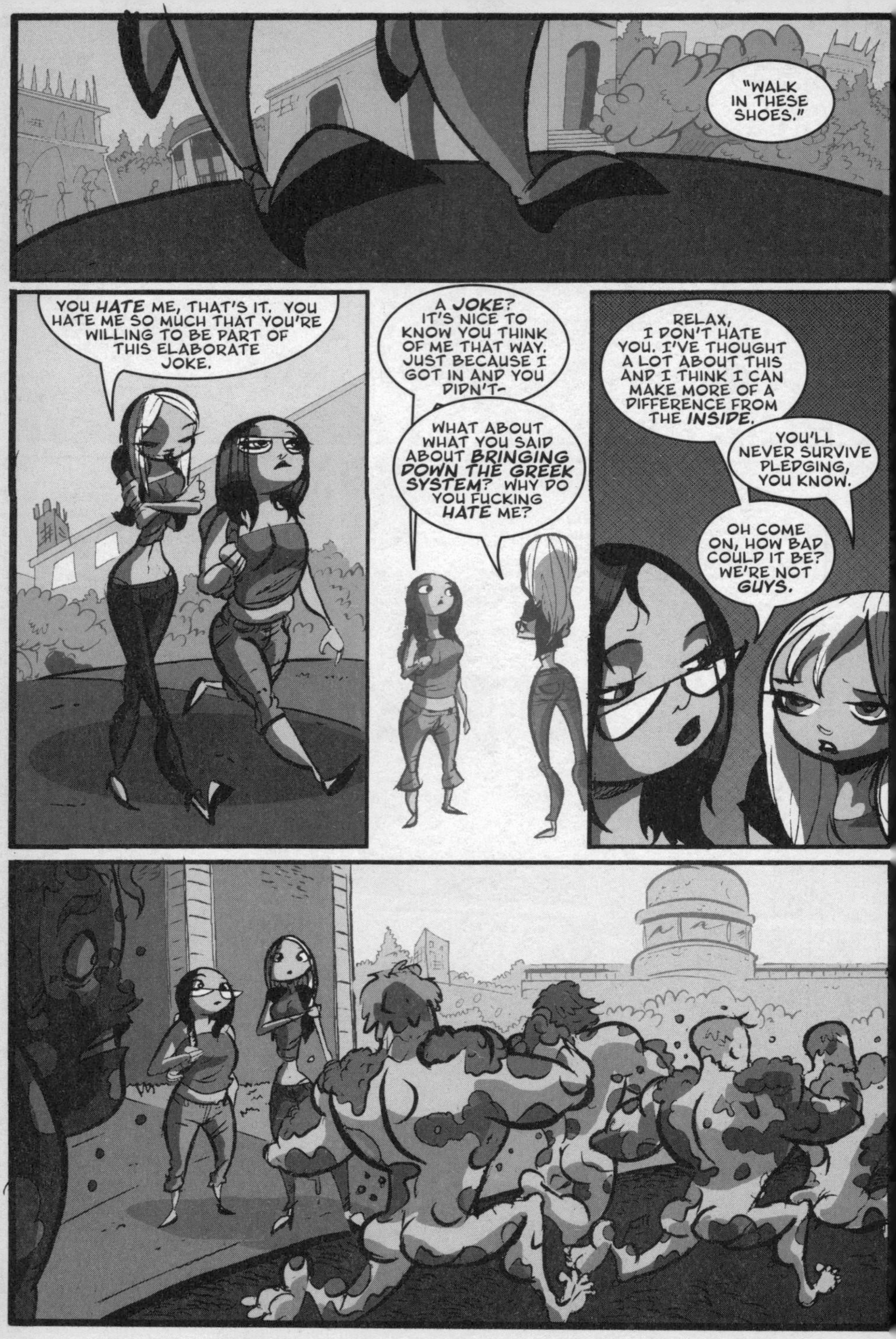
"WALK IN THESE SHOES."
YOU HATE ME, THAT'S IT. YOU HATE ME SO MUCH THAT YOU'RE WILLING TO BE PART OF THIS ELABORATE JOKE.
A JOKE? IT'S NICE TO KNOW YOU THINK OF ME THAT WAY. JUST BECAUSE I GOT IN AND YOU DIDN'T-
WHAT ABOUT WHAT YOU SAID ABOUT BRINGING DOWN THE GREEK SYSTEM? WHY DO YOU FUCKING HATE ME?
RELAX, I DON'T HATE YOU. I'VE THOUGHT A LOT ABOUT THIS AND I THINK I CAN MAKE MORE OF A DIFFERENCE FROM THE INSIDE.
YOU'LL NEVER SURVIVE PLEDGING, YOU KNOW.
OH COME ON, HOW BAD COULD IT BE? WE'RE NOT GUYS.

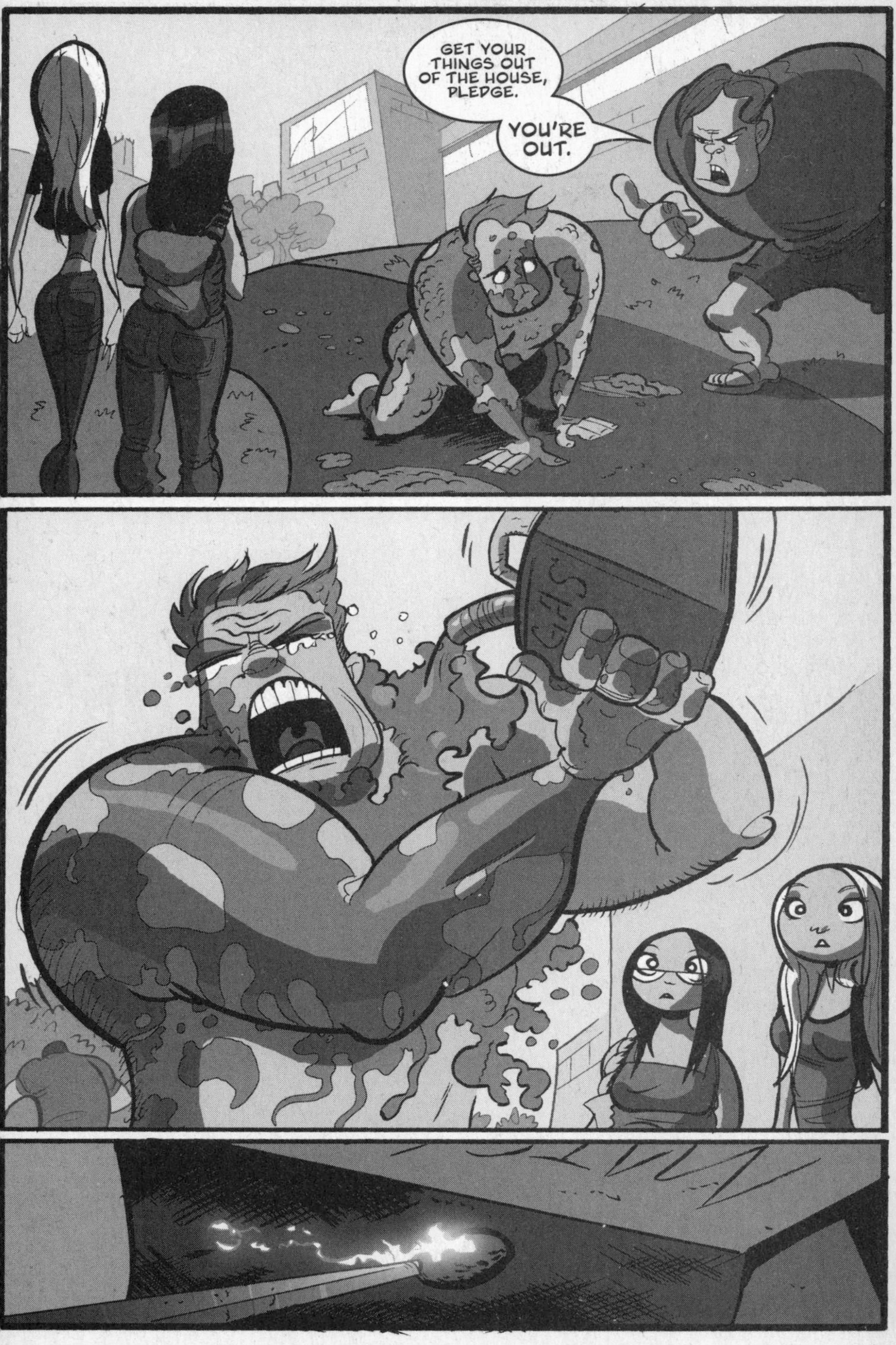
GET YOUR THINGS OUT OF THE HOUSE, PLEDGE.
YOU'RE OUT.

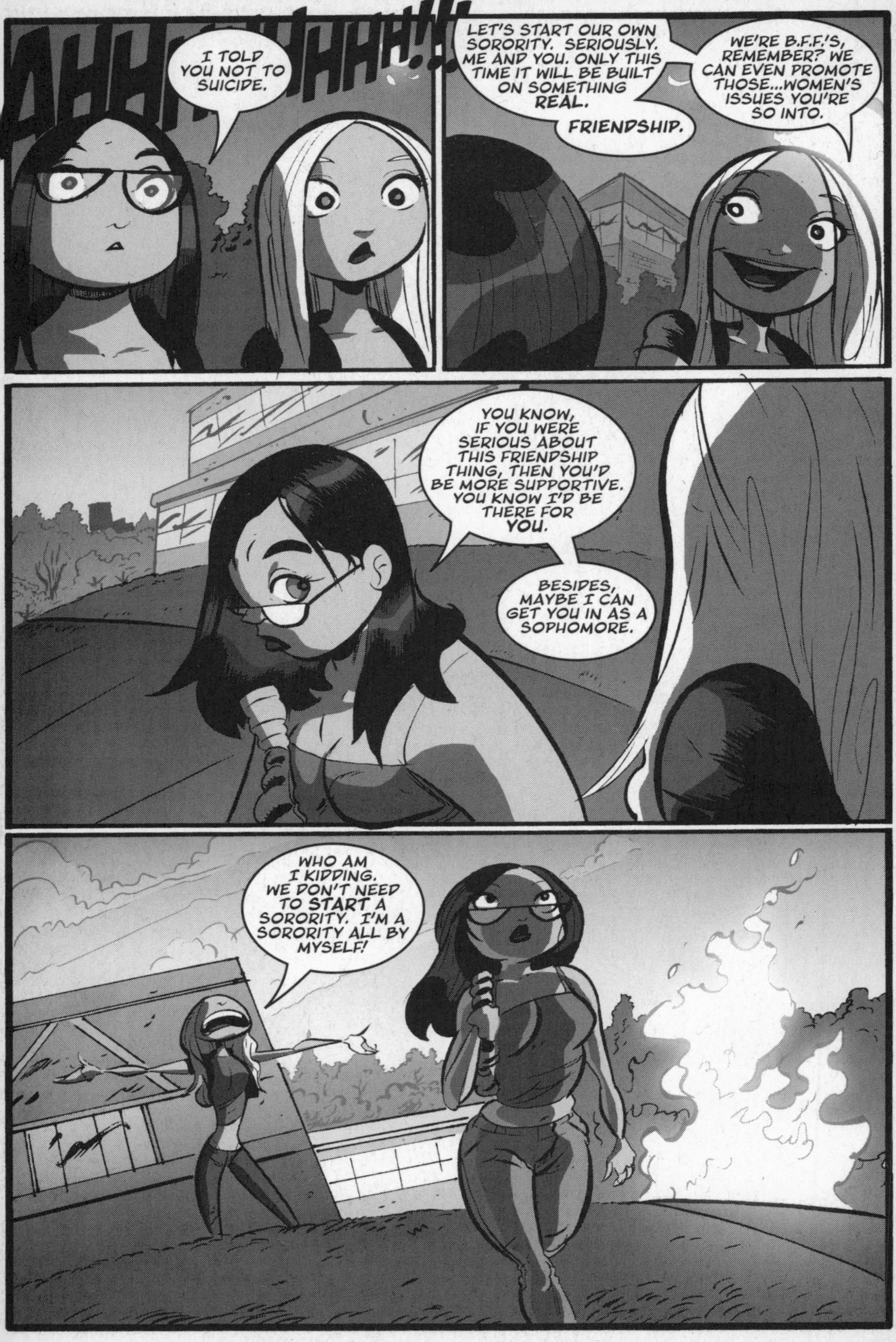
I TOLD YOU NOT TO SUICIDE.
LET'S START OUR OWN SORORITY. SERIOUSLY. ME AND YOU. ONLY THIS TIME IT WILL BE BUILT ON SOMETHING REAL.
FRIENDSHIP.
WE'RE B.F.F.'S, REMEMBER? WE CAN EVEN PROMOTE THOSE...WOMEN'S ISSUES YOU'RE SO INTO.
YOU KNOW, IF YOU WERE SERIOUS ABOUT THIS FRIENDSHIP THING, THEN YOU'D BE MORE SUPPORTIVE. YOU KNOW I'D BE THERE FOR YOU.
BESIDES, MAYBE I CAN GET YOU IN AS A SOPHOMORE.
WHO AM I KIDDING. WE DON'T NEED TO START A SORORITY. I'M A SORORITY ALL BY MYSELF!

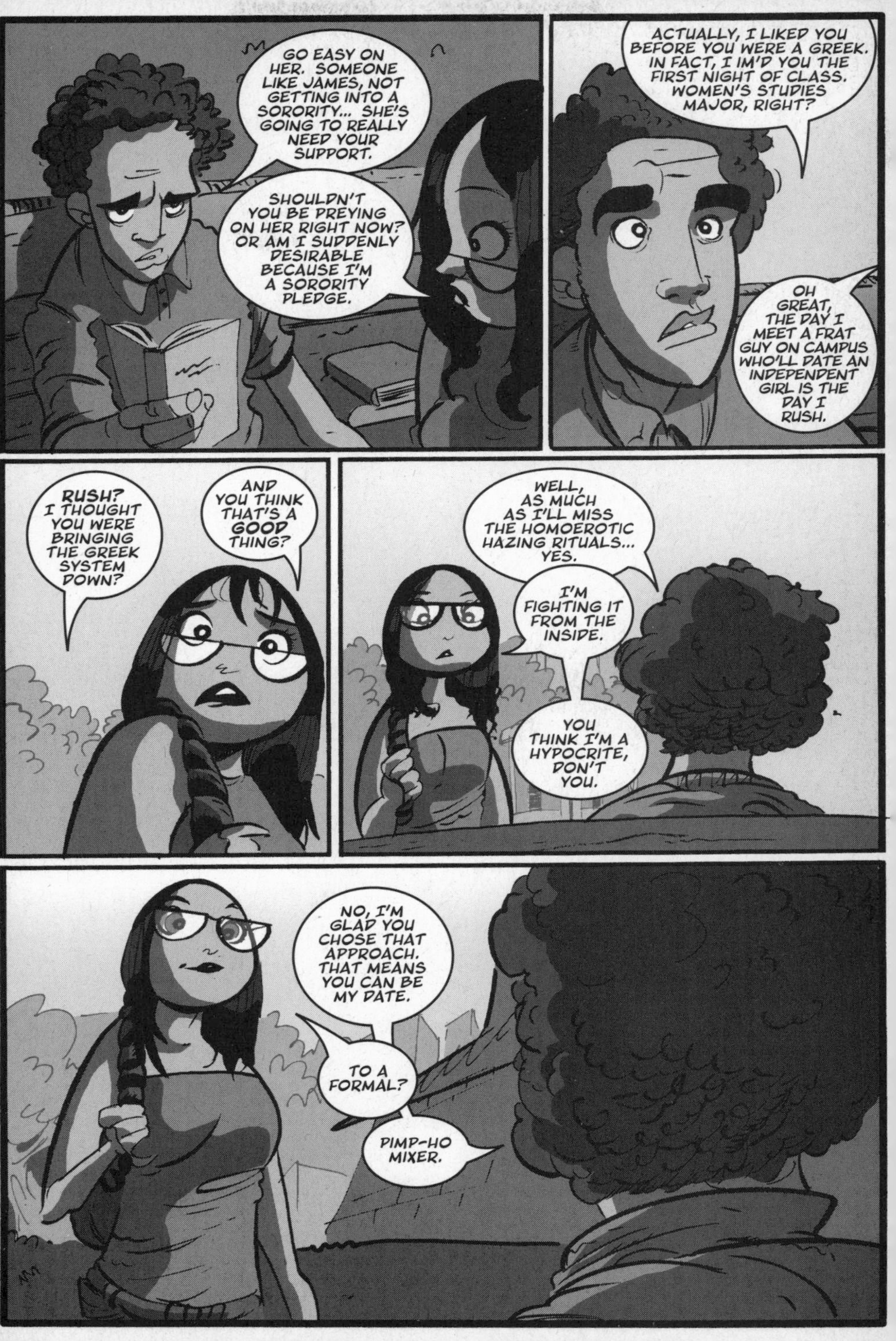
GO EASY ON HER. SOMEONE LIKE JAMES, NOT GETTING INTO A SORORITY... SHE'S GOING TO REALLY NEED YOUR SUPPORT.
SHOULDN'T YOU BE PREYING ON HER RIGHT NOW? OR AM I SUDDENLY DESIRABLE BECAUSE I'M A SORORITY PLEDGE.
ACTUALLY, I LIKED YOU BEFORE YOU WERE A GREEK. IN FACT, I IM'D YOU THE FIRST NIGHT OF CLASS. WOMEN'S STUDIES MAJOR, RIGHT?
OH GREAT, THE DAY I MEET A FRAT GUY ON CAMPUS WHO'LL DATE AN INDEPENDENT GIRL IS THE DAY I RUSH.
RUSH? I THOUGHT YOU WERE BRINGING THE GREEK SYSTEM DOWN?
AND YOU THINK THAT'S A GOOD THING?
WELL, AS MUCH AS I'LL MISS THE HOMOEROTIC HAZING RITUALS... YES.
I'M FIGHTING IT FROM THE INSIDE.
YOU THINK I'M A HYPOCRITE, DON'T YOU.
NO, I'M GLAD YOU CHOSE THAT APPROACH. THAT MEANS YOU CAN BE MY DATE.
TO A FORMAL?
PIMP-HO MIXER.

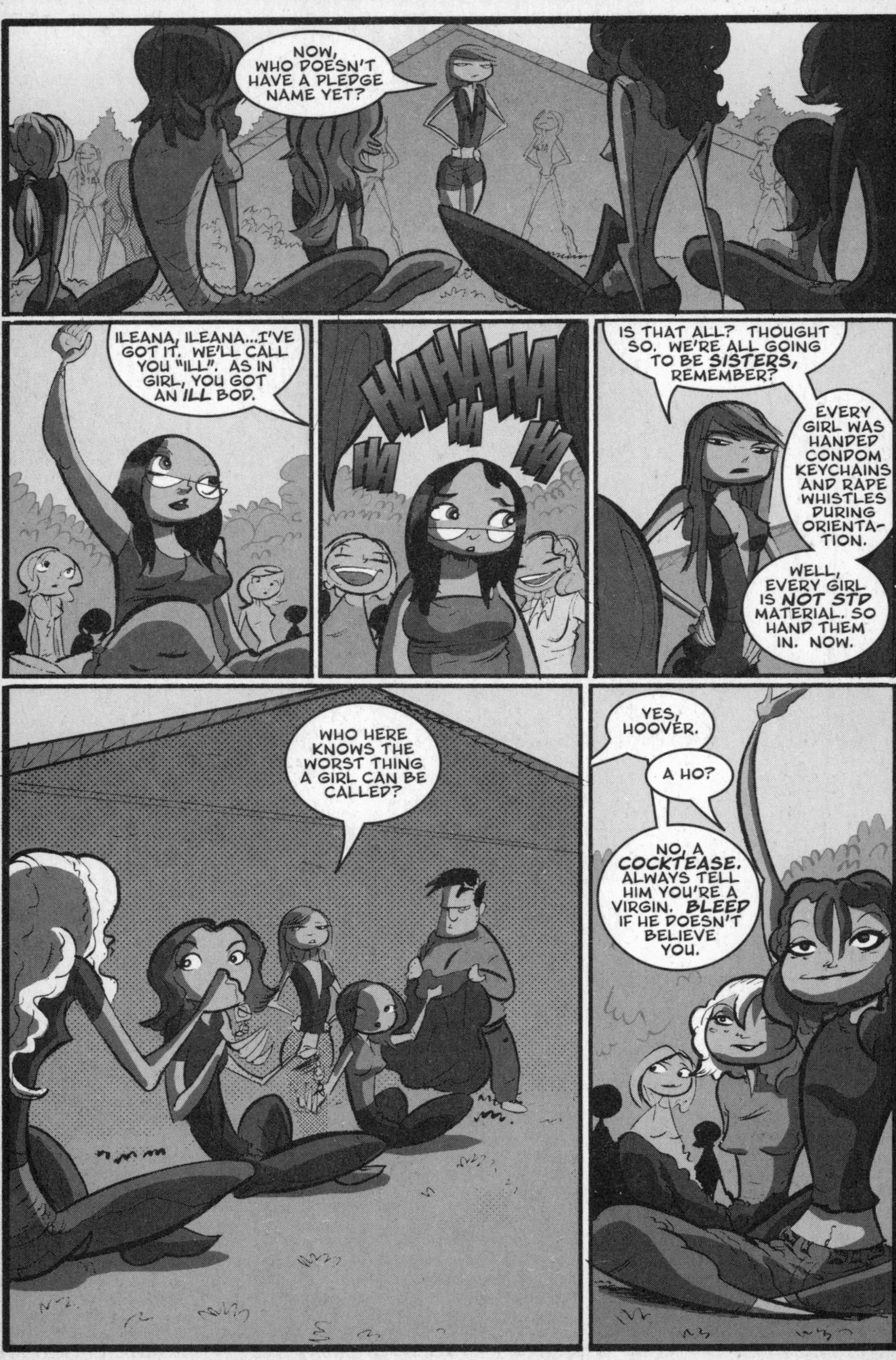
NOW, WHO DOESN'T HAVE A PLEDGE NAME YET?
ILEANA, ILEANA...I'VE GOT IT. WE'LL CALL YOU "ILL". AS IN GIRL, YOU GOT AN ILL BOD.
HAHAHA HA HA HA HA
IS THAT ALL? THOUGHT SO. WE'RE ALL GOING TO BE SISTERS, REMEMBER?
EVERY GIRL WAS HANDED CONDOM KEYCHAINS AND RAPE WHISTLES DURING ORIENTATION.
WELL, EVERY GIRL IS NOT STD MATERIAL. SO HAND THEM IN. NOW.
WHO HERE KNOWS THE WORST THING A GIRL CAN BE CALLED?
YES, HOOVER.
A HO?
NO, A COCKTEASE. ALWAYS TELL HIM YOU'RE A VIRGIN. BLEED IF HE DOESN'T BELIEVE YOU.

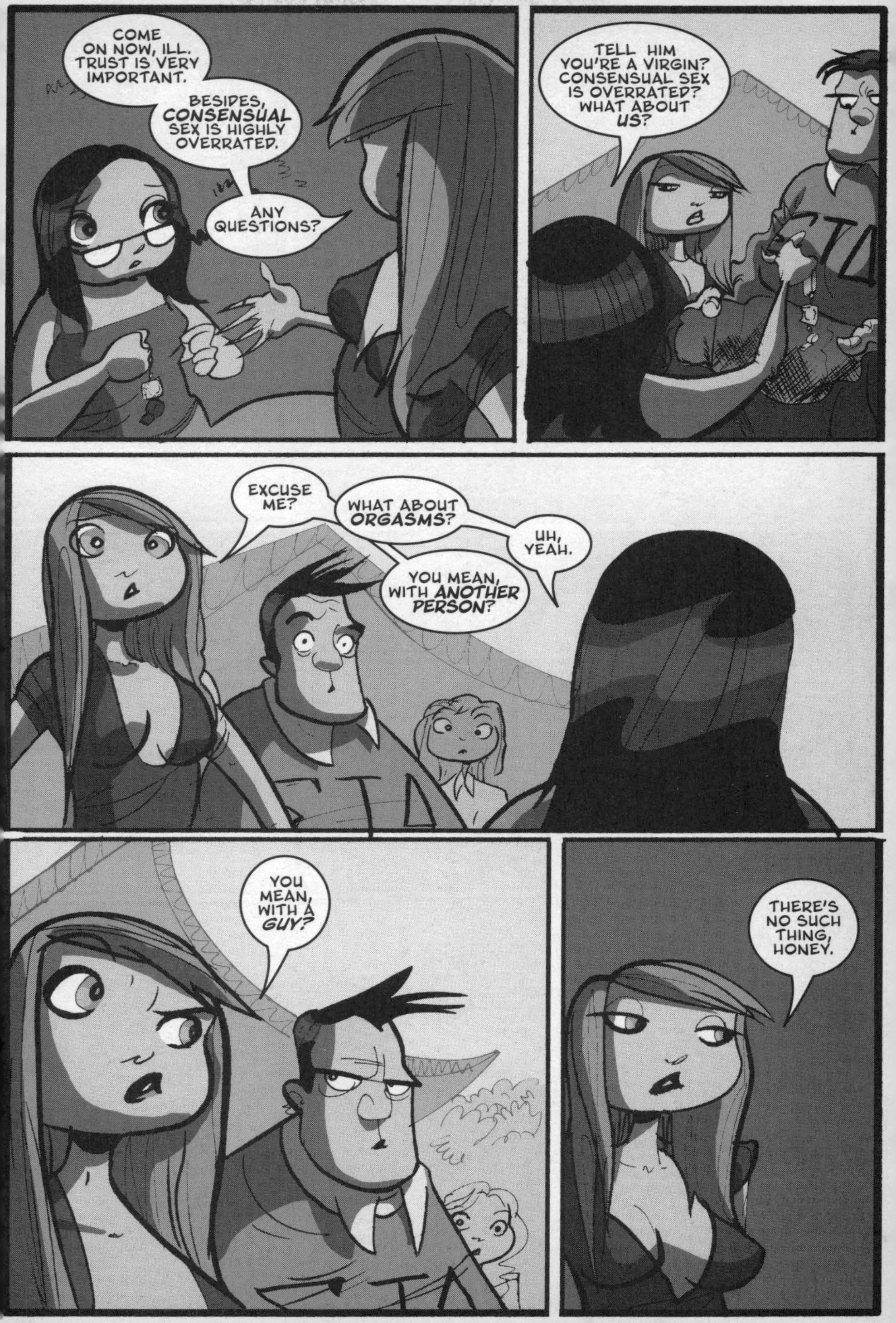
COME ON NOW, ILL. TRUST IS VERY IMPORTANT.
BESIDES, CONSENSUAL SEX IS HIGHLY OVERRATED.
ANY QUESTIONS?
TELL HIM YOU'RE A VIRGIN? CONSENSUAL SEX IS OVERRATED? WHAT ABOUT US?
EXCUSE ME?
WHAT ABOUT ORGASMS?
UH, YEAH.
YOU MEAN, WITH ANOTHER PERSON?
YOU MEAN, WITH A GUY?
THERE'S NO SUCH THING, HONEY.

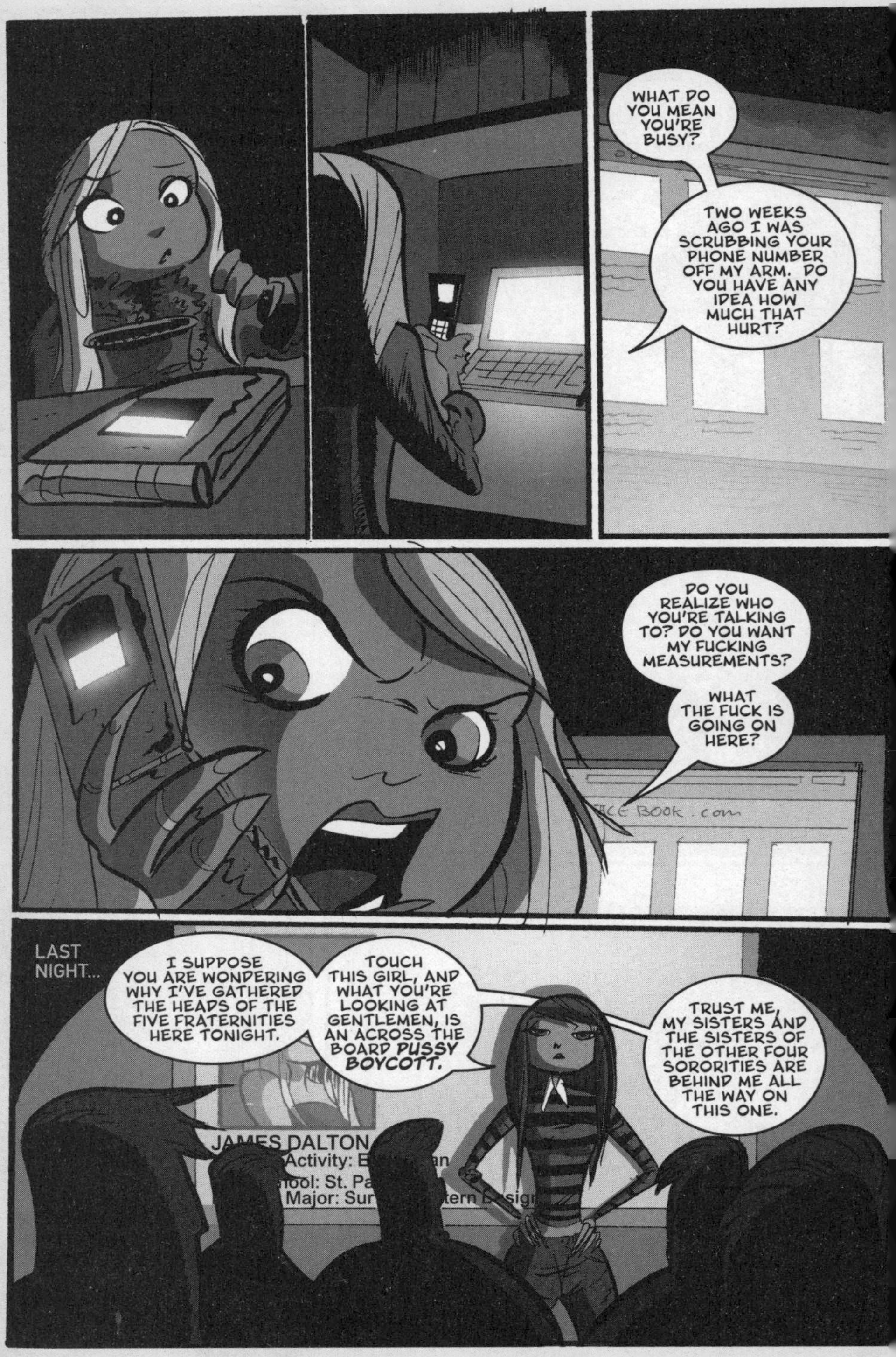
WHAT DO YOU MEAN YOU'RE BUSY?
TWO WEEKS AGO I WAS SCRUBBING YOUR PHONE NUMBER OFF MY ARM. DO YOU HAVE ANY IDEA HOW MUCH THAT HURT?
DO YOU REALIZE WHO YOU'RE TALKING TO? DO YOU WANT MY FUCKING MEASUREMENTS?
WHAT THE FUCK IS GOING ON HERE?
LAST NIGHT...
I SUPPOSE YOU ARE WONDERING WHY I'VE GATHERED THE HEADS OF THE FIVE FRATERNITIES HERE TONIGHT.
TOUCH THIS GIRL, AND WHAT YOU'RE LOOKING AT GENTLEMEN, IS AN ACROSS THE BOARD *PUSSY BOYCOTT.*
TRUST ME, MY SISTERS AND THE SISTERS OF THE OTHER FOUR SORORITIES ARE BEHIND ME ALL THE WAY ON THIS ONE.
JAMES DALTON

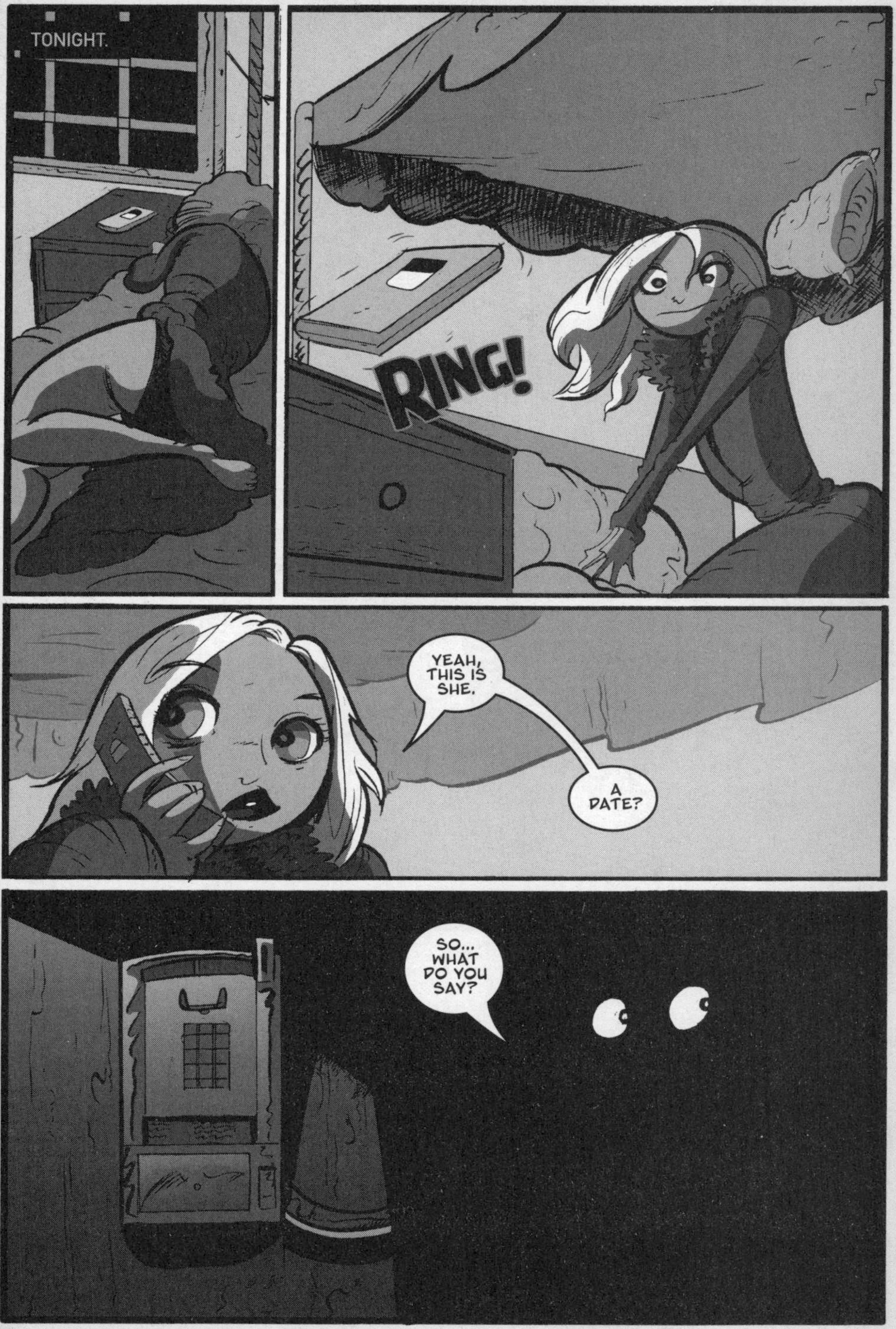
TONIGHT.
RING!
YEAH, THIS IS SHE.
A DATE?
SO... WHAT DO YOU SAY?

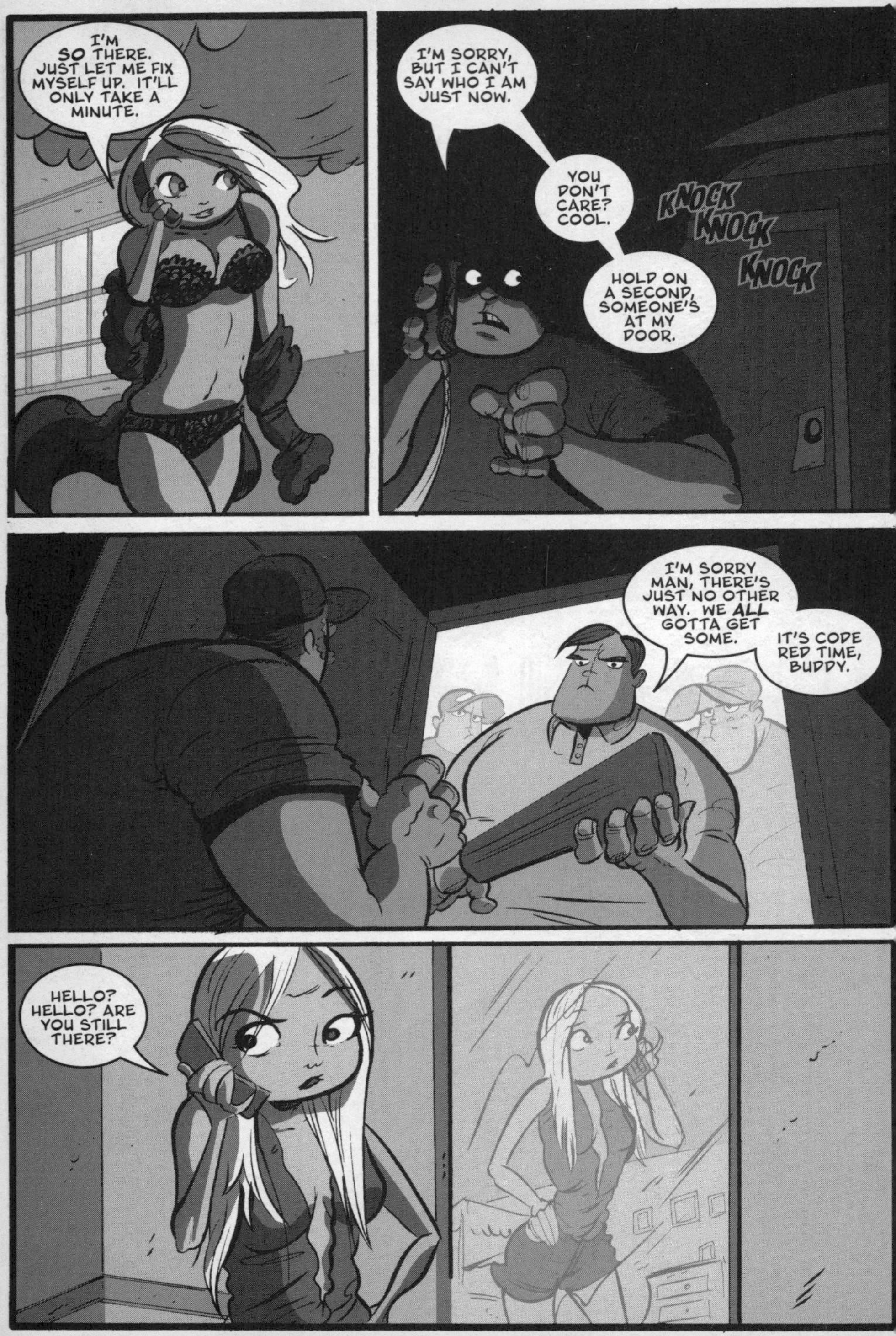
I'M SO THERE. JUST LET ME FIX MYSELF UP. IT'LL ONLY TAKE A MINUTE.
I'M SORRY, BUT I CAN'T SAY WHO I AM JUST NOW.
YOU DON'T CARE? COOL.
HOLD ON A SECOND, SOMEONE'S AT MY DOOR.
KNOCK KNOCK KNOCK
I'M SORRY MAN, THERE'S JUST NO OTHER WAY. WE ALL GOTTA GET SOME.
IT'S CODE RED TIME, BUDDY.
HELLO? HELLO? ARE YOU STILL THERE?

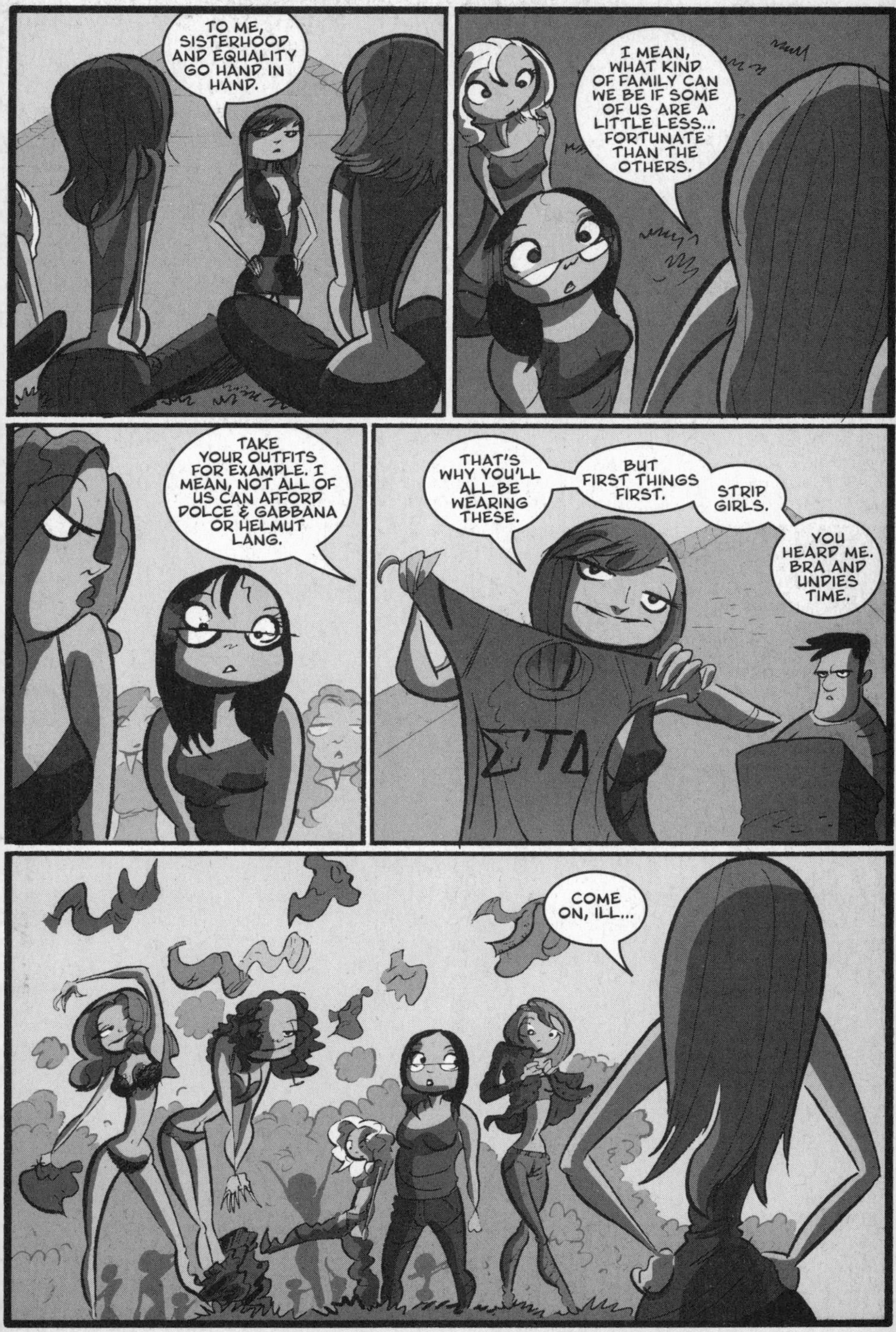
TO ME, SISTERHOOD AND EQUALITY GO HAND IN HAND.
I MEAN, WHAT KIND OF FAMILY CAN WE BE IF SOME OF US ARE A LITTLE LESS... FORTUNATE THAN THE OTHERS.
TAKE YOUR OUTFITS FOR EXAMPLE. I MEAN, NOT ALL OF US CAN AFFORD DOLCE & GABBANA OR HELMUT LANG.
THAT'S WHY YOU'LL ALL BE WEARING THESE.
BUT FIRST THINGS FIRST.
STRIP GIRLS.
YOU HEARD ME. BRA AND UNDIES TIME.
ΣΤΔ
COME ON, ILL...

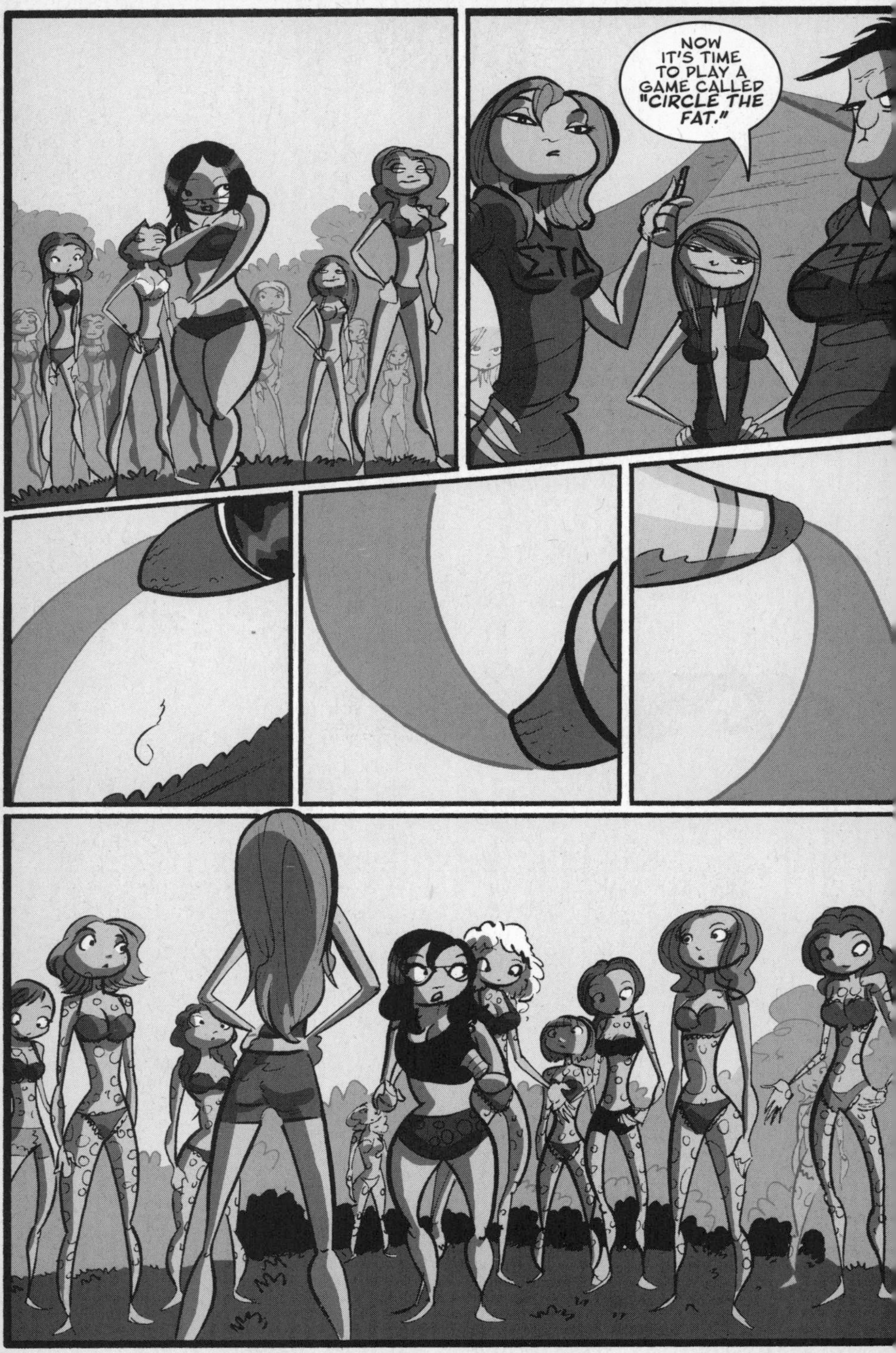
NOW IT'S TIME TO PLAY A GAME CALLED "CIRCLE THE FAT."

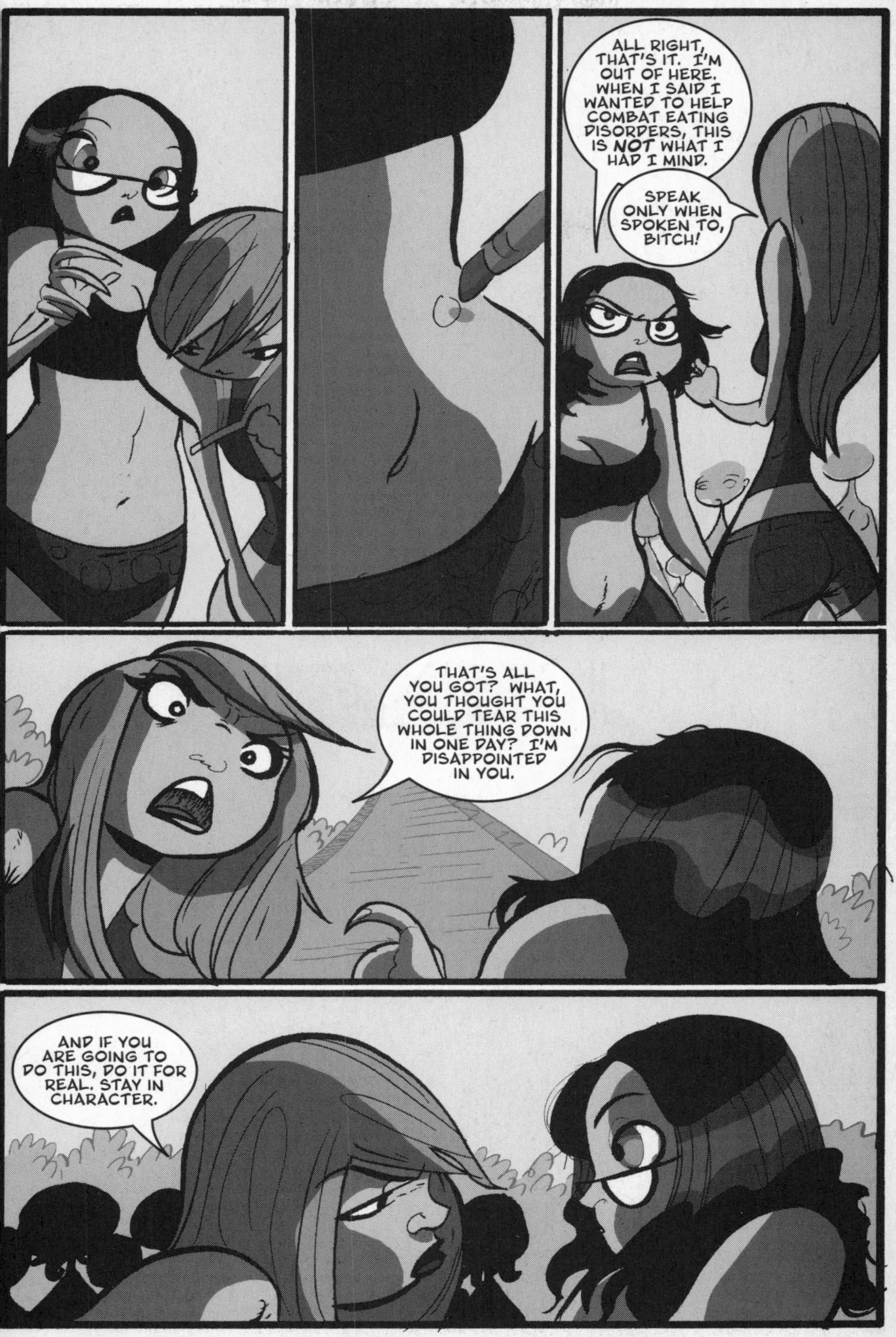
ALL RIGHT, THAT'S IT. I'M OUT OF HERE. WHEN I SAID I WANTED TO HELP COMBAT EATING DISORDERS, THIS IS **NOT** WHAT I HAD I MIND.
SPEAK ONLY WHEN SPOKEN TO, BITCH!
THAT'S ALL YOU GOT? WHAT, YOU THOUGHT YOU COULD TEAR THIS WHOLE THING DOWN IN ONE DAY? I'M DISAPPOINTED IN YOU.
AND IF YOU ARE GOING TO DO THIS, DO IT FOR REAL. STAY IN CHARACTER.

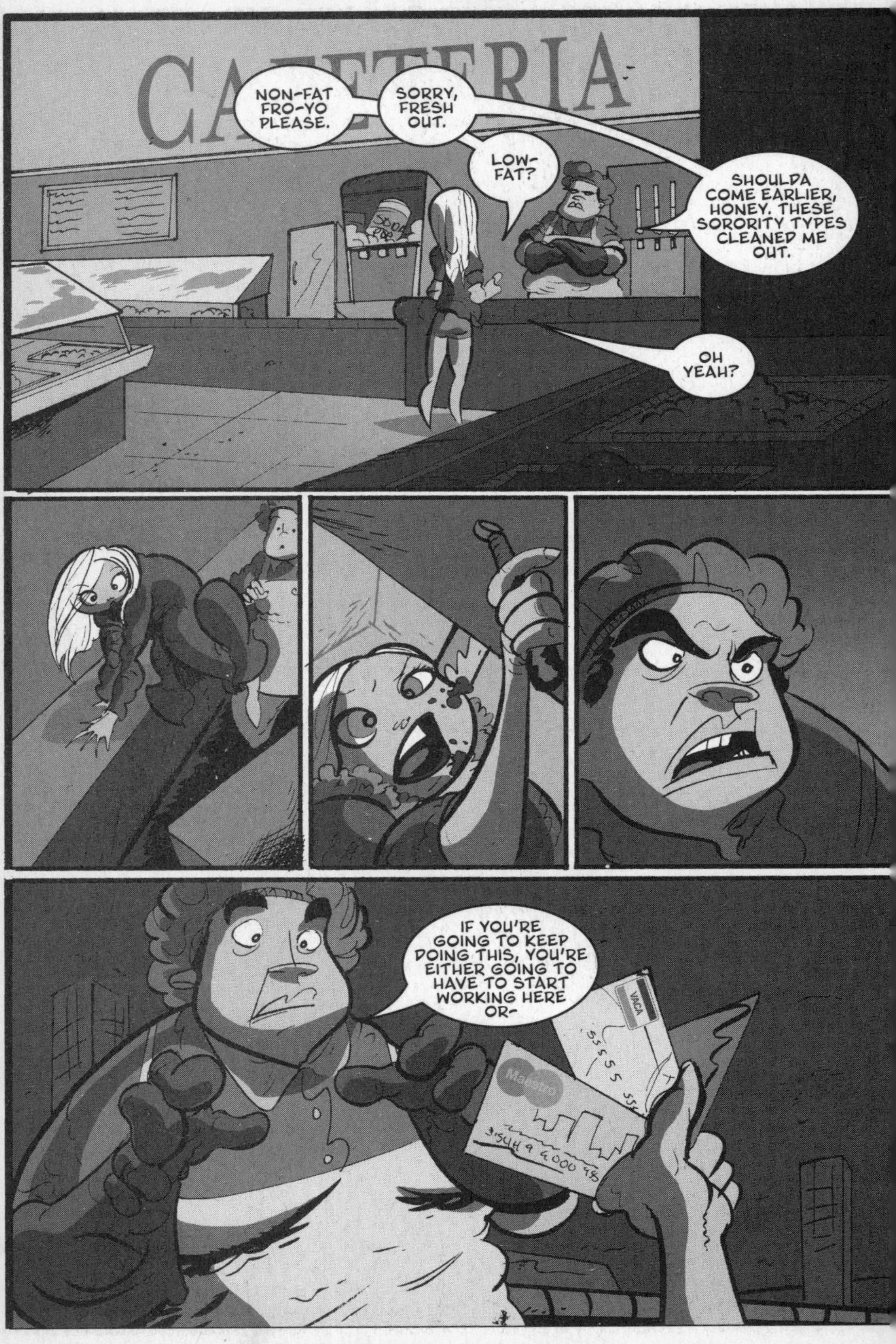
CAFETERIA
NON-FAT FRO-YO PLEASE.
SORRY, FRESH OUT.
LOW-FAT?
SHOULDA COME EARLIER, HONEY. THESE SORORITY TYPES CLEANED ME OUT.
OH YEAH?
IF YOU'RE GOING TO KEEP DOING THIS, YOU'RE EITHER HAVE TO START WORKING HERE OR-
Maestro
VACA

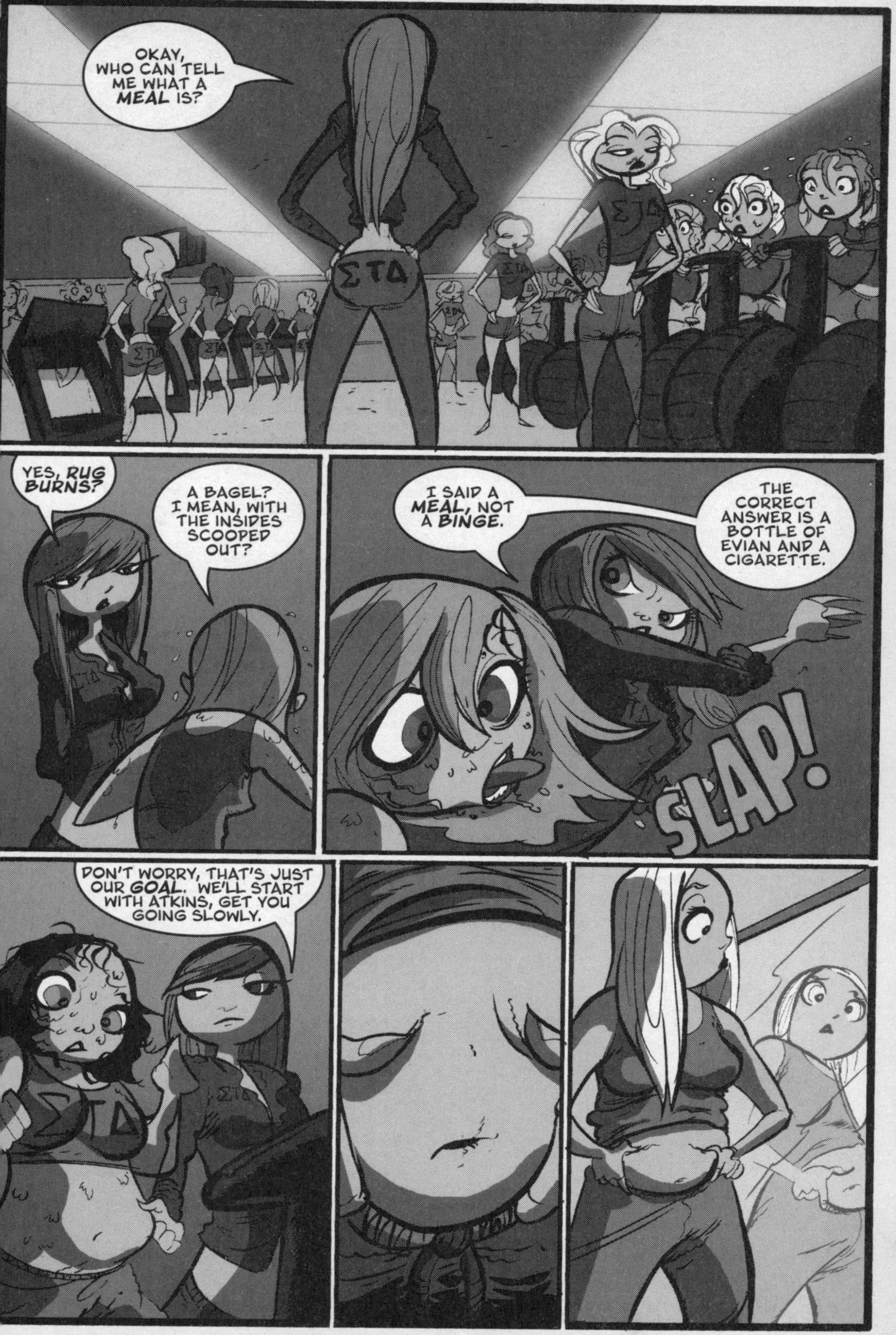
OKAY, WHO CAN TELL ME WHAT A MEAL IS?
YES, RUG BURNS?
A BAGEL? I MEAN, WITH THE INSIDES SCOOPED OUT?
I SAID A MEAL, NOT A BINGE.
THE CORRECT ANSWER IS A BOTTLE OF EVIAN AND A CIGARETTE.
SLAP!
DON'T WORRY, THAT'S JUST OUR GOAL. WE'LL START WITH ATKINS, GET YOU GOING SLOWLY.

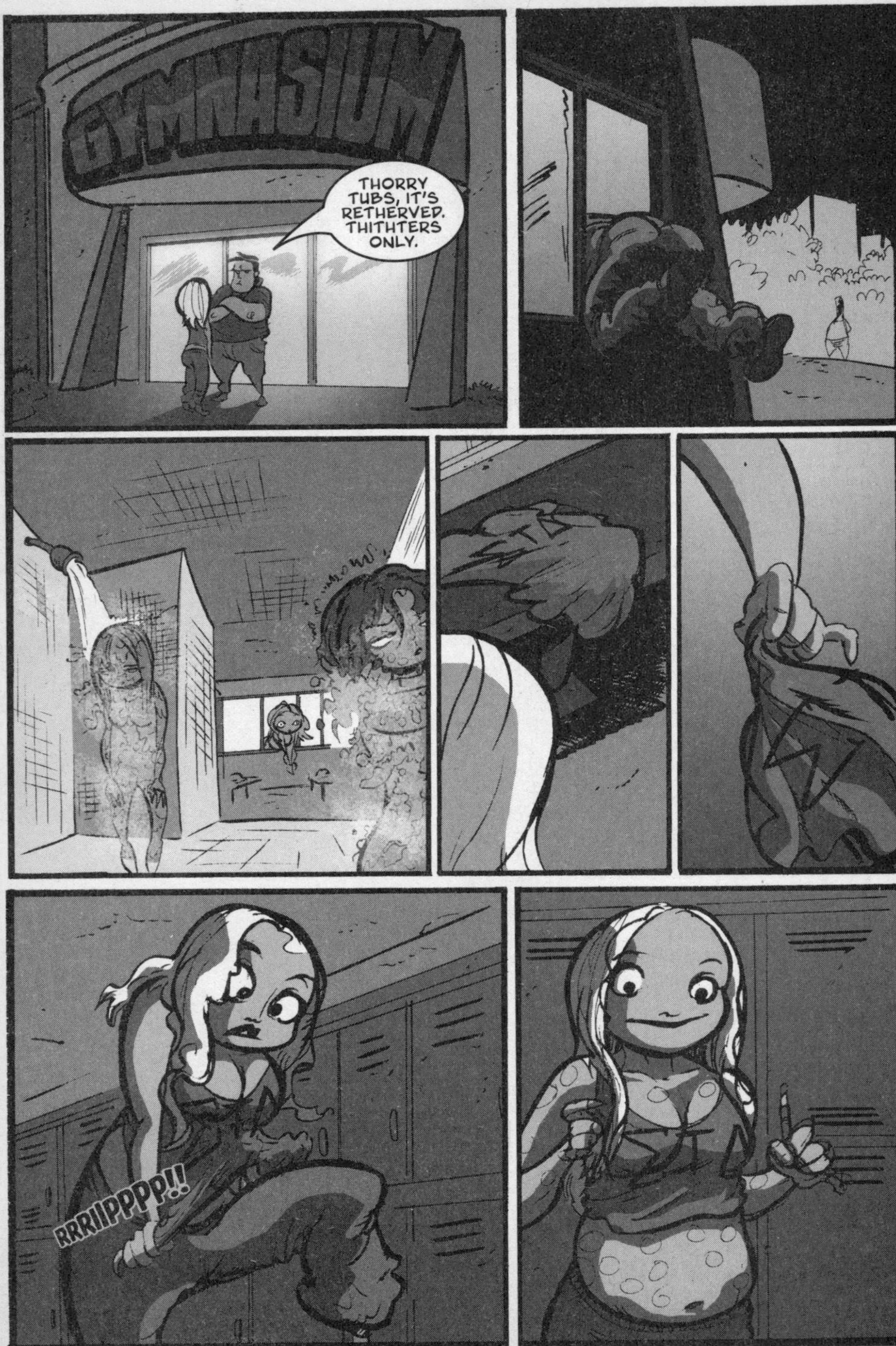
GYMNASIUM
THORRY TUBS, IT'S RETHERVED. THITHTERS ONLY.
RRRIIPPPPP!!

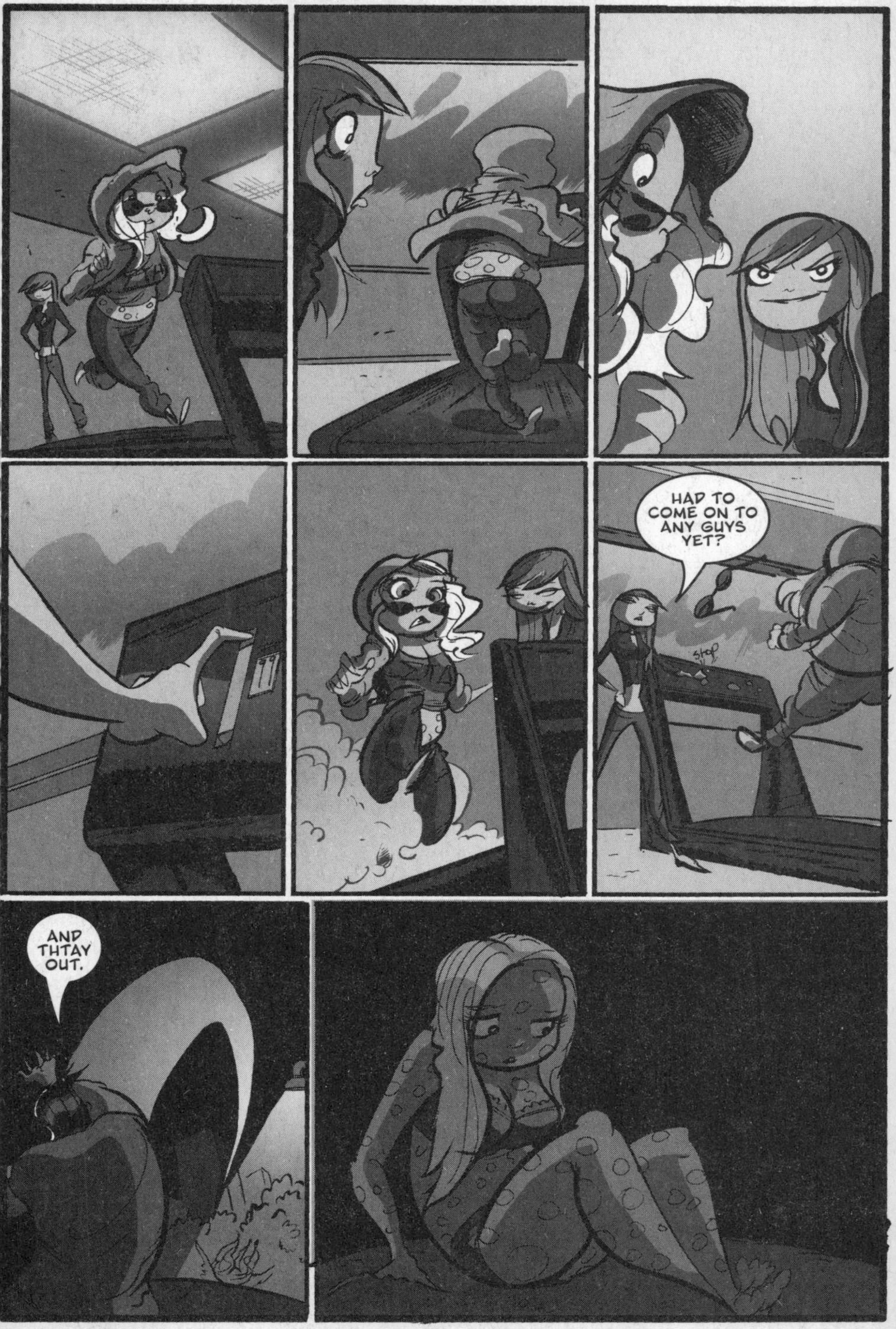
HAD TO COME ON TO ANY GUYS YET?
stop
AND THTAY OUT.

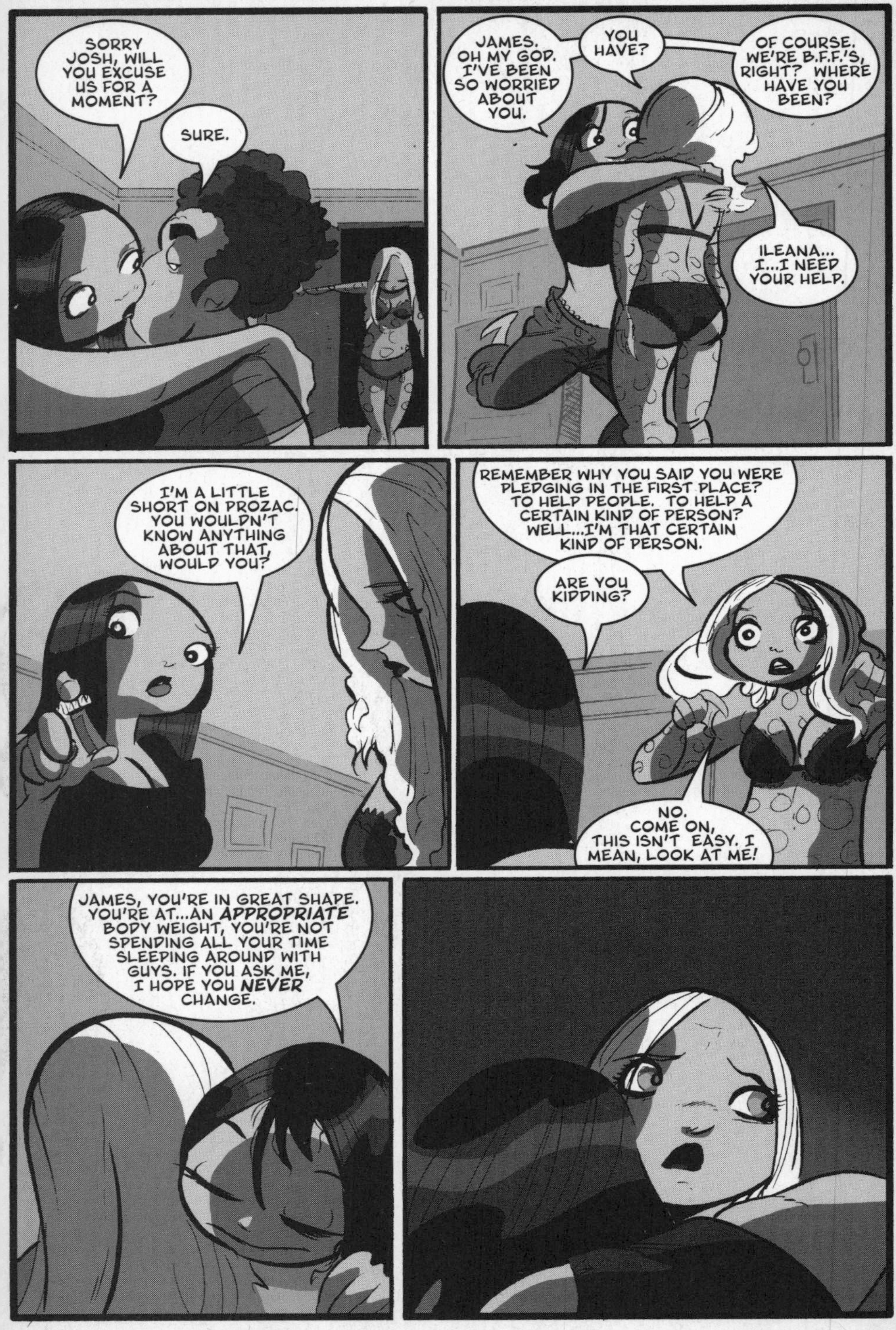
SORRY JOSH, WILL YOU EXCUSE US FOR A MOMENT?
SURE.
JAMES. OH MY GOD. I'VE BEEN SO WORRIED ABOUT YOU.
YOU HAVE?
OF COURSE. WE'RE B.F.F.'S, RIGHT? WHERE HAVE YOU BEEN?
ILEANA... I...I NEED YOUR HELP.
I'M A LITTLE SHORT ON PROZAC. YOU WOULDN'T KNOW ANYTHING ABOUT THAT, WOULD YOU?
REMEMBER WHY YOU SAID YOU WERE PLEDGING IN THE FIRST PLACE? TO HELP PEOPLE. TO HELP A CERTAIN KIND OF PERSON? WELL...I'M THAT CERTAIN KIND OF PERSON.
ARE YOU KIDDING?
NO. COME ON, THIS ISN'T EASY. I MEAN, LOOK AT ME!
JAMES, YOU'RE IN GREAT SHAPE. YOU'RE AT...AN *APPROPRIATE* BODY WEIGHT, YOU'RE NOT SPENDING ALL YOUR TIME SLEEPING AROUND WITH GUYS. IF YOU ASK ME, I HOPE YOU *NEVER* CHANGE.

CHAPTER
3

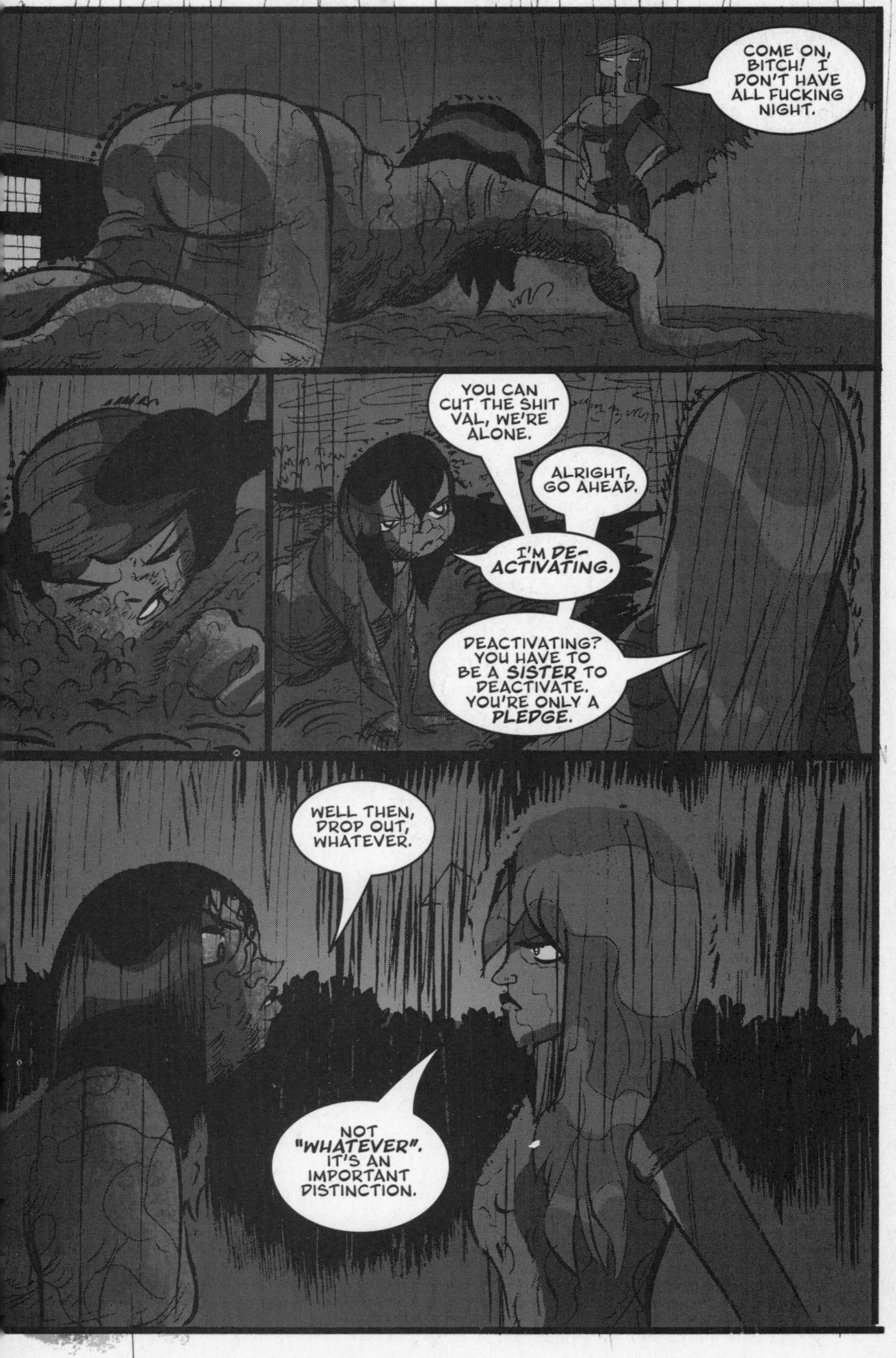
COME ON, BITCH! I DON'T HAVE ALL FUCKING NIGHT.
YOU CAN CUT THE SHIT VAL, WE'RE ALONE.
ALRIGHT, GO AHEAD.
I'M DE-ACTIVATING.
DEACTIVATING? YOU HAVE TO BE A SISTER TO DEACTIVATE. YOU'RE ONLY A PLEDGE.
WELL THEN, DROP OUT, WHATEVER.
NOT "WHATEVER". IT'S AN IMPORTANT DISTINCTION.

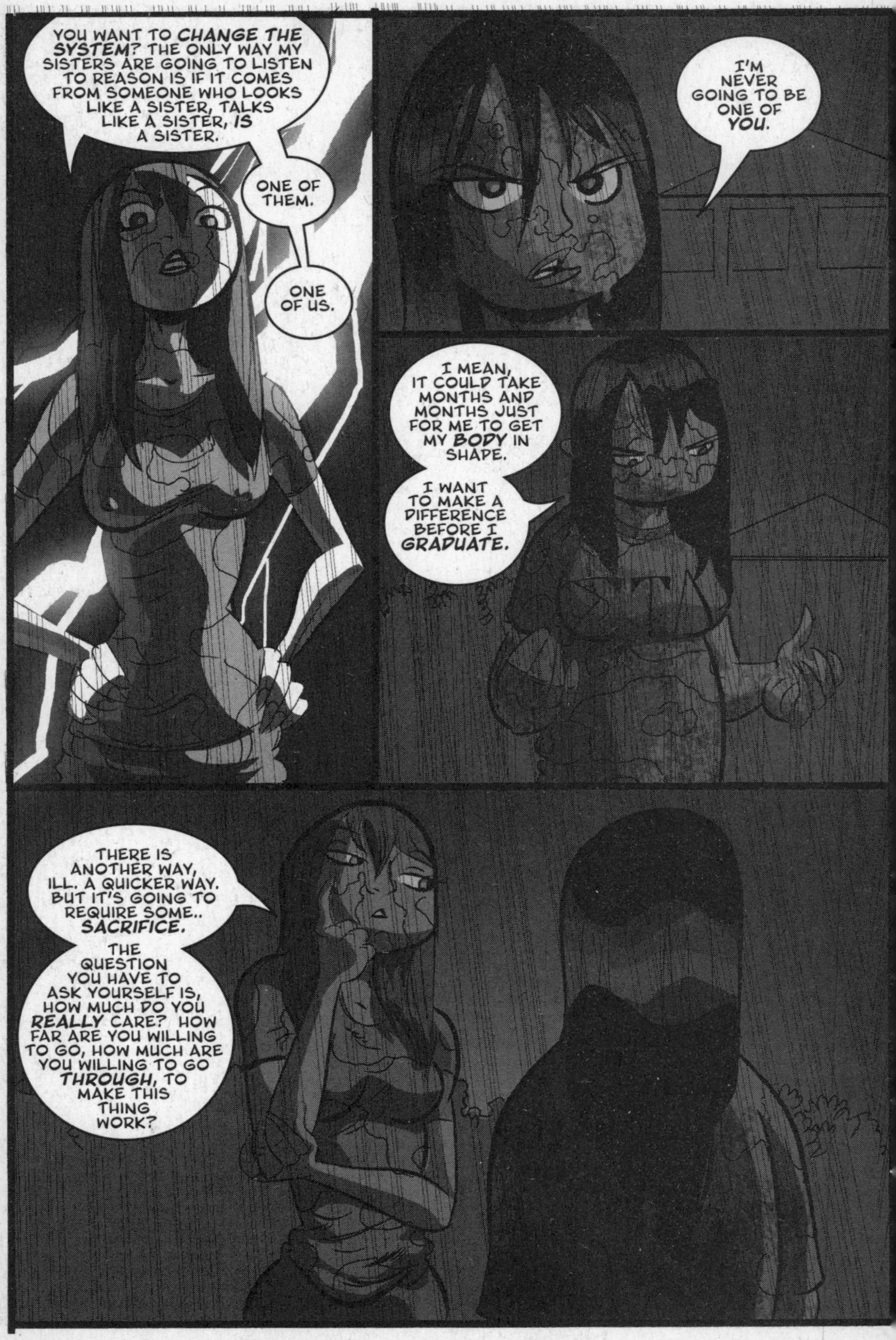
YOU WANT TO CHANGE THE SYSTEM? THE ONLY WAY MY SISTERS ARE GOING TO LISTEN TO REASON IS IF IT COMES FROM SOMEONE WHO LOOKS LIKE A SISTER, TALKS LIKE A SISTER, IS A SISTER.
ONE OF THEM.
ONE OF US.
I'M NEVER GOING TO BE ONE OF YOU.
I MEAN, IT COULD TAKE MONTHS AND MONTHS JUST FOR ME TO GET MY BODY IN SHAPE.
I WANT TO MAKE A DIFFERENCE BEFORE I GRADUATE.
THERE IS ANOTHER WAY, ILL. A QUICKER WAY. BUT IT'S GOING TO REQUIRE SOME.. SACRIFICE.
THE QUESTION YOU HAVE TO ASK YOURSELF IS, HOW MUCH DO YOU REALLY CARE? HOW FAR ARE YOU WILLING TO GO, HOW MUCH ARE YOU WILLING TO GO THROUGH, TO MAKE THIS THING WORK?

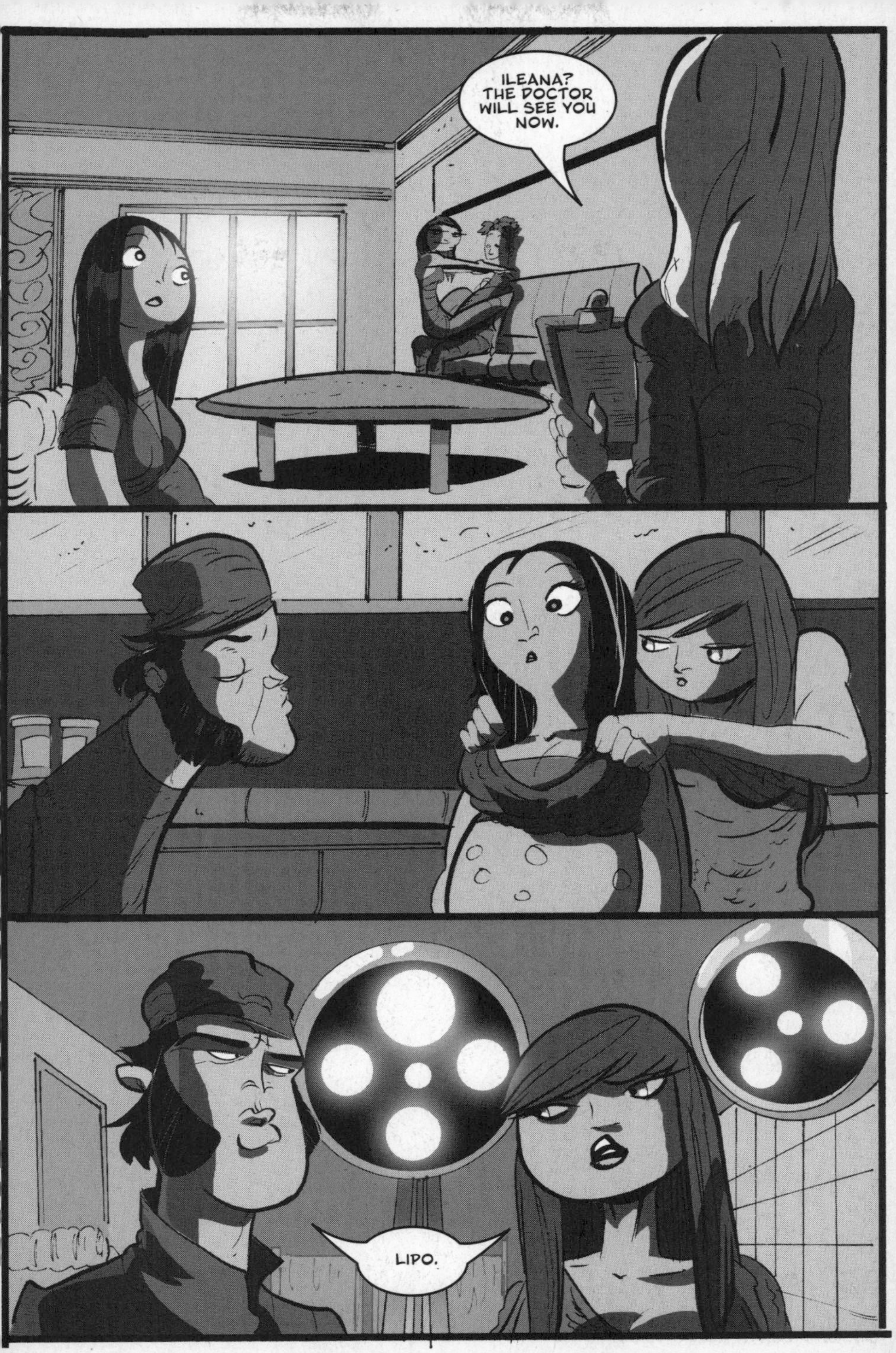
ILEANA? THE DOCTOR WILL SEE YOU NOW.
LIPO.

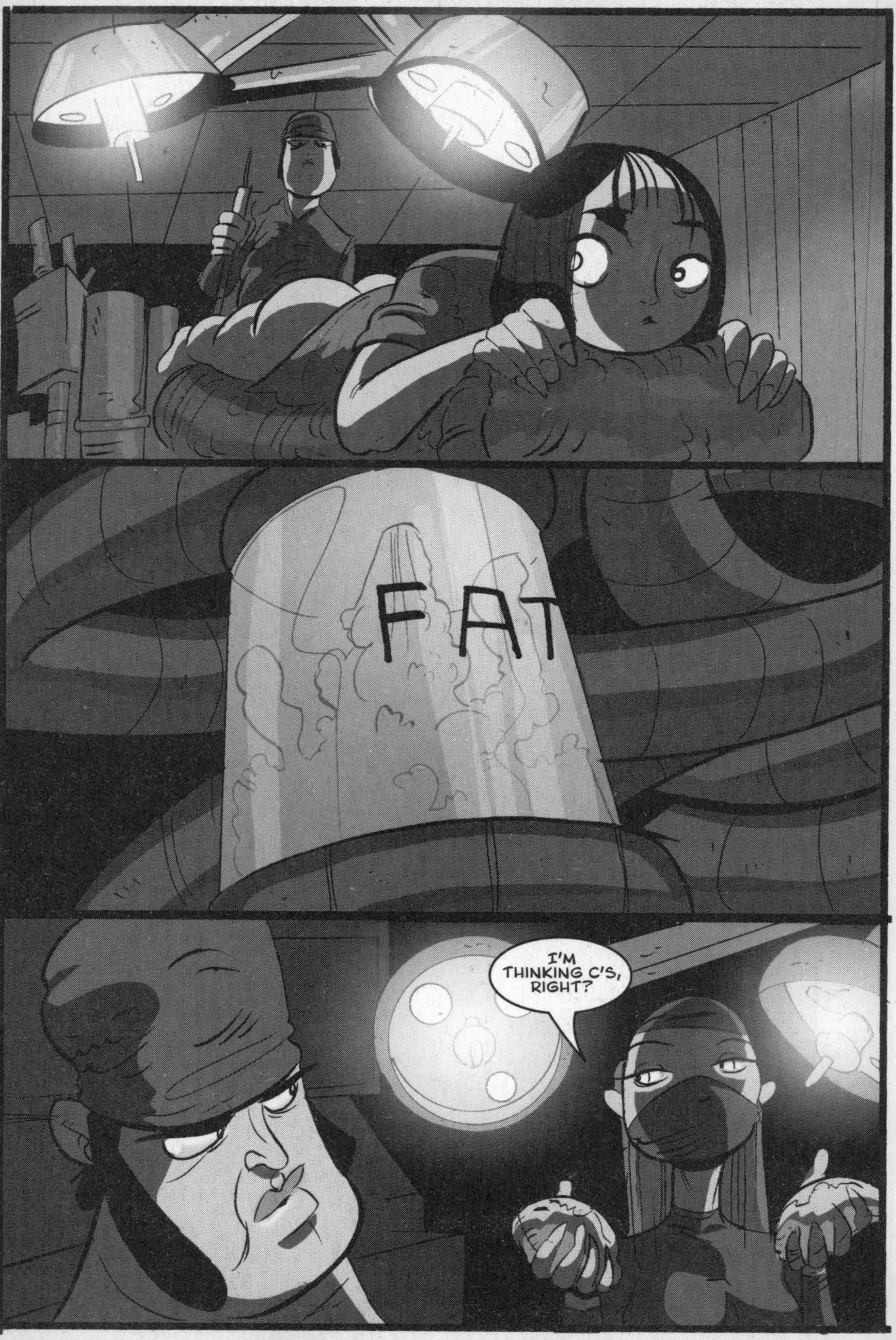
FAT
I'M THINKING C'S, RIGHT?

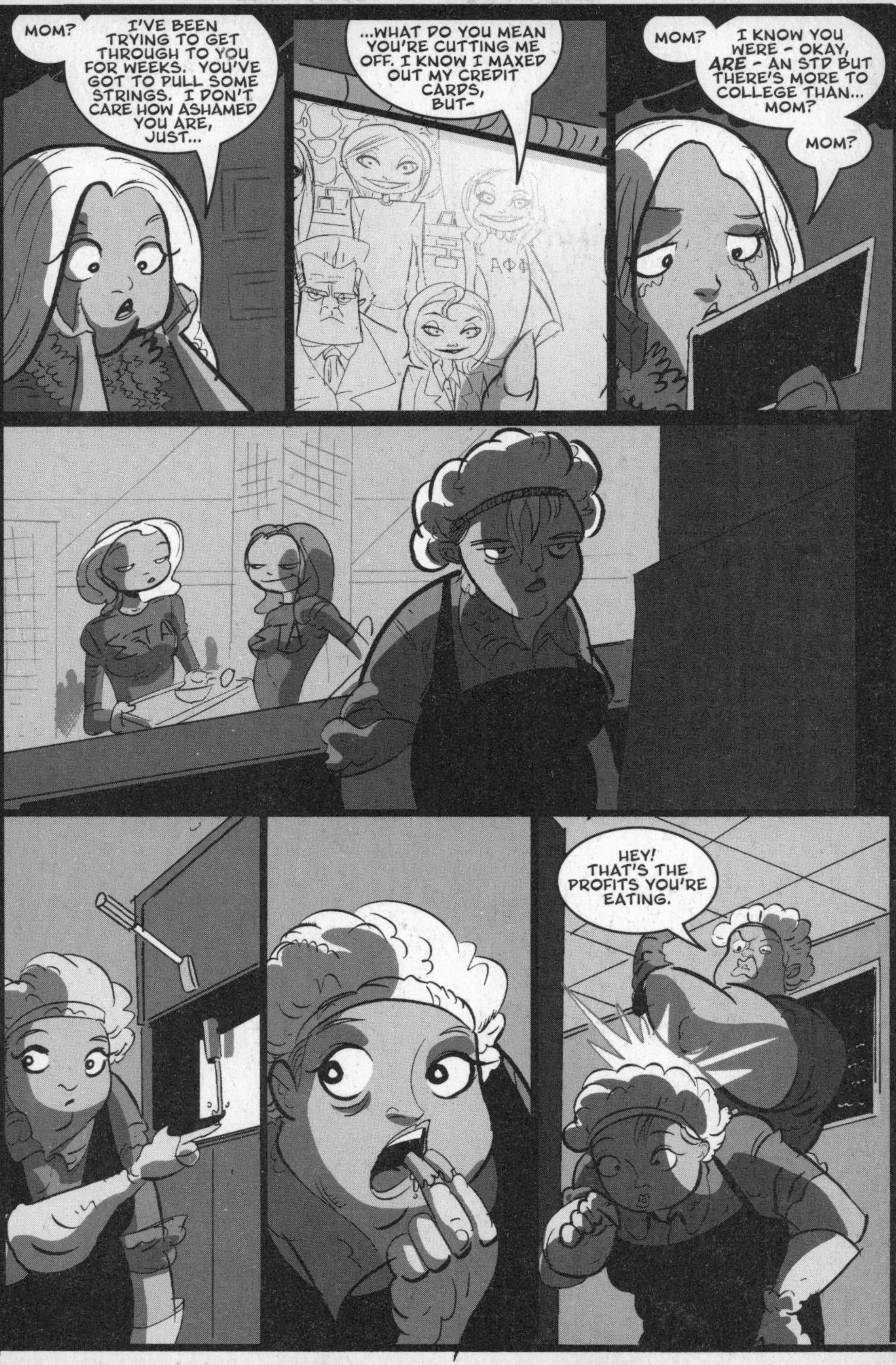
MOM?
I'VE BEEN TRYING TO GET THROUGH TO YOU FOR WEEKS. YOU'VE GOT TO PULL SOME STRINGS. I DON'T CARE HOW ASHAMED YOU ARE, JUST...
...WHAT DO YOU MEAN YOU'RE CUTTING ME OFF. I KNOW I MAXED OUT MY CREDIT CARDS, BUT-
ΑΦΦ
MOM?
I KNOW YOU WERE - OKAY, ARE - AN STD BUT THERE'S MORE TO COLLEGE THAN... MOM?
MOM?
HEY! THAT'S THE PROFITS YOU'RE EATING.

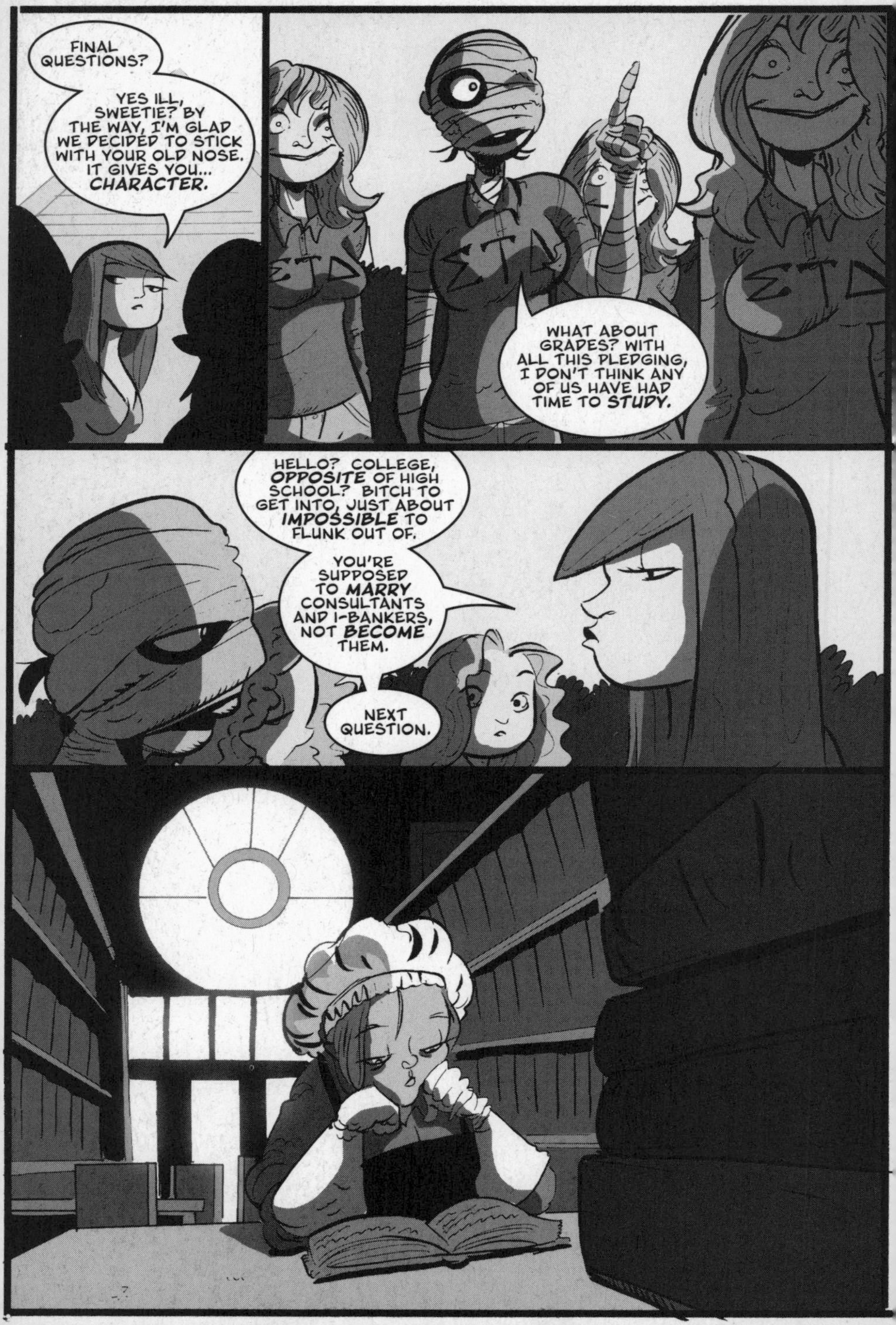
FINAL QUESTIONS?
YES ILL, SWEETIE? BY THE WAY, I'M GLAD WE DECIDED TO STICK WITH YOUR OLD NOSE. IT GIVES YOU... CHARACTER.
WHAT ABOUT GRADES? WITH ALL THIS PLEDGING, I DON'T THINK ANY OF US HAVE HAD TIME TO STUDY.
HELLO? COLLEGE, OPPOSITE OF HIGH SCHOOL? BITCH TO GET INTO, JUST ABOUT IMPOSSIBLE TO FLUNK OUT OF.
YOU'RE SUPPOSED TO MARRY CONSULTANTS AND I-BANKERS, NOT BECOME THEM.
NEXT QUESTION.

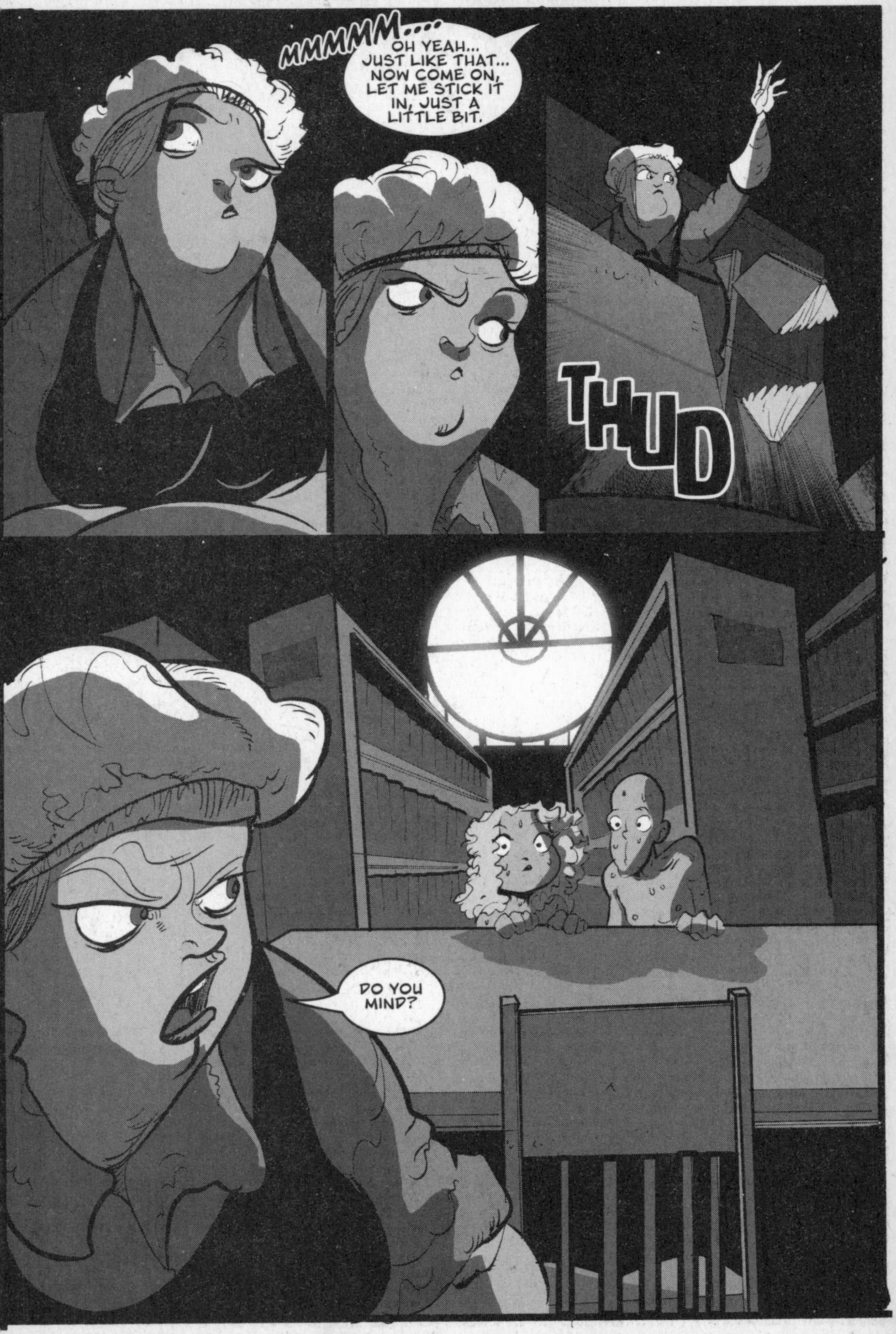
MMMMM....
OH YEAH... JUST LIKE THAT... NOW COME ON, LET ME STICK IT IN, JUST A LITTLE BIT.
THUD
DO YOU MIND?

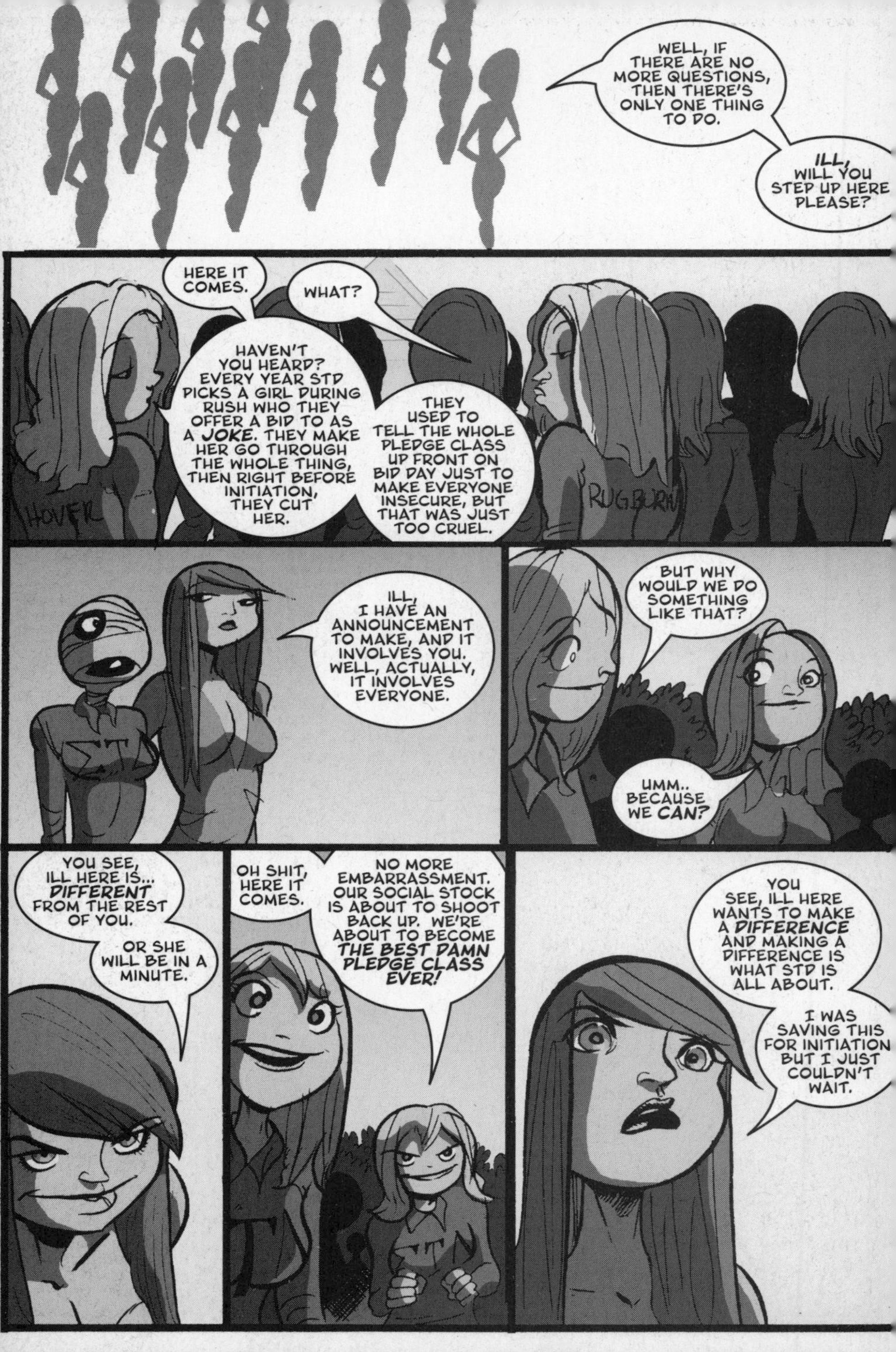
WELL, IF THERE ARE NO MORE QUESTIONS, THEN THERE'S ONLY ONE THING TO DO.
ILL, WILL YOU STEP UP HERE PLEASE?
HERE IT COMES.
WHAT?
HAVEN'T YOU HEARD? EVERY YEAR STD PICKS A GIRL DURING RUSH WHO THEY OFFER A BID TO AS A JOKE. THEY MAKE HER GO THROUGH THE WHOLE THING, THEN RIGHT BEFORE INITIATION, THEY CUT HER.
THEY USED TO TELL THE WHOLE PLEDGE CLASS UP FRONT ON BID DAY JUST TO MAKE EVERYONE INSECURE, BUT THAT WAS JUST TOO CRUEL.
HOVER
RUGBURN
ILL, I HAVE AN ANNOUNCEMENT TO MAKE, AND IT INVOLVES YOU. WELL, ACTUALLY, IT INVOLVES EVERYONE.
BUT WHY WOULD WE DO SOMETHING LIKE THAT?
UMM.. BECAUSE WE CAN?
YOU SEE, ILL HERE IS... DIFFERENT FROM THE REST OF YOU.
OR SHE WILL BE IN A MINUTE.
OH SHIT, HERE IT COMES.
NO MORE EMBARRASSMENT. OUR SOCIAL STOCK IS ABOUT TO SHOOT BACK UP. WE'RE ABOUT TO BECOME THE BEST DAMN PLEDGE CLASS EVER!
YOU SEE, ILL HERE WANTS TO MAKE A DIFFERENCE AND MAKING A DIFFERENCE IS WHAT STD IS ALL ABOUT.
I WAS SAVING THIS FOR INITIATION BUT I JUST COULDN'T WAIT.

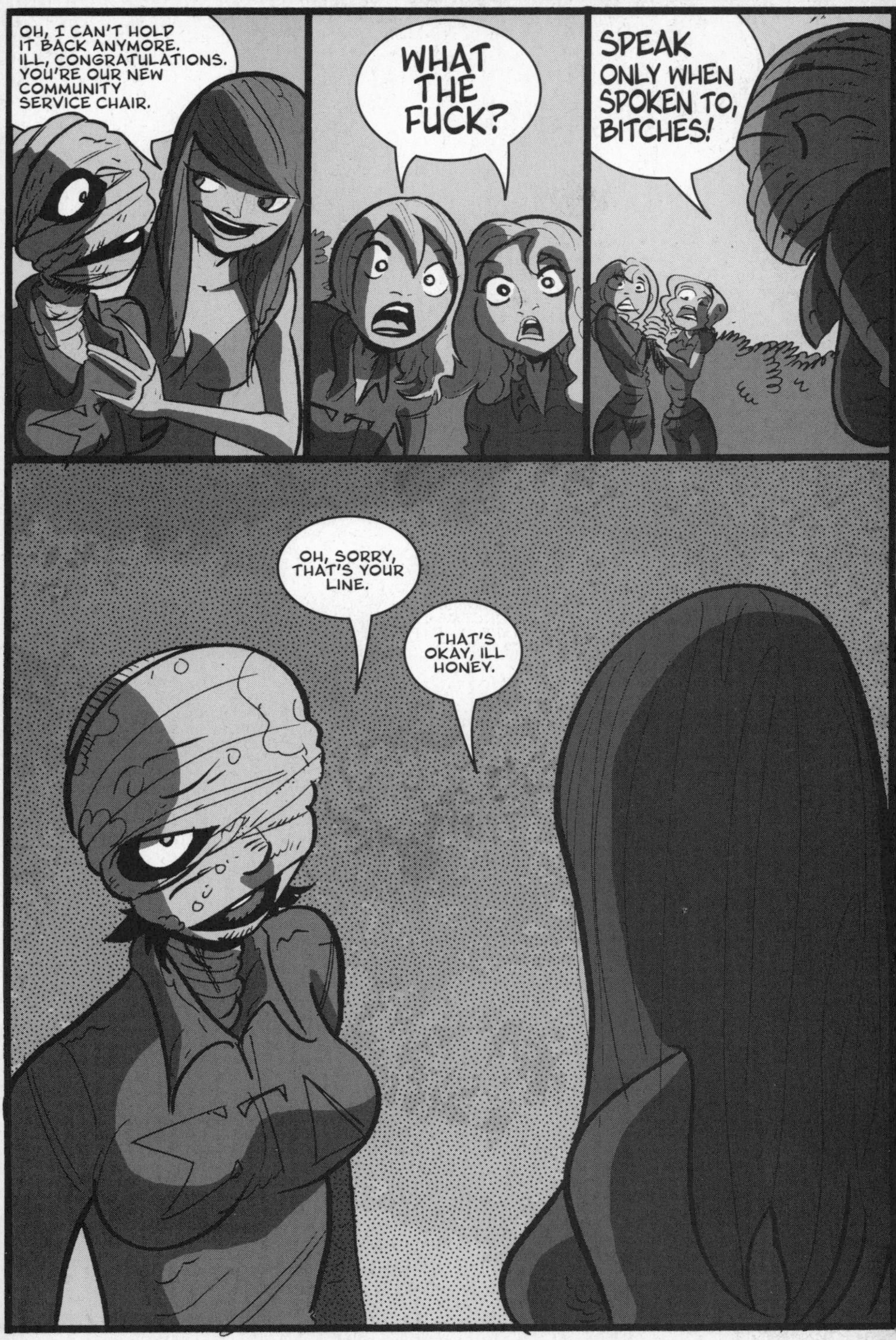
OH, I CAN'T HOLD IT BACK ANYMORE. ILL, CONGRATULATIONS. YOU'RE OUR NEW COMMUNITY SERVICE CHAIR.
WHAT THE FUCK?
SPEAK ONLY WHEN SPOKEN TO, BITCHES!
OH, SORRY, THAT'S YOUR LINE.
THAT'S OKAY, ILL HONEY.

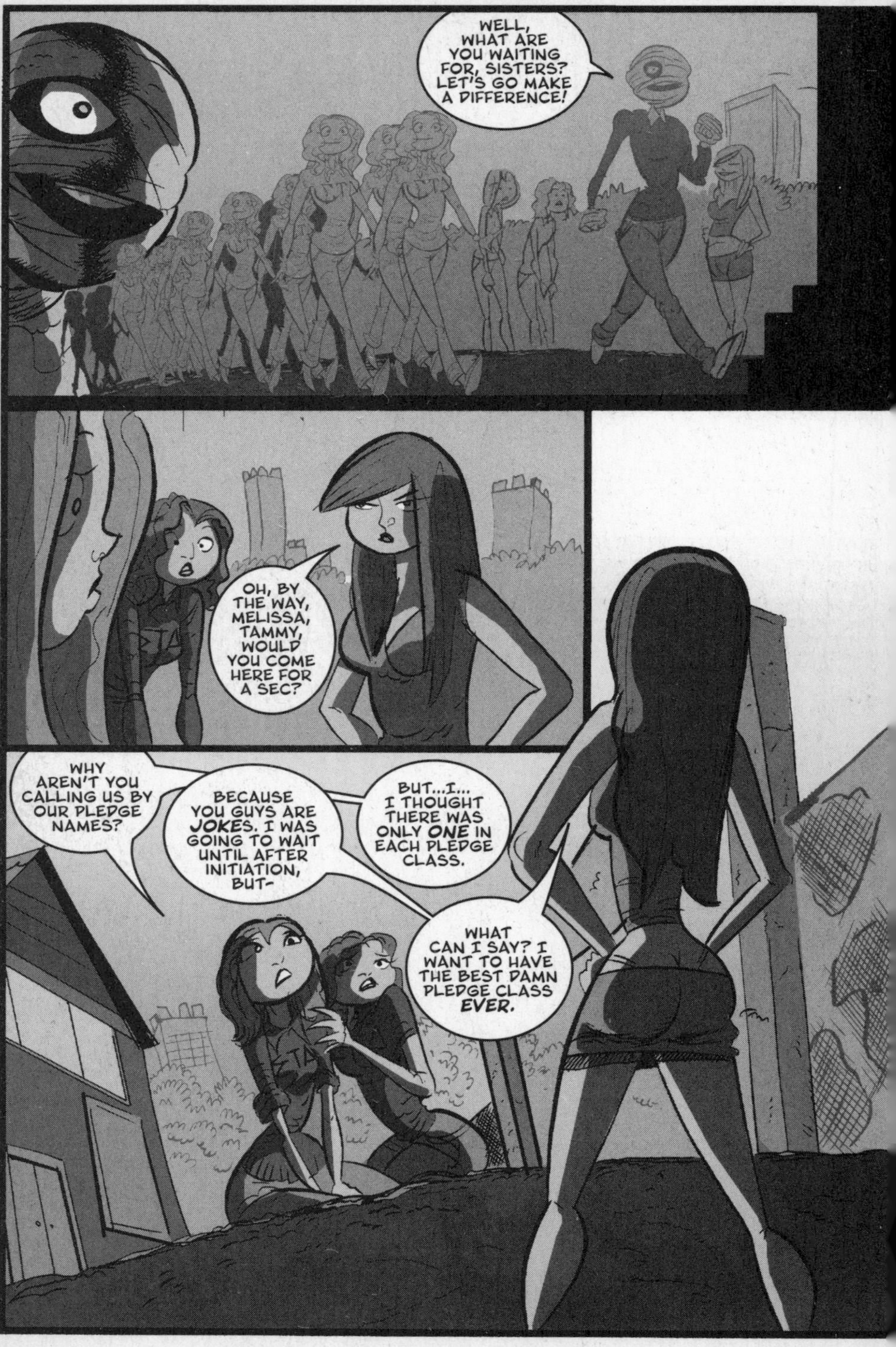

WELL, WHAT ARE YOU WAITING FOR, SISTERS? LET'S GO MAKE A DIFFERENCE!
OH, BY THE WAY, MELISSA, TAMMY, WOULD YOU COME HERE FOR A SEC?
WHY AREN'T YOU CALLING US BY OUR PLEDGE NAMES?
BECAUSE YOU GUYS ARE JOKES. I WAS GOING TO WAIT UNTIL AFTER INITIATION, BUT-
BUT...I... I THOUGHT THERE WAS ONLY ONE IN EACH PLEDGE CLASS.
WHAT CAN I SAY? I WANT TO HAVE THE BEST DAMN PLEDGE CLASS EVER.

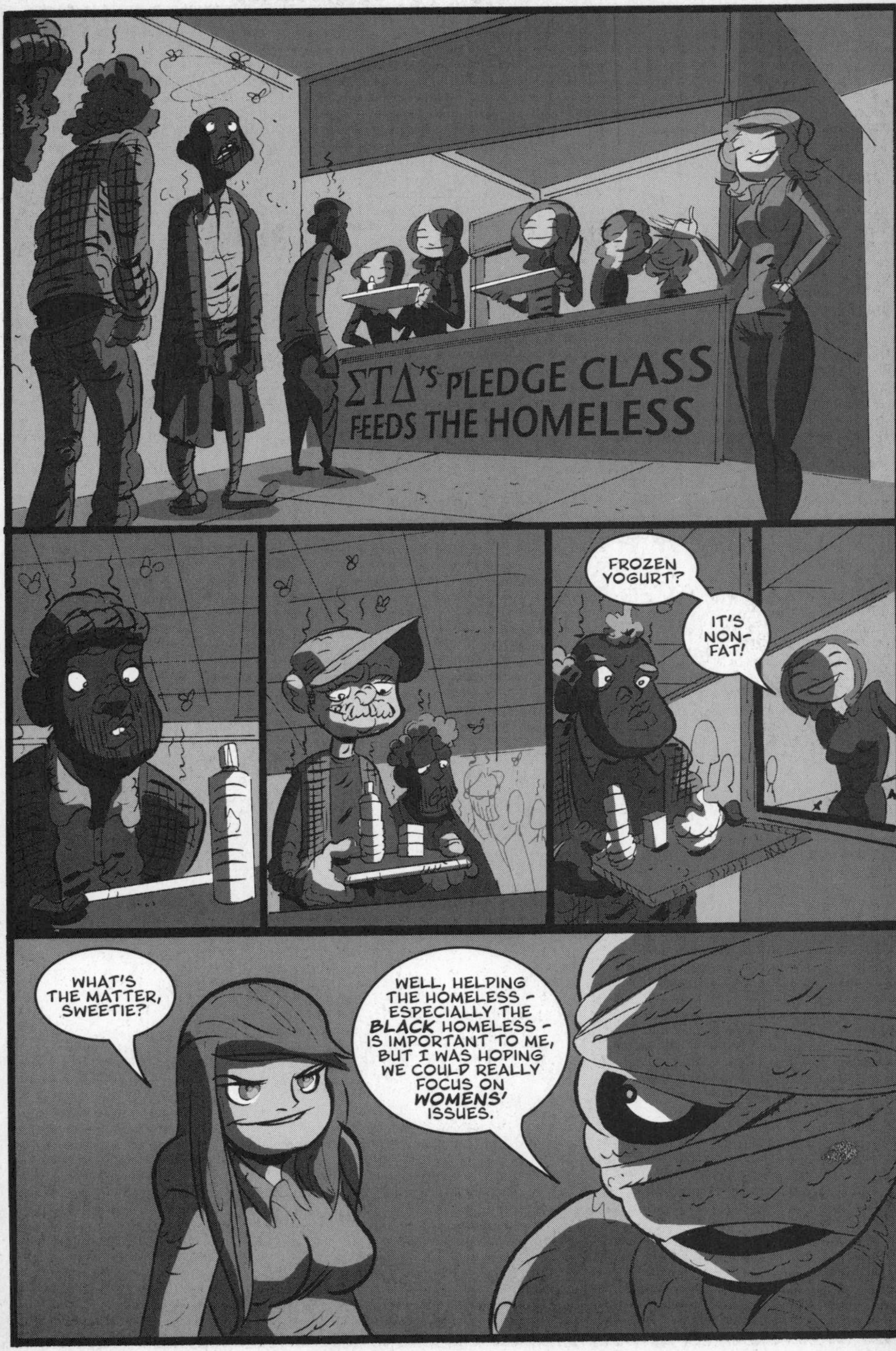
ΣΤΔ'S PLEDGE CLASS FEEDS THE HOMELESS
FROZEN YOGURT?
IT'S NON-FAT!
WHAT'S THE MATTER, SWEETIE?
WELL, HELPING THE HOMELESS - ESPECIALLY THE BLACK HOMELESS - IS IMPORTANT TO ME, BUT I WAS HOPING WE COULD REALLY FOCUS ON WOMENS' ISSUES.

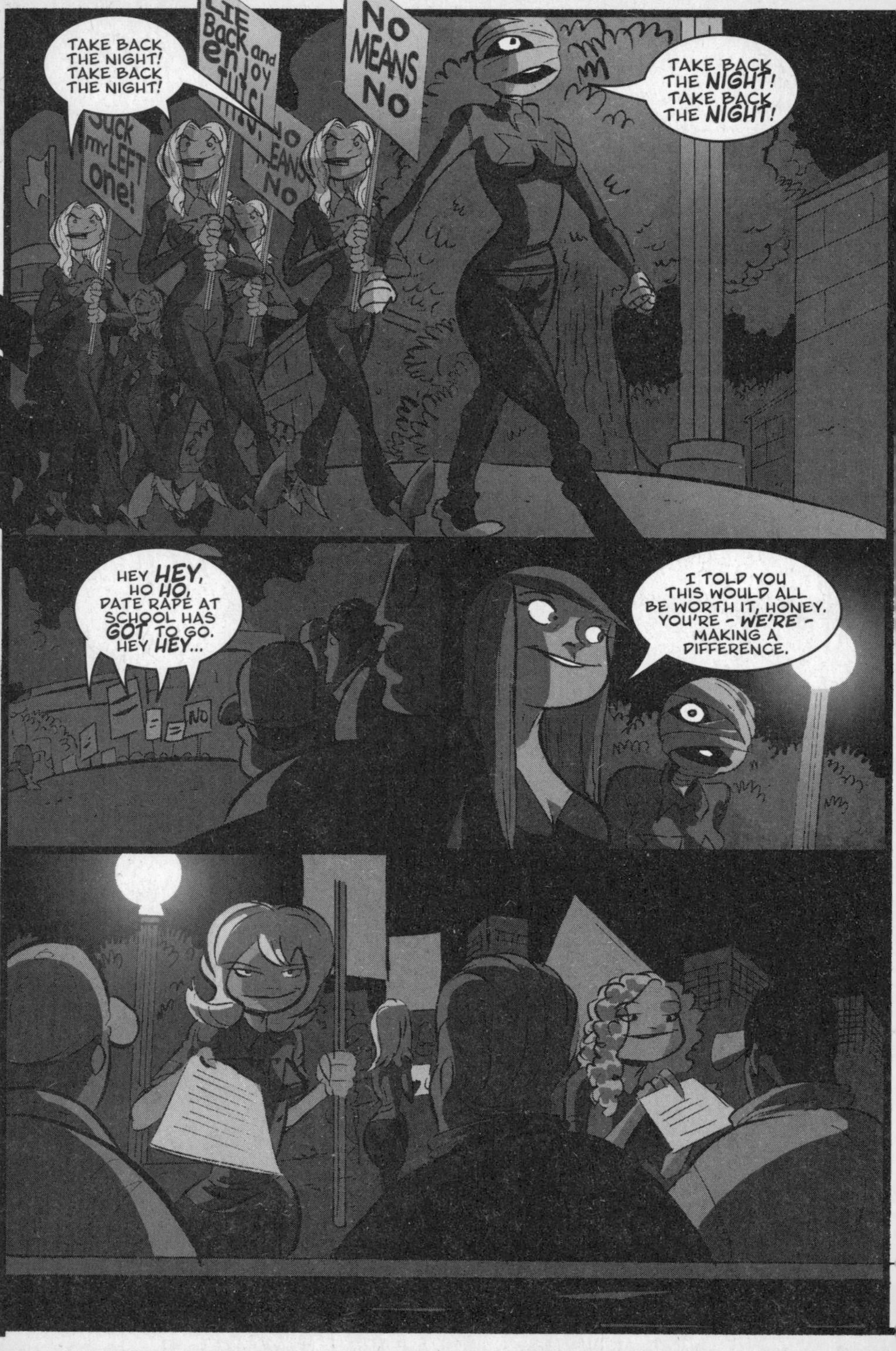
TAKE BACK THE NIGHT! TAKE BACK THE NIGHT!
LIE Back and enjoy
NO MEANS NO
Suck my LEFT one!
TAKE BACK THE NIGHT! TAKE BACK THE NIGHT!
HEY HEY, HO HO, DATE RAPE AT SCHOOL HAS GOT TO GO. HEY HEY...
I TOLD YOU THIS WOULD ALL BE WORTH IT, HONEY. YOU'RE - WE'RE - MAKING A DIFFERENCE.

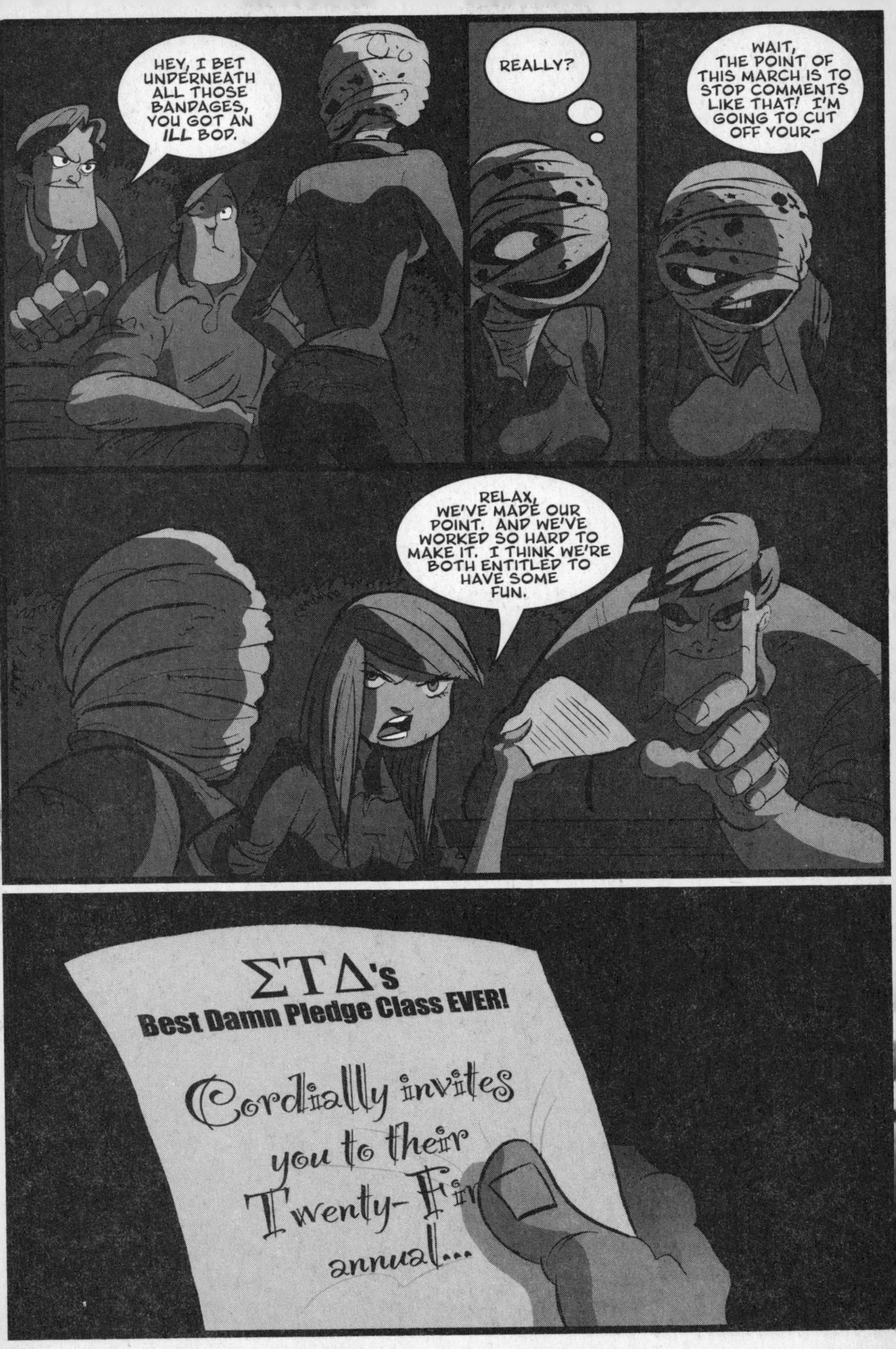
HEY, I BET UNDERNEATH ALL THOSE BANDAGES, YOU GOT AN ILL BOD.
REALLY?
WAIT, THE POINT OF THIS MARCH IS TO STOP COMMENTS LIKE THAT! I'M GOING TO CUT OFF YOUR-
RELAX, WE'VE MADE OUR POINT. AND WE'VE WORKED SO HARD TO MAKE IT. I THINK WE'RE BOTH ENTITLED TO HAVE SOME FUN.
ΣΤΔ's
Best Damn Pledge Class EVER!
Cordially invites you to their Twenty-Fi
annual...

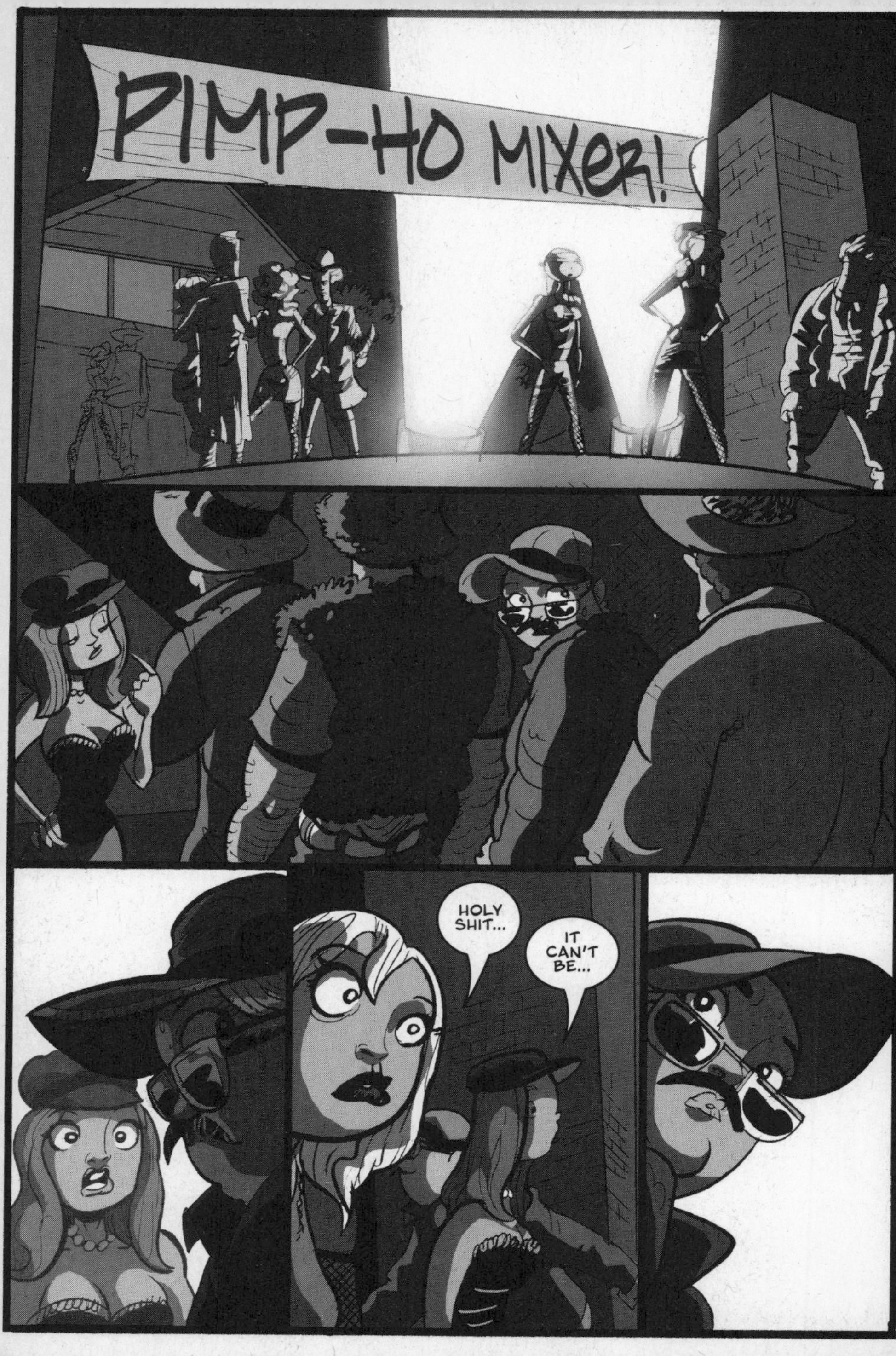
PIMP-HO MIXER!
HOLY SHIT...
IT CAN'T BE...

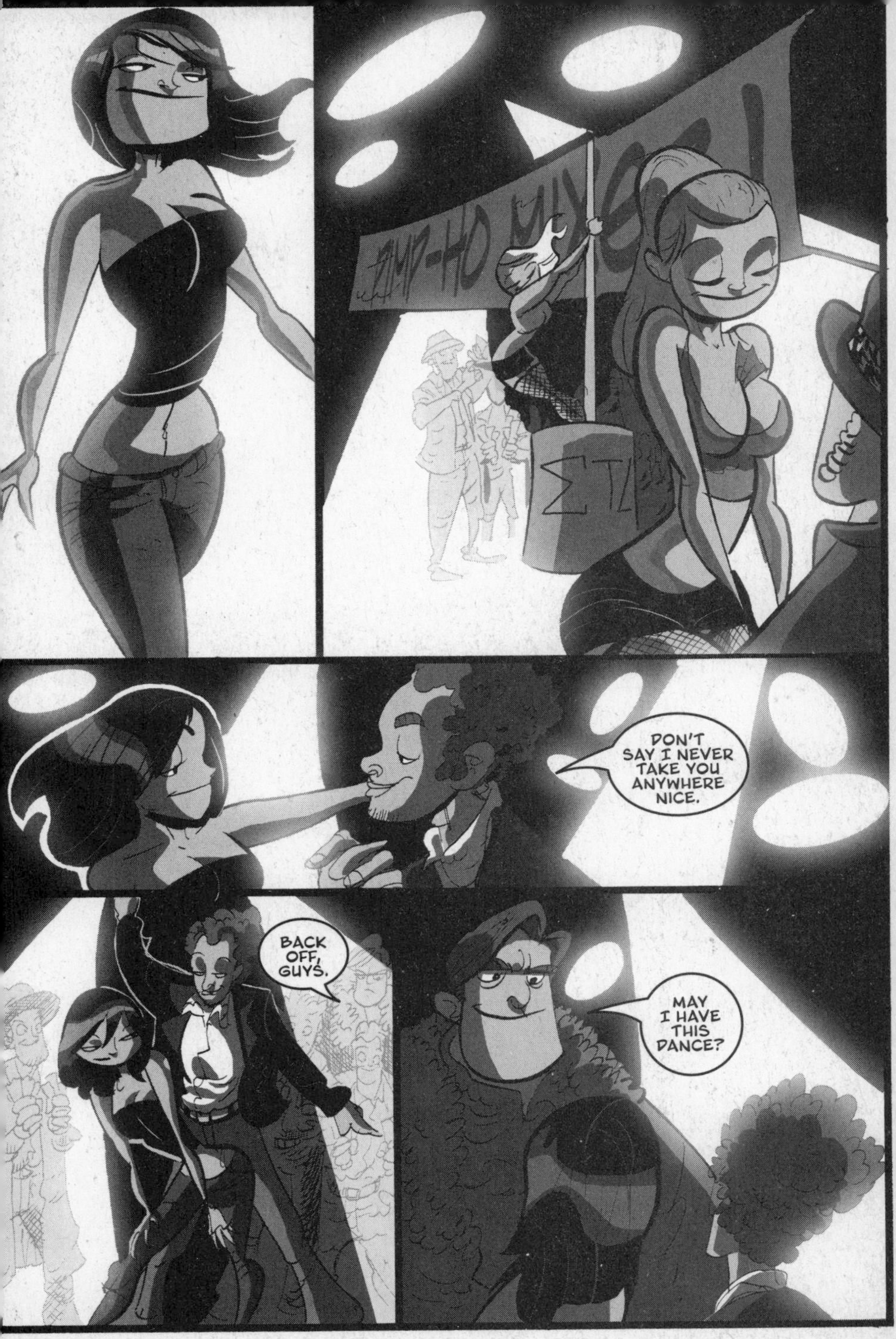
DON'T SAY I NEVER TAKE YOU ANYWHERE NICE.
BACK OFF, GUYS.
MAY I HAVE THIS DANCE?

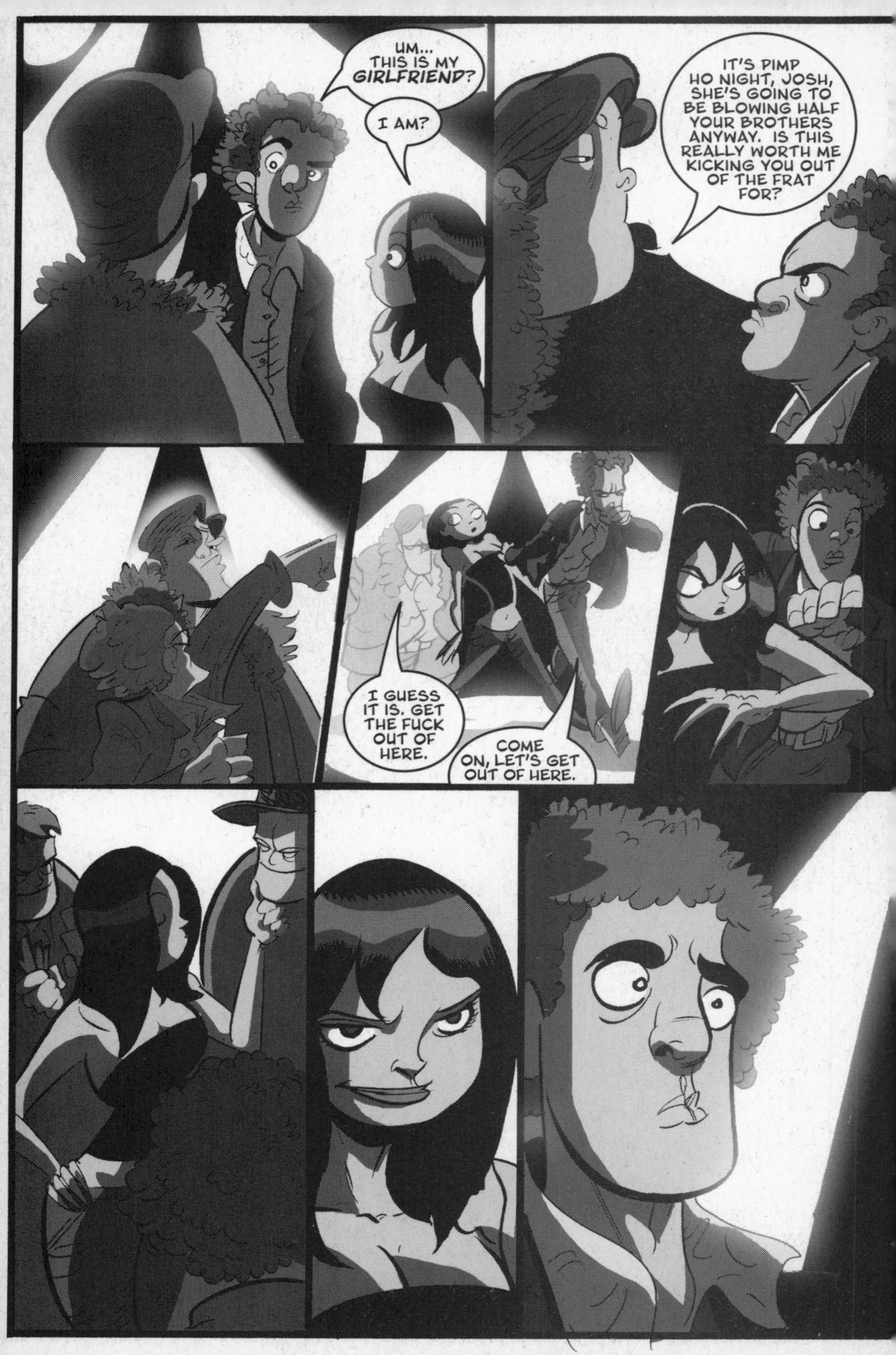
UM... THIS IS MY GIRLFRIEND?
I AM?
IT'S PIMP HO NIGHT, JOSH, SHE'S GOING TO BE BLOWING HALF YOUR BROTHERS ANYWAY. IS THIS REALLY WORTH ME KICKING YOU OUT OF THE FRAT FOR?
I GUESS IT IS. GET THE FUCK OUT OF HERE.
COME ON, LET'S GET OUT OF HERE.

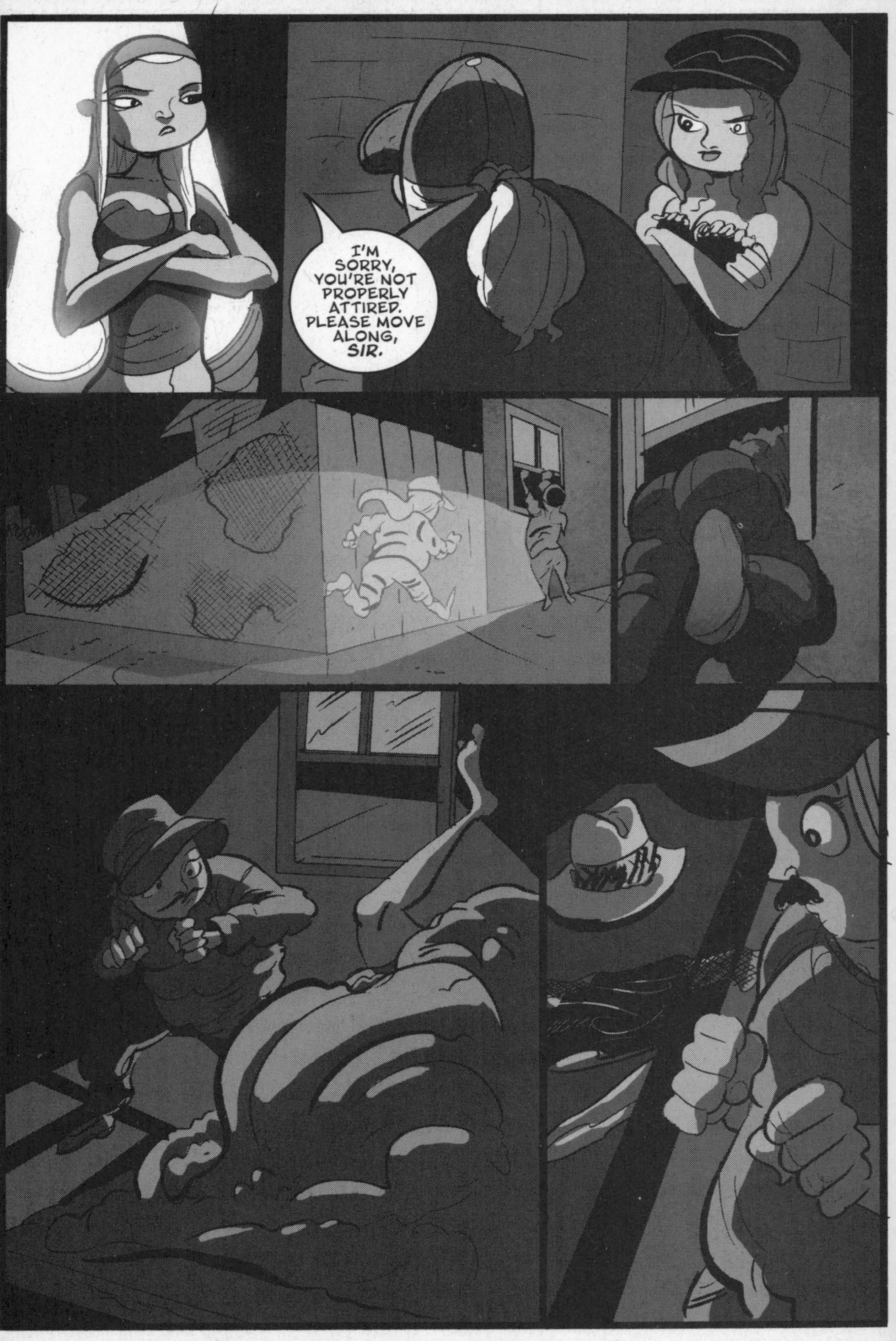
I'M SORRY, YOU'RE NOT PROPERLY ATTIRED. PLEASE MOVE ALONG, SIR.

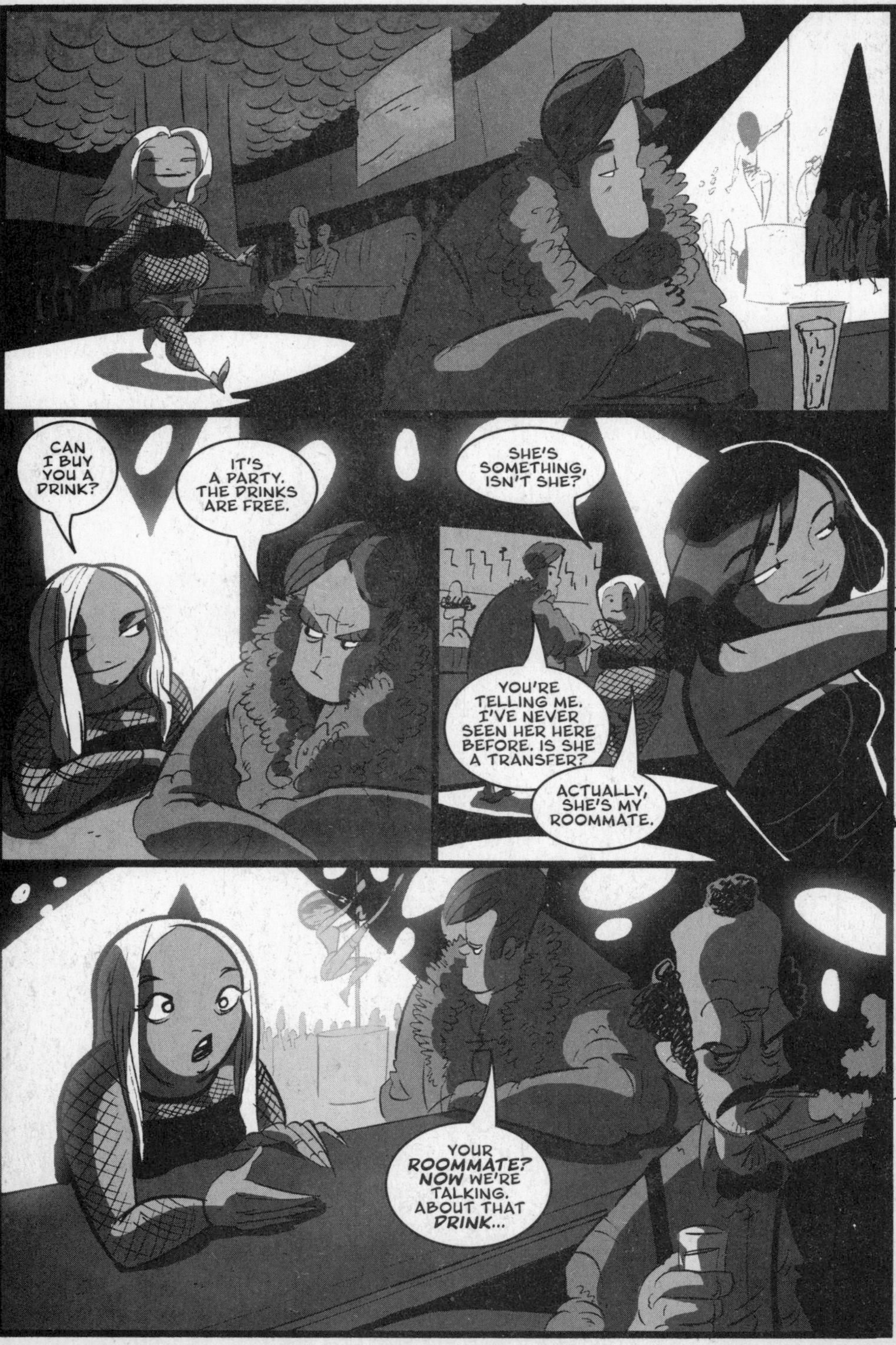
CAN I BUY YOU A DRINK?
IT'S A PARTY. THE DRINKS ARE FREE.
SHE'S SOMETHING, ISN'T SHE?
YOU'RE TELLING ME. I'VE NEVER SEEN HER HERE BEFORE. IS SHE A TRANSFER?
ACTUALLY, SHE'S MY ROOMMATE.
YOUR ROOMMATE? NOW WE'RE TALKING. ABOUT THAT DRINK...

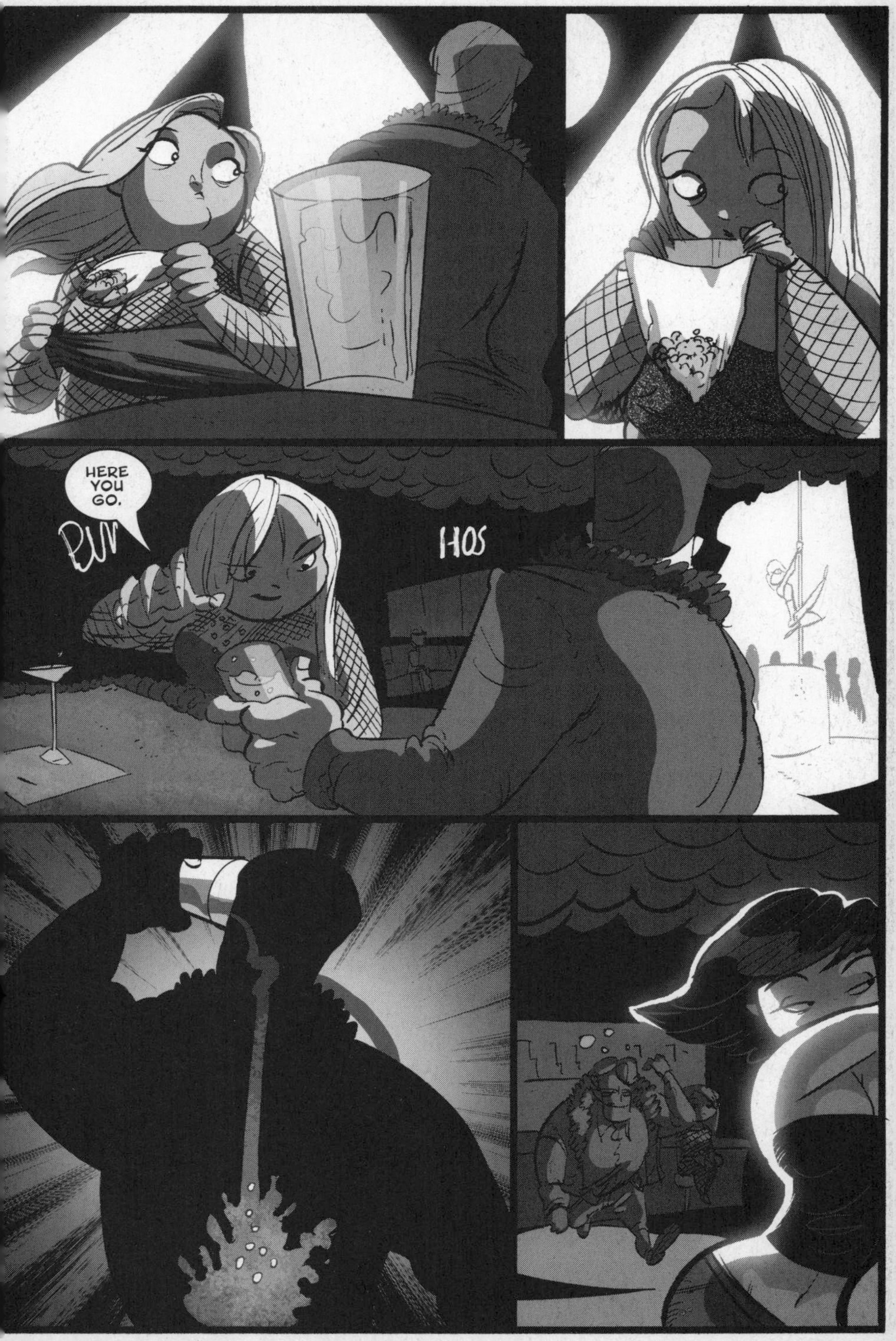
HERE YOU GO.

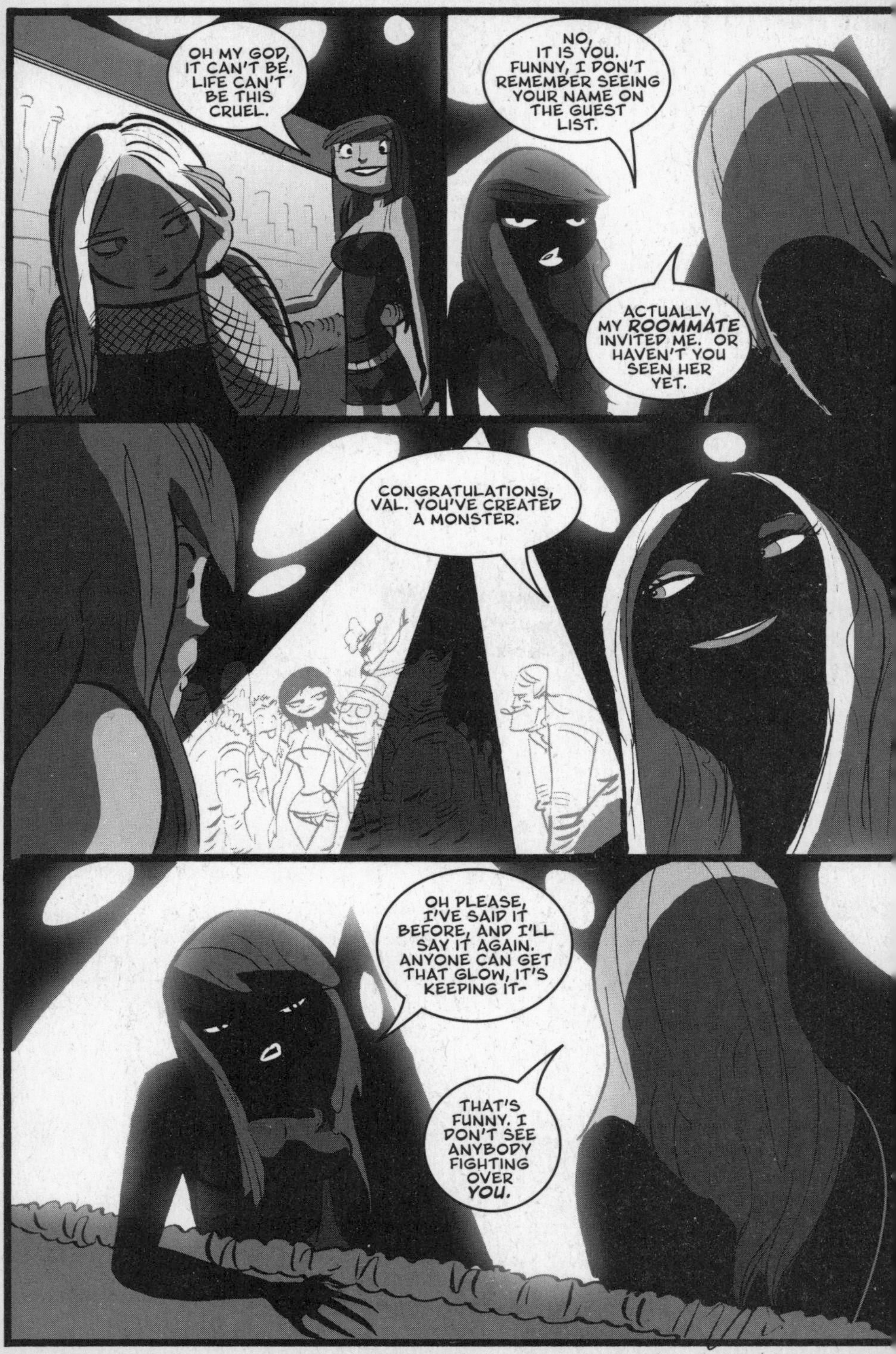
OH MY GOD, IT CAN'T BE. LIFE CAN'T BE THIS CRUEL.
NO, IT IS YOU. FUNNY, I DON'T REMEMBER SEEING YOUR NAME ON THE GUEST LIST.
ACTUALLY, MY ROOMMATE INVITED ME. OR HAVEN'T YOU SEEN HER YET.
CONGRATULATIONS, VAL. YOU'VE CREATED A MONSTER.
OH PLEASE, I'VE SAID IT BEFORE, AND I'LL SAY IT AGAIN. ANYONE CAN GET THAT GLOW, IT'S KEEPING IT-
THAT'S FUNNY. I DON'T SEE ANYBODY FIGHTING OVER YOU.

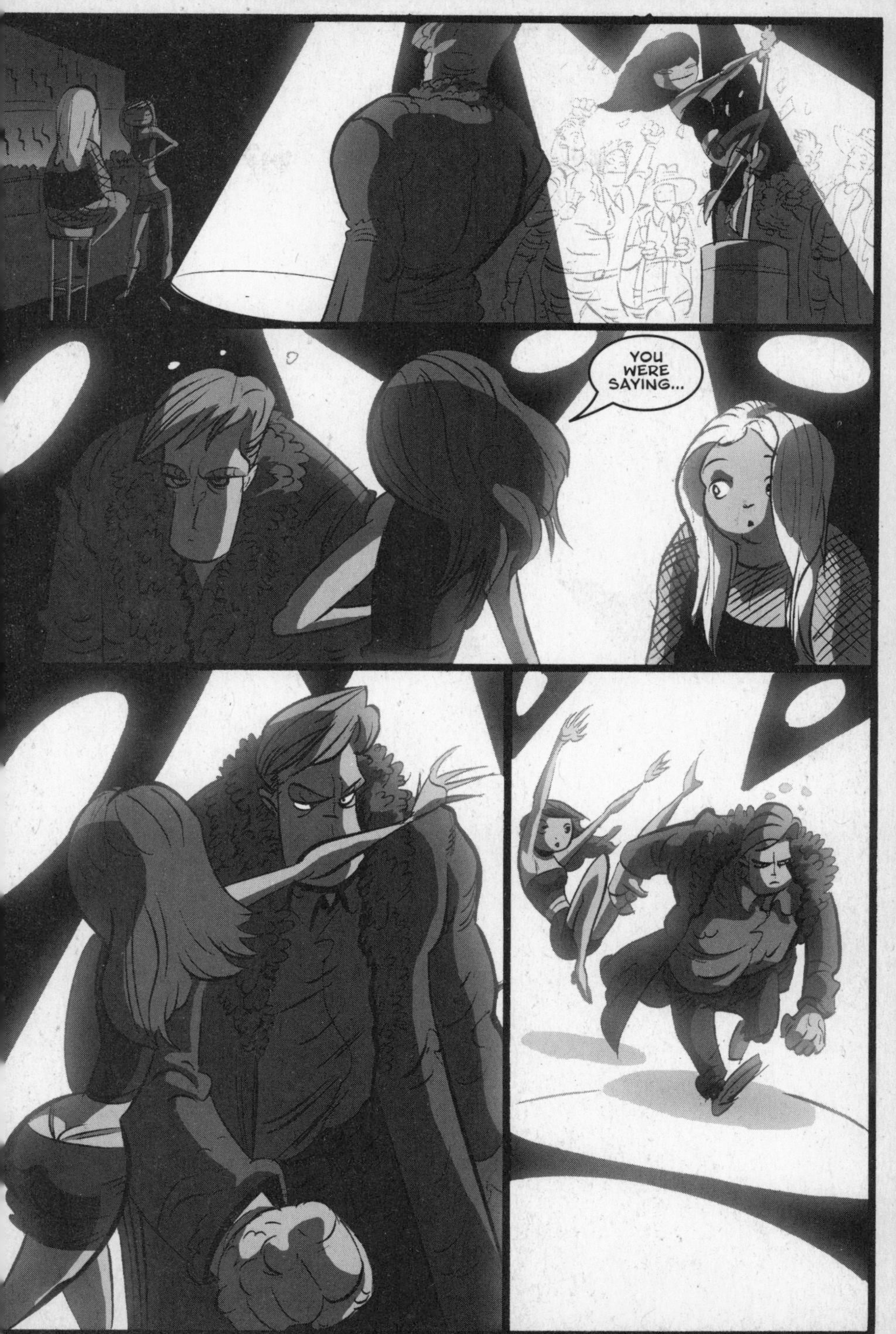
YOU WERE SAYING...

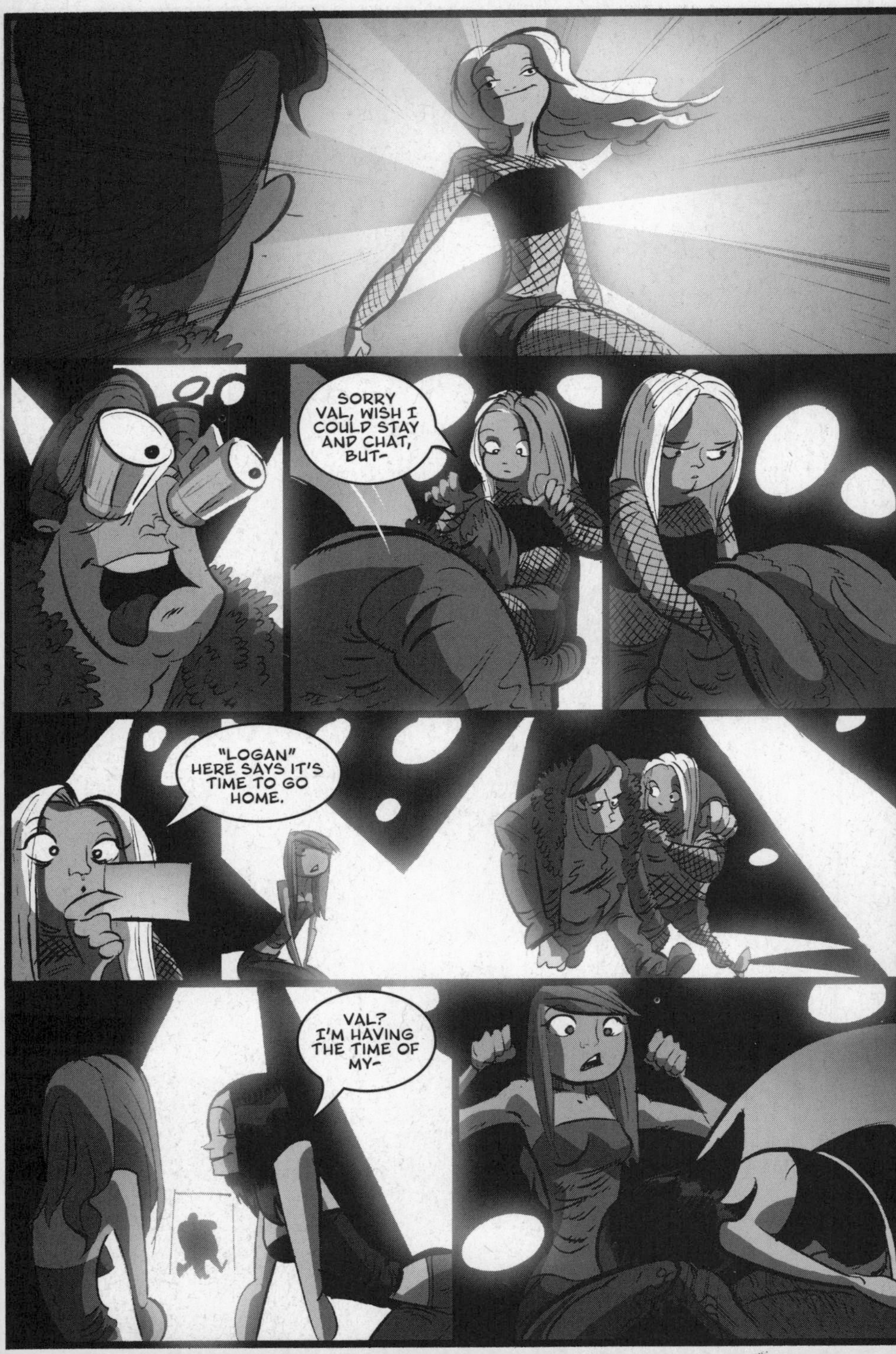
SORRY VAL, WISH I COULD STAY AND CHAT, BUT-
"LOGAN" HERE SAYS IT'S TIME TO GO HOME.
VAL? I'M HAVING THE TIME OF MY-

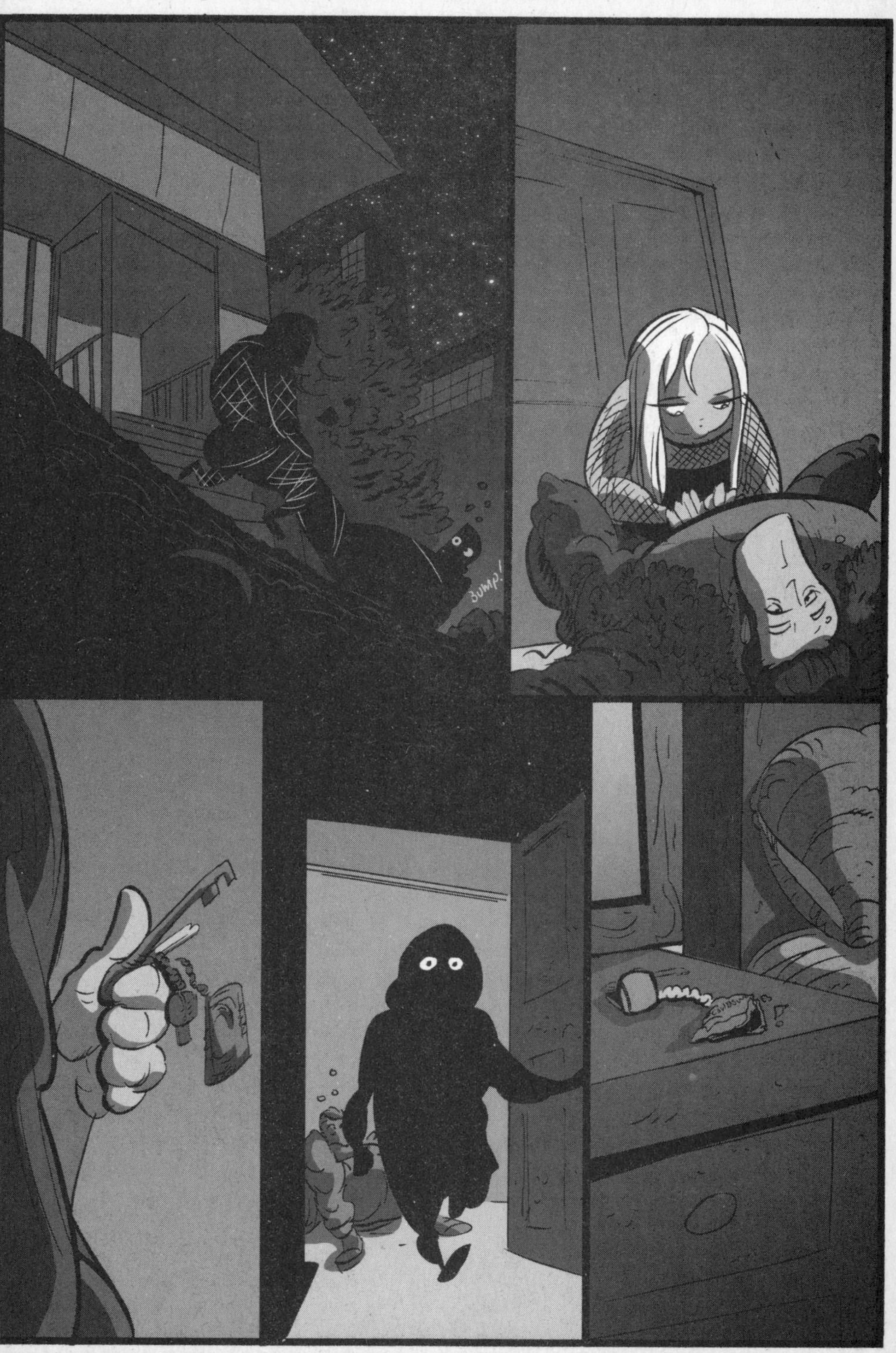
BUMP!

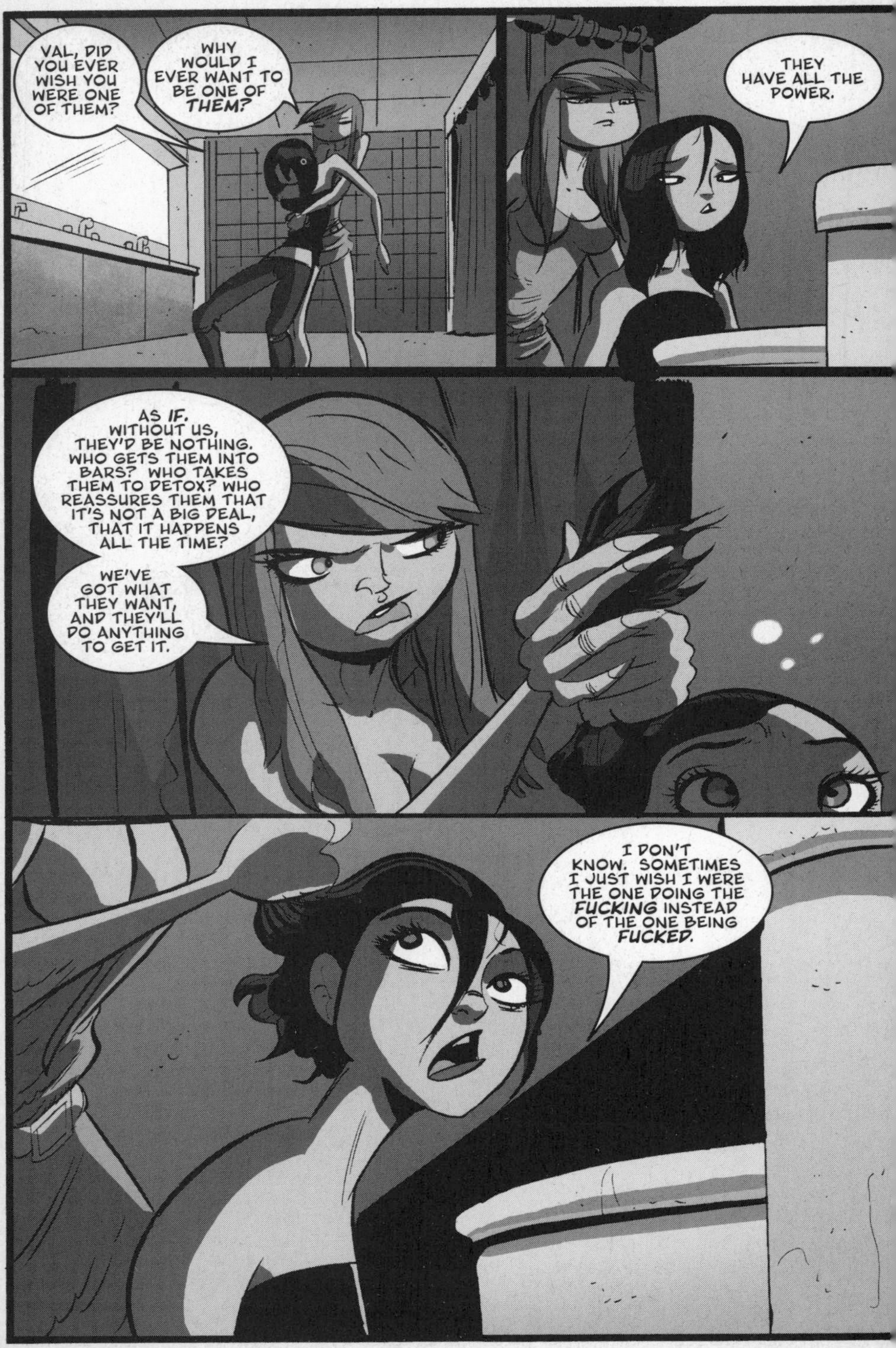
VAL, DID YOU EVER WISH YOU WERE ONE OF THEM?
WHY WOULD I EVER WANT TO BE ONE OF *THEM?*
THEY HAVE ALL THE POWER.
AS *IF.* WITHOUT US, THEY'D BE NOTHING. WHO GETS THEM INTO BARS? WHO TAKES THEM TO DETOX? WHO REASSURES THEM THAT IT'S NOT A BIG DEAL, THAT IT HAPPENS ALL THE TIME?
WE'VE GOT WHAT THEY WANT, AND THEY'LL DO ANYTHING TO GET IT.
I DON'T KNOW. SOMETIMES I JUST WISH I WERE THE ONE DOING THE **FUCKING** INSTEAD OF THE ONE BEING **FUCKED**.

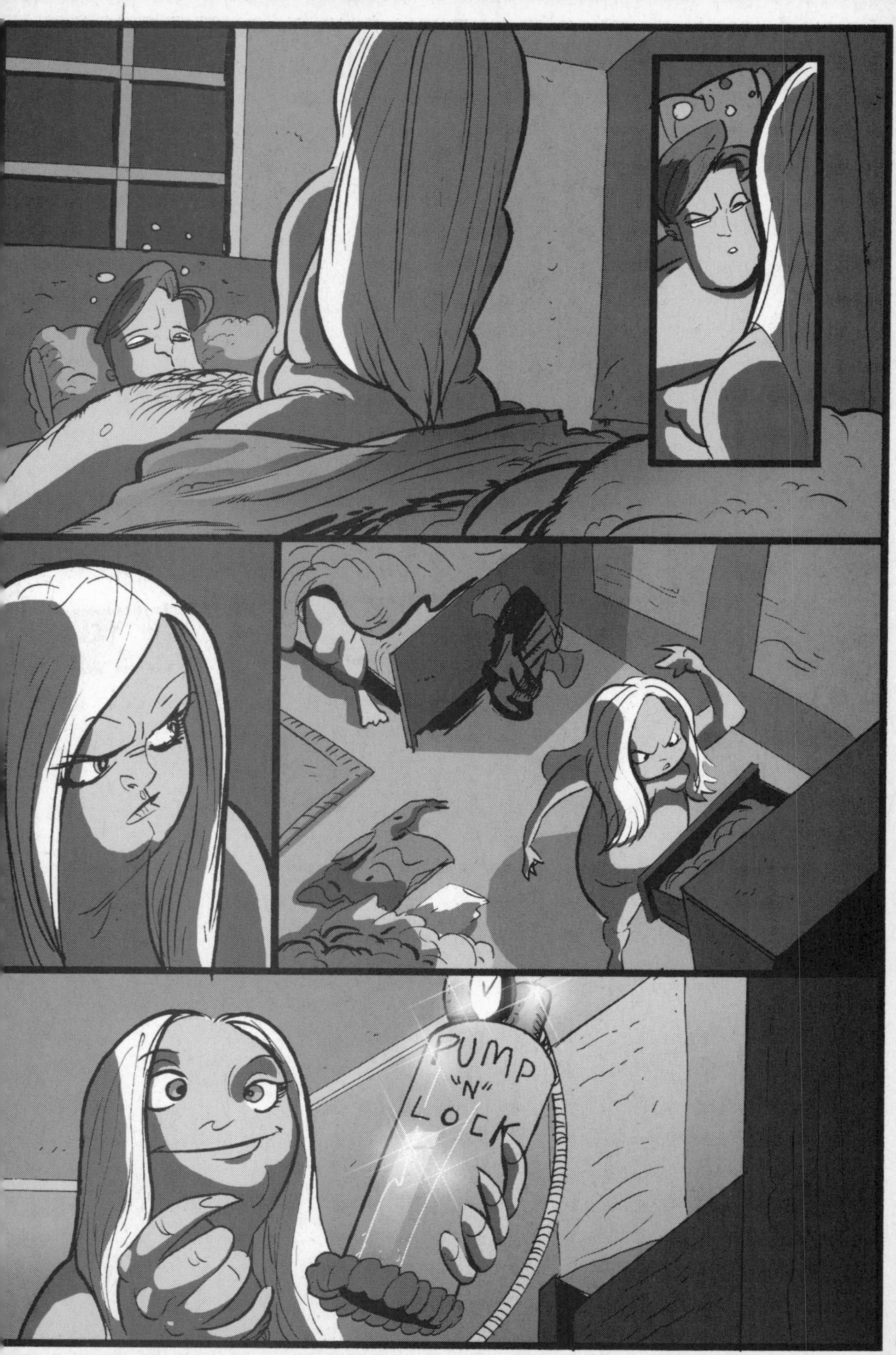
PUMP
"N"
LOCK

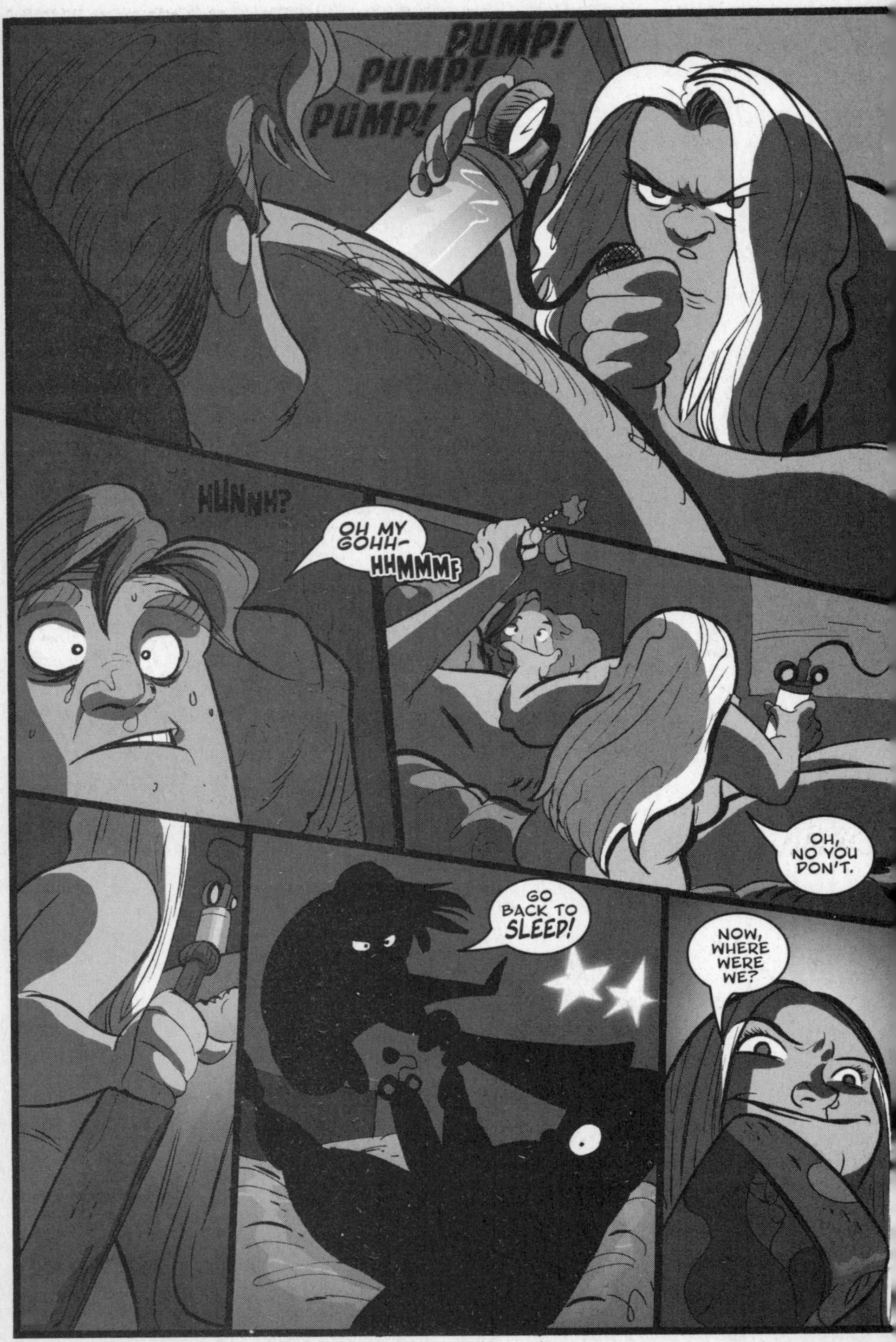
PUMP!
PUMP!
PUMP!
HUNNH?
OH MY GOHH-
HHMMMF
OH, NO YOU DON'T.
GO BACK TO SLEEP!
NOW, WHERE WERE WE?

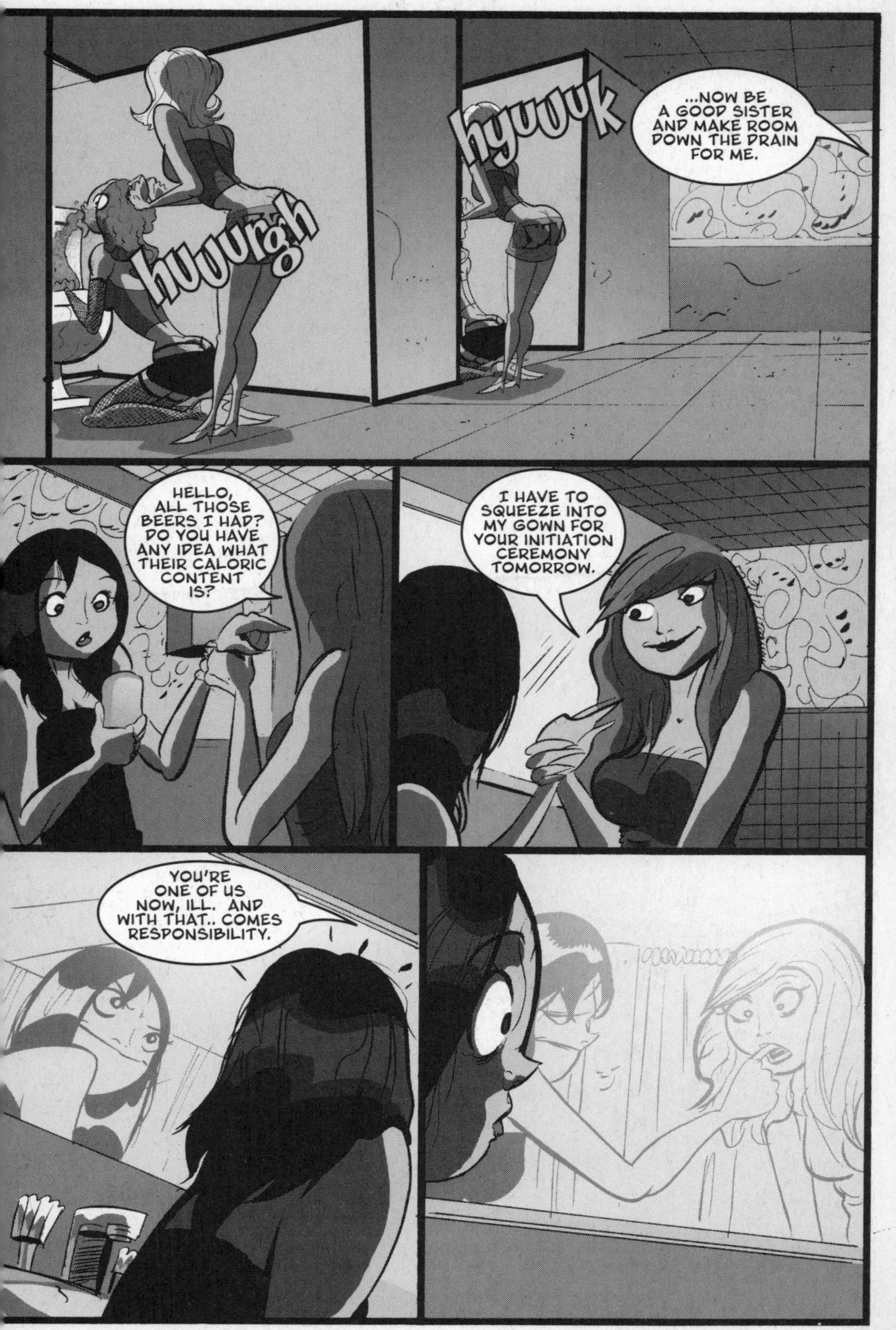
huuurgh
hyuuuk
...NOW BE A GOOD SISTER AND MAKE ROOM DOWN THE DRAIN FOR ME.
HELLO, ALL THOSE BEERS I HAD? DO YOU HAVE ANY IDEA WHAT THEIR CALORIC CONTENT IS?
I HAVE TO SQUEEZE INTO MY GOWN FOR YOUR INITIATION CEREMONY TOMORROW.
YOU'RE ONE OF US NOW, ILL. AND WITH THAT.. COMES RESPONSIBILITY.

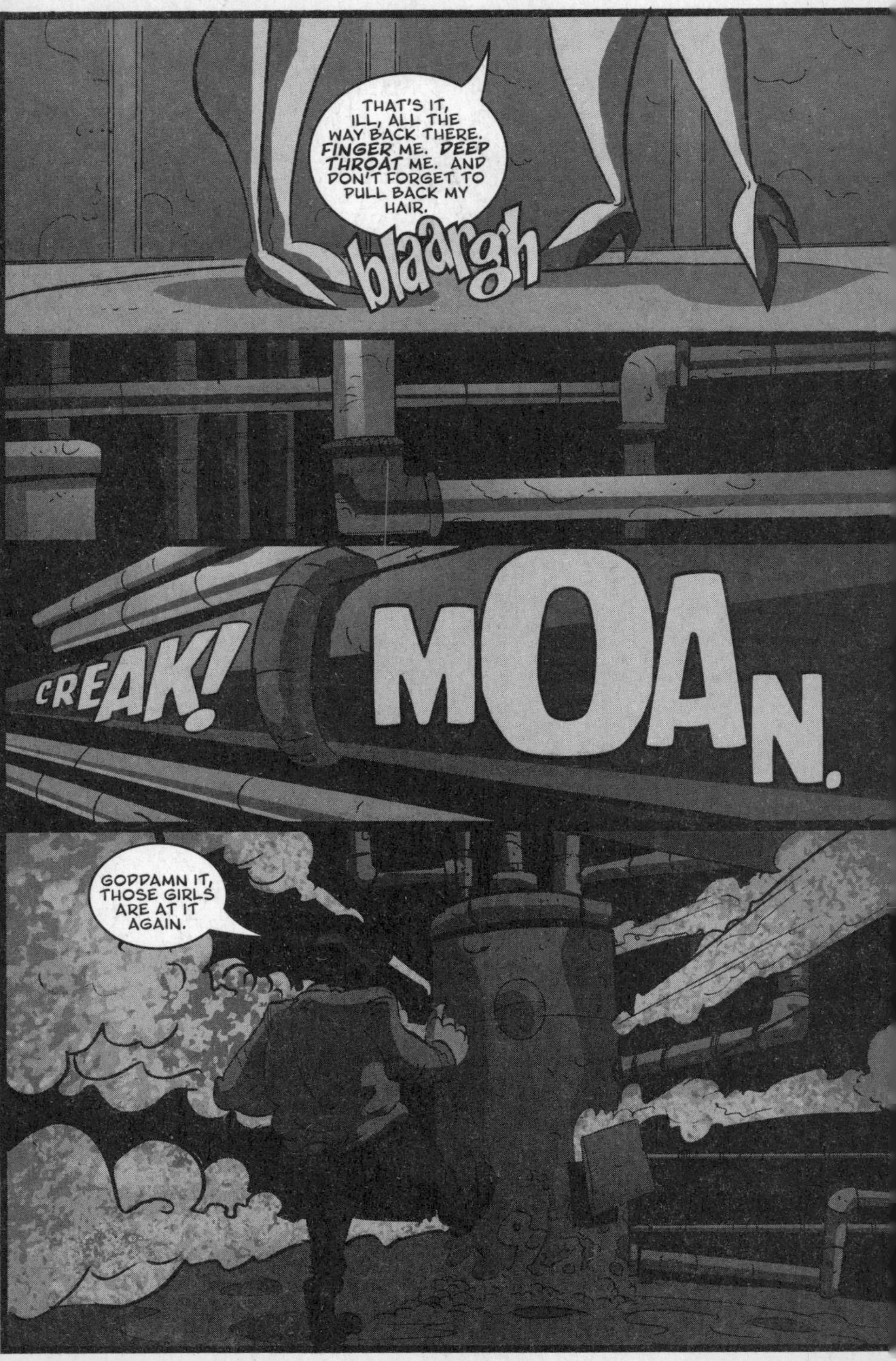
THAT'S IT, ILL, ALL THE WAY BACK THERE. FINGER ME. DEEP THROAT ME. AND DON'T FORGET TO PULL BACK MY HAIR.
blaargh
CREAK!
MOAN.
GODDAMN IT, THOSE GIRLS ARE AT IT AGAIN.

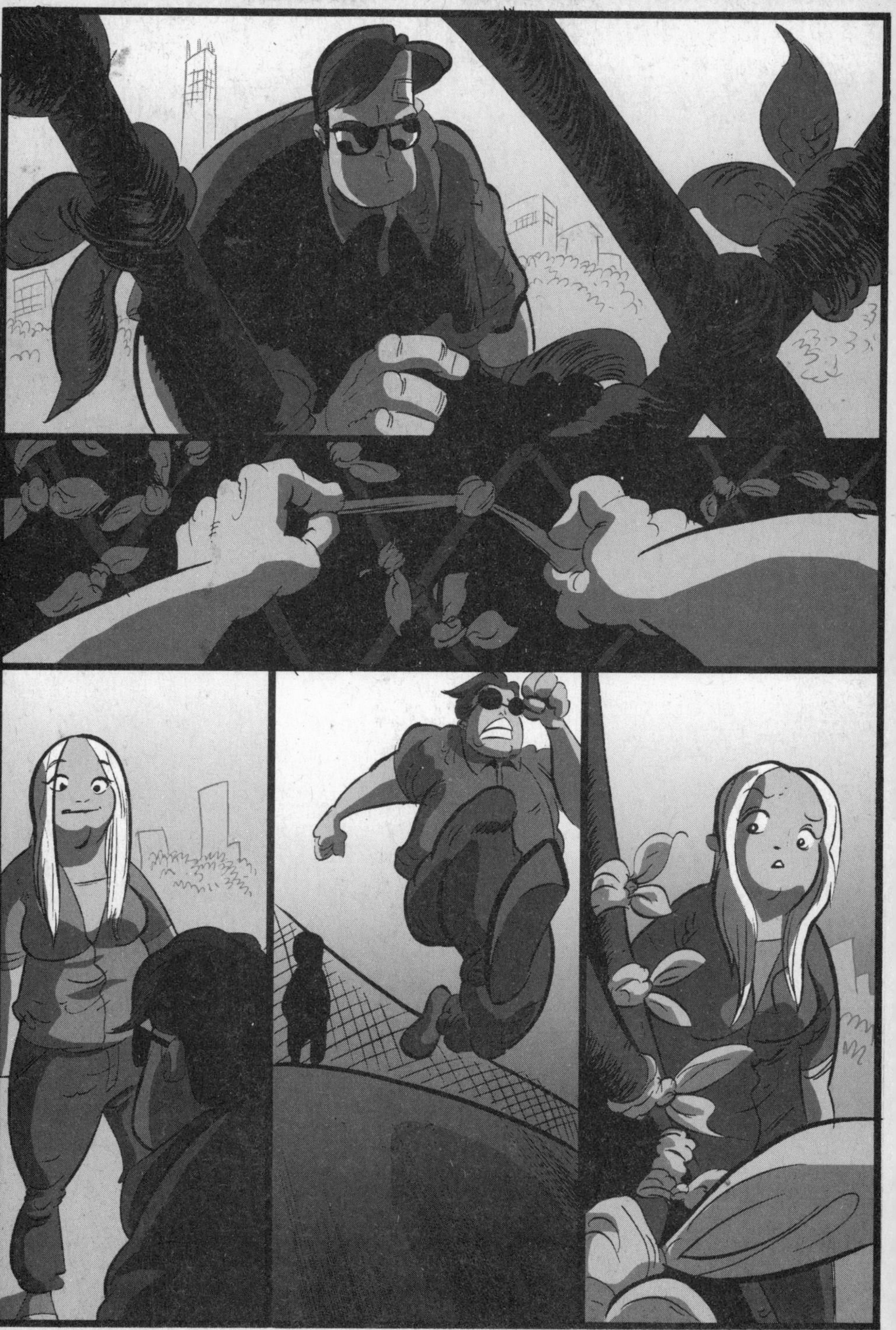

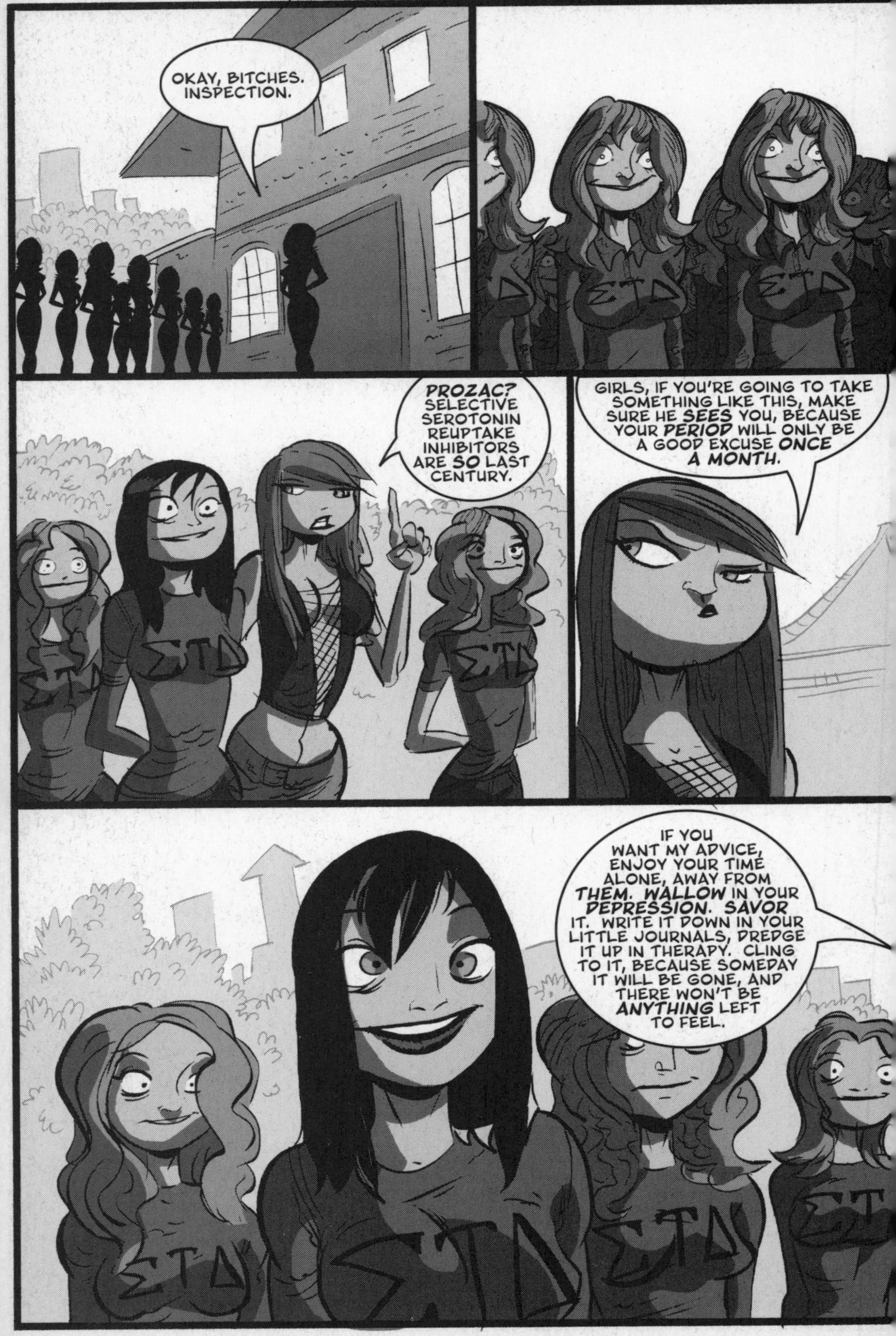
OKAY, BITCHES. INSPECTION.
PROZAC? SELECTIVE SEROTONIN REUPTAKE INHIBITORS ARE SO LAST CENTURY.
GIRLS, IF YOU'RE GOING TO TAKE SOMETHING LIKE THIS, MAKE SURE HE SEES YOU, BECAUSE YOUR PERIOD WILL ONLY BE A GOOD EXCUSE ONCE A MONTH.
IF YOU WANT MY ADVICE, ENJOY YOUR TIME ALONE, AWAY FROM THEM. WALLOW IN YOUR DEPRESSION. SAVOR IT. WRITE IT DOWN IN YOUR LITTLE JOURNALS, DREDGE IT UP IN THERAPY. CLING TO IT, BECAUSE SOMEDAY IT WILL BE GONE, AND THERE WON'T BE ANYTHING LEFT TO FEEL.

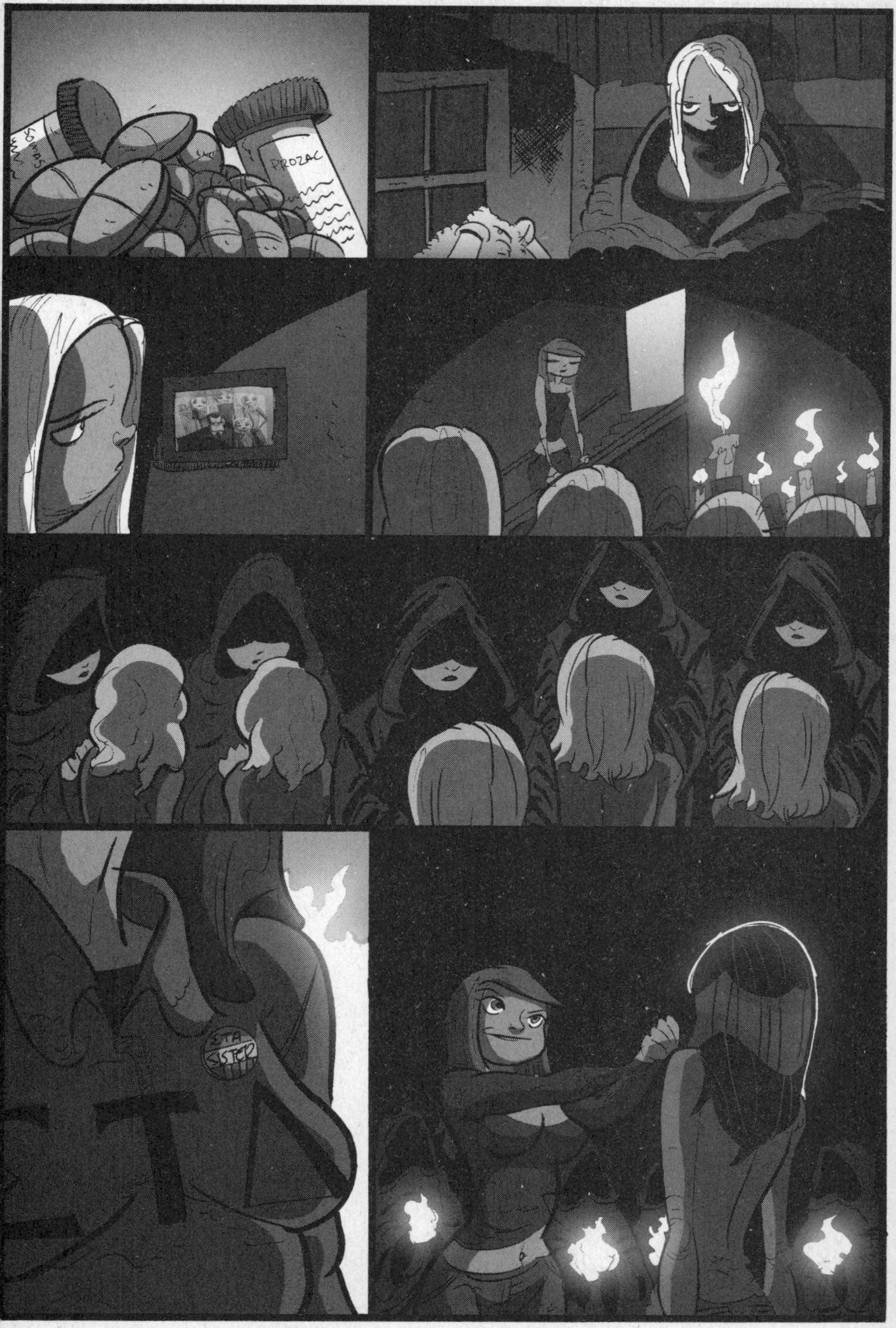
PROZAC
SISTER

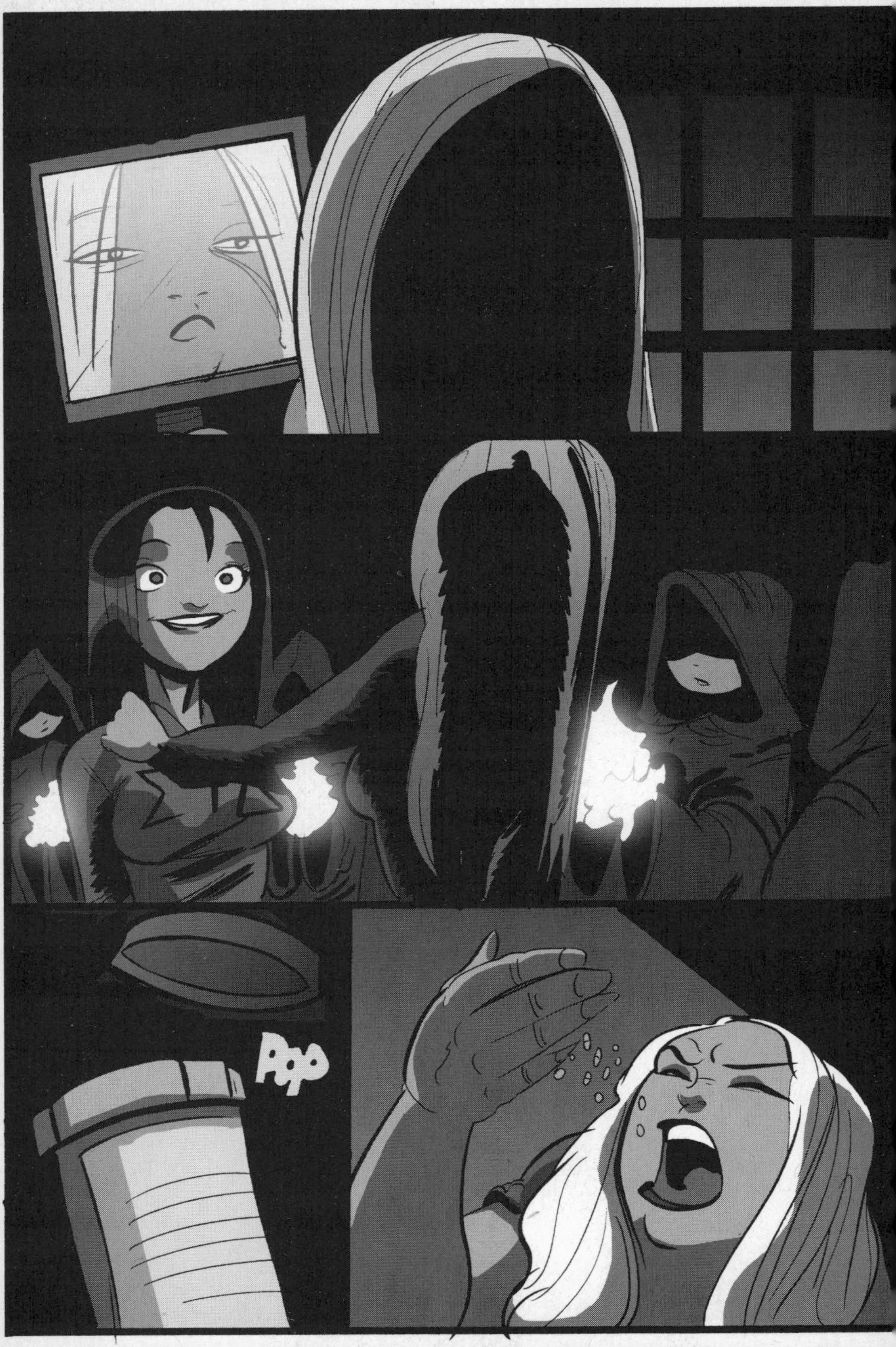
POP

CHAPTER
4

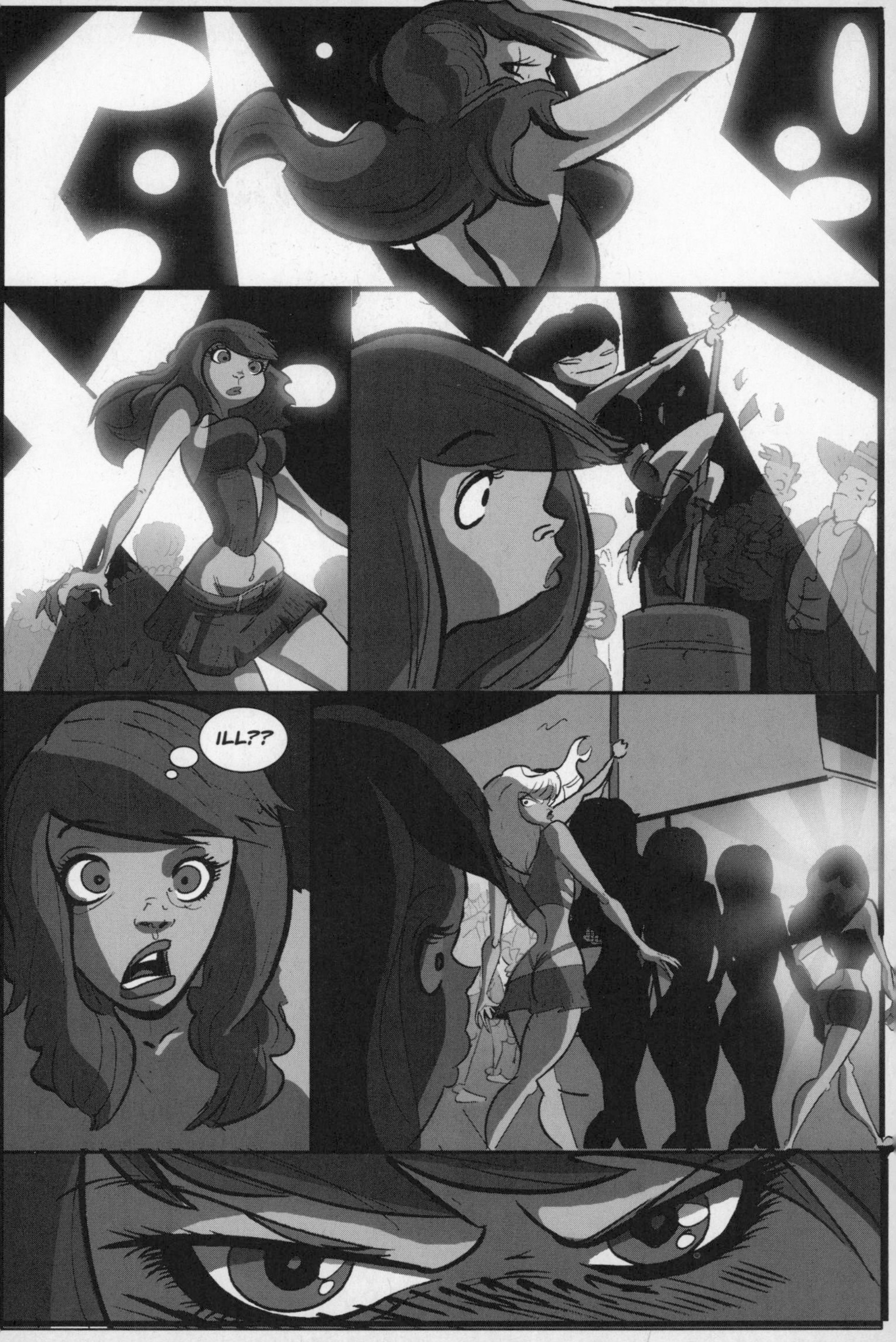
ILL??

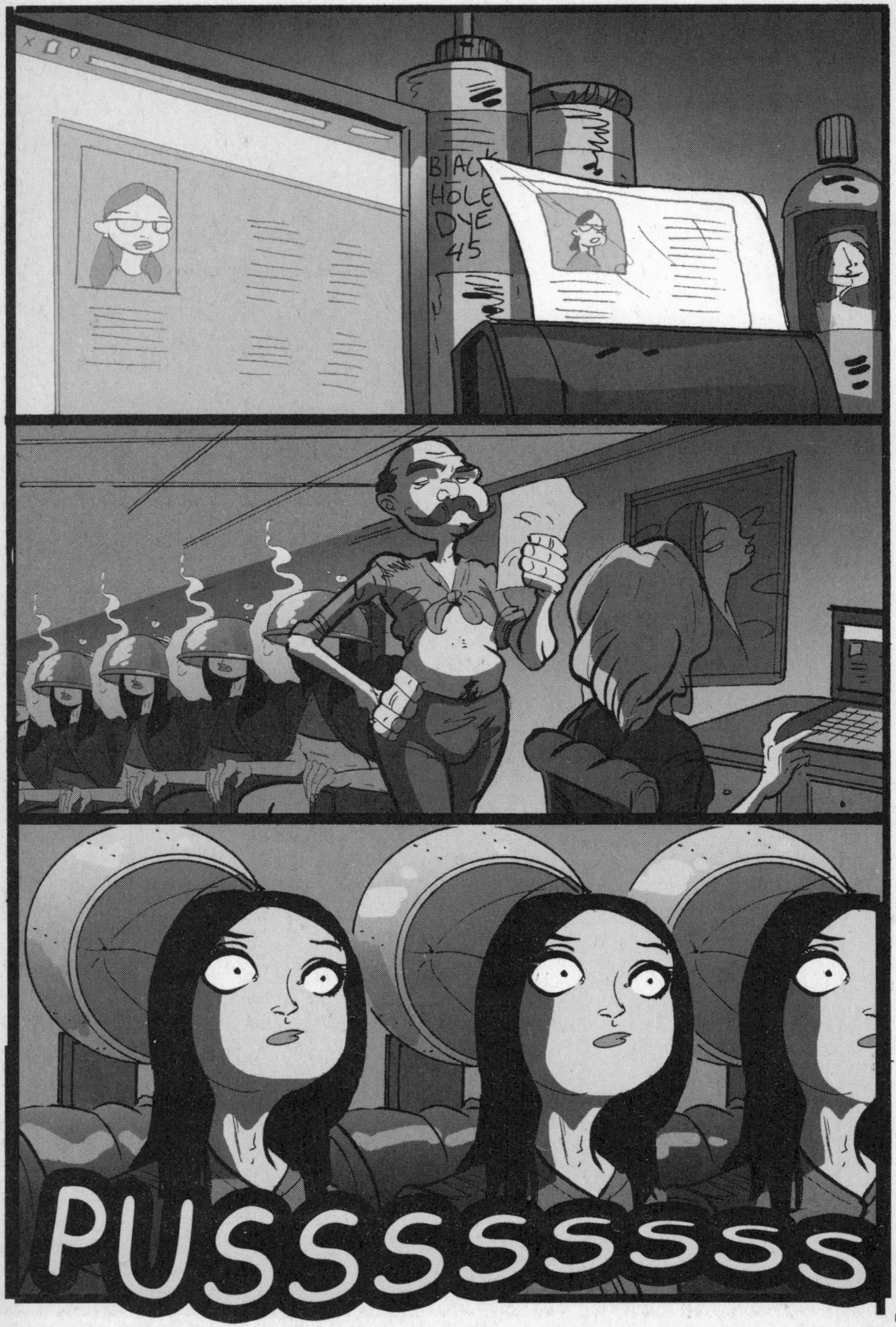
BLACK HOLE DYE 45
PUSSSSSSSS

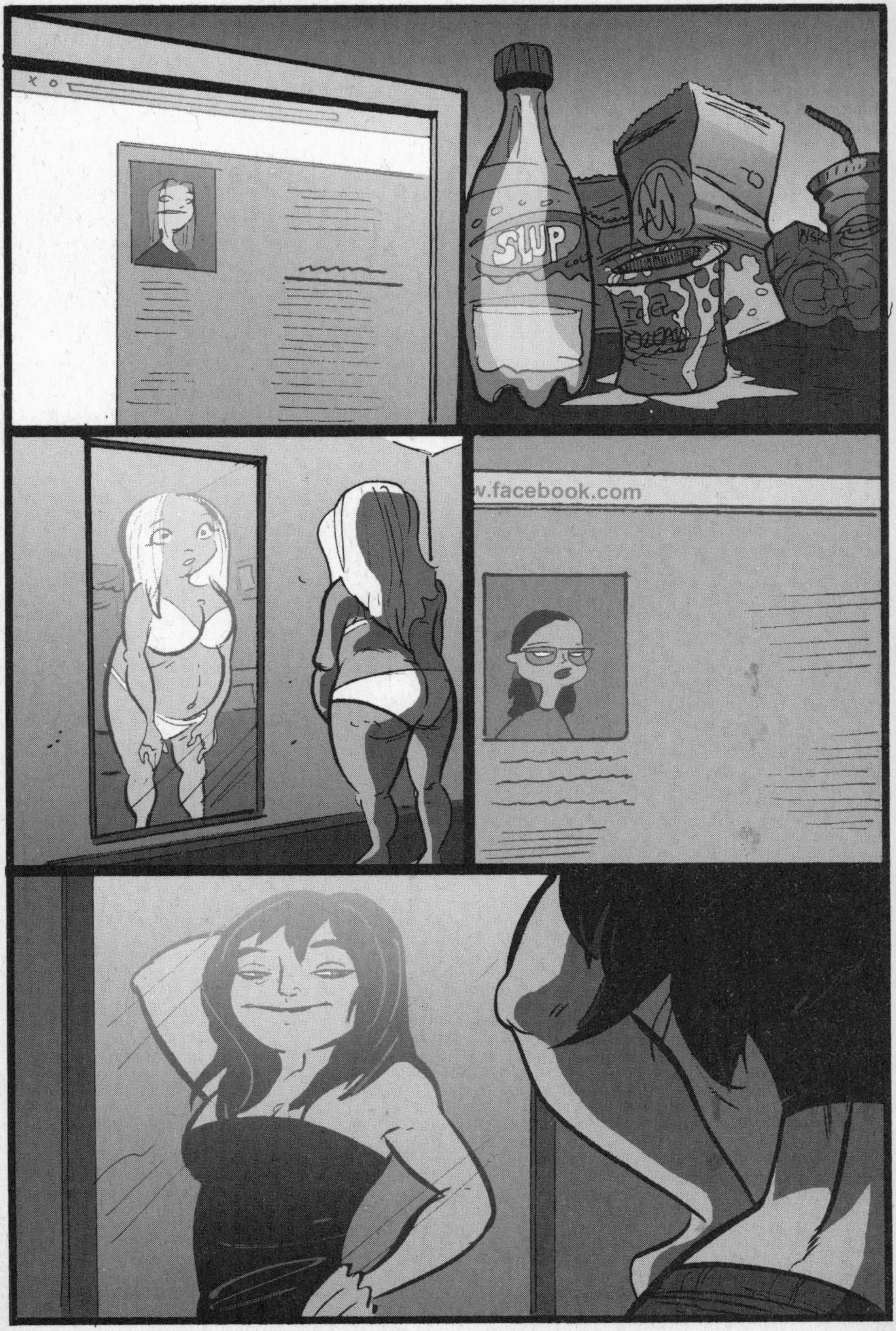
SLUP
w.facebook.com

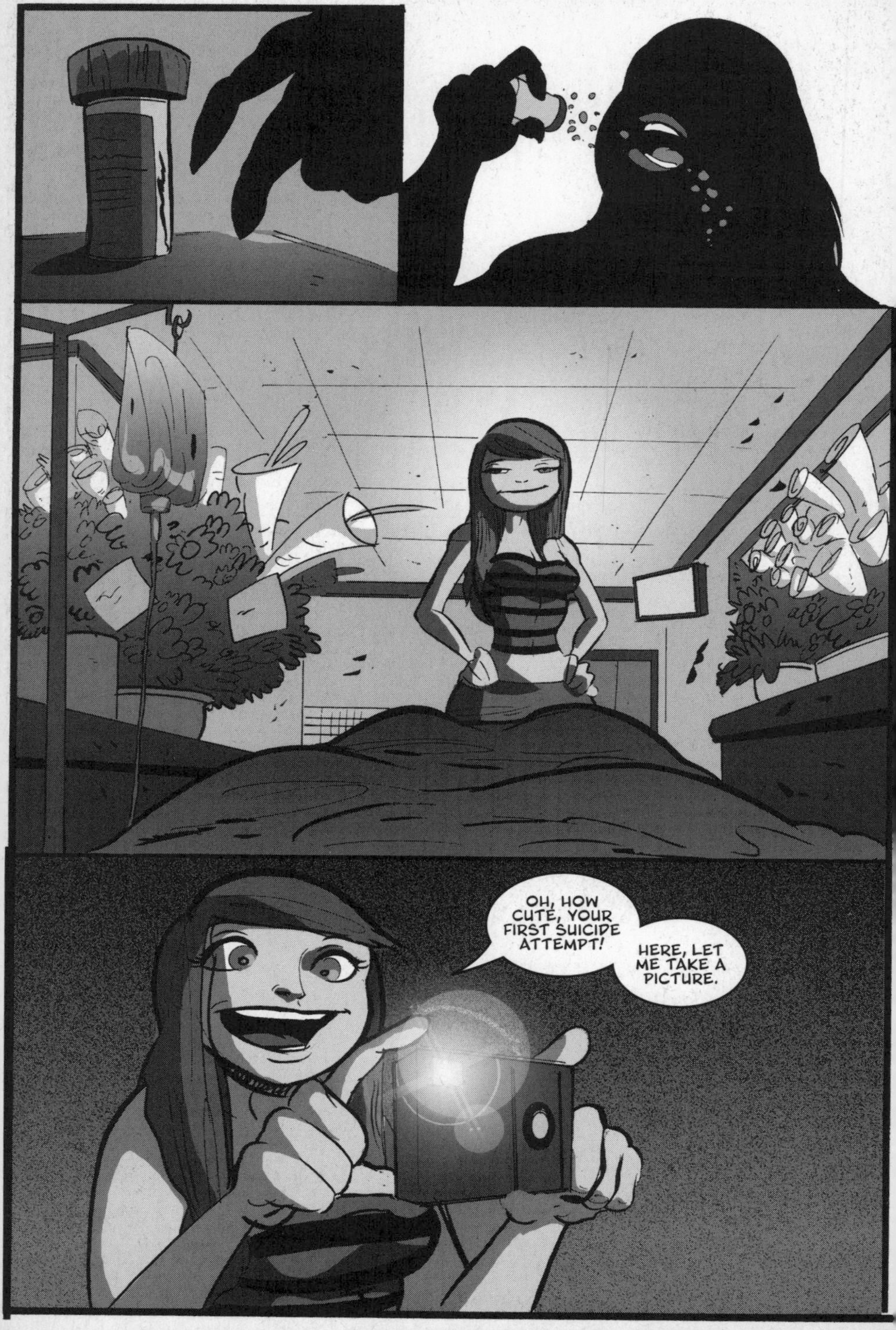
OH, HOW CUTE, YOUR FIRST SUICIDE ATTEMPT!
HERE, LET ME TAKE A PICTURE.

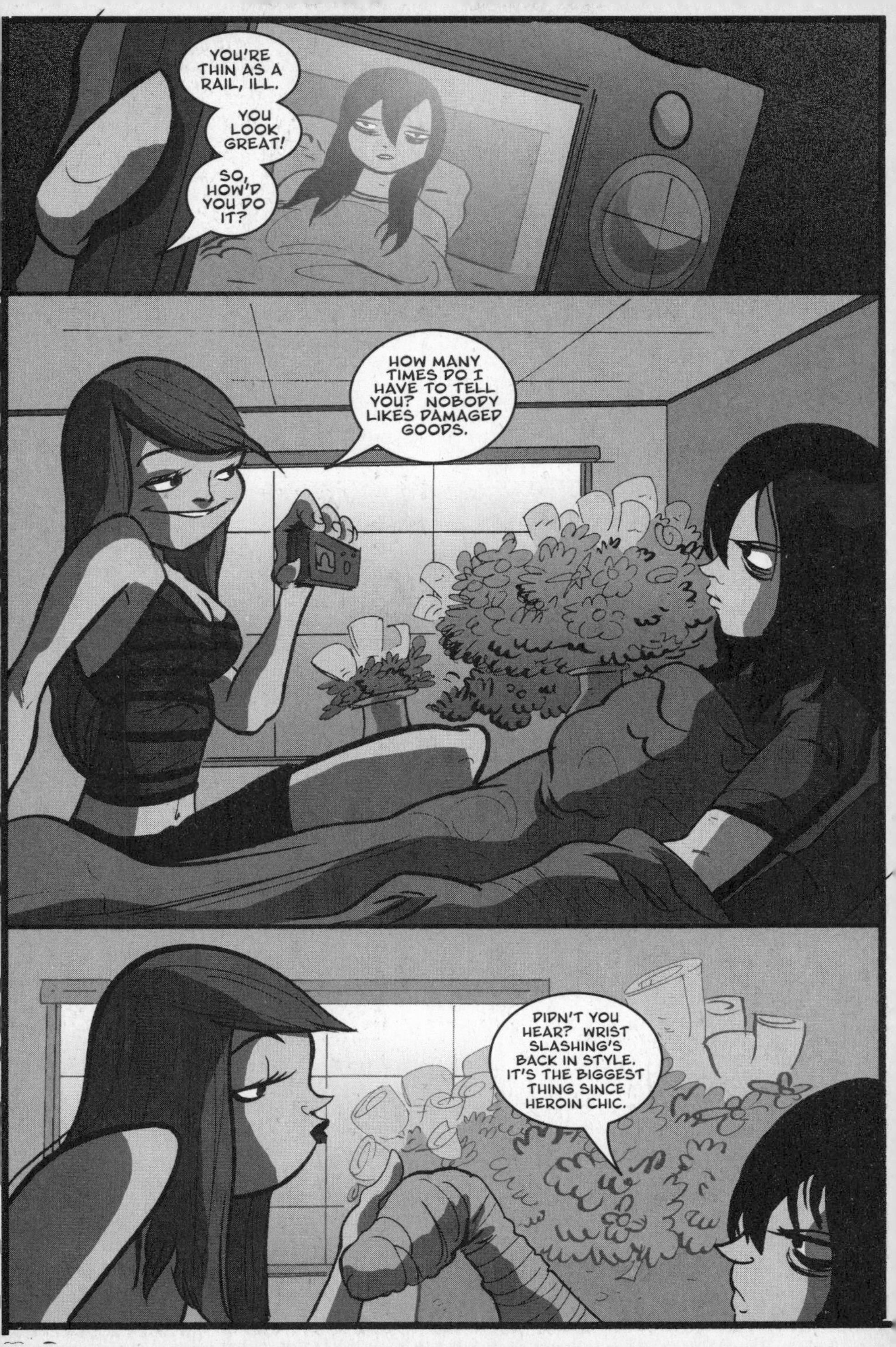

YOU'RE THIN AS A RAIL, ILL.
YOU LOOK GREAT!
SO, HOW'D YOU DO IT?
HOW MANY TIMES DO I HAVE TO TELL YOU? NOBODY LIKES DAMAGED GOODS.
DIDN'T YOU HEAR? WRIST SLASHING'S BACK IN STYLE. IT'S THE BIGGEST THING SINCE HEROIN CHIC.

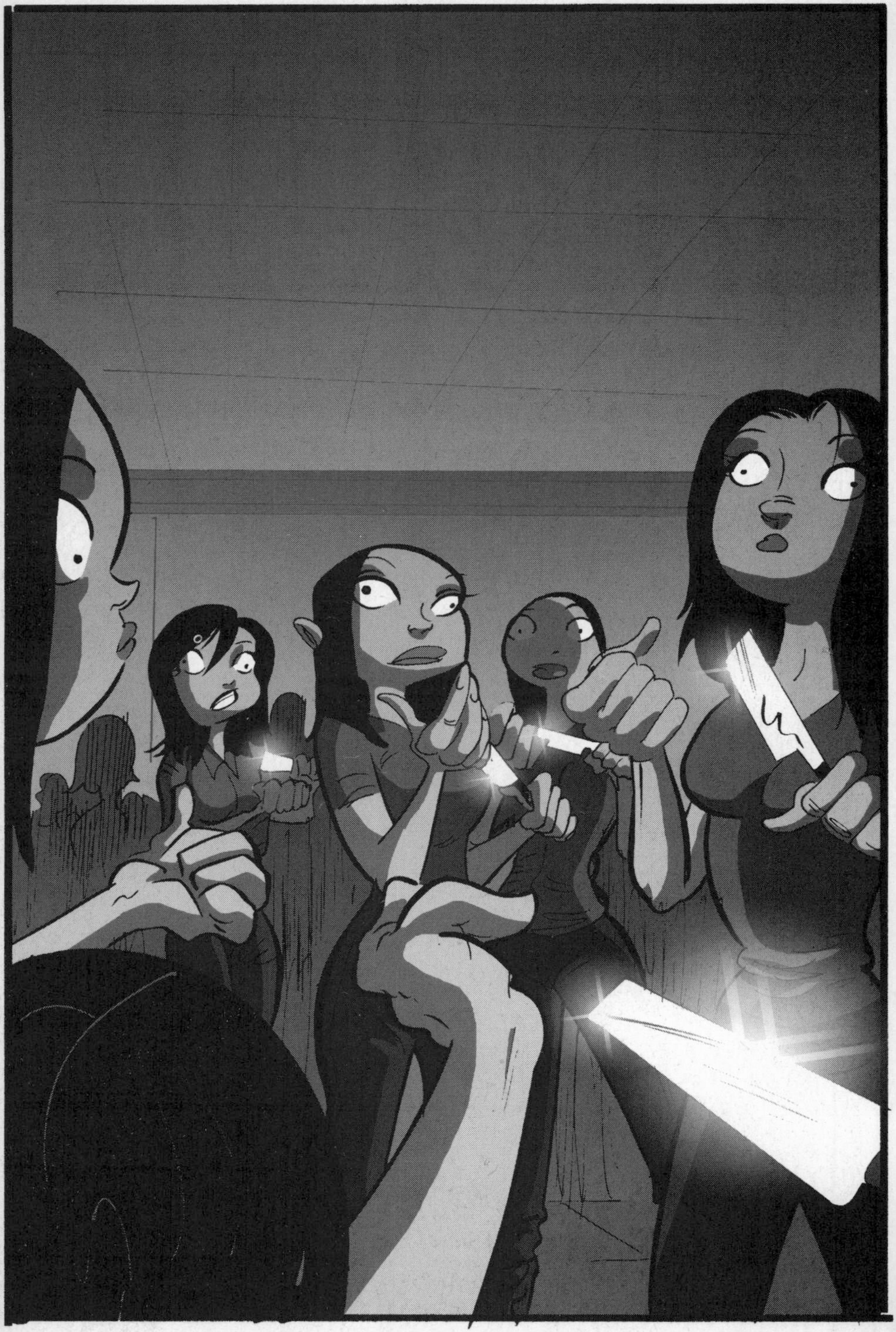

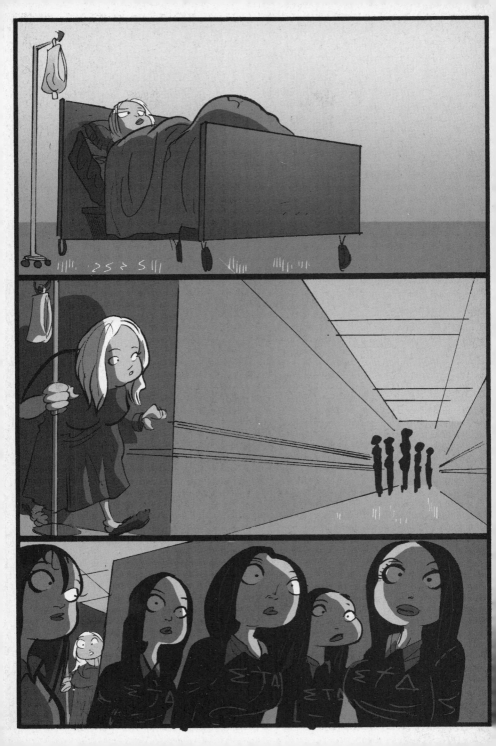

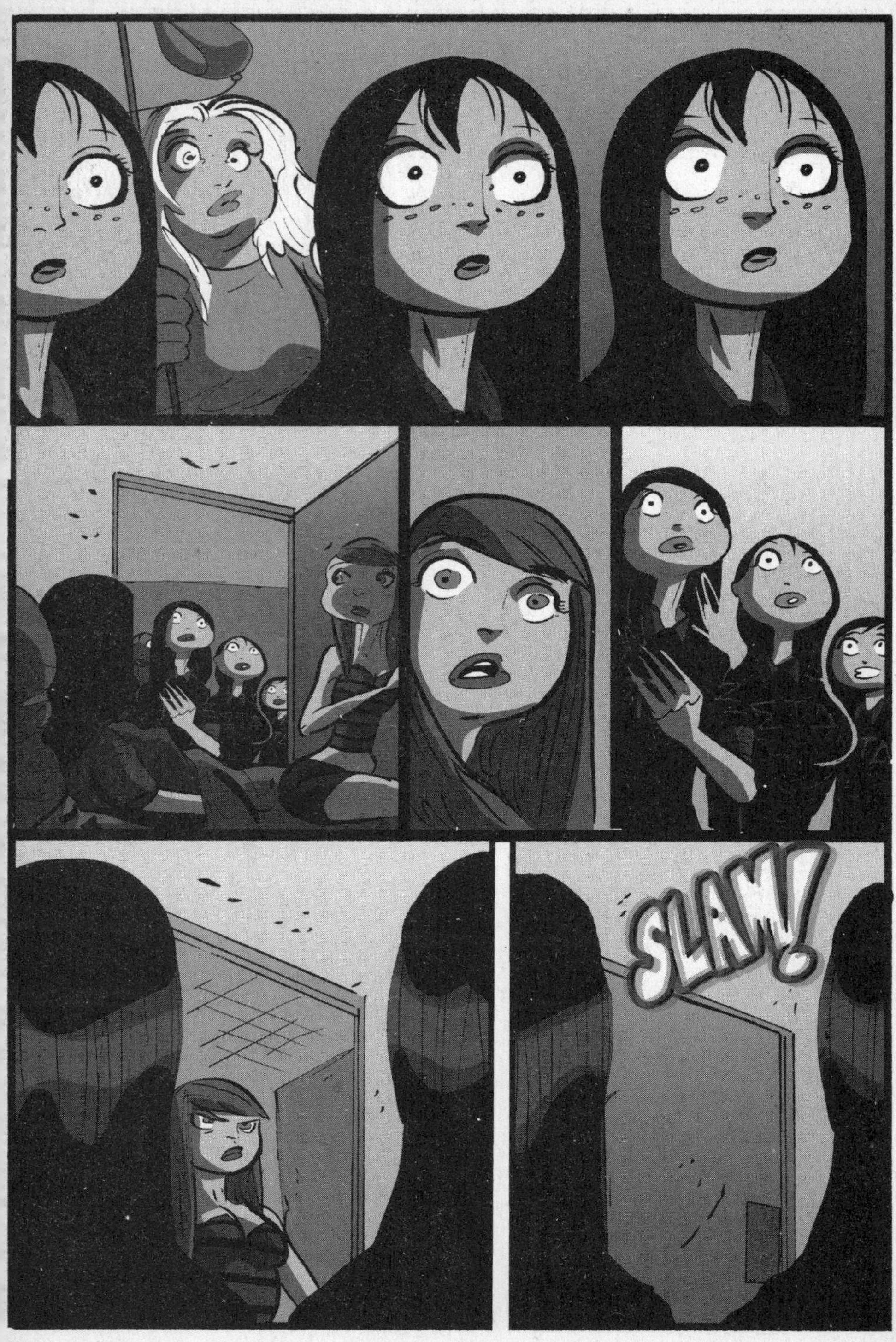
SLAM!

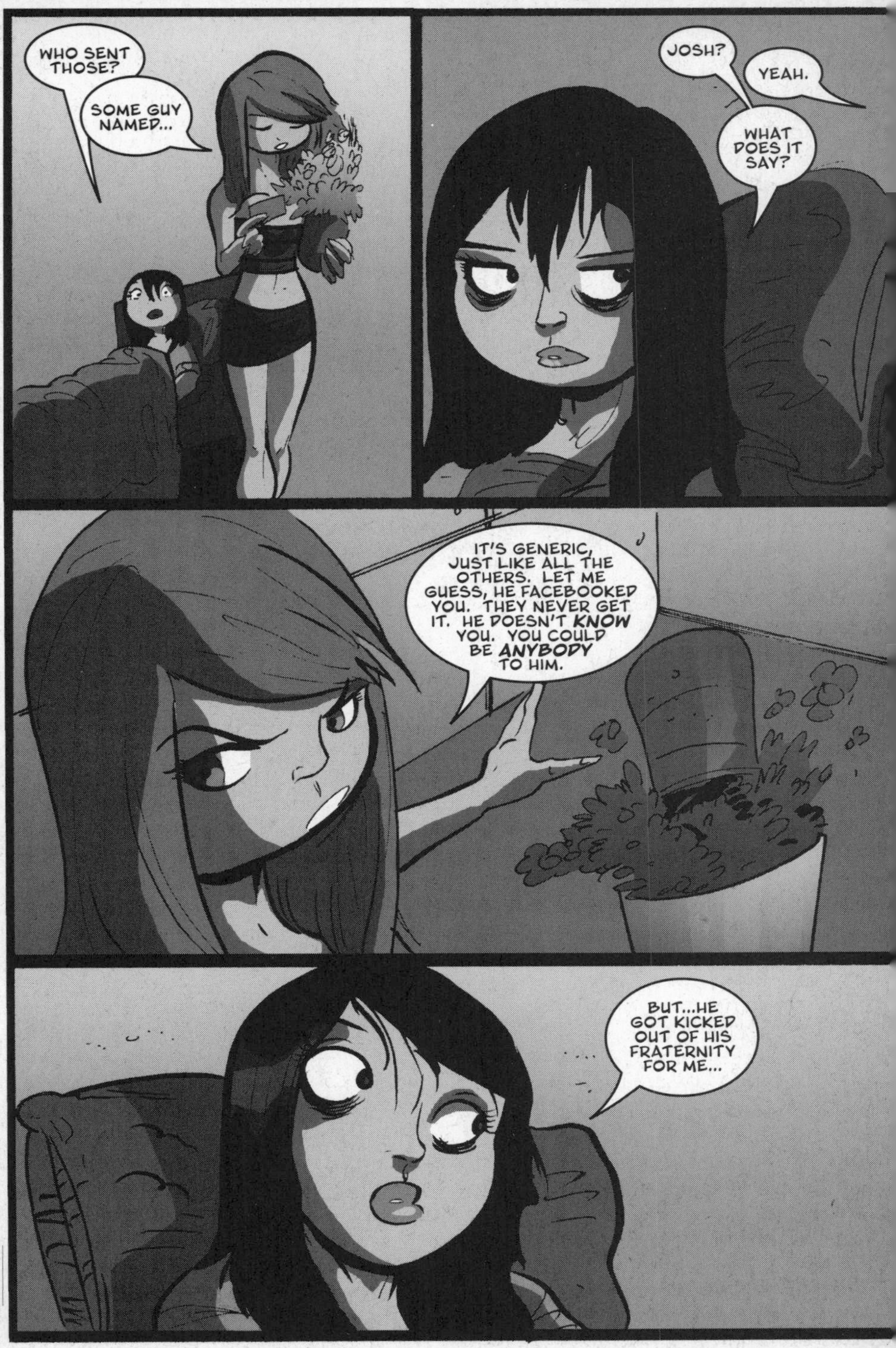

WHO SENT THOSE?
SOME GUY NAMED...
JOSH?
YEAH.
WHAT DOES IT SAY?
IT'S GENERIC, JUST LIKE ALL THE OTHERS. LET ME GUESS, HE FACEBOOKED YOU. THEY NEVER GET IT. HE DOESN'T **KNOW** YOU. YOU COULD BE **ANYBODY** TO HIM.
BUT...HE GOT KICKED OUT OF HIS FRATERNITY FOR ME...

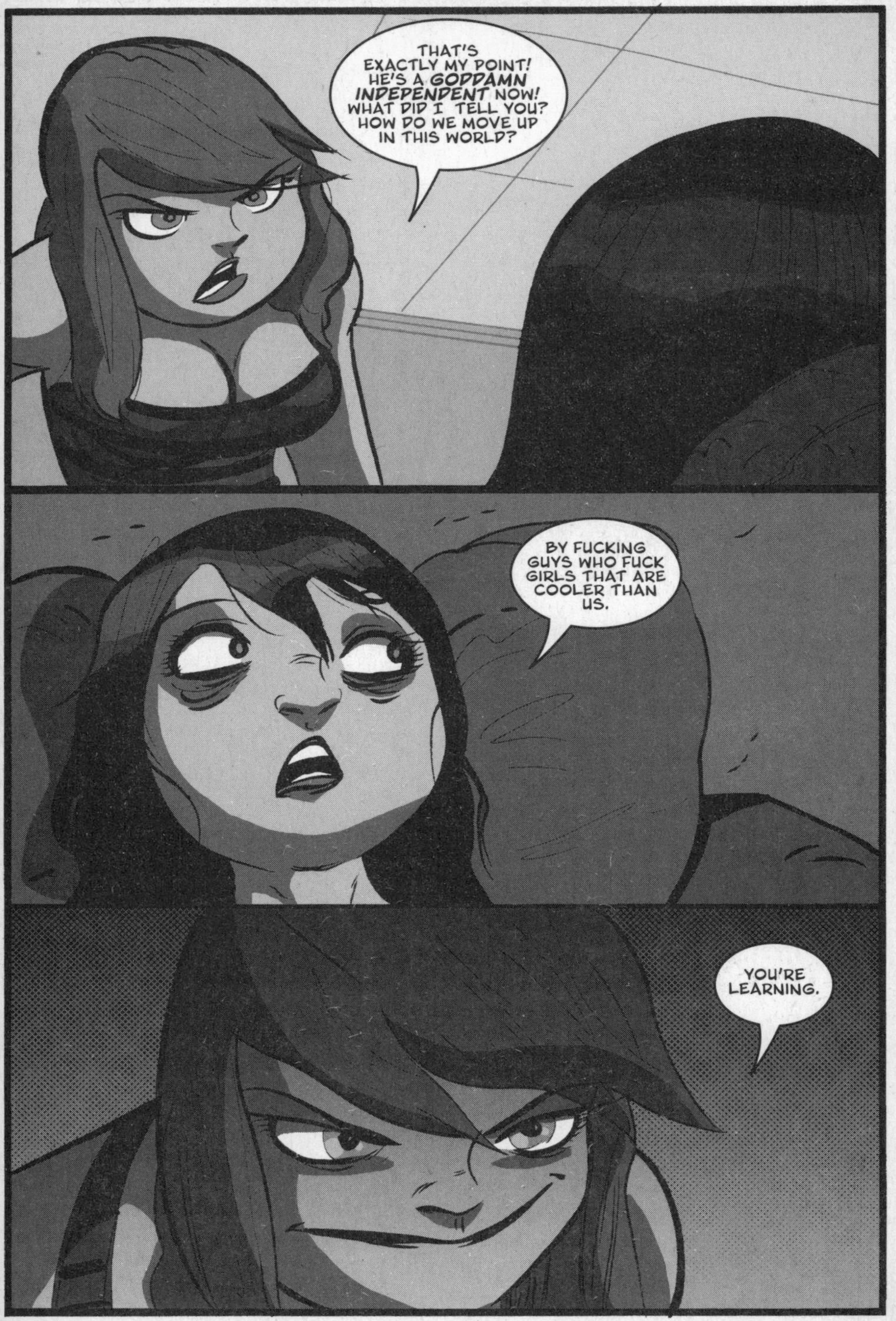
THAT'S EXACTLY MY POINT! HE'S A GODDAMN INDEPENDENT NOW! WHAT DID I TELL YOU? HOW DO WE MOVE UP IN THIS WORLD?
BY FUCKING GUYS WHO FUCK GIRLS THAT ARE COOLER THAN US.
YOU'RE LEARNING.

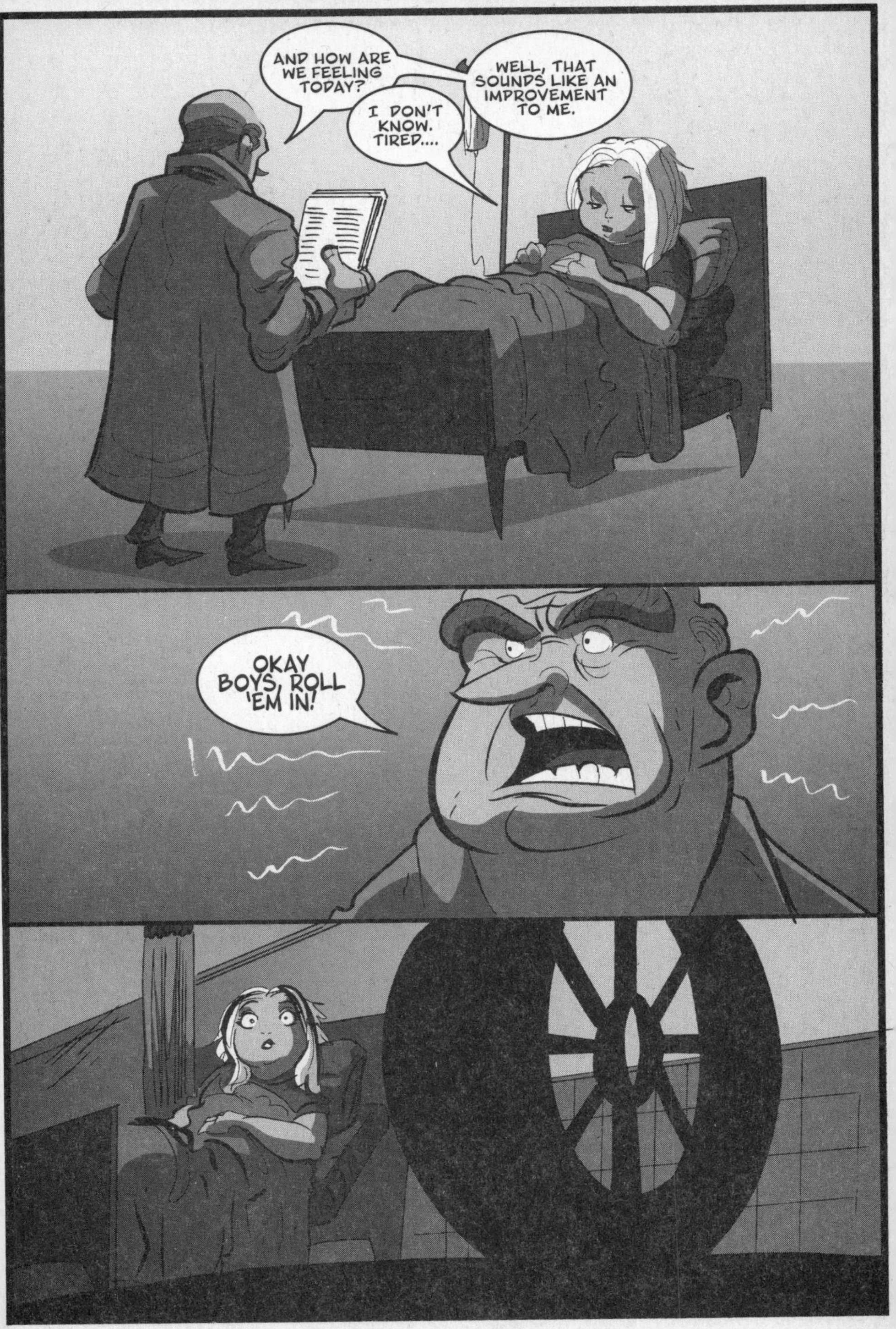
AND HOW ARE WE FEELING TODAY?
I DON'T KNOW. TIRED....
WELL, THAT SOUNDS LIKE AN IMPROVEMENT TO ME.
OKAY BOYS, ROLL 'EM IN!

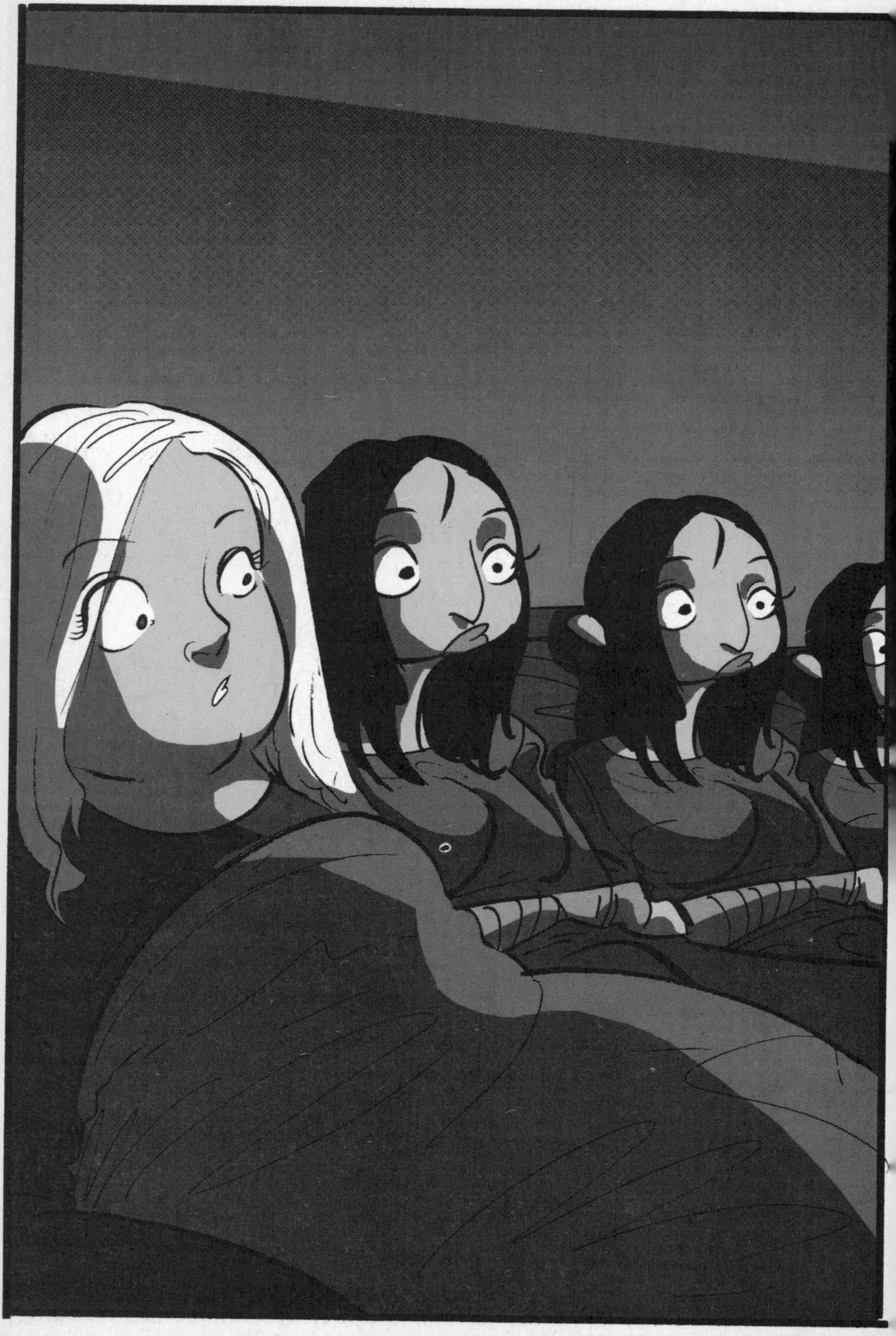

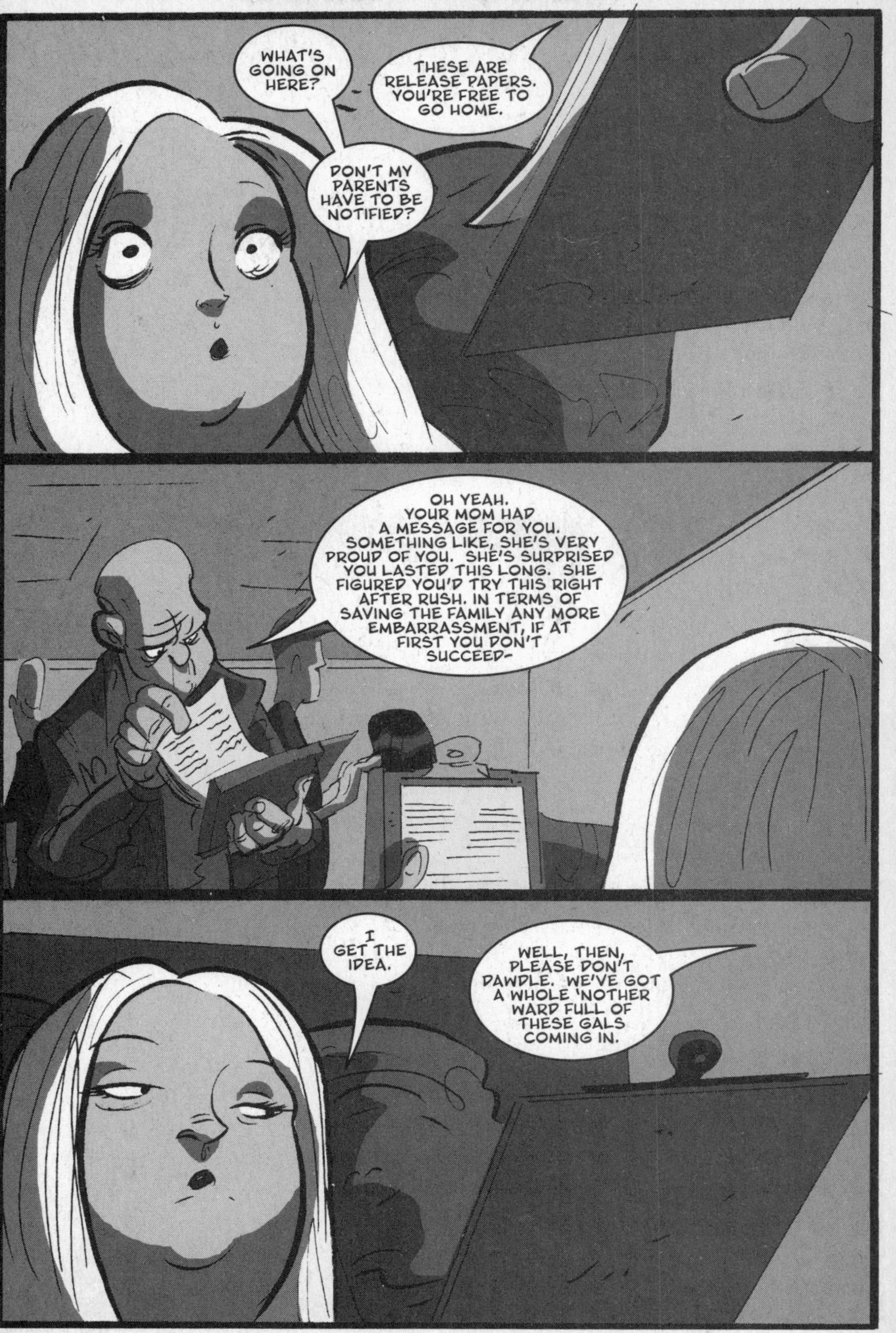

WHAT'S GOING ON HERE?
THESE ARE RELEASE PAPERS. YOU'RE FREE TO GO HOME.
DON'T MY PARENTS HAVE TO BE NOTIFIED?
OH YEAH. YOUR MOM HAD A MESSAGE FOR YOU. SOMETHING LIKE, SHE'S VERY PROUD OF YOU. SHE'S SURPRISED YOU LASTED THIS LONG. SHE FIGURED YOU'D TRY THIS RIGHT AFTER RUSH. IN TERMS OF SAVING THE FAMILY ANY MORE EMBARRASSMENT, IF AT FIRST YOU DON'T SUCCEED-
I GET THE IDEA.
WELL, THEN, PLEASE DON'T DAWDLE. WE'VE GOT A WHOLE 'NOTHER WARD FULL OF THESE GALS COMING IN.

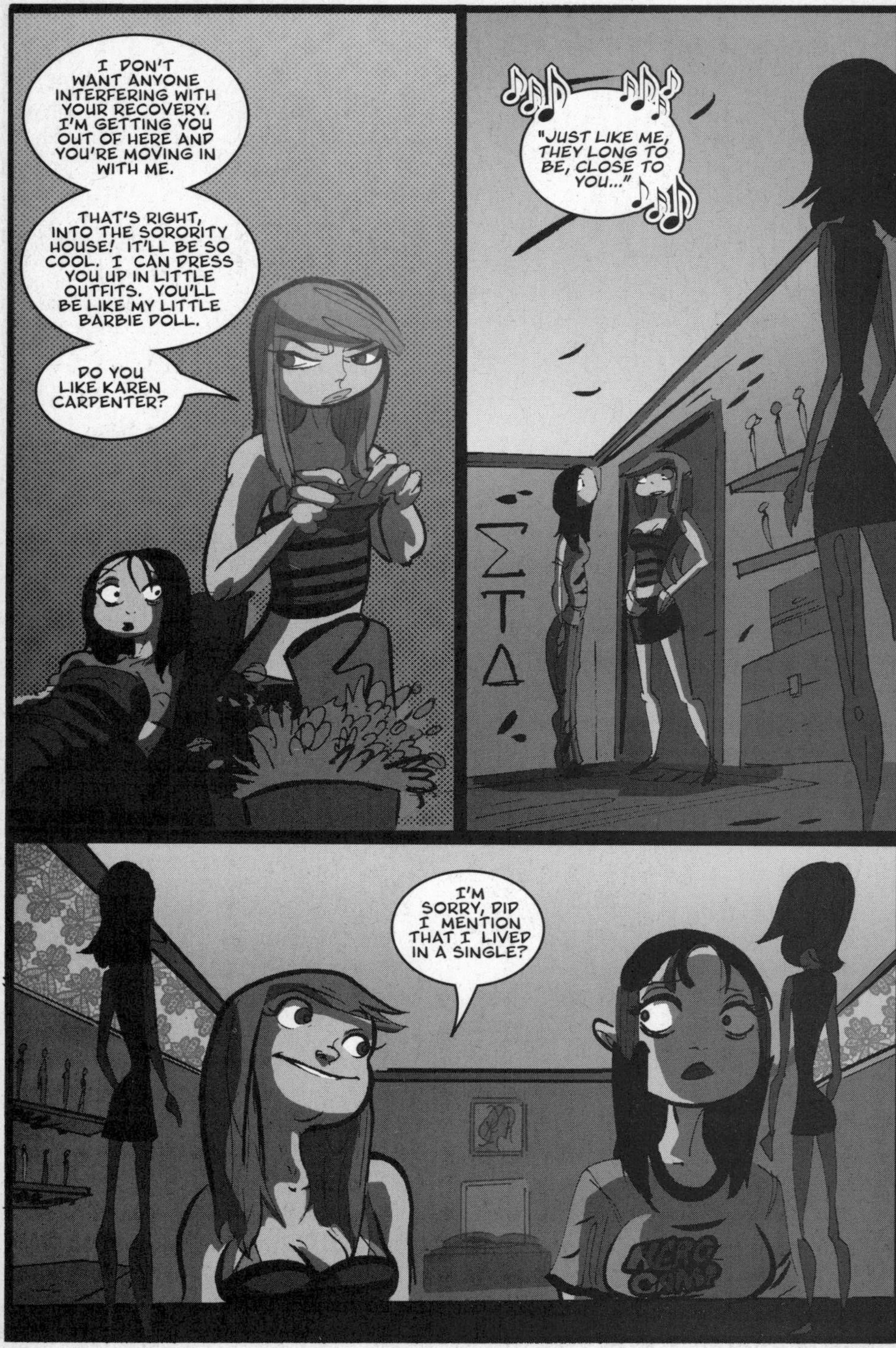
I DON'T WANT ANYONE INTERFERING WITH YOUR RECOVERY. I'M GETTING YOU OUT OF HERE AND YOU'RE MOVING IN WITH ME.
THAT'S RIGHT, INTO THE SORORITY HOUSE! IT'LL BE SO COOL. I CAN DRESS YOU UP IN LITTLE OUTFITS. YOU'LL BE LIKE MY LITTLE BARBIE DOLL.
DO YOU LIKE KAREN CARPENTER?
"JUST LIKE ME, THEY LONG TO BE, CLOSE TO YOU..."
ΣΤΔ
I'M SORRY, DID I MENTION THAT I LIVED IN A SINGLE?

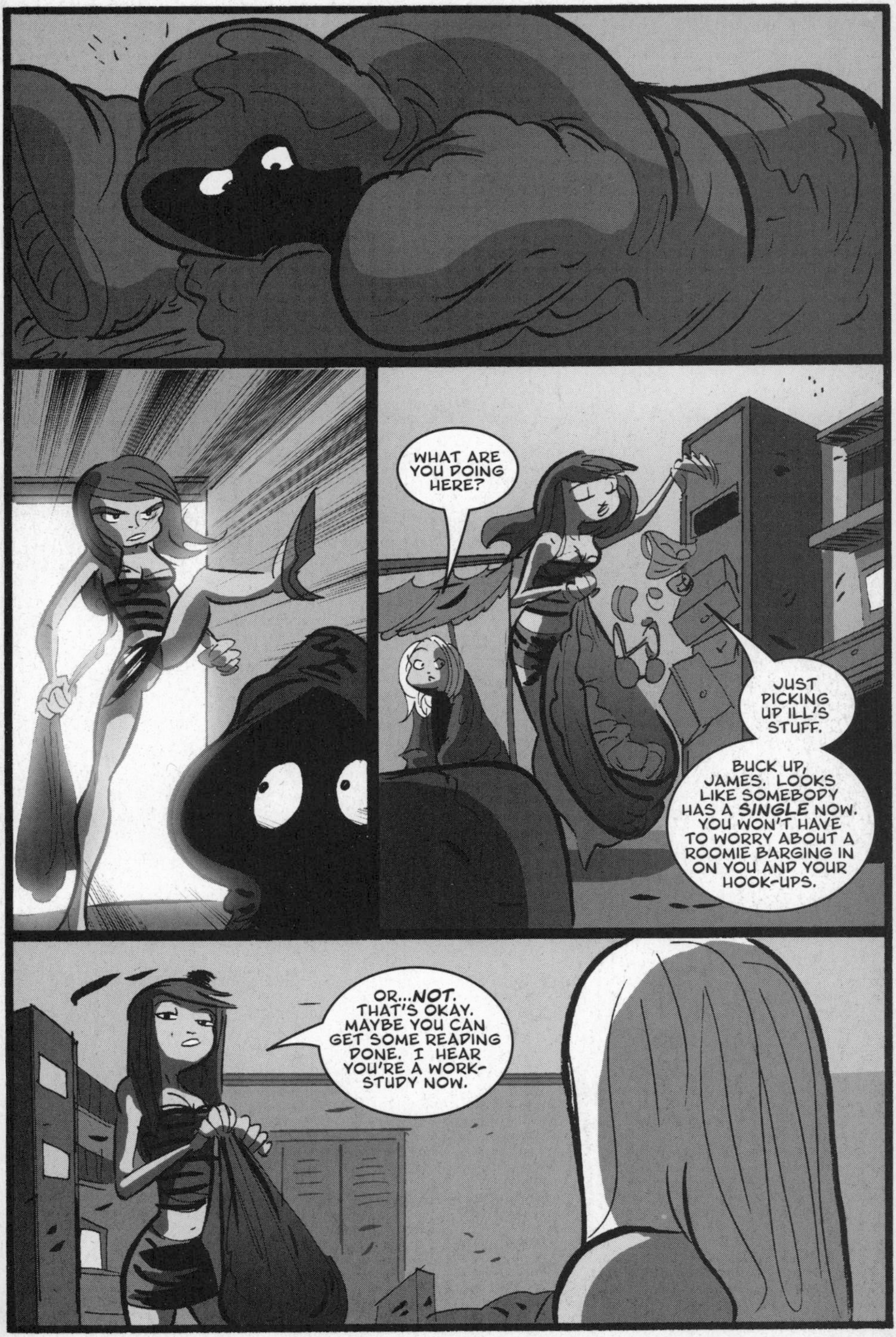
WHAT ARE YOU DOING HERE?
JUST PICKING UP ILL'S STUFF.
BUCK UP, JAMES. LOOKS LIKE SOMEBODY HAS A *SINGLE* NOW. YOU WON'T HAVE TO WORRY ABOUT A ROOMIE BARGING IN ON YOU AND YOUR HOOK-UPS.
OR...*NOT*. THAT'S OKAY. MAYBE YOU CAN GET SOME READING DONE. I HEAR YOU'RE A WORK-STUDY NOW.

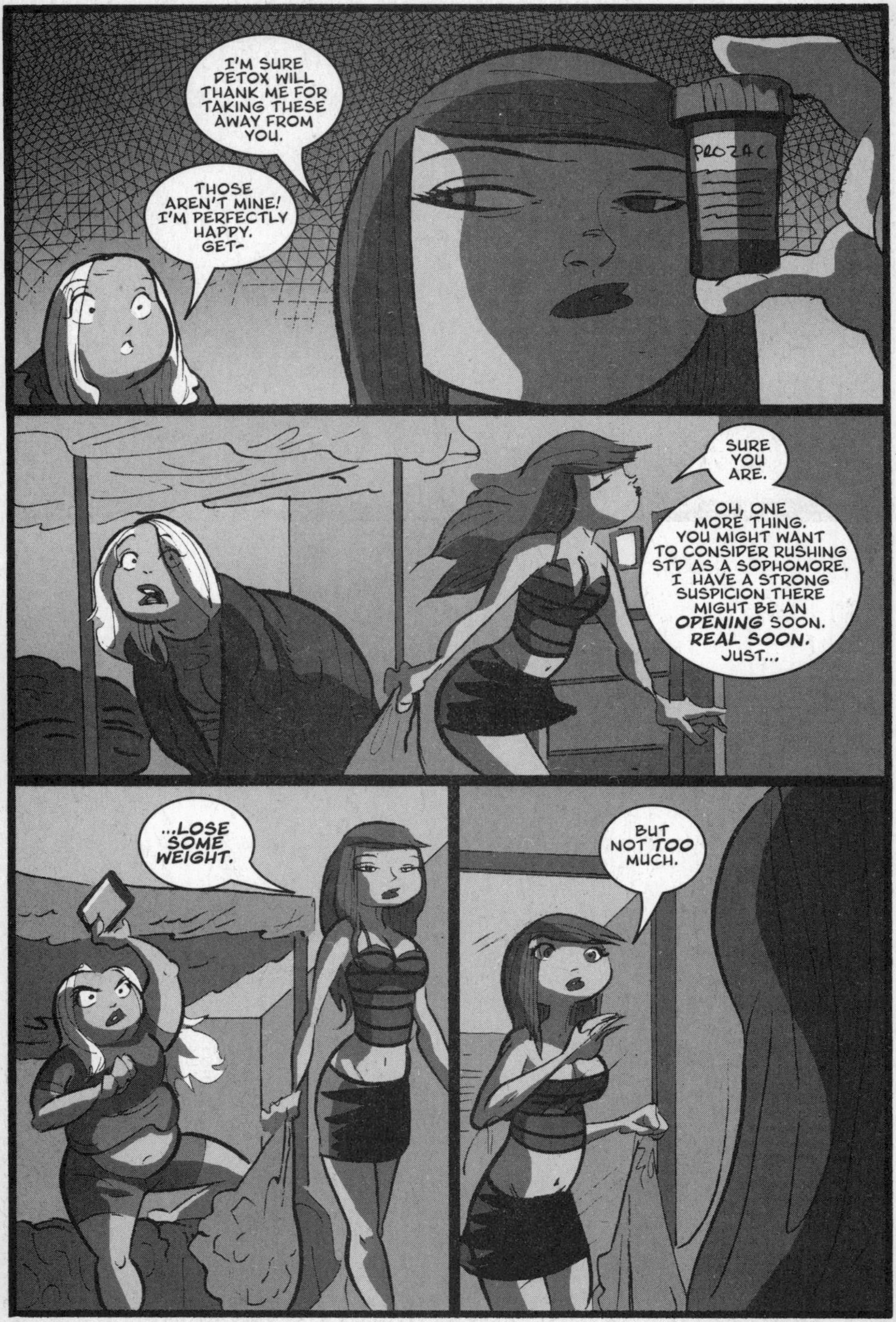
I'M SURE DETOX WILL THANK ME FOR TAKING THESE AWAY FROM YOU.
PROZAC
THOSE AREN'T MINE! I'M PERFECTLY HAPPY. GET-
SURE YOU ARE.
OH, ONE MORE THING. YOU MIGHT WANT TO CONSIDER RUSHING STD AS A SOPHOMORE. I HAVE A STRONG SUSPICION THERE MIGHT BE AN OPENING SOON. REAL SOON. JUST...
...LOSE SOME WEIGHT.
BUT NOT TOO MUCH.

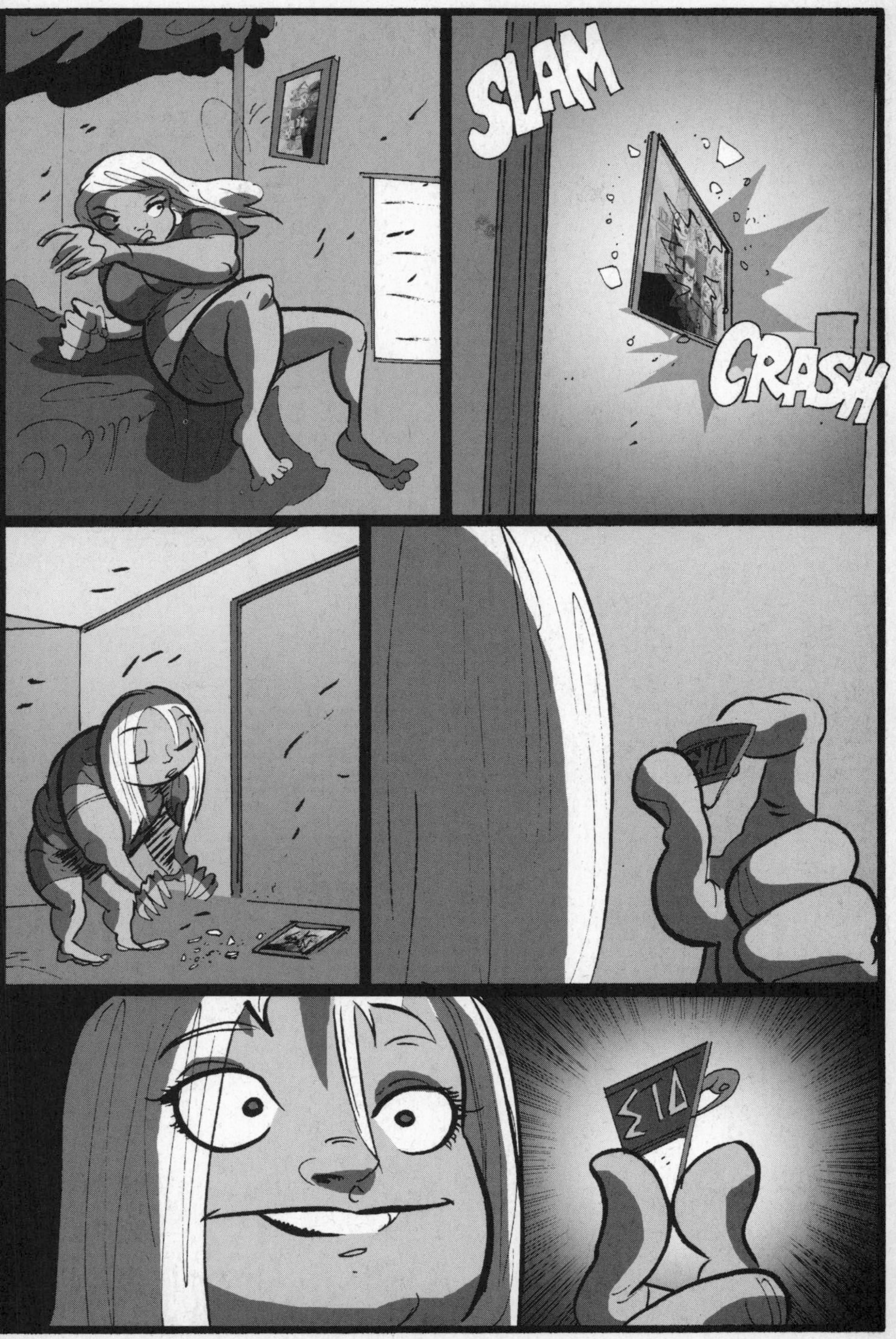
SLAM
CRASH
ΣIΔ

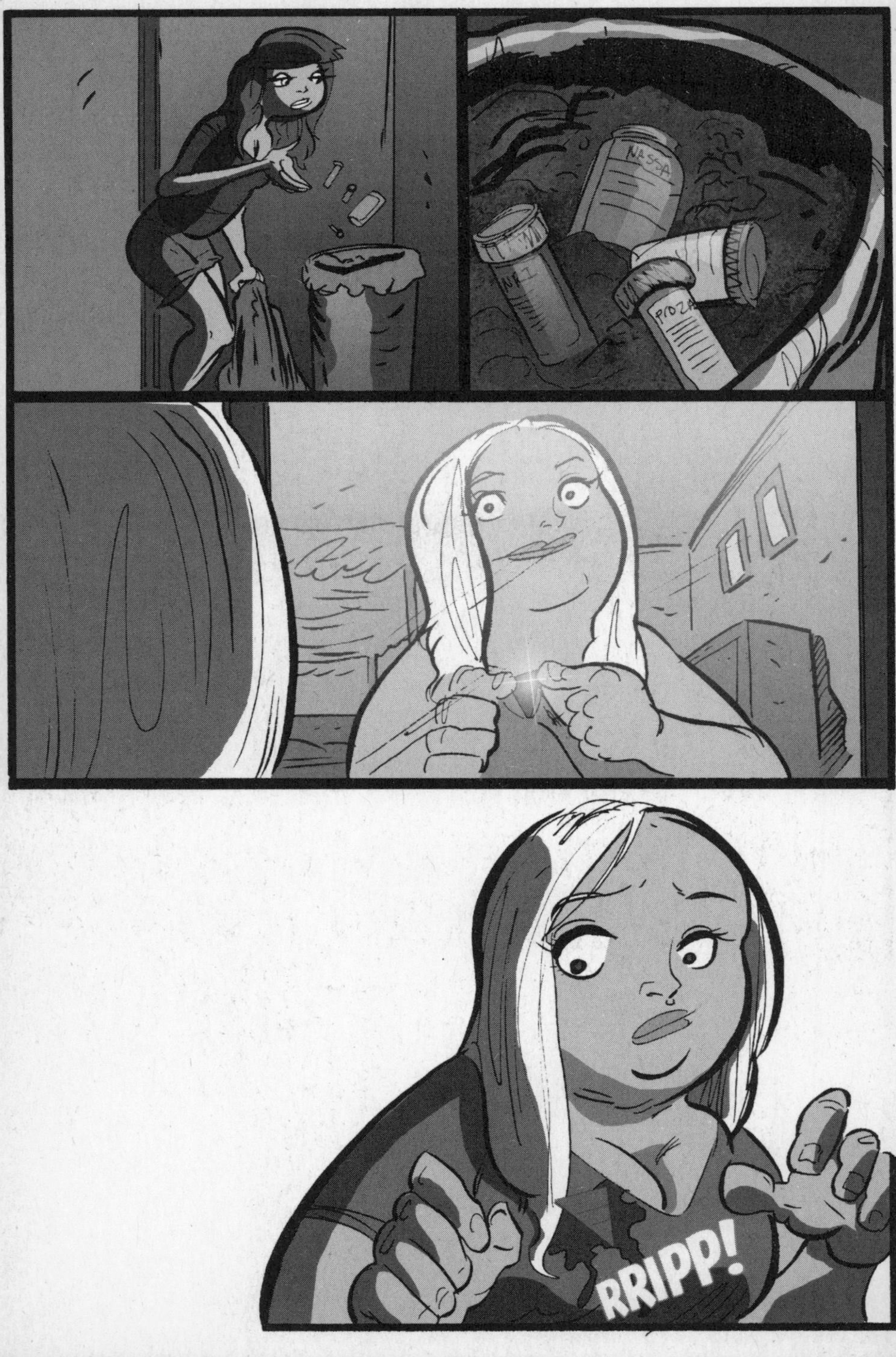
NASSA
PROZA
RRIPP!

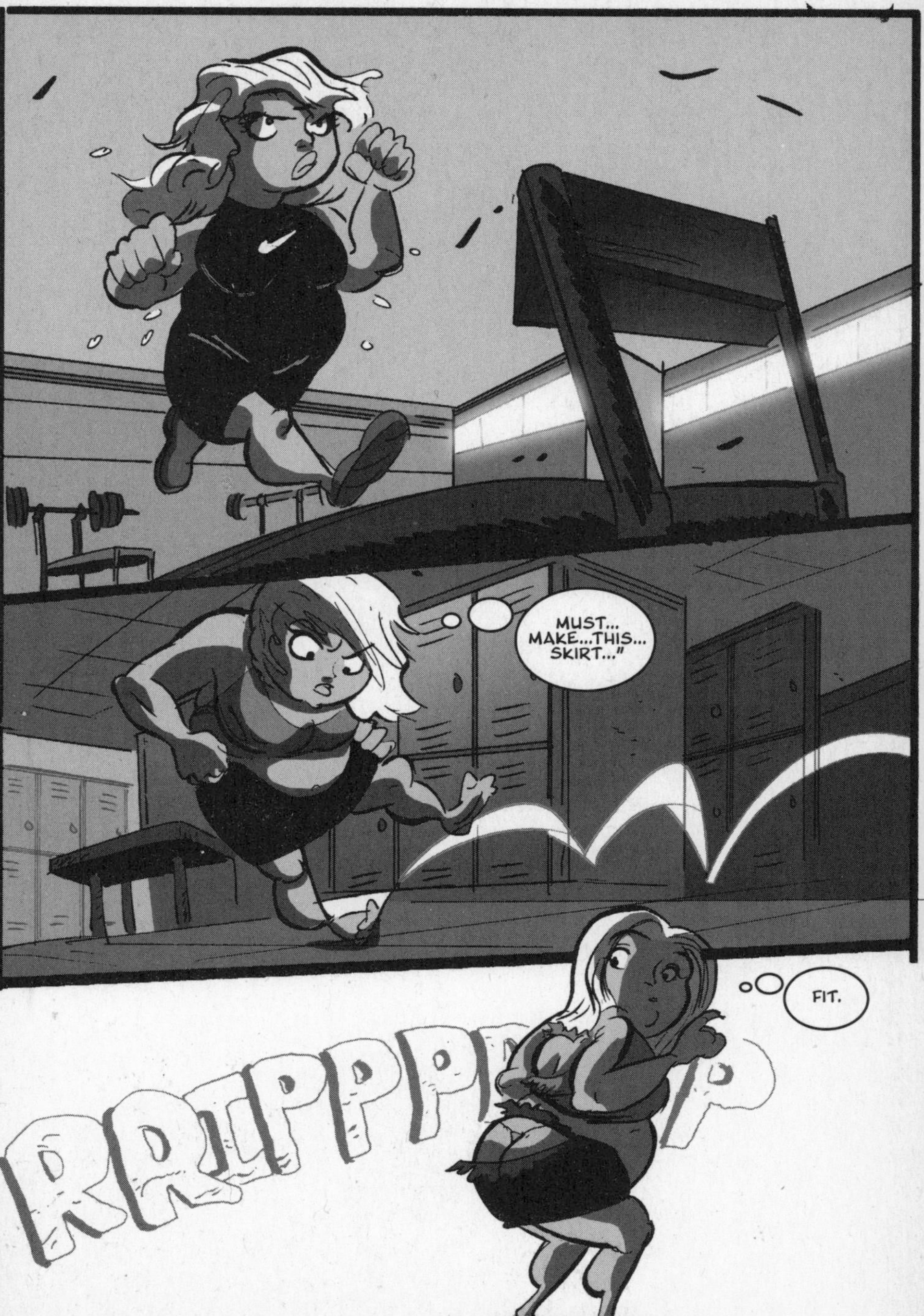
MUST...
MAKE...THIS...
SKIRT..."
FIT.
RRIPPPP

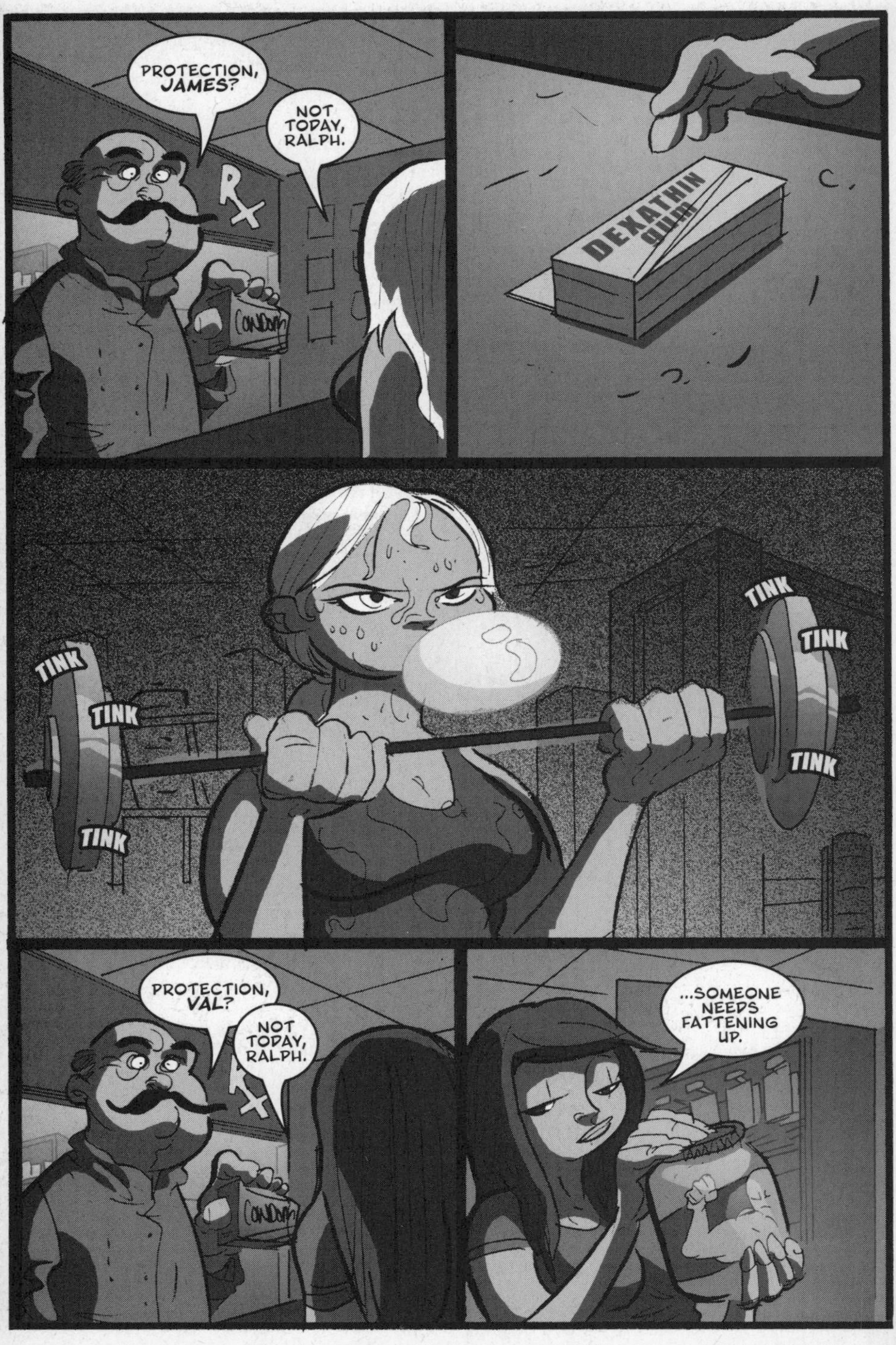
PROTECTION, JAMES?
NOT TODAY, RALPH.
CONDOM
DEXATHIN
TINK
TINK
TINK
TINK
TINK
TINK
PROTECTION, VAL?
NOT TODAY, RALPH.
CONDOM
...SOMEONE NEEDS FATTENING UP.

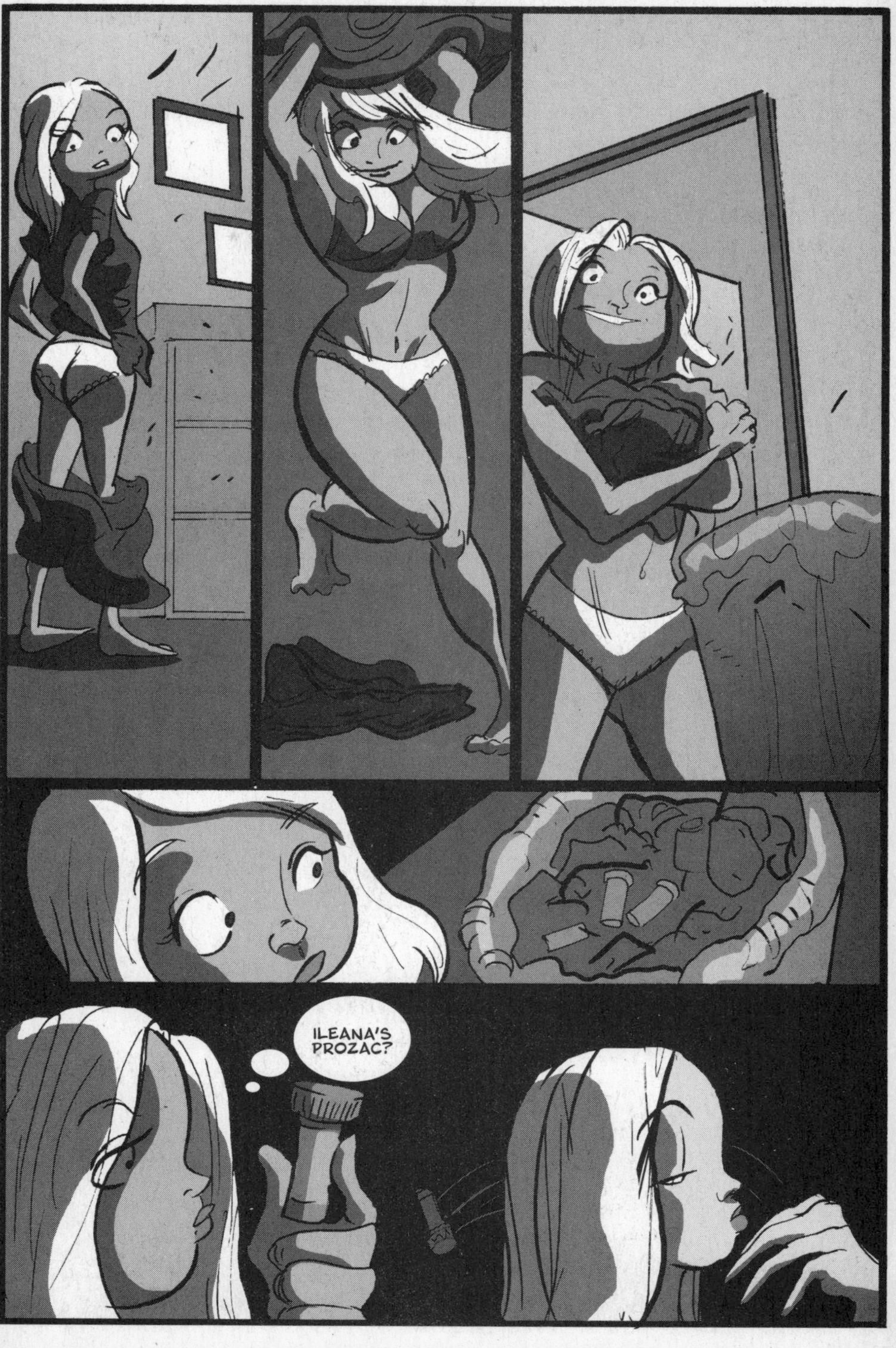
ILEANA'S PROZAC?

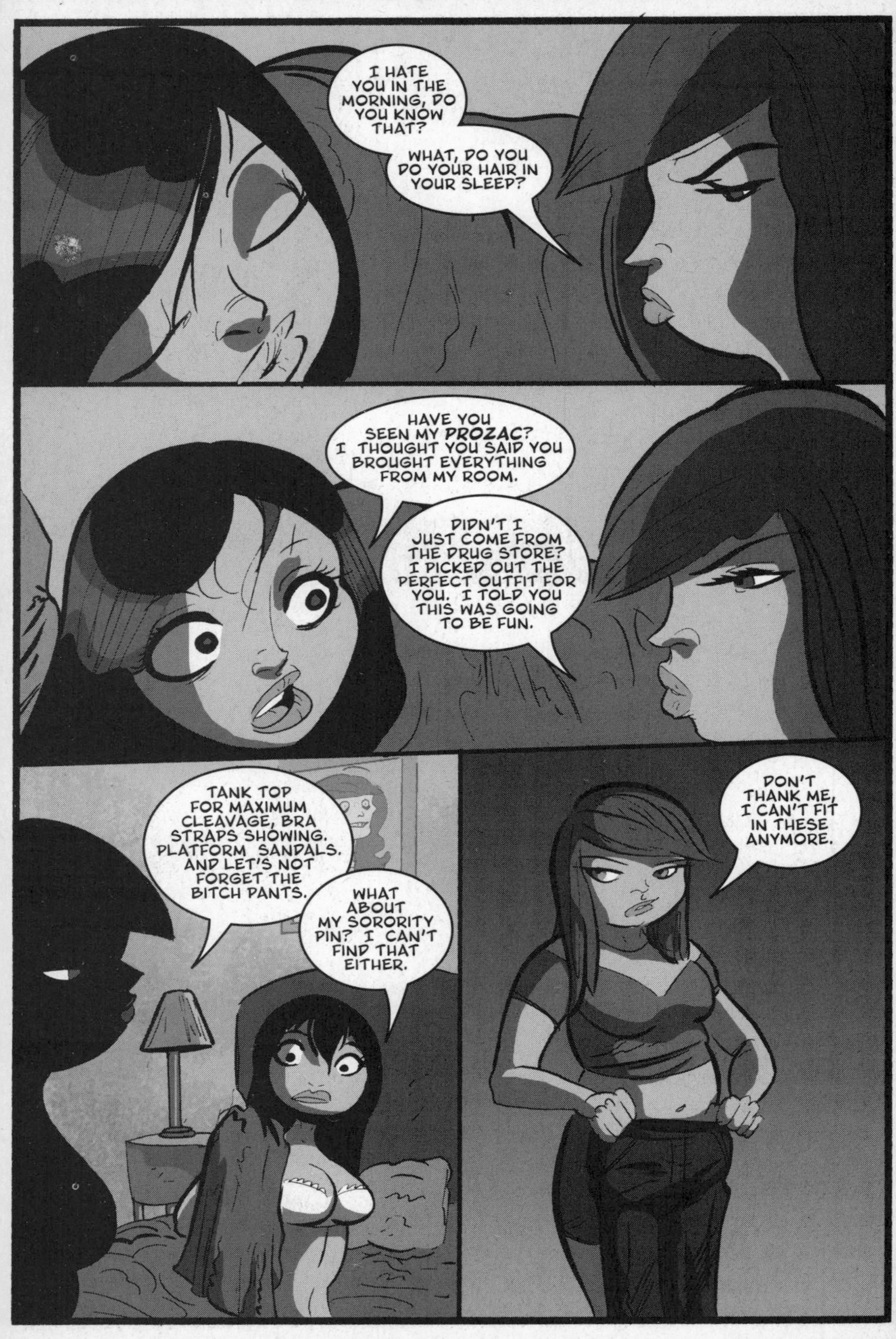
I HATE YOU IN THE MORNING, DO YOU KNOW THAT?
WHAT, DO YOU DO YOUR HAIR IN YOUR SLEEP?
HAVE YOU SEEN MY PROZAC? I THOUGHT YOU SAID YOU BROUGHT EVERYTHING FROM MY ROOM.
DIDN'T I JUST COME FROM THE DRUG STORE? I PICKED OUT THE PERFECT OUTFIT FOR YOU. I TOLD YOU THIS WAS GOING TO BE FUN.
TANK TOP FOR MAXIMUM CLEAVAGE, BRA STRAPS SHOWING. PLATFORM SANDALS. AND LET'S NOT FORGET THE BITCH PANTS.
WHAT ABOUT MY SORORITY PIN? I CAN'T FIND THAT EITHER.
DON'T THANK ME, I CAN'T FIT IN THESE ANYMORE.

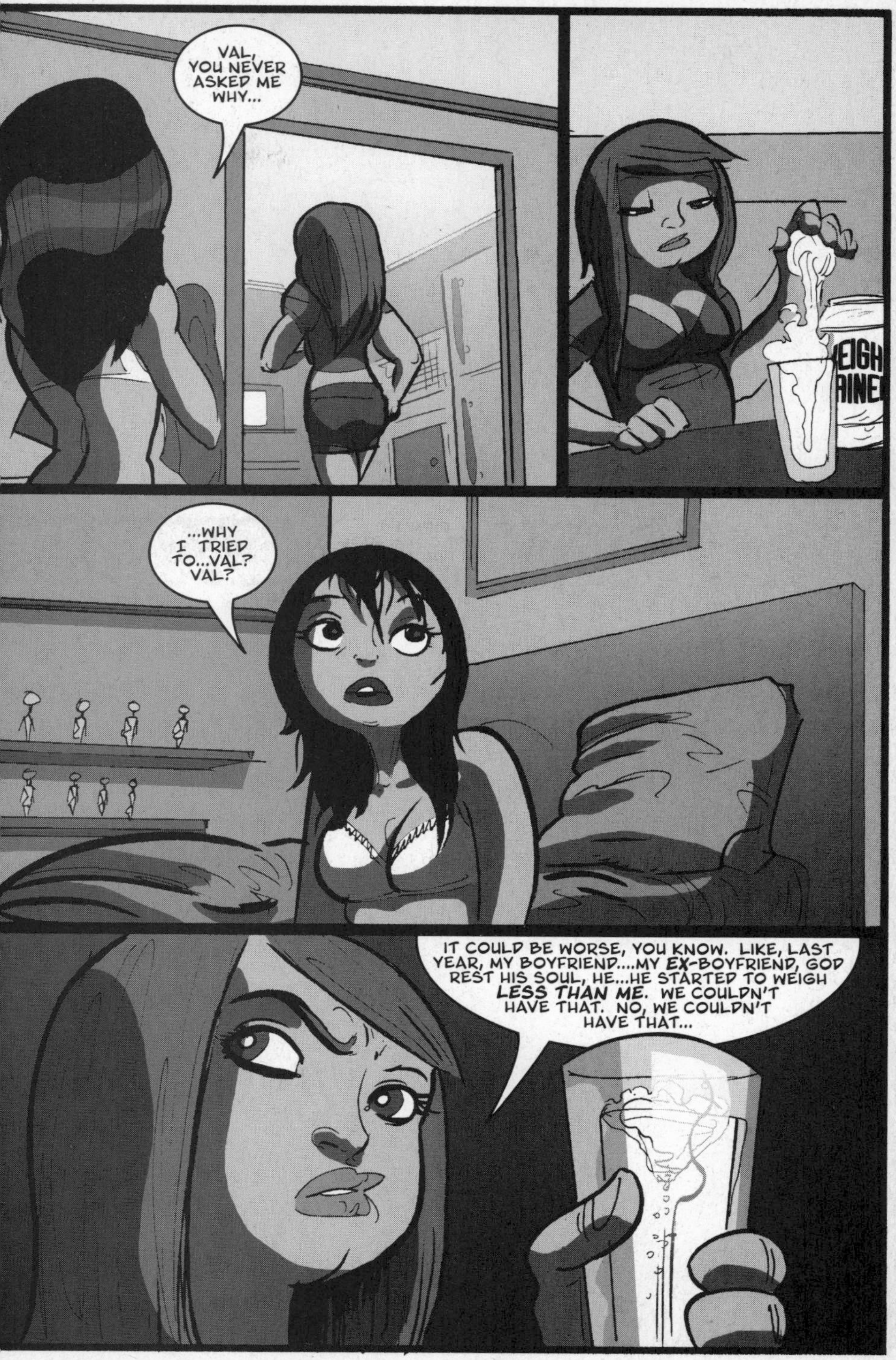
VAL, YOU NEVER ASKED ME WHY...
...WHY I TRIED TO...VAL? VAL?
IT COULD BE WORSE, YOU KNOW. LIKE, LAST YEAR, MY BOYFRIEND....MY **EX**-BOYFRIEND, GOD REST HIS SOUL, HE...HE STARTED TO WEIGH **LESS THAN ME.** WE COULDN'T HAVE THAT. NO, WE COULDN'T HAVE THAT...

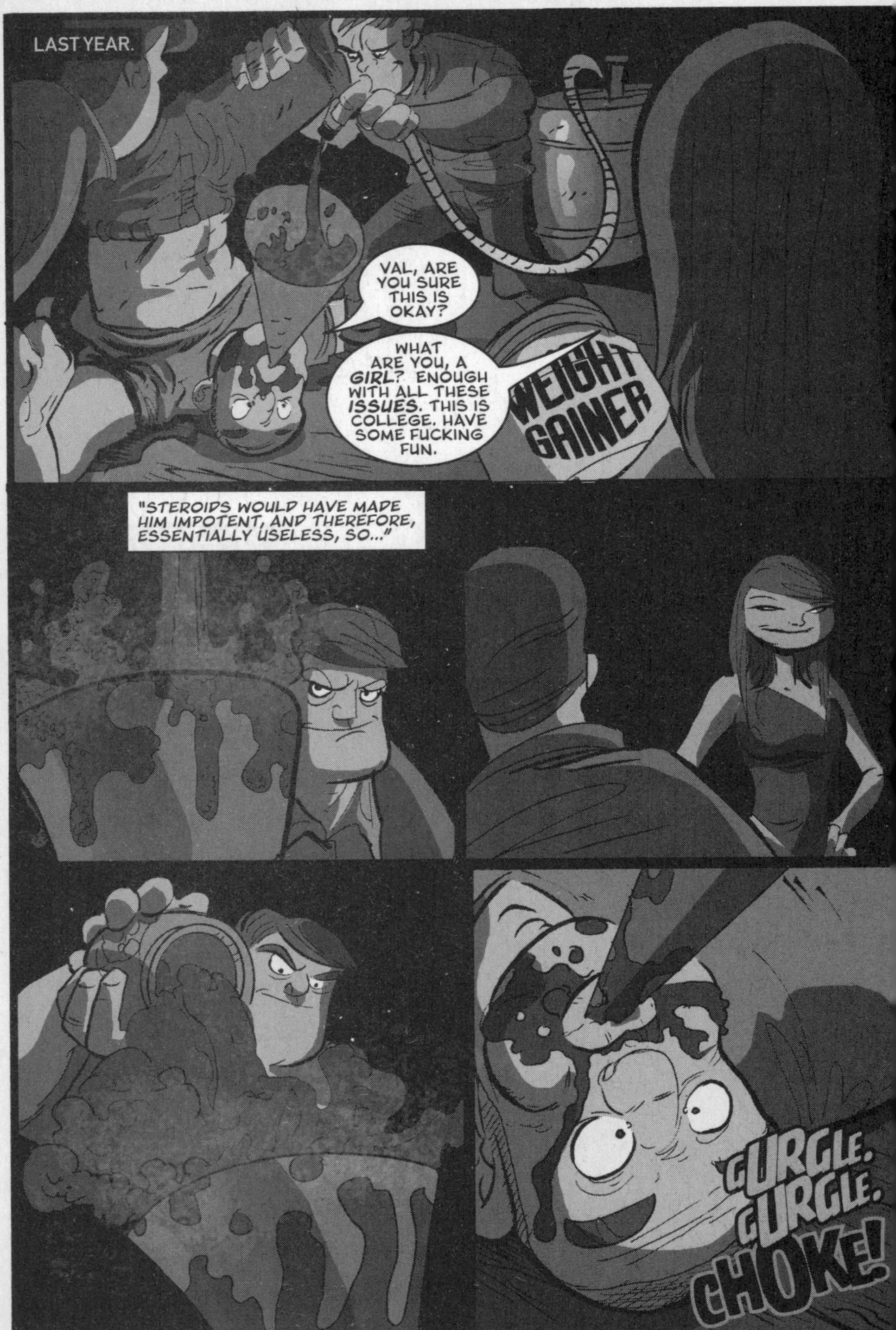
LAST YEAR.
VAL, ARE YOU SURE THIS IS OKAY?
WHAT ARE YOU, A GIRL? ENOUGH WITH ALL THESE ISSUES. THIS IS COLLEGE. HAVE SOME FUCKING FUN.
WEIGHT GAINER
"STEROIDS WOULD HAVE MADE HIM IMPOTENT, AND THEREFORE, ESSENTIALLY USELESS, SO..."
GURGLE. GURGLE. CHOKE!

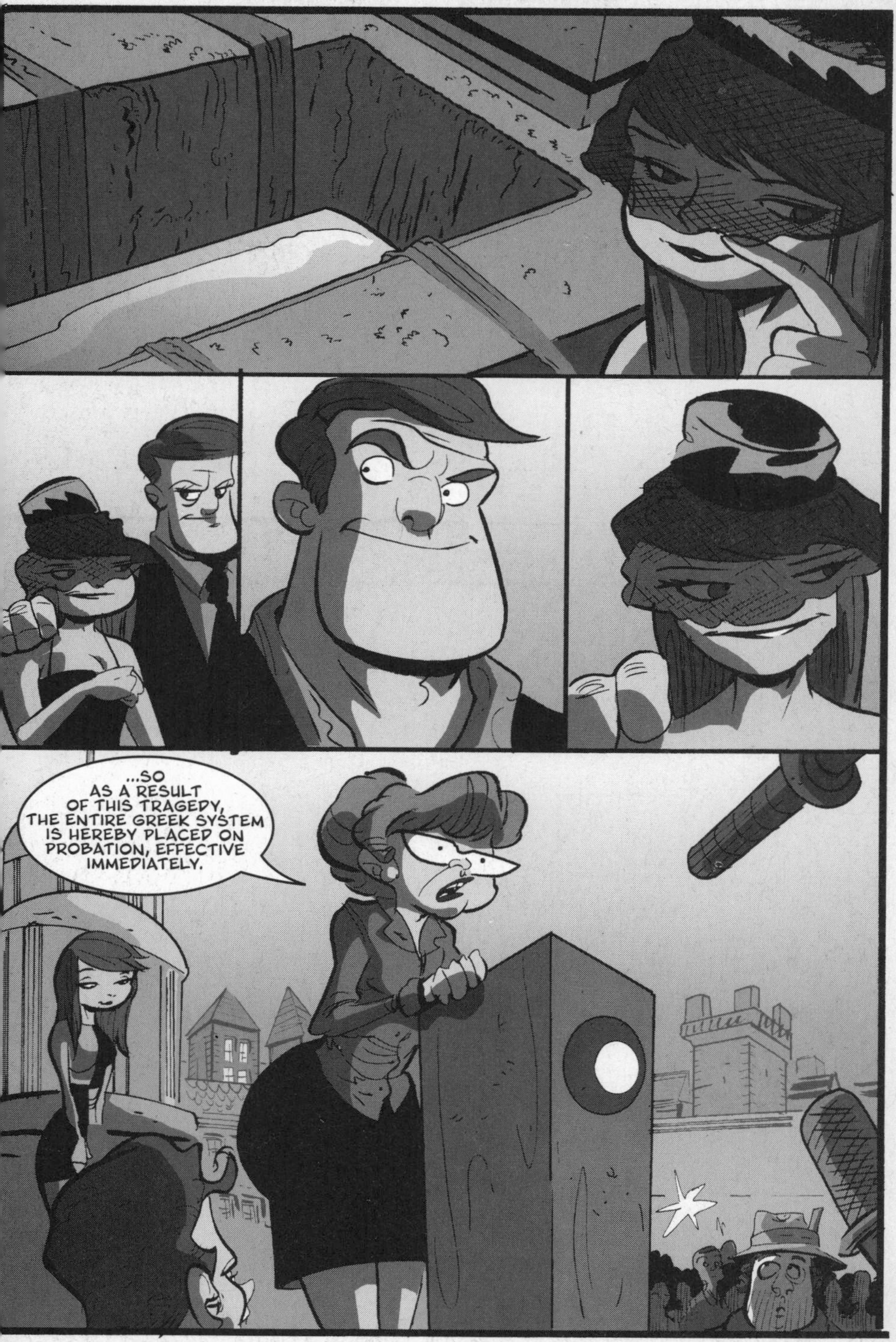
...SO AS A RESULT OF THIS TRAGEDY, THE ENTIRE GREEK SYSTEM IS HEREBY PLACED ON PROBATION, EFFECTIVE IMMEDIATELY.

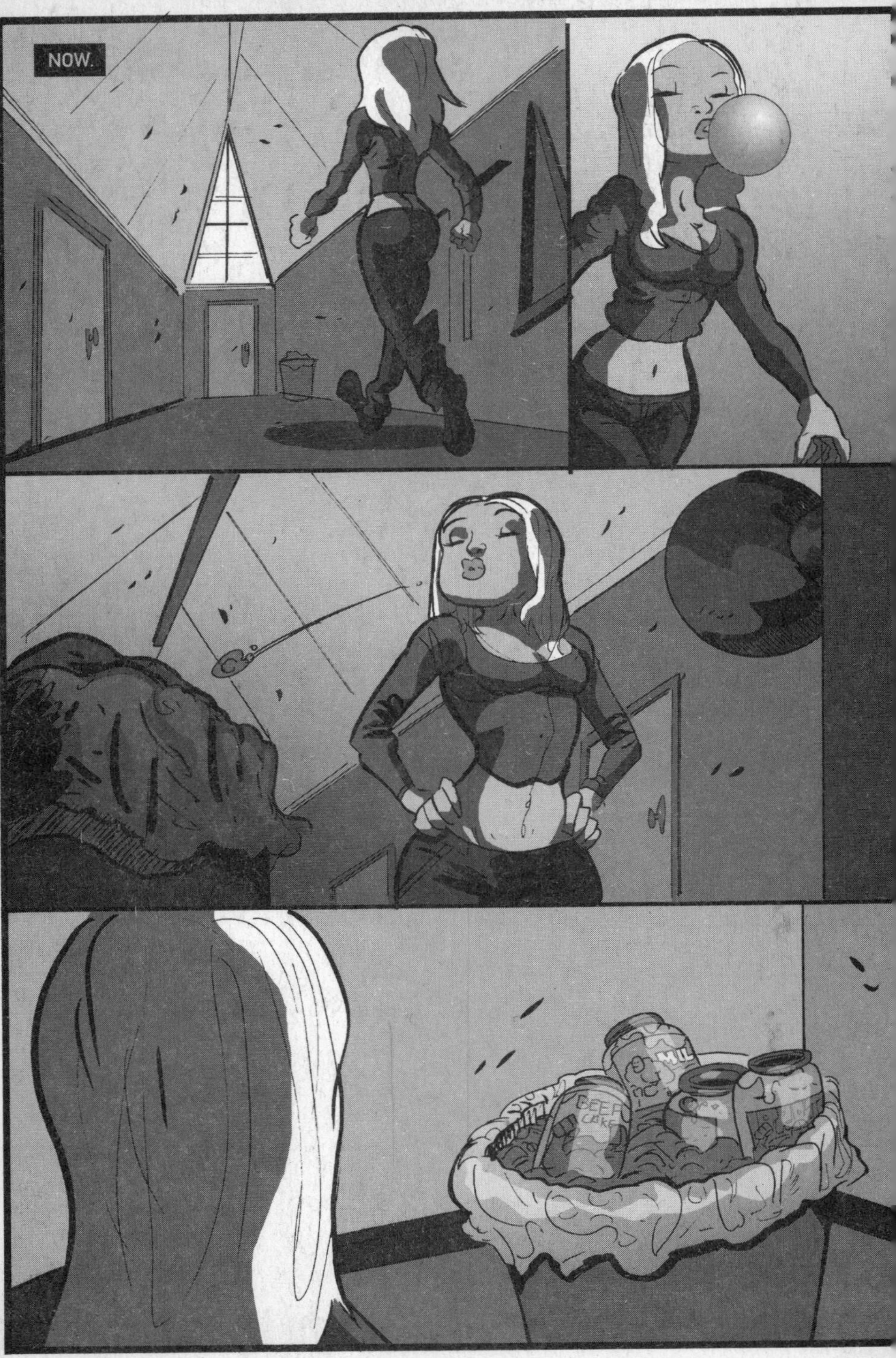
NOW.
BEER

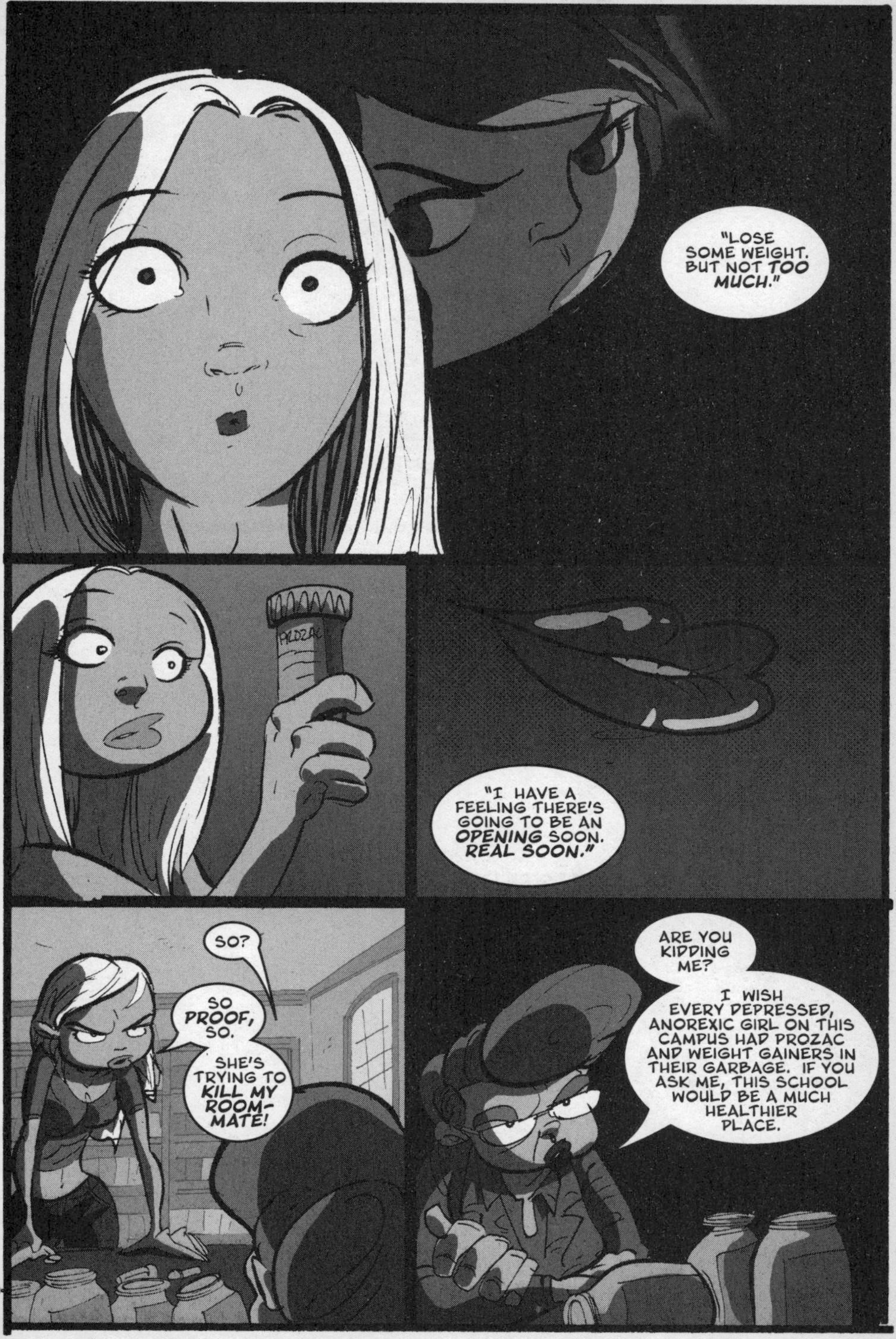
"LOSE SOME WEIGHT. BUT NOT TOO MUCH."
PROZAC
"I HAVE A FEELING THERE'S GOING TO BE AN OPENING SOON. REAL SOON."
SO?
SO PROOF, SO.
SHE'S TRYING TO KILL MY ROOM-MATE!
ARE YOU KIDDING ME?
I WISH EVERY DEPRESSED, ANOREXIC GIRL ON THIS CAMPUS HAD PROZAC AND WEIGHT GAINERS IN THEIR GARBAGE. IF YOU ASK ME, THIS SCHOOL WOULD BE A MUCH HEALTHIER PLACE.

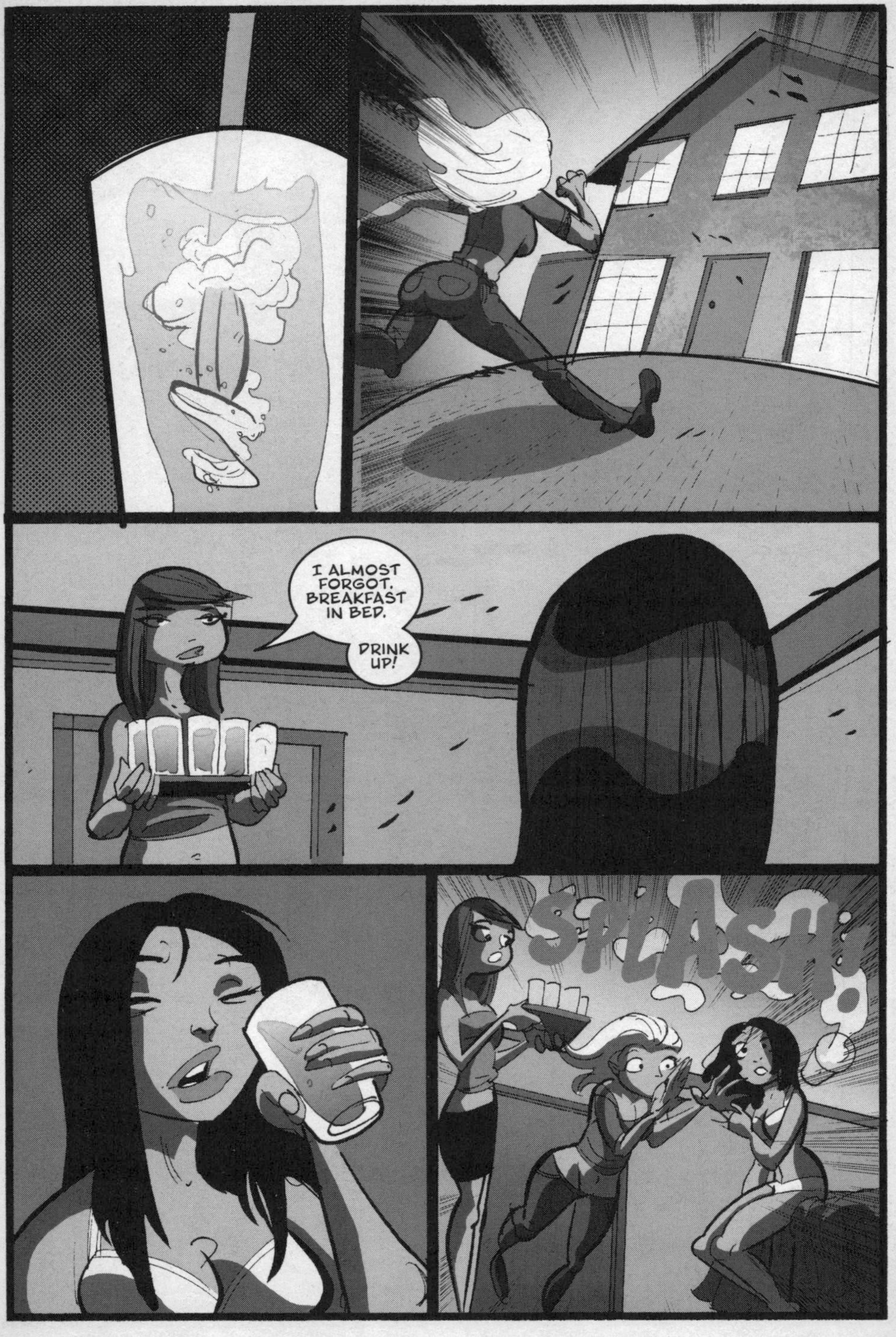
I ALMOST FORGOT. BREAKFAST IN BED.
DRINK UP!
SPLASH!

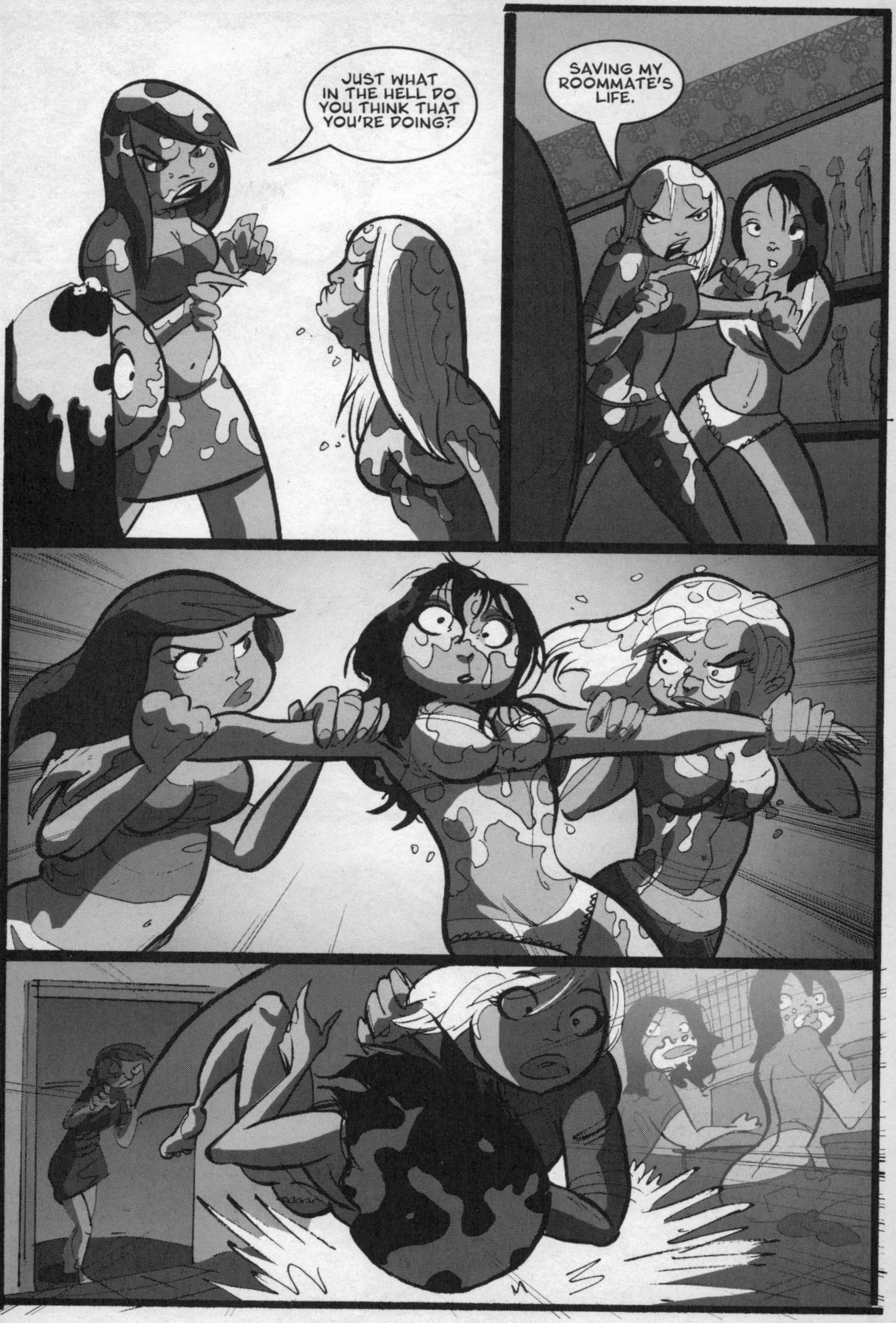
JUST WHAT IN THE HELL DO YOU THINK THAT YOU'RE DOING?
SAVING MY ROOMMATE'S LIFE.

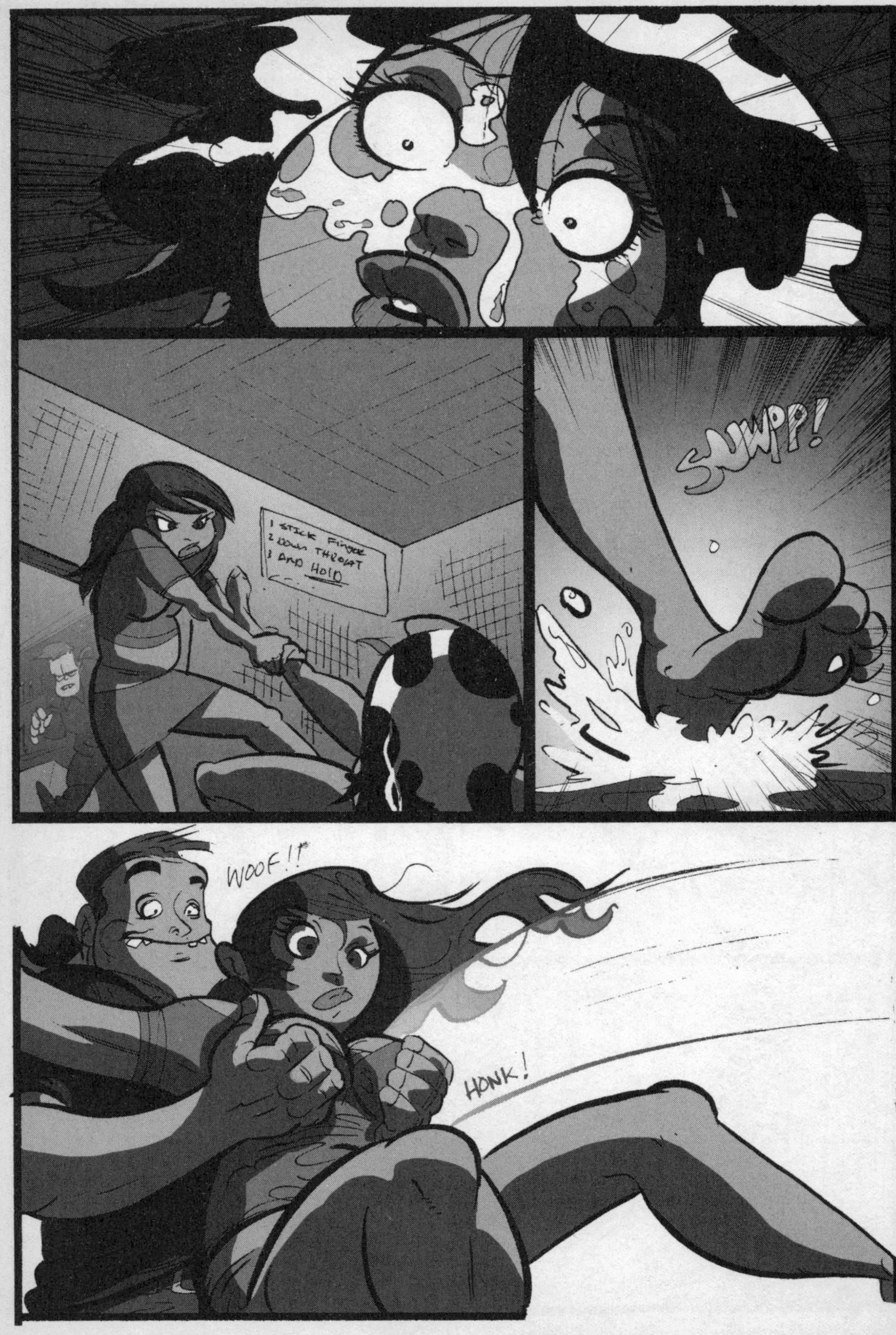

1 STICK FINGER
2 DOWN THROAT
3 AND HOLD
SWPP!
WOOF!!
HONK!

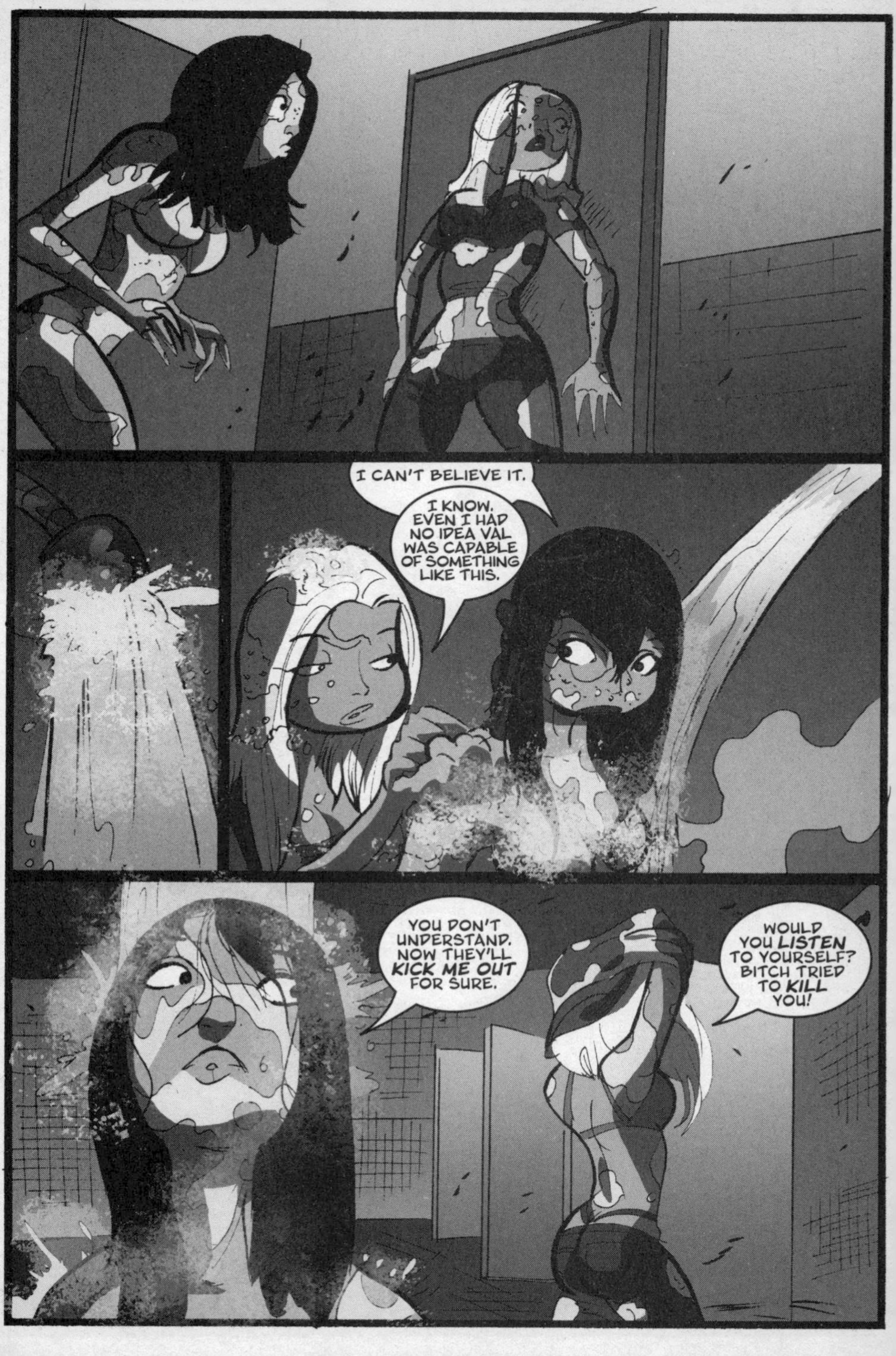
I CAN'T BELIEVE IT.
I KNOW. EVEN I HAD NO IDEA VAL WAS CAPABLE OF SOMETHING LIKE THIS.
YOU DON'T UNDERSTAND. NOW THEY'LL KICK ME OUT FOR SURE.
WOULD YOU LISTEN TO YOURSELF? BITCH TRIED TO KILL YOU!

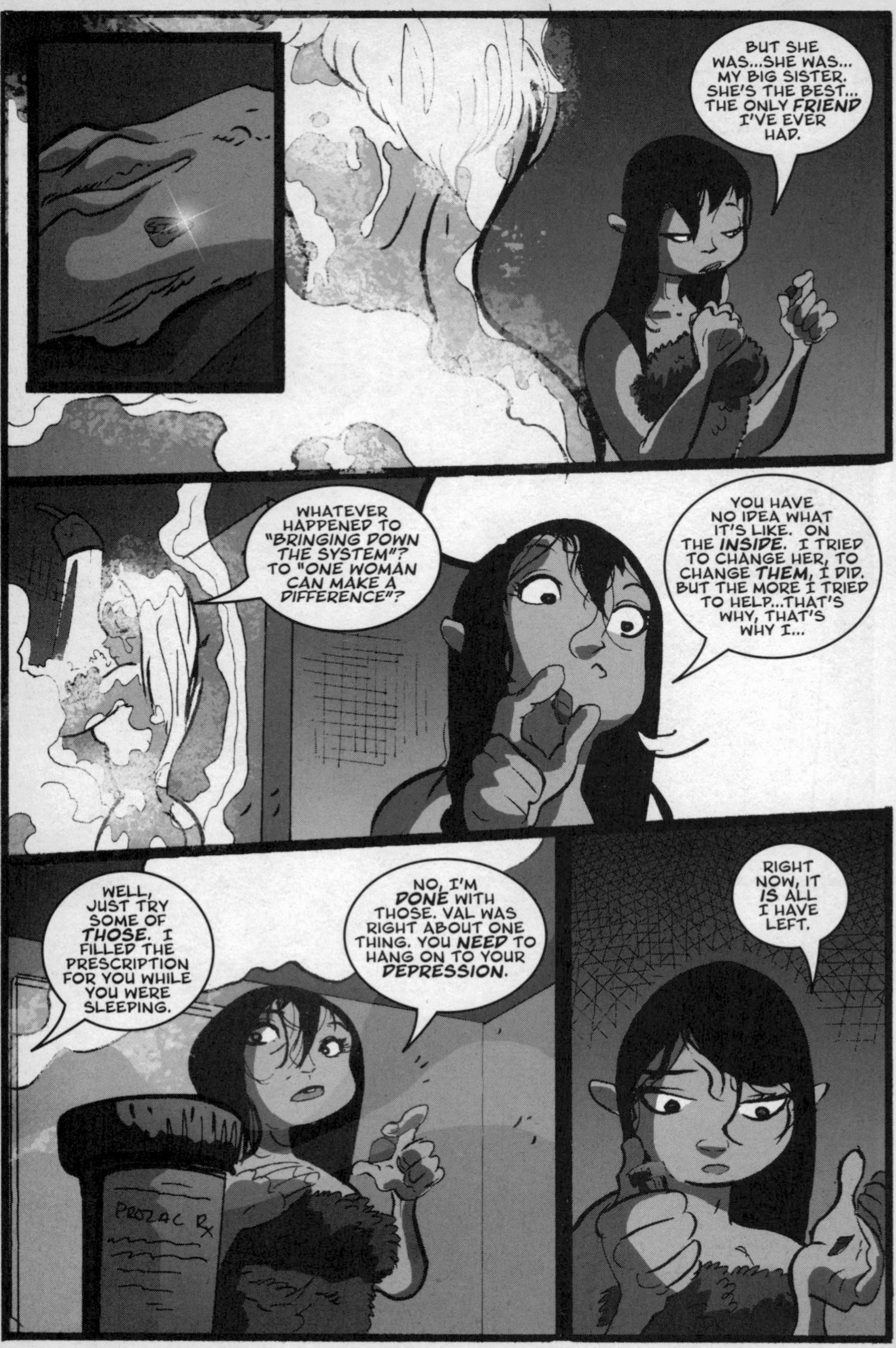
BUT SHE WAS...SHE WAS... MY BIG SISTER. SHE'S THE BEST... THE ONLY FRIEND I'VE EVER HAD.
WHATEVER HAPPENED TO "BRINGING DOWN THE SYSTEM"? TO "ONE WOMAN CAN MAKE A DIFFERENCE"?
YOU HAVE NO IDEA WHAT IT'S LIKE. ON THE INSIDE. I TRIED TO CHANGE HER, TO CHANGE THEM, I DID. BUT THE MORE I TRIED TO HELP...THAT'S WHY, THAT'S WHY I...
WELL, JUST TRY SOME OF THOSE. I FILLED THE PRESCRIPTION FOR YOU WHILE YOU WERE SLEEPING.
NO, I'M DONE WITH THOSE. VAL WAS RIGHT ABOUT ONE THING. YOU NEED TO HANG ON TO YOUR DEPRESSION.
RIGHT NOW, IT IS ALL I HAVE LEFT.
PROZAC Rx

CHAPTER 5

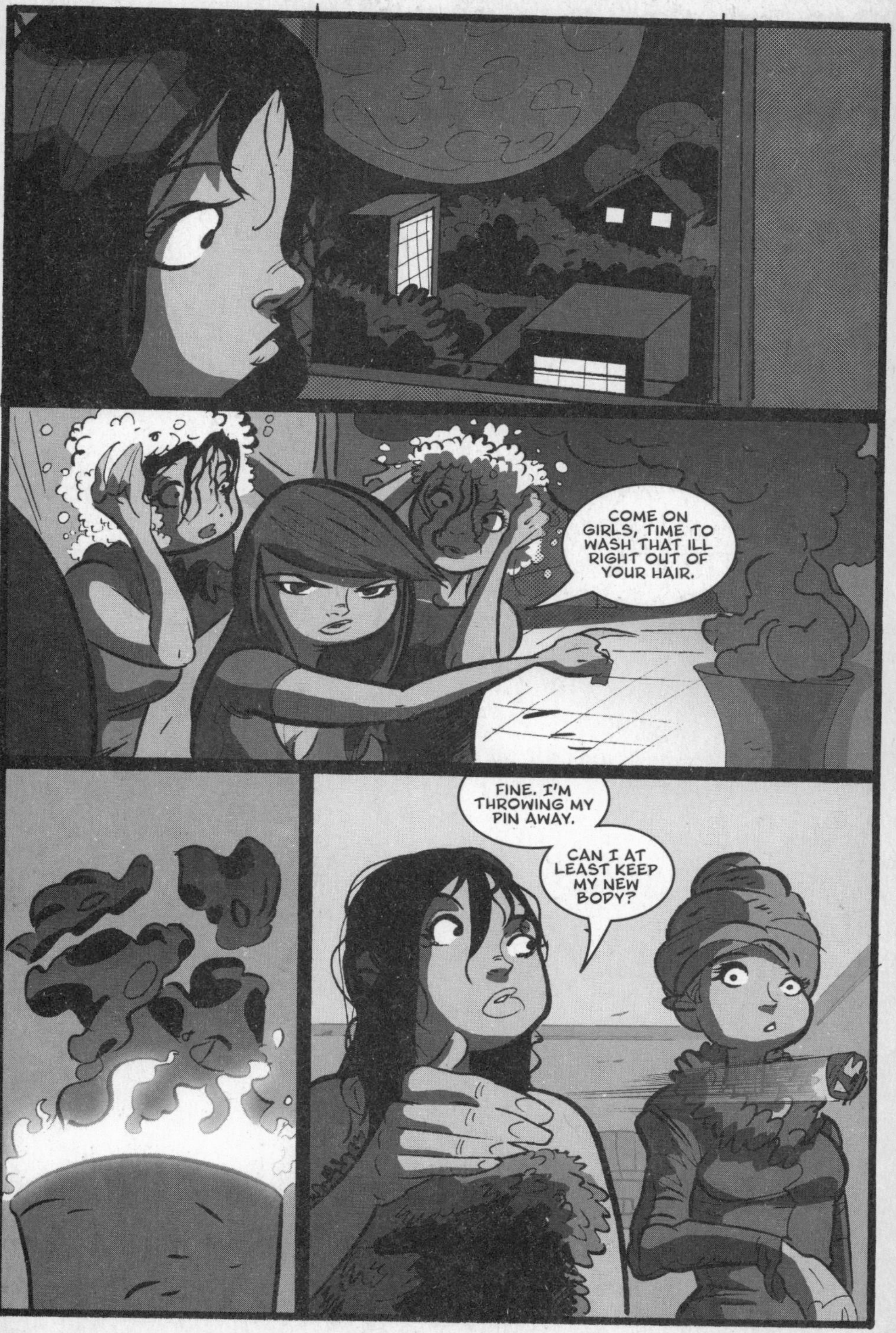
COME ON GIRLS, TIME TO WASH THAT ILL RIGHT OUT OF YOUR HAIR.
FINE. I'M THROWING MY PIN AWAY.
CAN I AT LEAST KEEP MY NEW BODY?

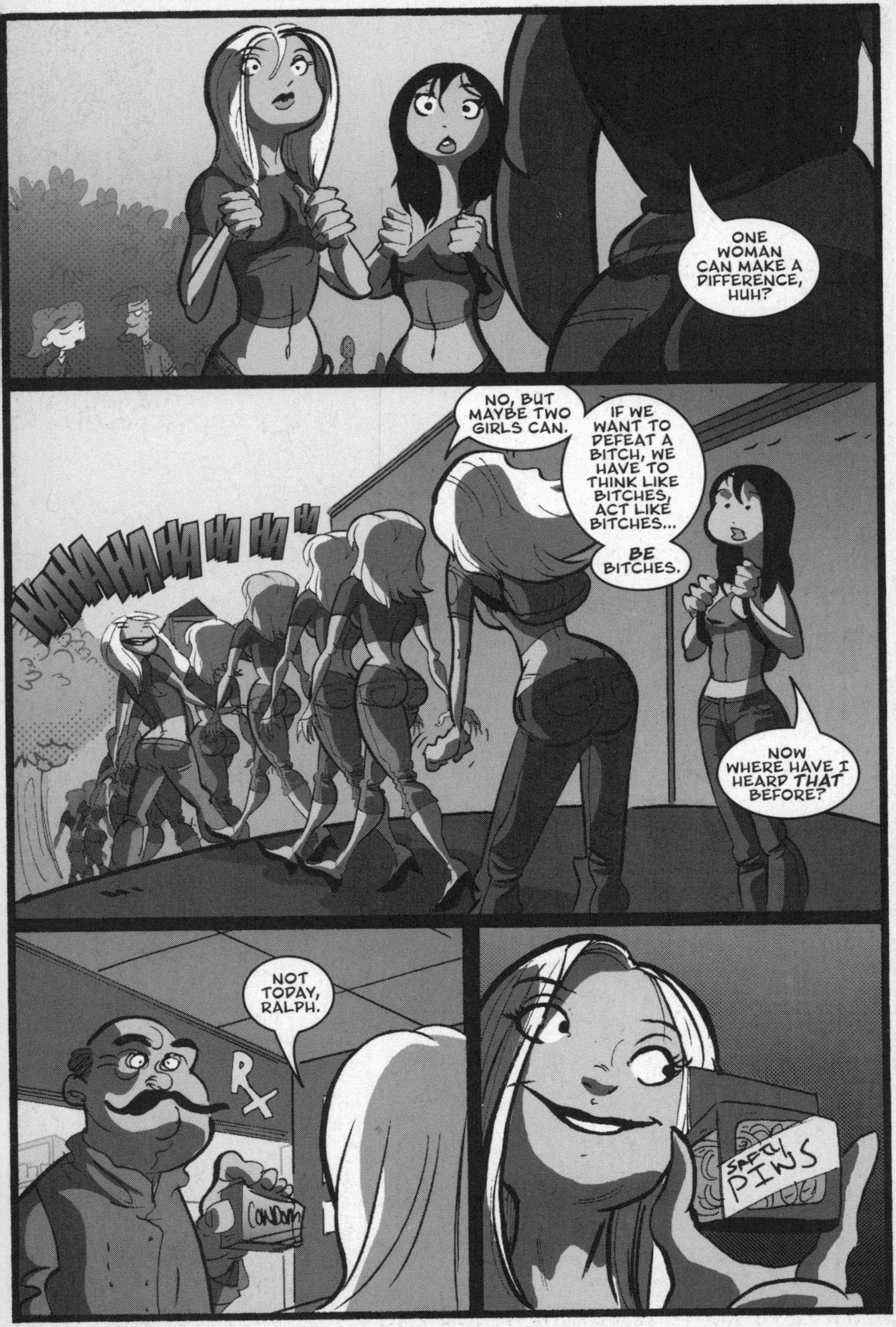
ONE WOMAN CAN MAKE A DIFFERENCE, HUH?
NO, BUT MAYBE TWO GIRLS CAN.
IF WE WANT TO DEFEAT A BITCH, WE HAVE TO THINK LIKE BITCHES, ACT LIKE BITCHES...
BE BITCHES.
HAHAHAHA HA HA HA
NOW WHERE HAVE I HEARD THAT BEFORE?
NOT TODAY, RALPH.
Rx
CONDOM
SAFTY PINS

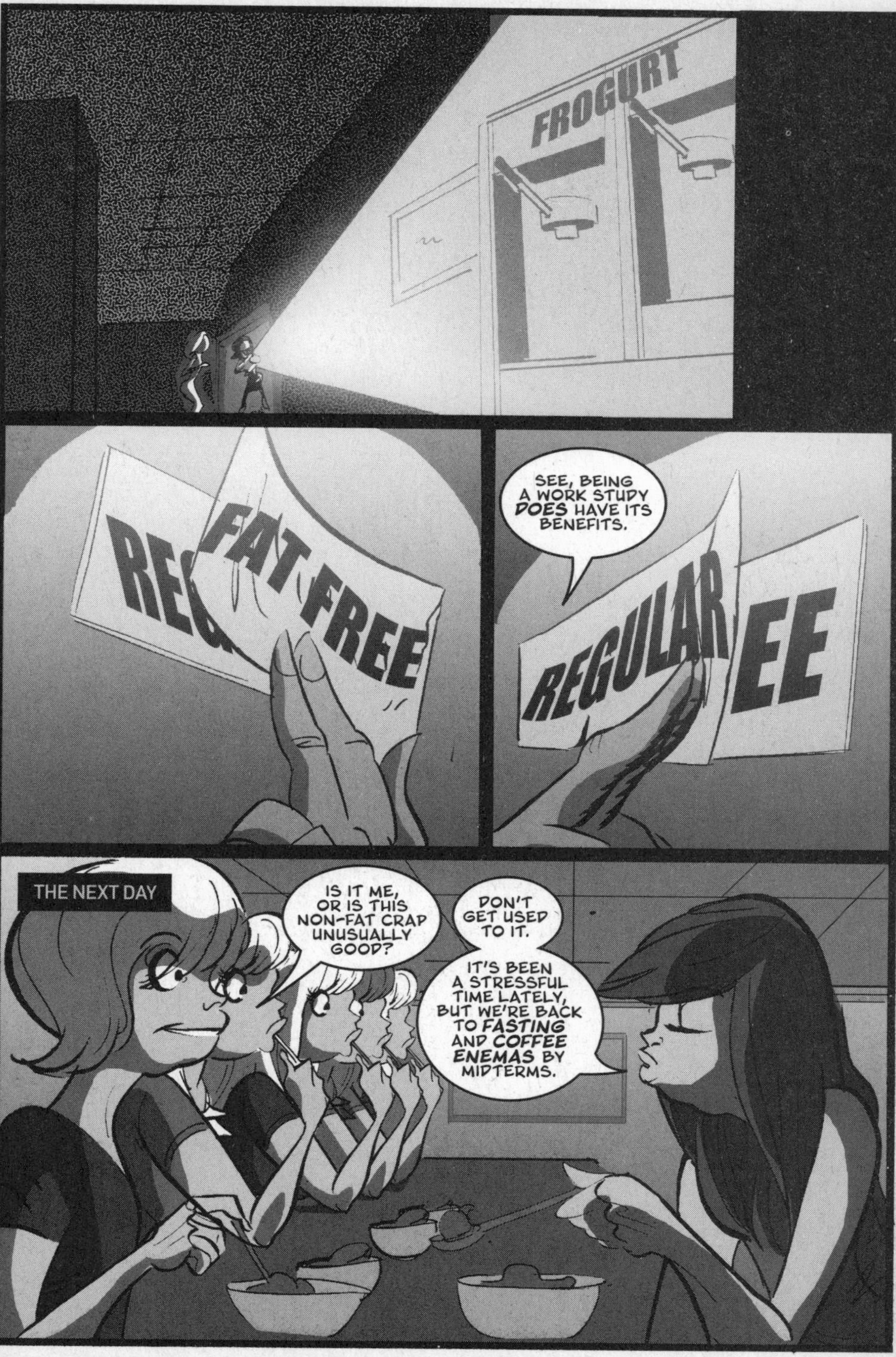
FROGURT
FROGURT
REGU
FAT FREE
SEE, BEING A WORK STUDY DOES HAVE ITS BENEFITS.
REGULAR
EE
THE NEXT DAY
IS IT ME, OR IS THIS NON-FAT CRAP UNUSUALLY GOOD?
DON'T GET USED TO IT.
IT'S BEEN A STRESSFUL TIME LATELY, BUT WE'RE BACK TO FASTING AND COFFEE ENEMAS BY MIDTERMS.

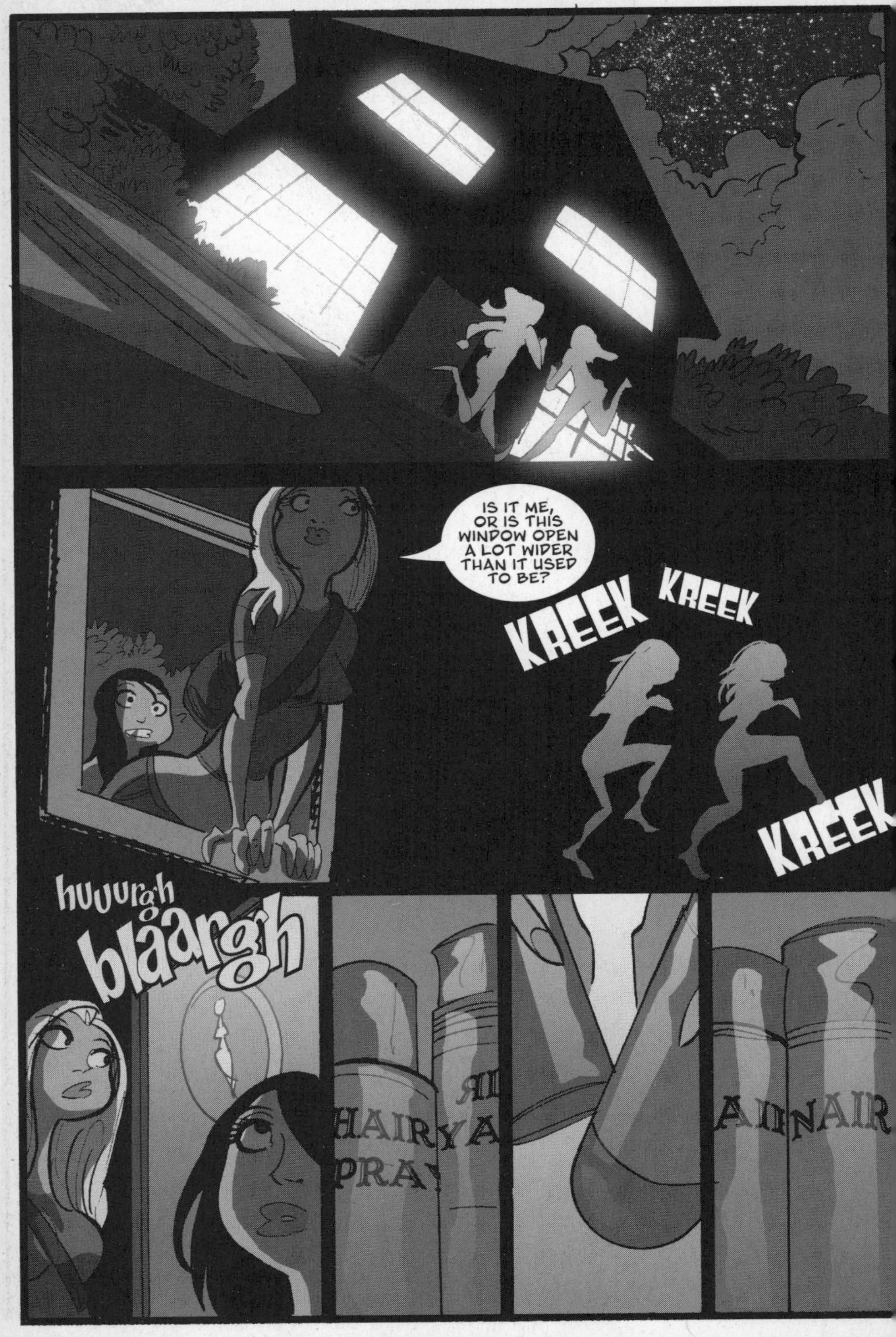
IS IT ME, OR IS THIS WINDOW OPEN A LOT WIDER THAN IT USED TO BE?
KREEK
KREEK
KREEK
huuurgh
blaargh

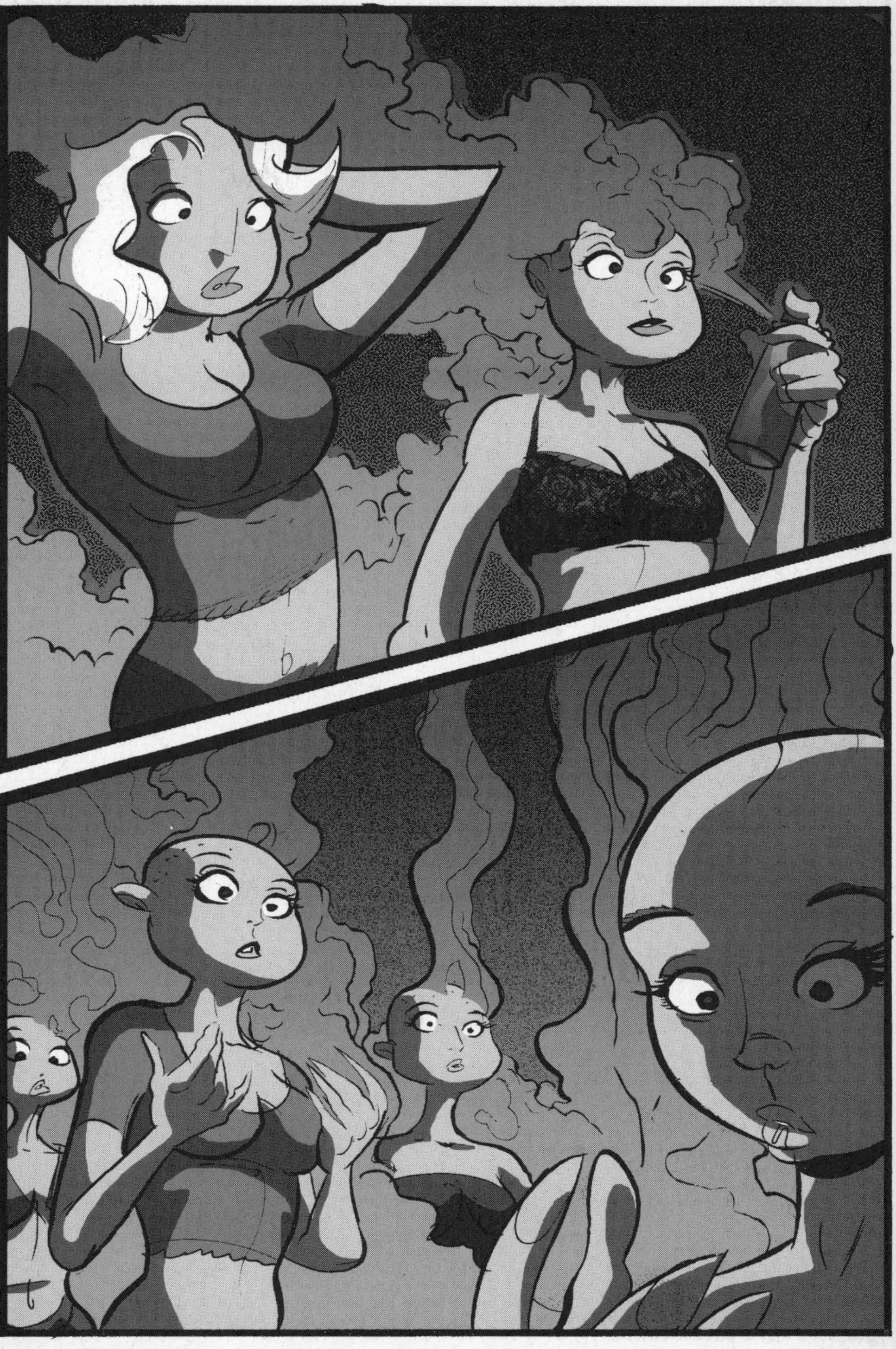

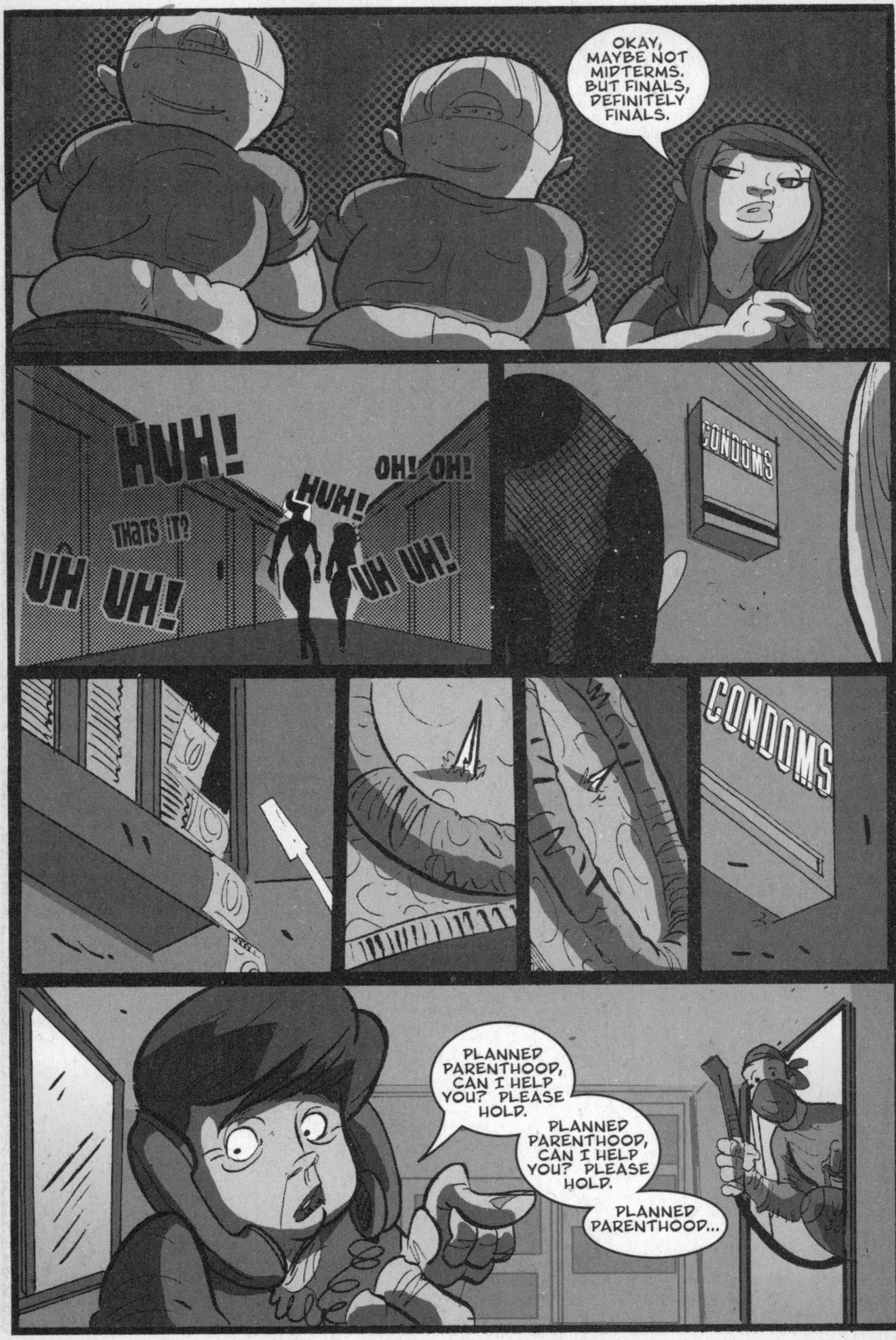
OKAY, MAYBE NOT MIDTERMS. BUT FINALS, DEFINITELY FINALS.
HUH!
THATS IT?
UH UH!
HUH!
OH! OH!
UH UH!
CONDOMS
CONDOMS
PLANNED PARENTHOOD, CAN I HELP YOU? PLEASE HOLD.
PLANNED PARENTHOOD, CAN I HELP YOU? PLEASE HOLD.
PLANNED PARENTHOOD...

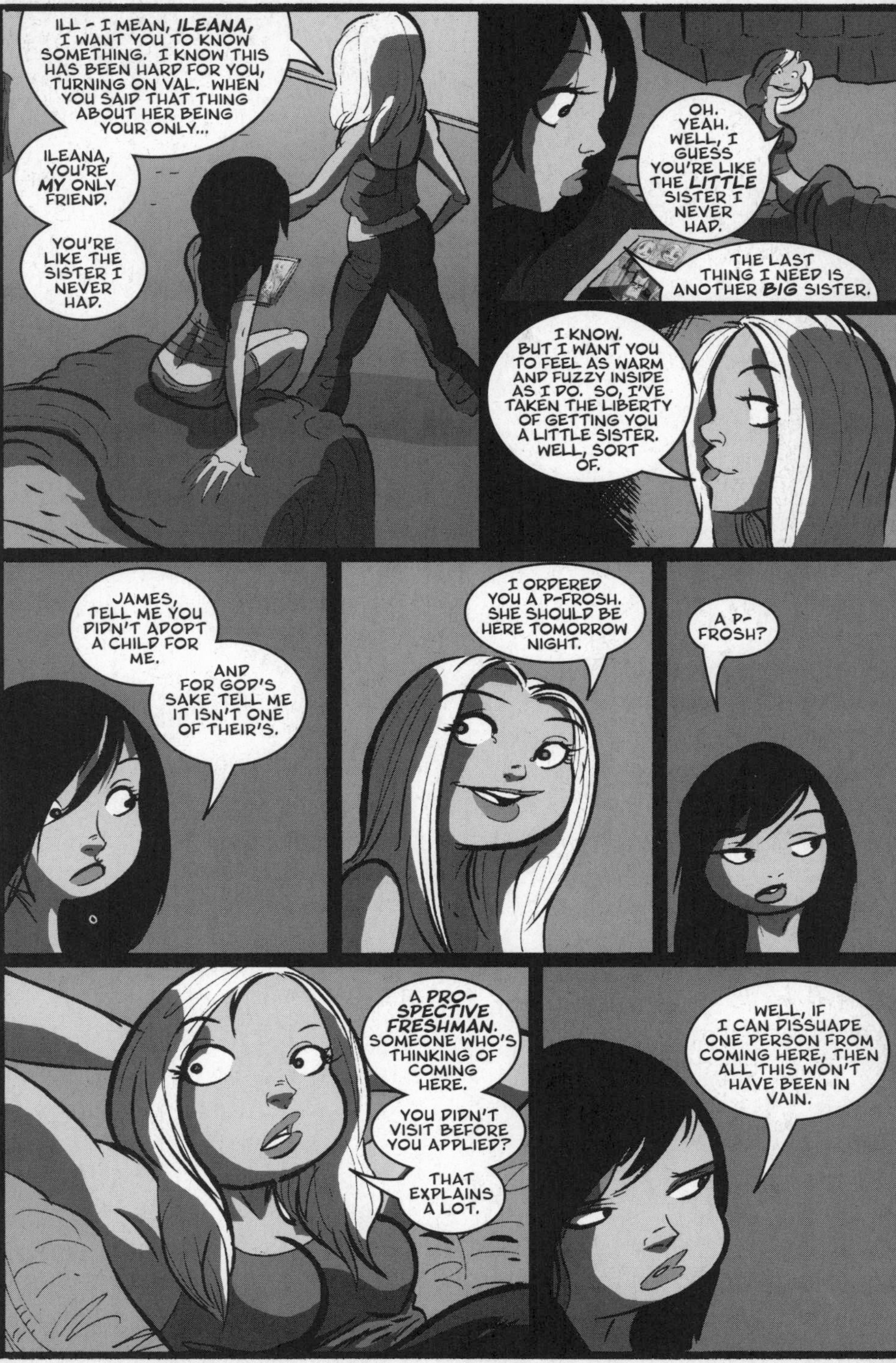
ILL - I MEAN, ILEANA, I WANT YOU TO KNOW SOMETHING. I KNOW THIS HAS BEEN HARD FOR YOU, TURNING ON VAL. WHEN YOU SAID THAT THING ABOUT HER BEING YOUR ONLY...
ILEANA, YOU'RE MY ONLY FRIEND.
YOU'RE LIKE THE SISTER I NEVER HAD.
OH. YEAH. WELL, I GUESS YOU'RE LIKE THE LITTLE SISTER I NEVER HAD.
THE LAST THING I NEED IS ANOTHER BIG SISTER.
I KNOW. BUT I WANT YOU TO FEEL AS WARM AND FUZZY INSIDE AS I DO. SO, I'VE TAKEN THE LIBERTY OF GETTING YOU A LITTLE SISTER. WELL, SORT OF.
JAMES, TELL ME YOU DIDN'T ADOPT A CHILD FOR ME.
AND FOR GOD'S SAKE TELL ME IT ISN'T ONE OF THEIR'S.
I ORDERED YOU A P-FROSH. SHE SHOULD BE HERE TOMORROW NIGHT.
A P-FROSH?
A PRO-SPECTIVE FRESHMAN. SOMEONE WHO'S THINKING OF COMING HERE.
YOU DIDN'T VISIT BEFORE YOU APPLIED?
THAT EXPLAINS A LOT.
WELL, IF I CAN DISSUADE ONE PERSON FROM COMING HERE, THEN ALL THIS WON'T HAVE BEEN IN VAIN.

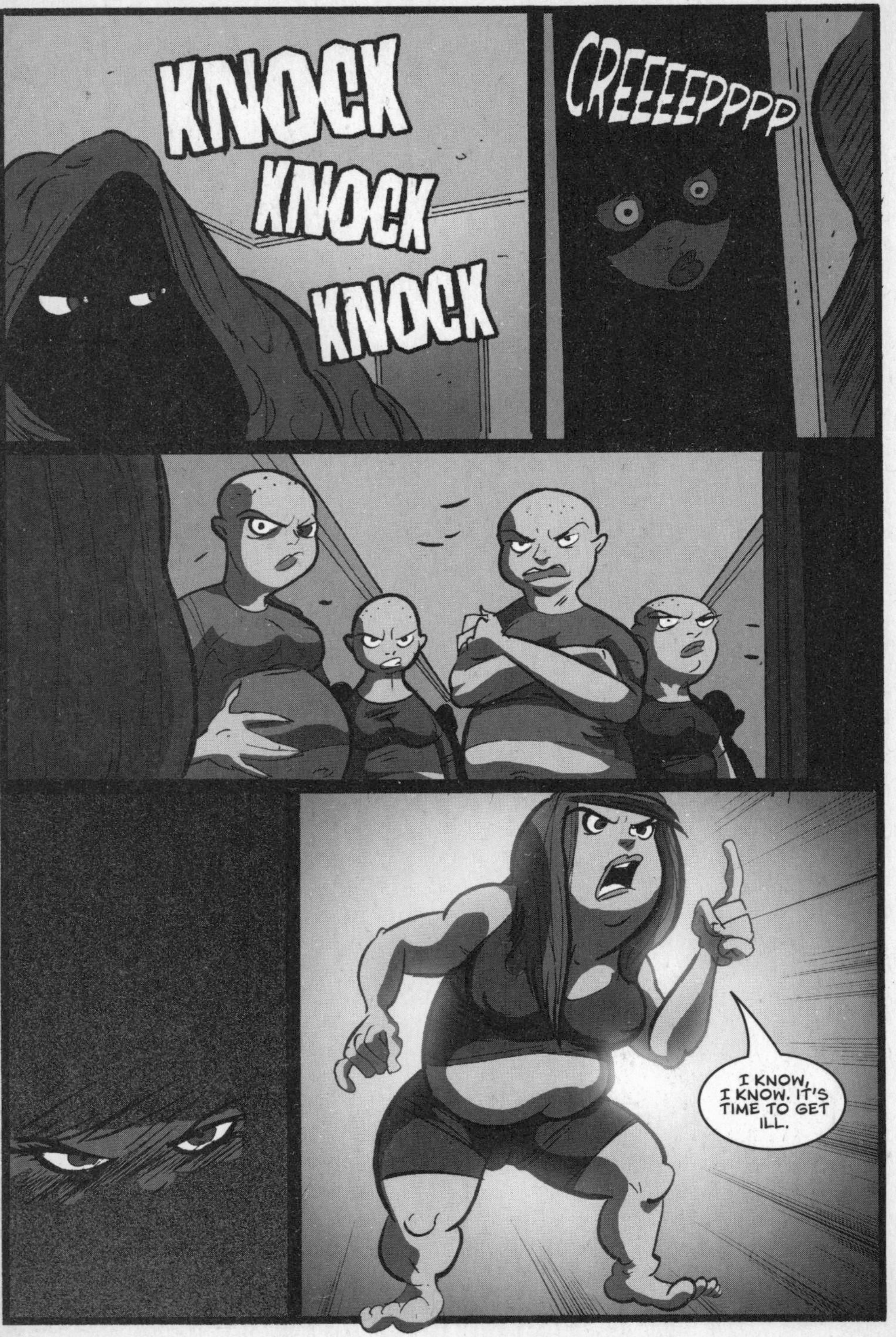
KNOCK
KNOCK
KNOCK
CREEEEEPPPP
I KNOW, I KNOW. IT'S TIME TO GET ILL.

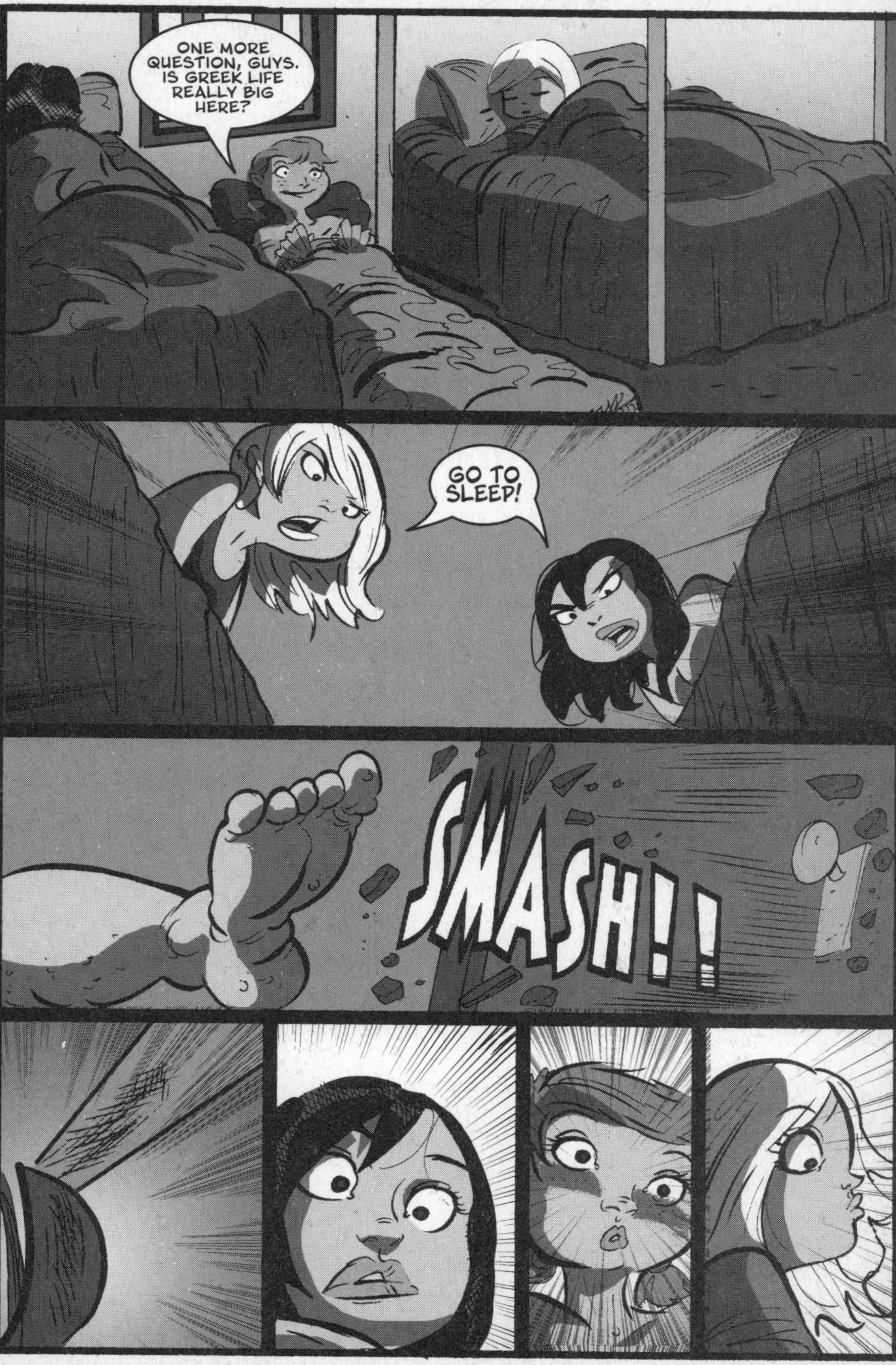
ONE MORE QUESTION, GUYS. IS GREEK LIFE REALLY BIG HERE?
GO TO SLEEP!
SMASH!!

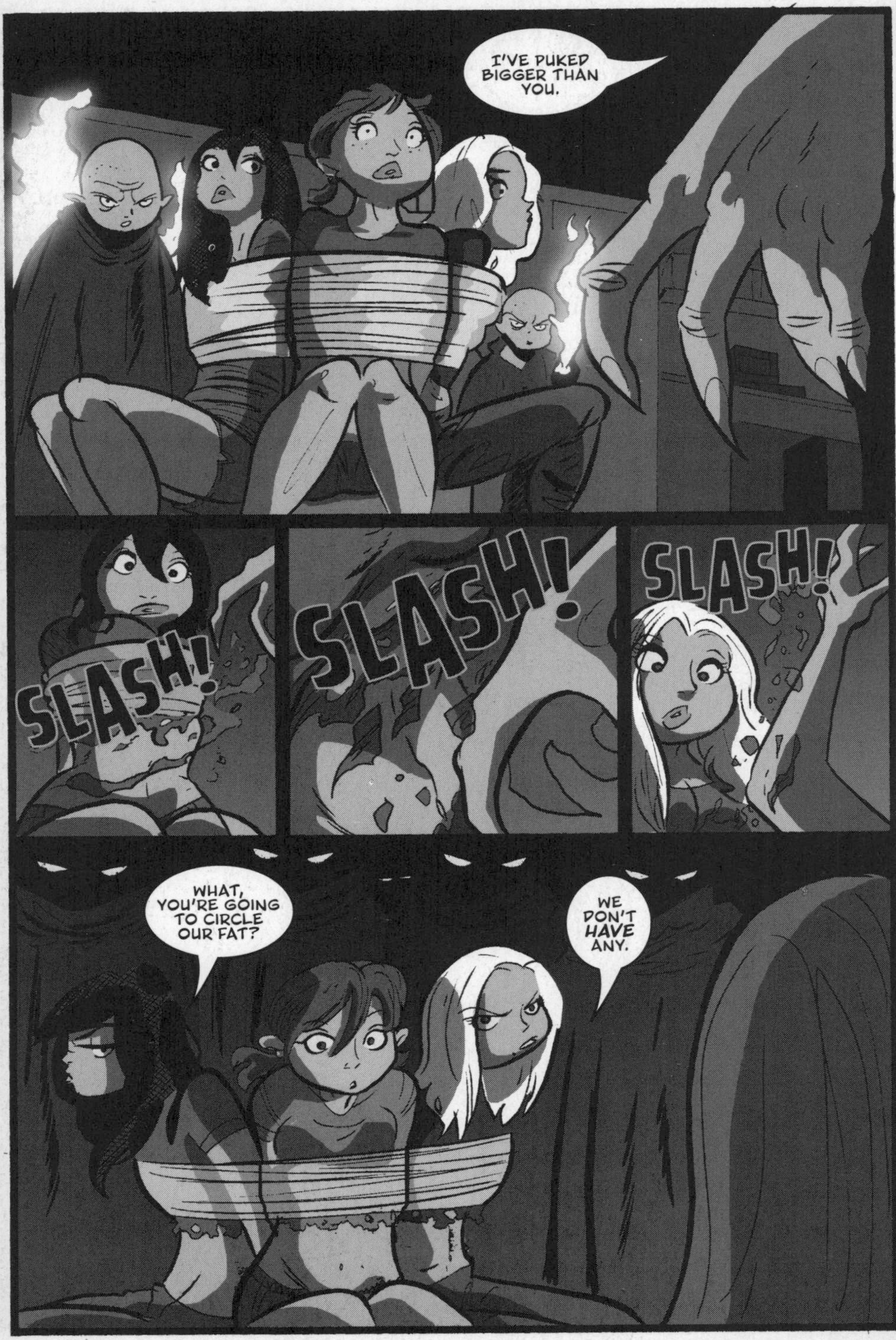
I'VE PUKED BIGGER THAN YOU.
SLASH!
SLASH!
SLASH!
WHAT, YOU'RE GOING TO CIRCLE OUR FAT?
WE DON'T HAVE ANY.

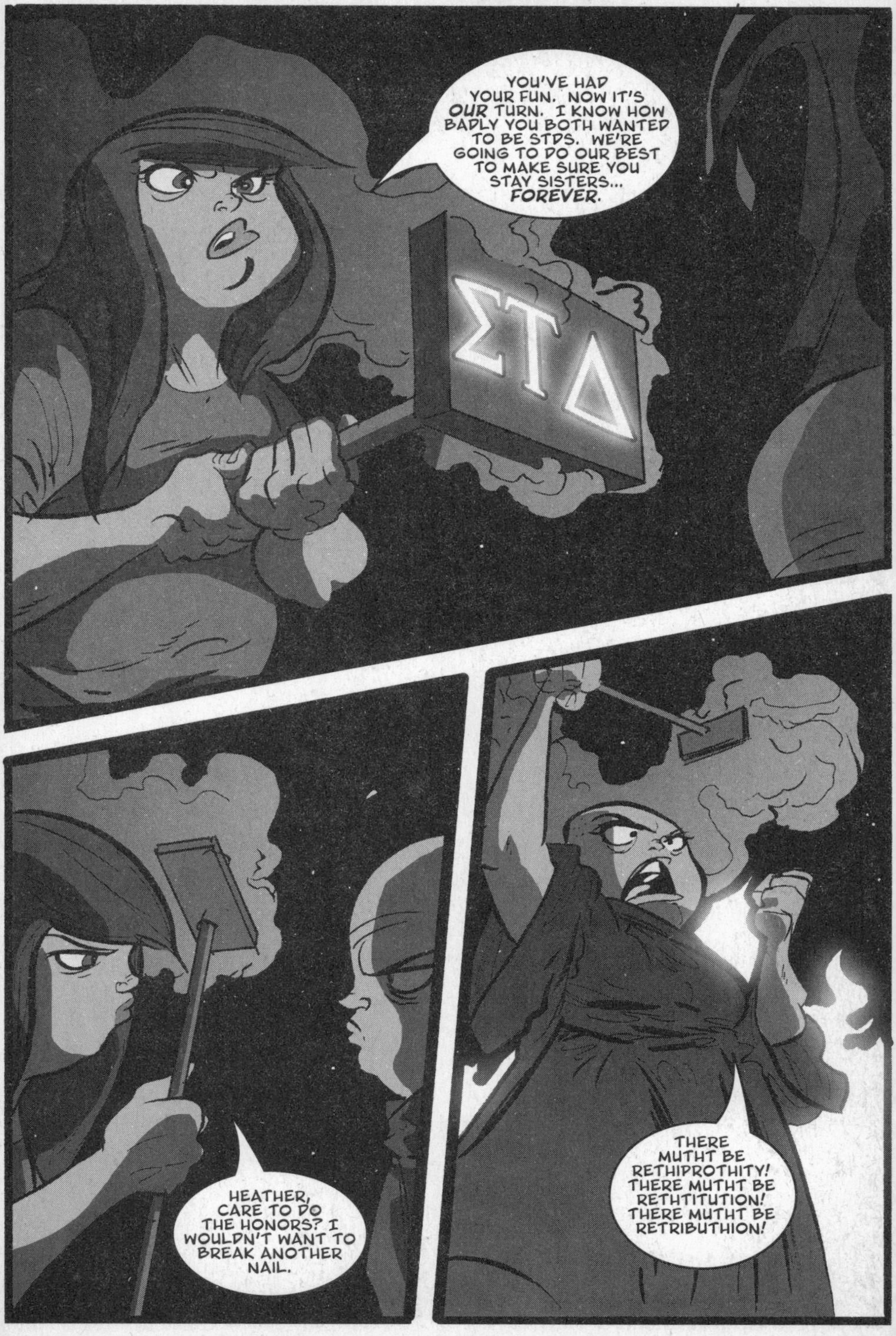

YOU'VE HAD YOUR FUN. NOW IT'S OUR TURN. I KNOW HOW BADLY YOU BOTH WANTED TO BE STDS. WE'RE GOING TO DO OUR BEST TO MAKE SURE YOU STAY SISTERS... FOREVER.
ΣΤΔ
HEATHER, CARE TO DO THE HONORS? I WOULDN'T WANT TO BREAK ANOTHER NAIL.
THERE MUTHT BE RETHIPROTHITY! THERE MUTHT BE RETHTITUTION! THERE MUTHT BE RETRIBUTHION!

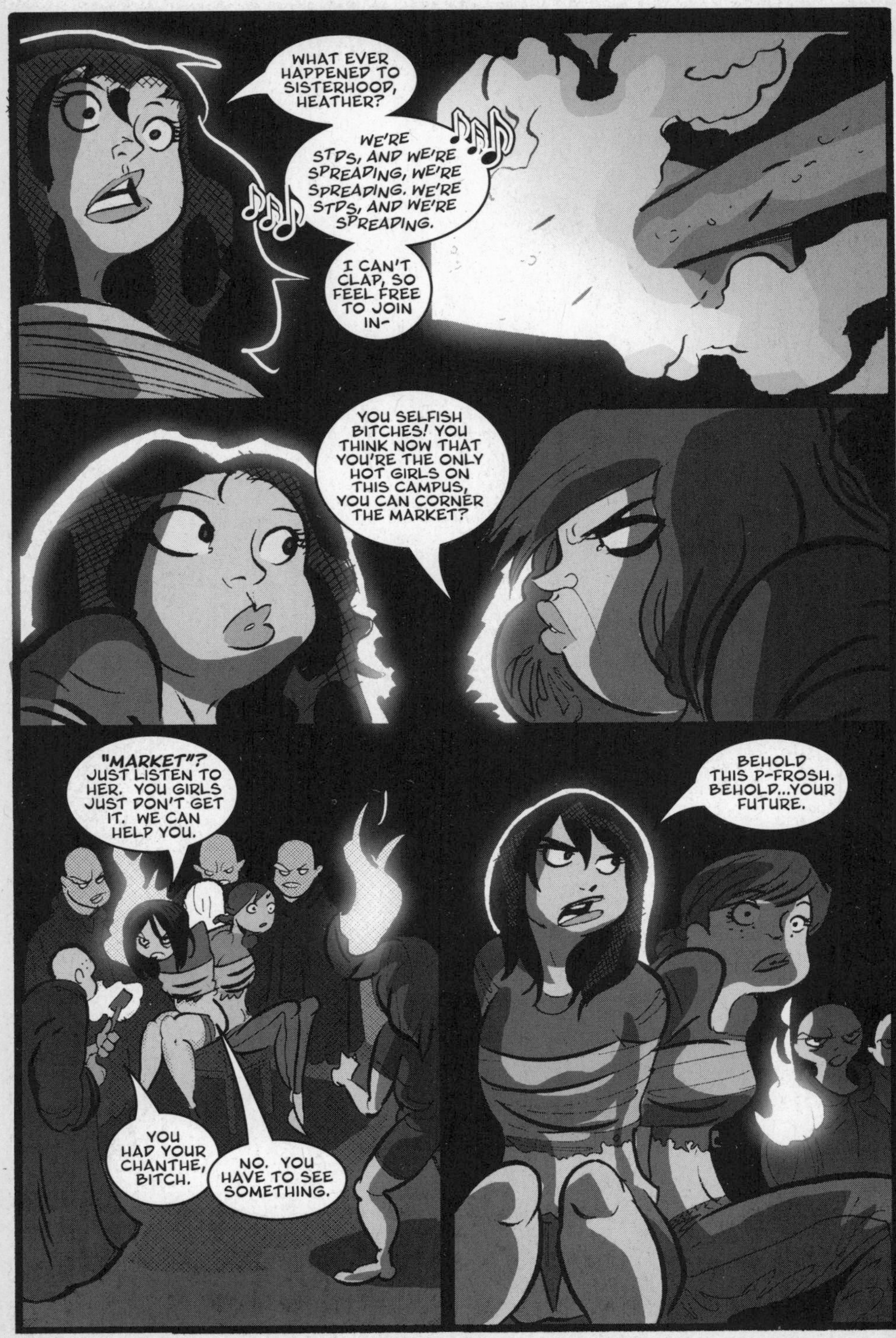
WHAT EVER HAPPENED TO SISTERHOOD, HEATHER?
WE'RE STDS, AND WE'RE SPREADING, WE'RE SPREADING. WE'RE STDS, AND WE'RE SPREADING.
I CAN'T CLAP, SO FEEL FREE TO JOIN IN-
YOU SELFISH BITCHES! YOU THINK NOW THAT YOU'RE THE ONLY HOT GIRLS ON THIS CAMPUS, YOU CAN CORNER THE MARKET?
"MARKET"? JUST LISTEN TO HER. YOU GIRLS JUST DON'T GET IT. WE CAN HELP YOU.
YOU HAD YOUR CHANTHE, BITCH.
NO. YOU HAVE TO SEE SOMETHING.
BEHOLD THIS P-FROSH. BEHOLD...YOUR FUTURE.

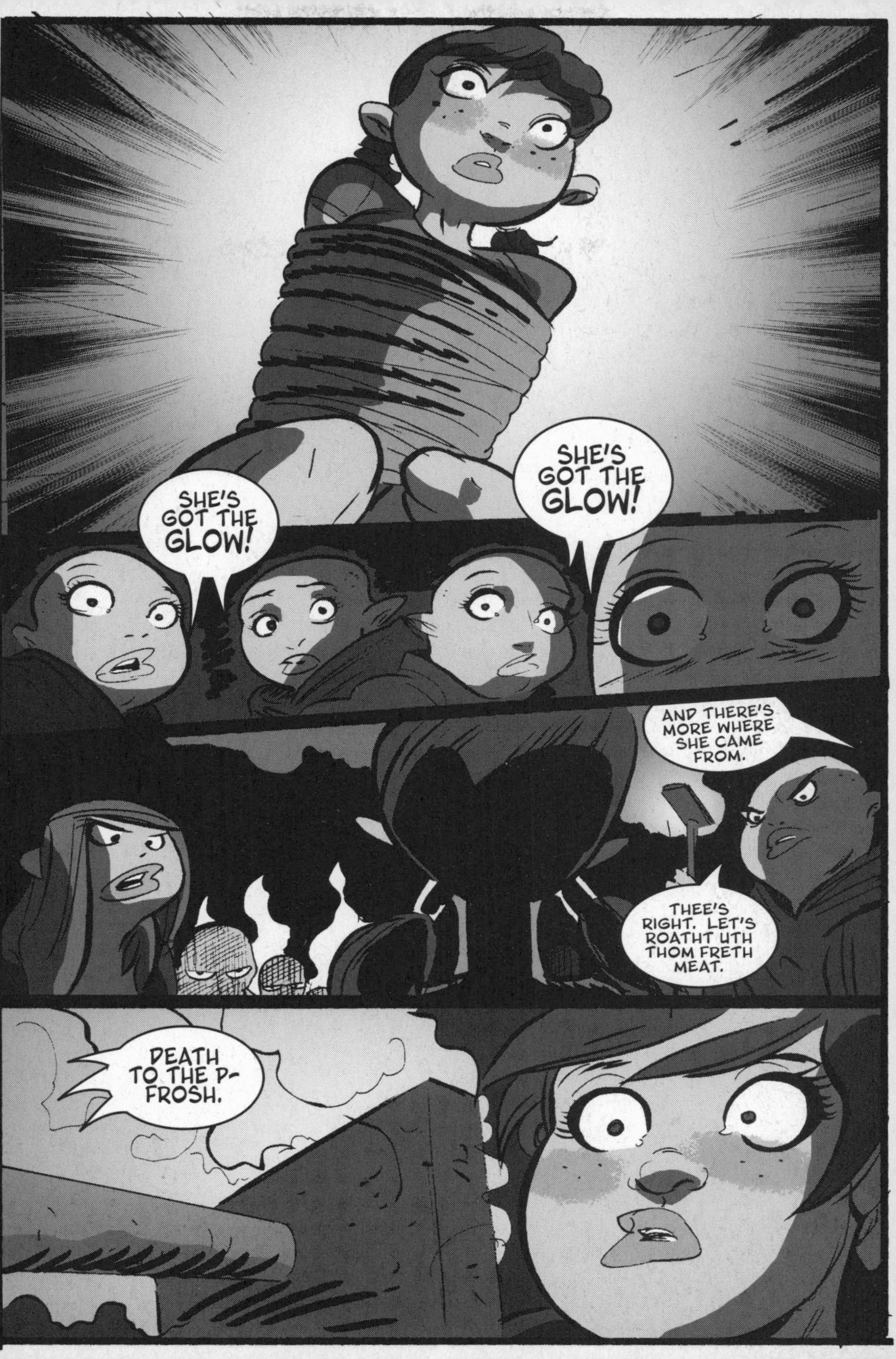
SHE'S GOT THE GLOW!
SHE'S GOT THE GLOW!
AND THERE'S MORE WHERE SHE CAME FROM.
THEE'S RIGHT. LET'S ROATHT UTH THOM FRETH MEAT.
DEATH TO THE P-FROSH.

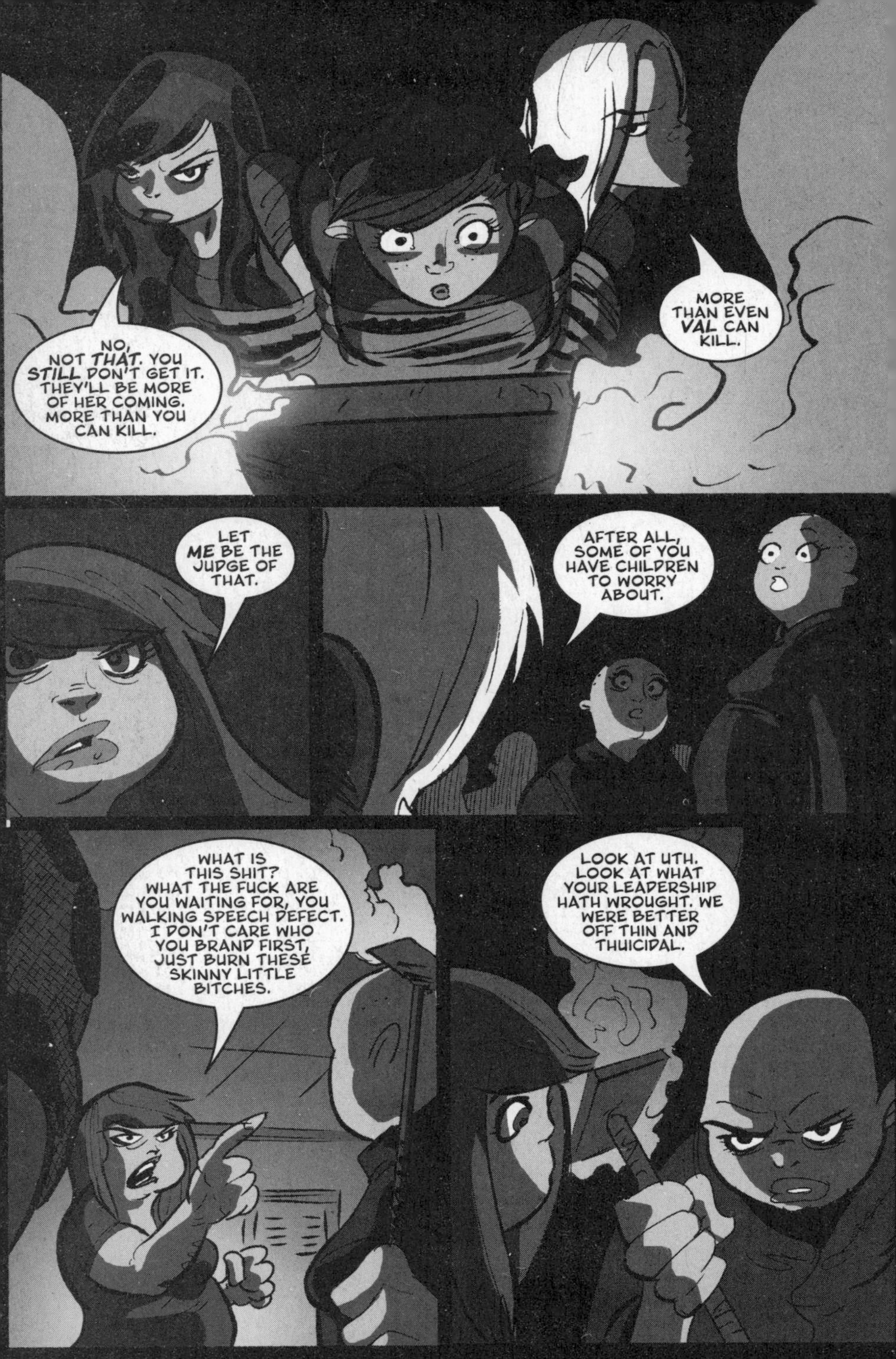

NO, NOT THAT. YOU STILL DON'T GET IT. THEY'LL BE MORE OF HER COMING. MORE THAN YOU CAN KILL.
MORE THAN EVEN VAL CAN KILL.
LET ME BE THE JUDGE OF THAT.
AFTER ALL, SOME OF YOU HAVE CHILDREN TO WORRY ABOUT.
WHAT IS THIS SHIT? WHAT THE FUCK ARE YOU WAITING FOR, YOU WALKING SPEECH DEFECT. I DON'T CARE WHO YOU BRAND FIRST, JUST BURN THESE SKINNY LITTLE BITCHES.
LOOK AT UTH. LOOK AT WHAT YOUR LEADERSHIP HATH WROUGHT. WE WERE BETTER OFF THIN AND THUICIDAL.

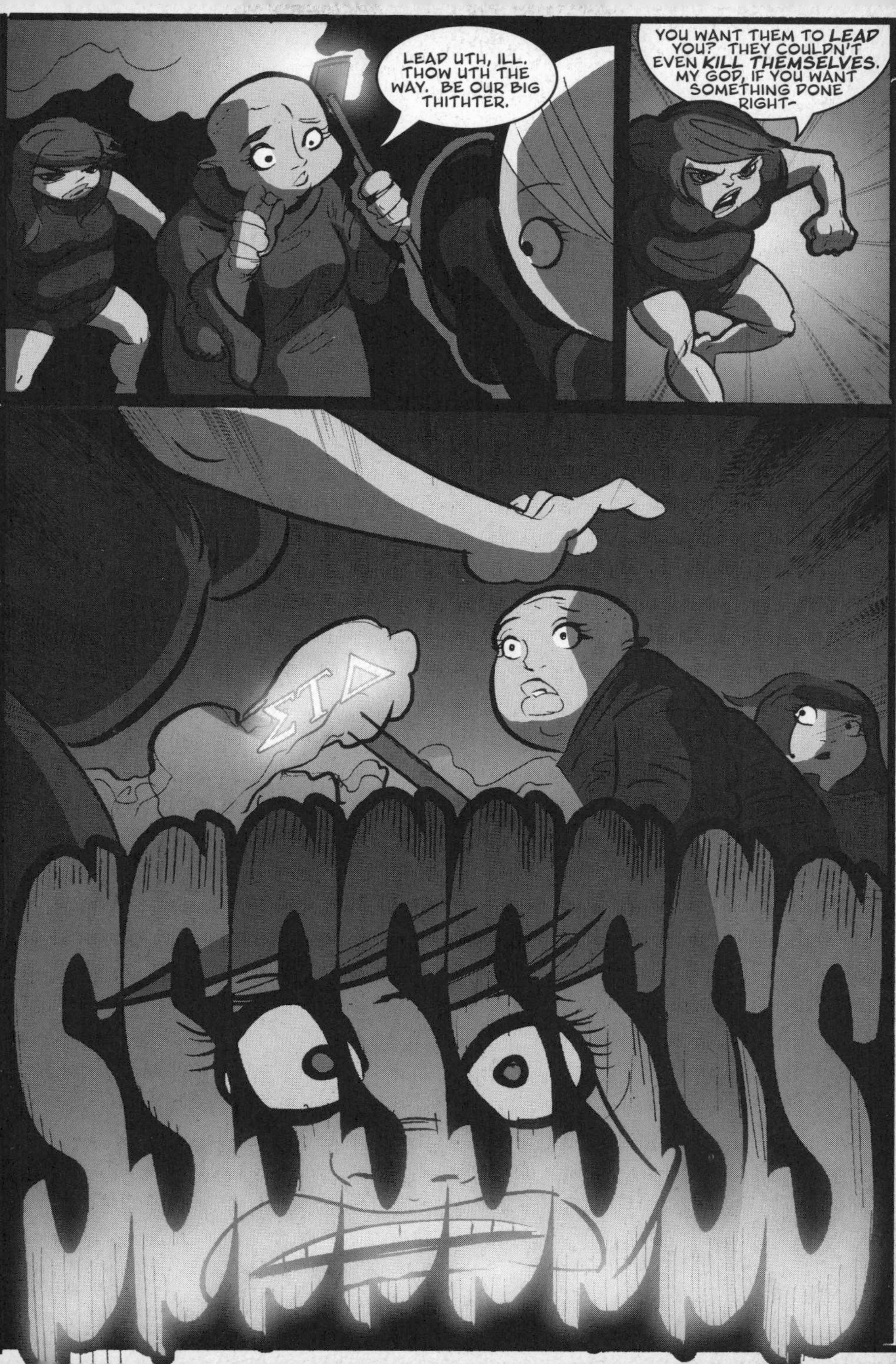
LEAD UTH, ILL. THOW UTH THE WAY. BE OUR BIG THITHTER.
YOU WANT THEM TO LEAD YOU? THEY COULDN'T EVEN KILL THEMSELVES. MY GOD, IF YOU WANT SOMETHING DONE RIGHT-
ΣΤΔ

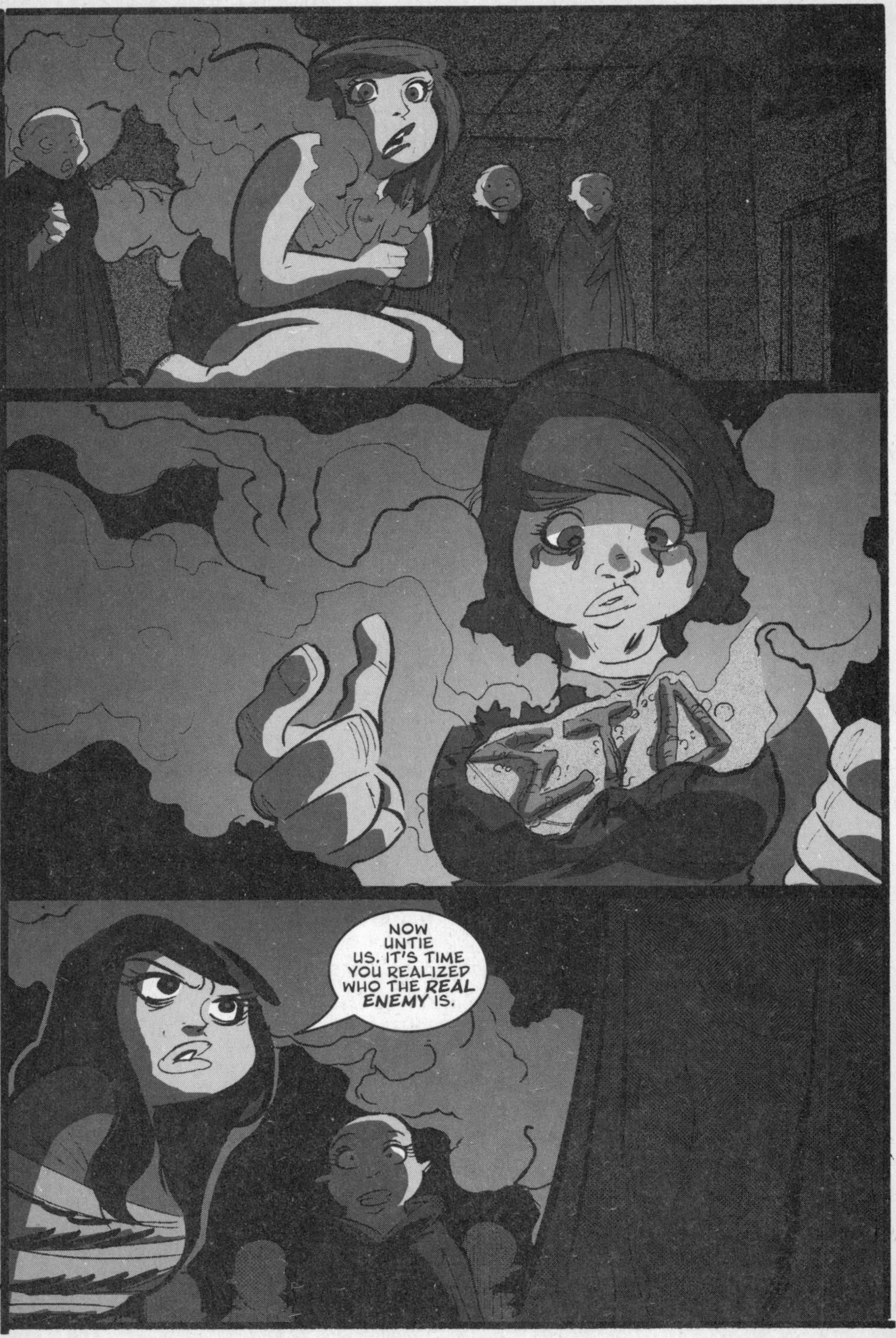
NOW UNTIE US. IT'S TIME YOU REALIZED WHO THE REAL ENEMY IS.

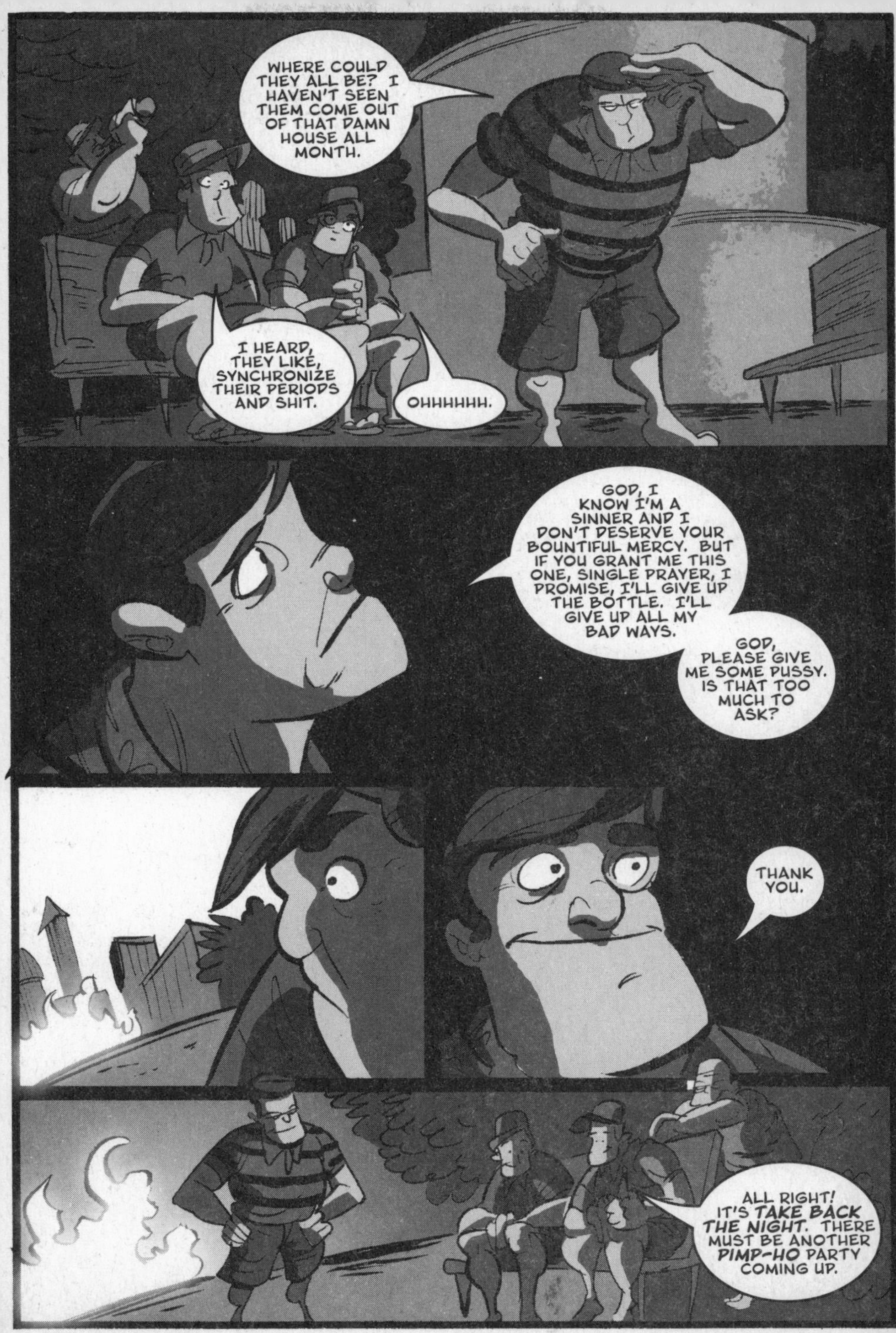
WHERE COULD THEY ALL BE? I HAVEN'T SEEN THEM COME OUT OF THAT DAMN HOUSE ALL MONTH.
I HEARD, THEY LIKE, SYNCHRONIZE THEIR PERIODS AND SHIT.
OHHHHHH.
GOD, I KNOW I'M A SINNER AND I DON'T DESERVE YOUR BOUNTIFUL MERCY. BUT IF YOU GRANT ME THIS ONE, SINGLE PRAYER, I PROMISE, I'LL GIVE UP THE BOTTLE. I'LL GIVE UP ALL MY BAD WAYS.
GOD, PLEASE GIVE ME SOME PUSSY. IS THAT TOO MUCH TO ASK?
THANK YOU.
ALL RIGHT! IT'S *TAKE BACK THE NIGHT*. THERE MUST BE ANOTHER *PIMP-HO* PARTY COMING UP.

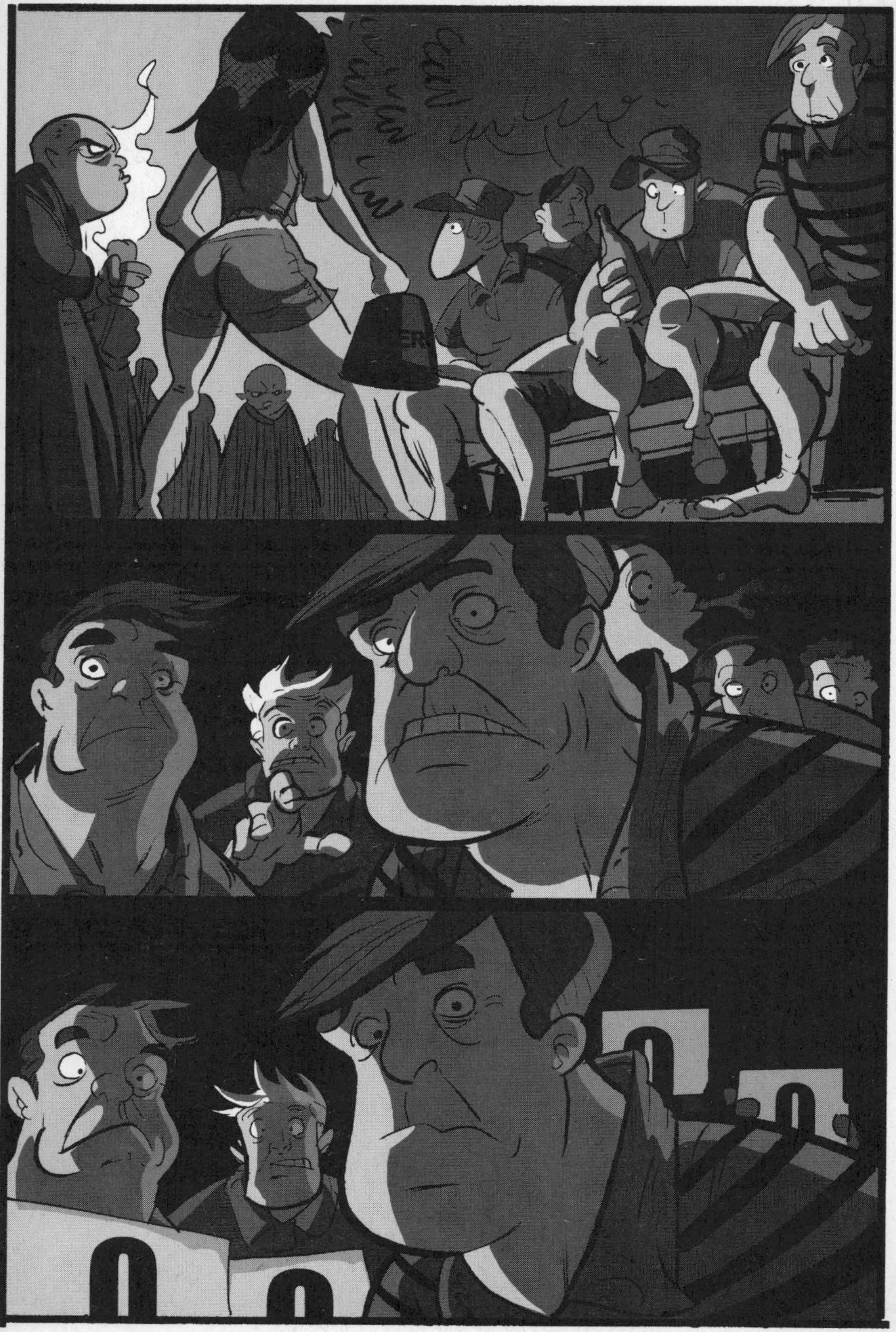

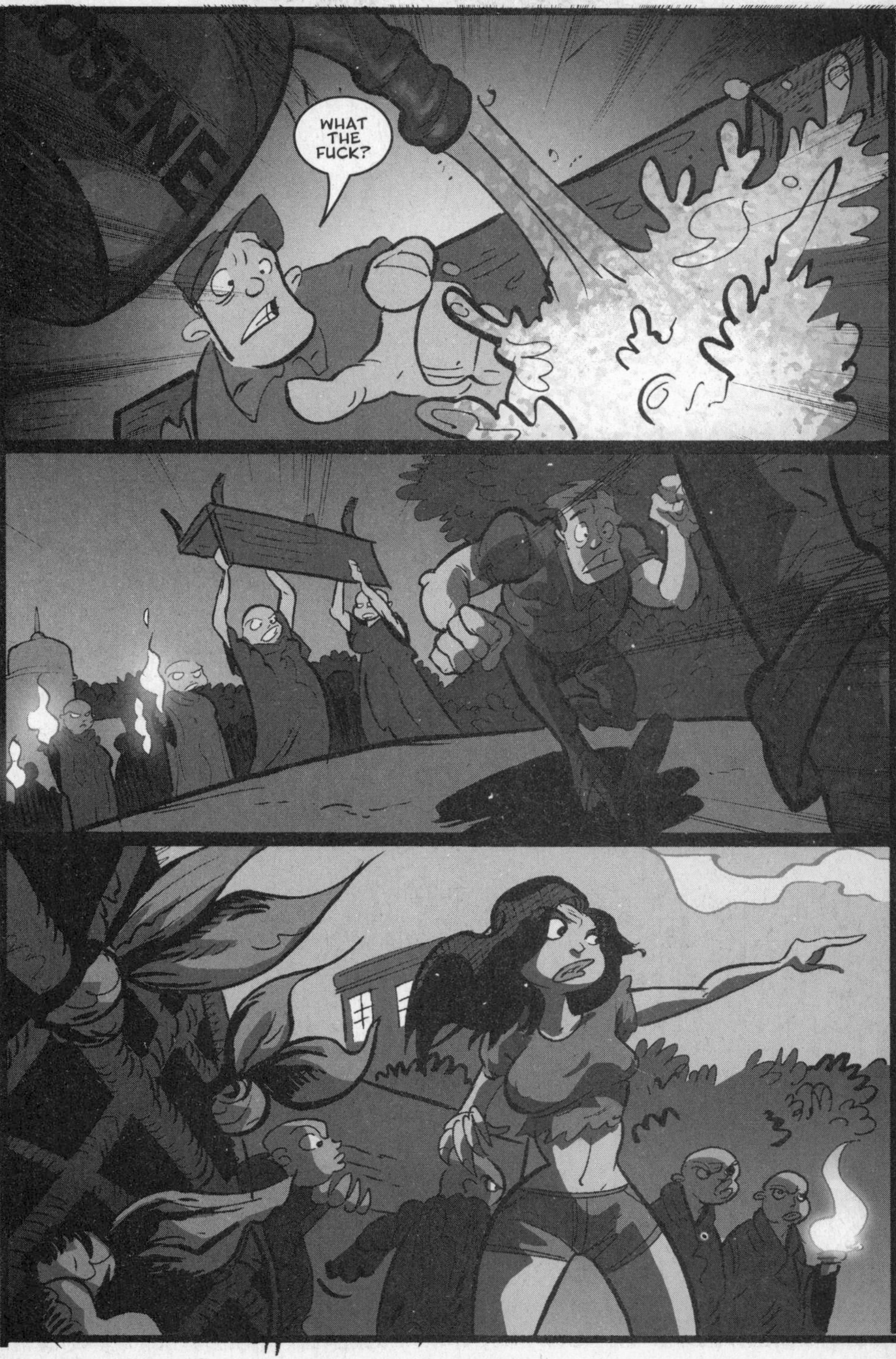
WHAT THE FUCK?

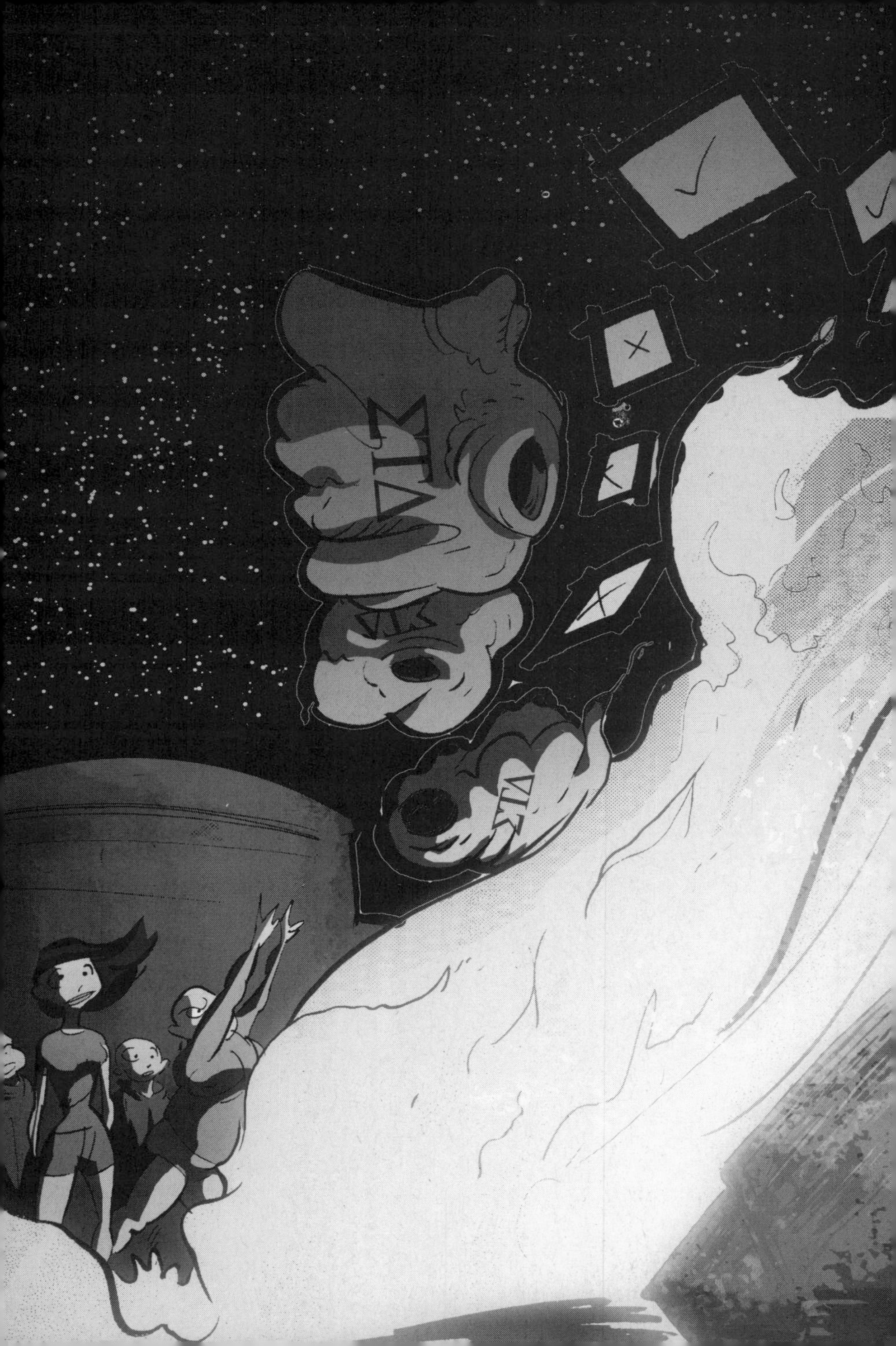

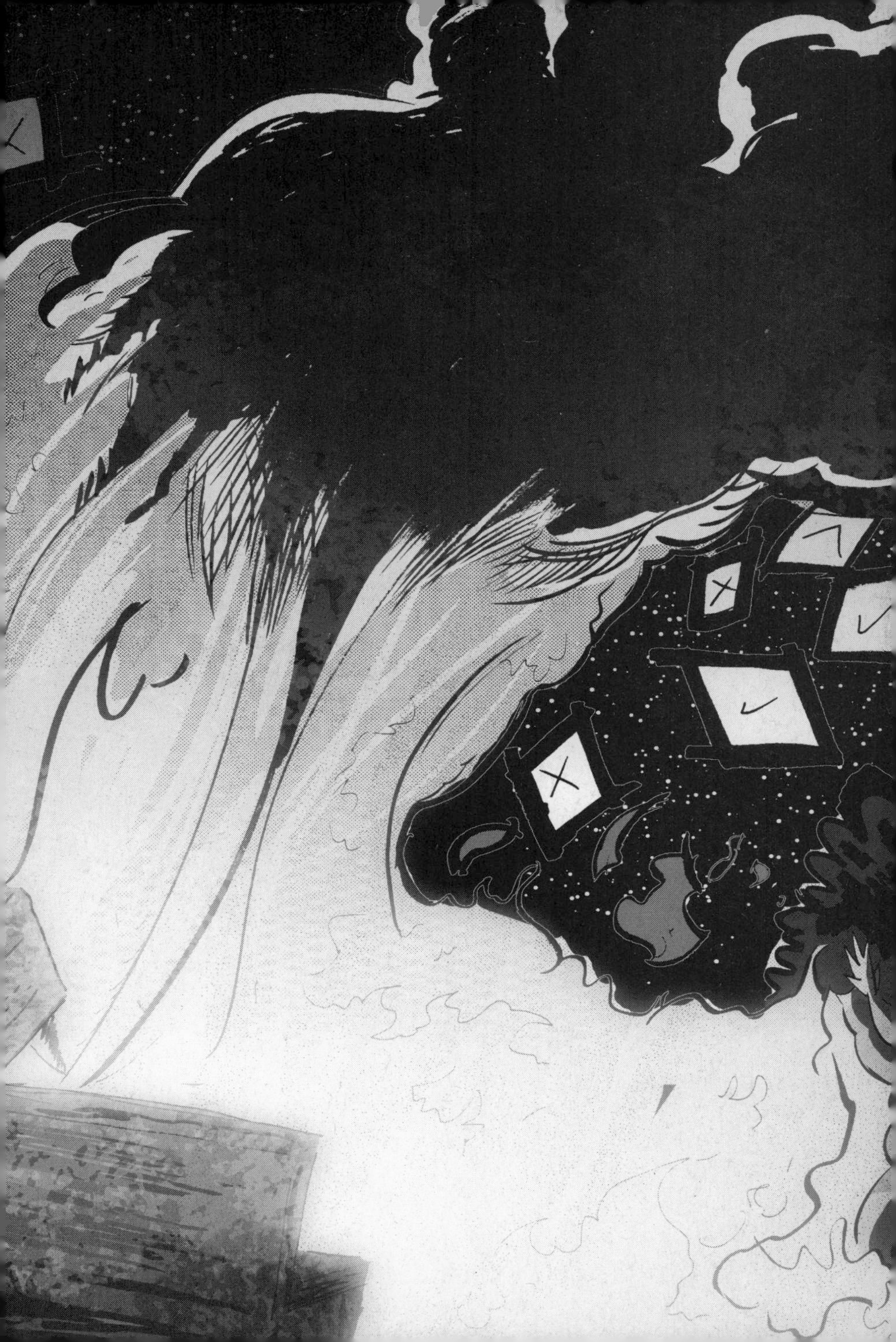

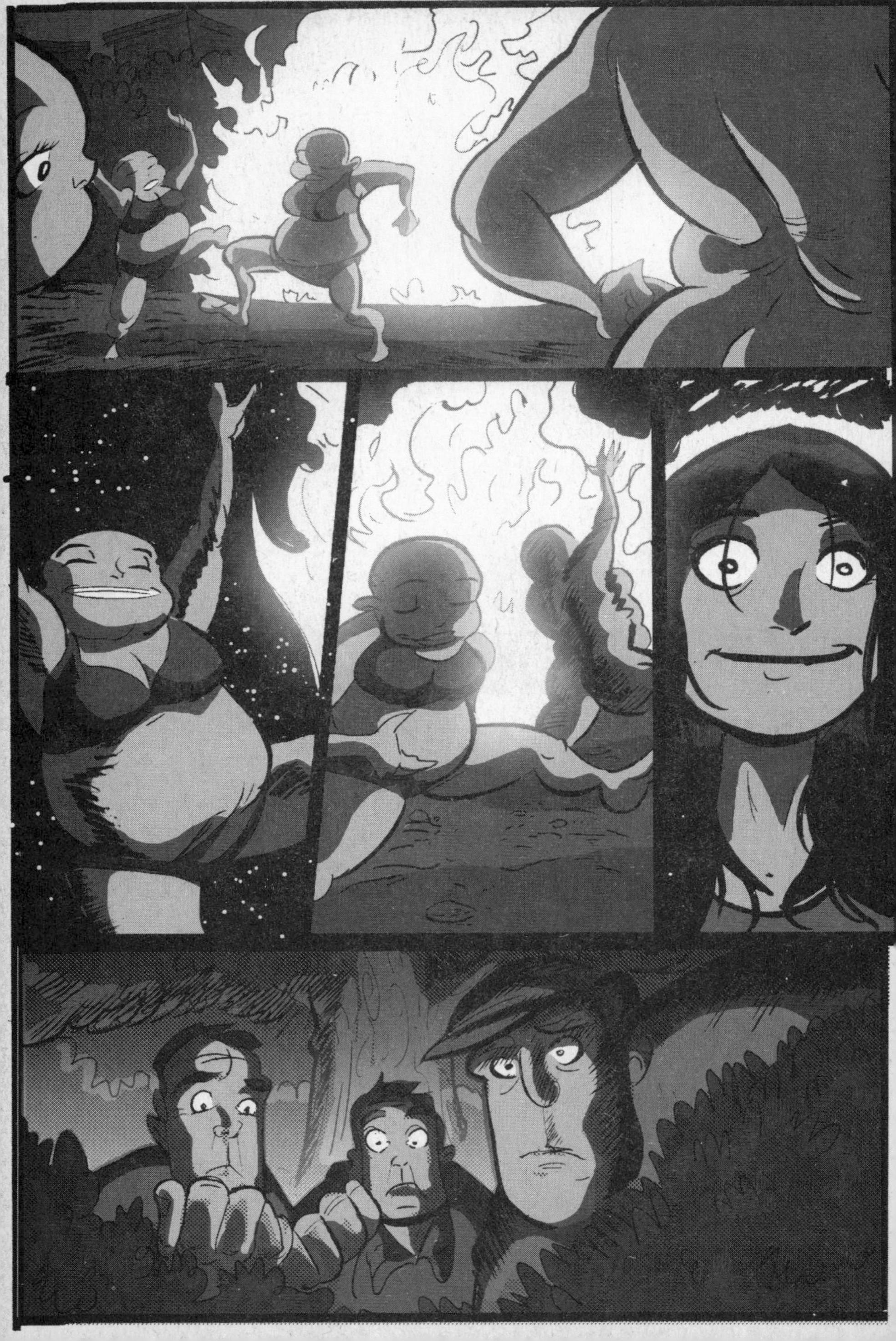

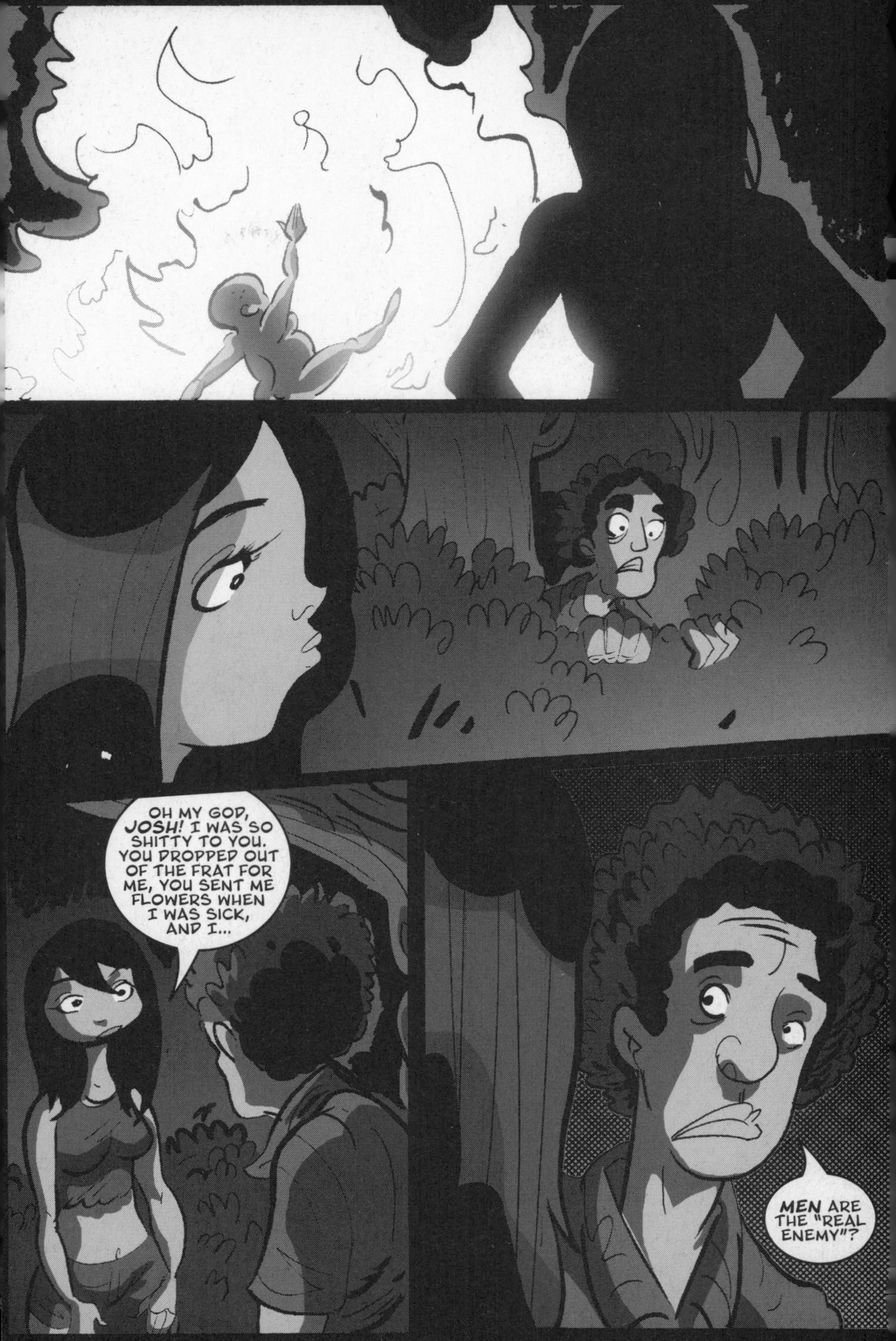
OH MY GOD, JOSH! I WAS SO SHITTY TO YOU. YOU DROPPED OUT OF THE FRAT FOR ME, YOU SENT ME FLOWERS WHEN I WAS SICK, AND I...
MEN ARE THE "REAL ENEMY"?

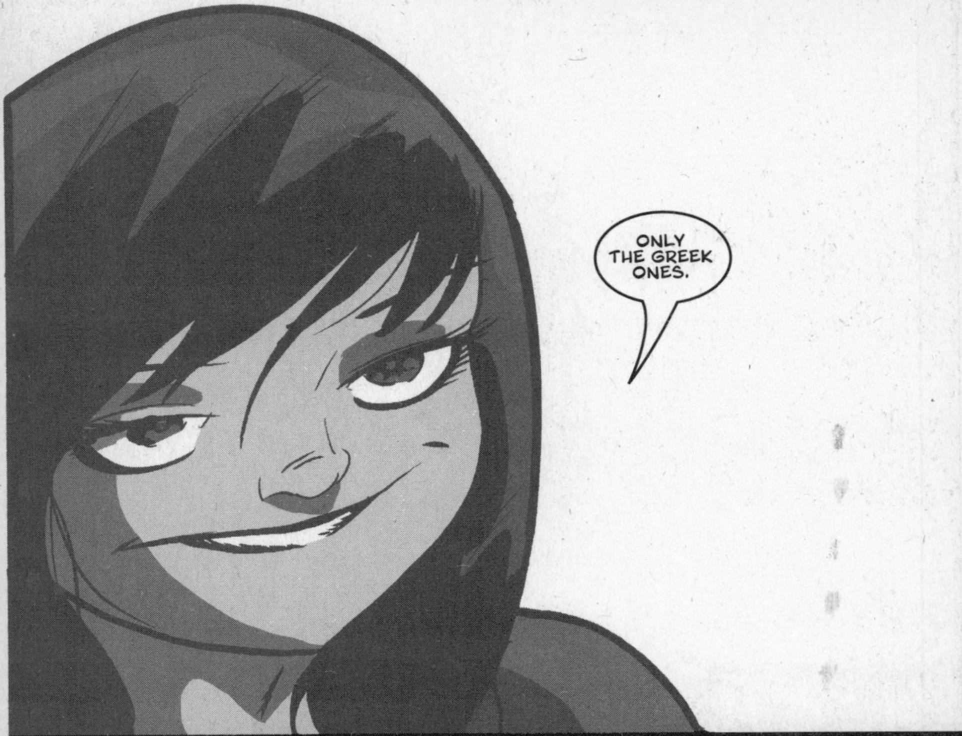
ONLY THE GREEK ONES.

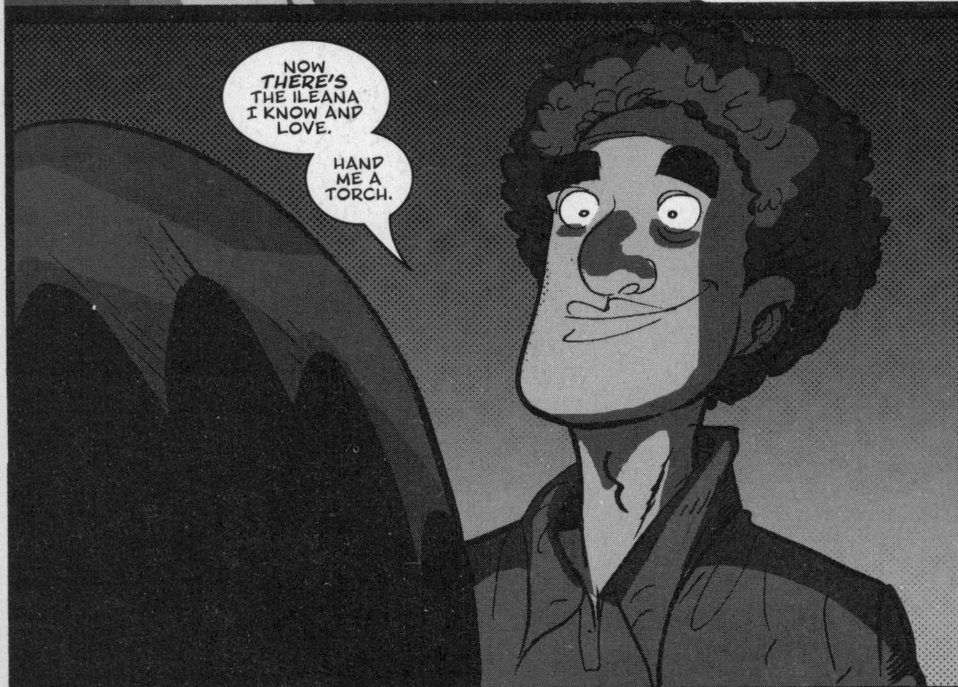
NOW THERE'S THE ILEANA I KNOW AND LOVE.
HAND ME A TORCH.

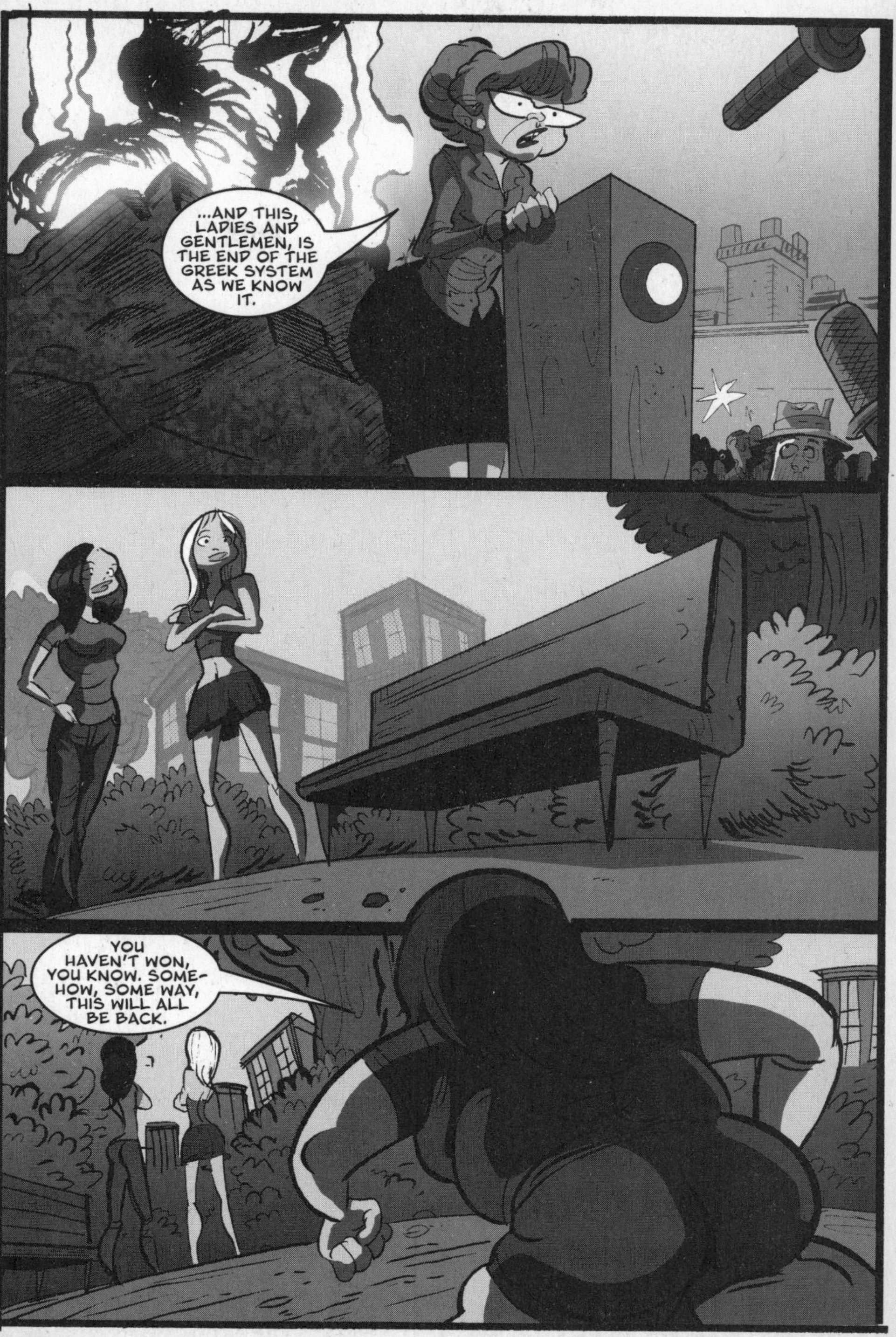
...AND THIS, LADIES AND GENTLEMEN, IS THE END OF THE GREEK SYSTEM AS WE KNOW IT.
YOU HAVEN'T WON, YOU KNOW. SOME-HOW, SOME WAY, THIS WILL ALL BE BACK.

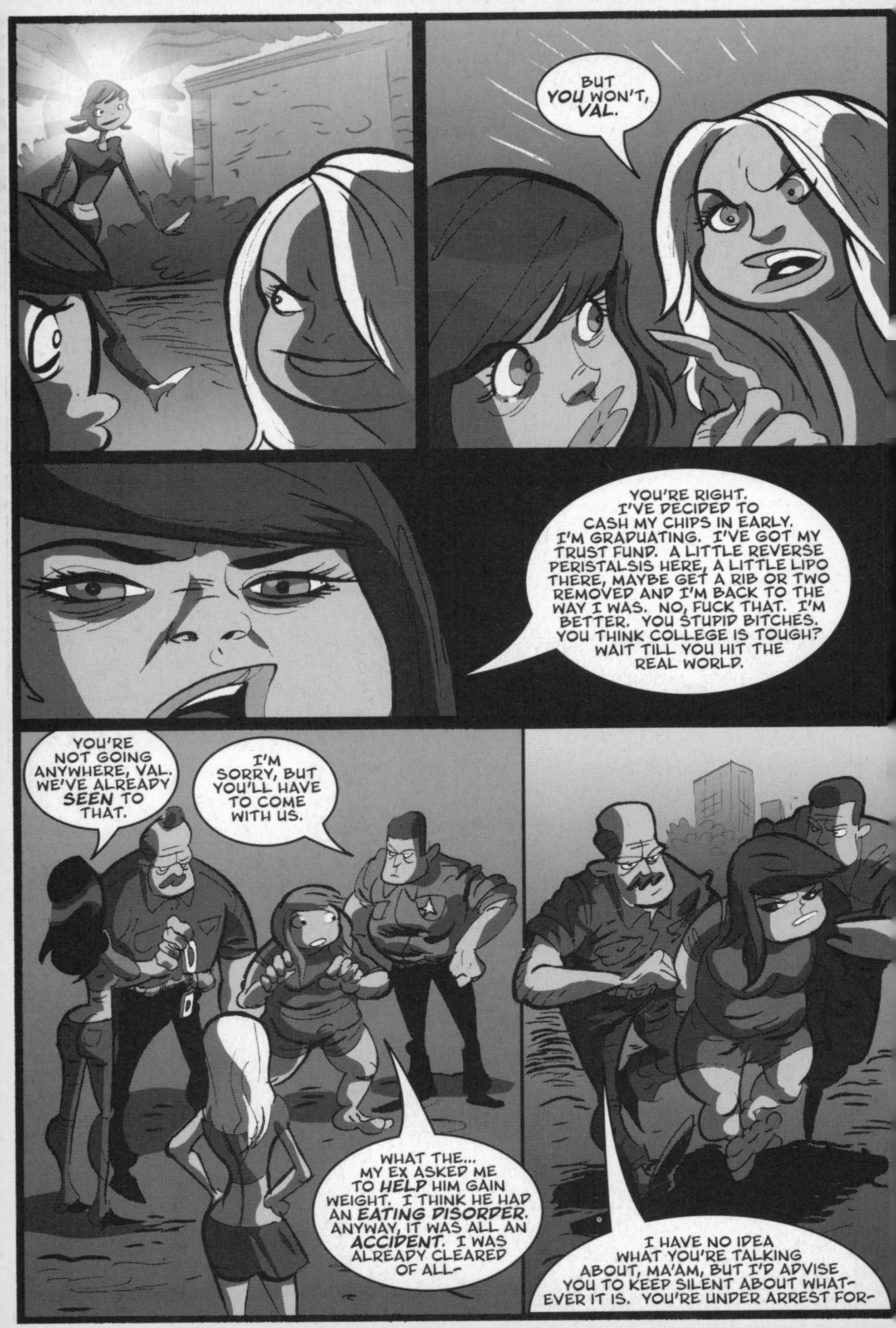
BUT YOU WON'T, VAL.
YOU'RE RIGHT. I'VE DECIDED TO CASH MY CHIPS IN EARLY. I'M GRADUATING. I'VE GOT MY TRUST FUND. A LITTLE REVERSE PERISTALSIS HERE, A LITTLE LIPO THERE, MAYBE GET A RIB OR TWO REMOVED AND I'M BACK TO THE WAY I WAS. NO, FUCK THAT. I'M BETTER. YOU STUPID BITCHES. YOU THINK COLLEGE IS TOUGH? WAIT TILL YOU HIT THE REAL WORLD.
YOU'RE NOT GOING ANYWHERE, VAL. WE'VE ALREADY SEEN TO THAT.
I'M SORRY, BUT YOU'LL HAVE TO COME WITH US.
WHAT THE... MY EX ASKED ME TO HELP HIM GAIN WEIGHT. I THINK HE HAD AN EATING DISORDER. ANYWAY, IT WAS ALL AN ACCIDENT. I WAS ALREADY CLEARED OF ALL-
I HAVE NO IDEA WHAT YOU'RE TALKING ABOUT, MA'AM, BUT I'D ADVISE YOU TO KEEP SILENT ABOUT WHAT-EVER IT IS. YOU'RE UNDER ARREST FOR-

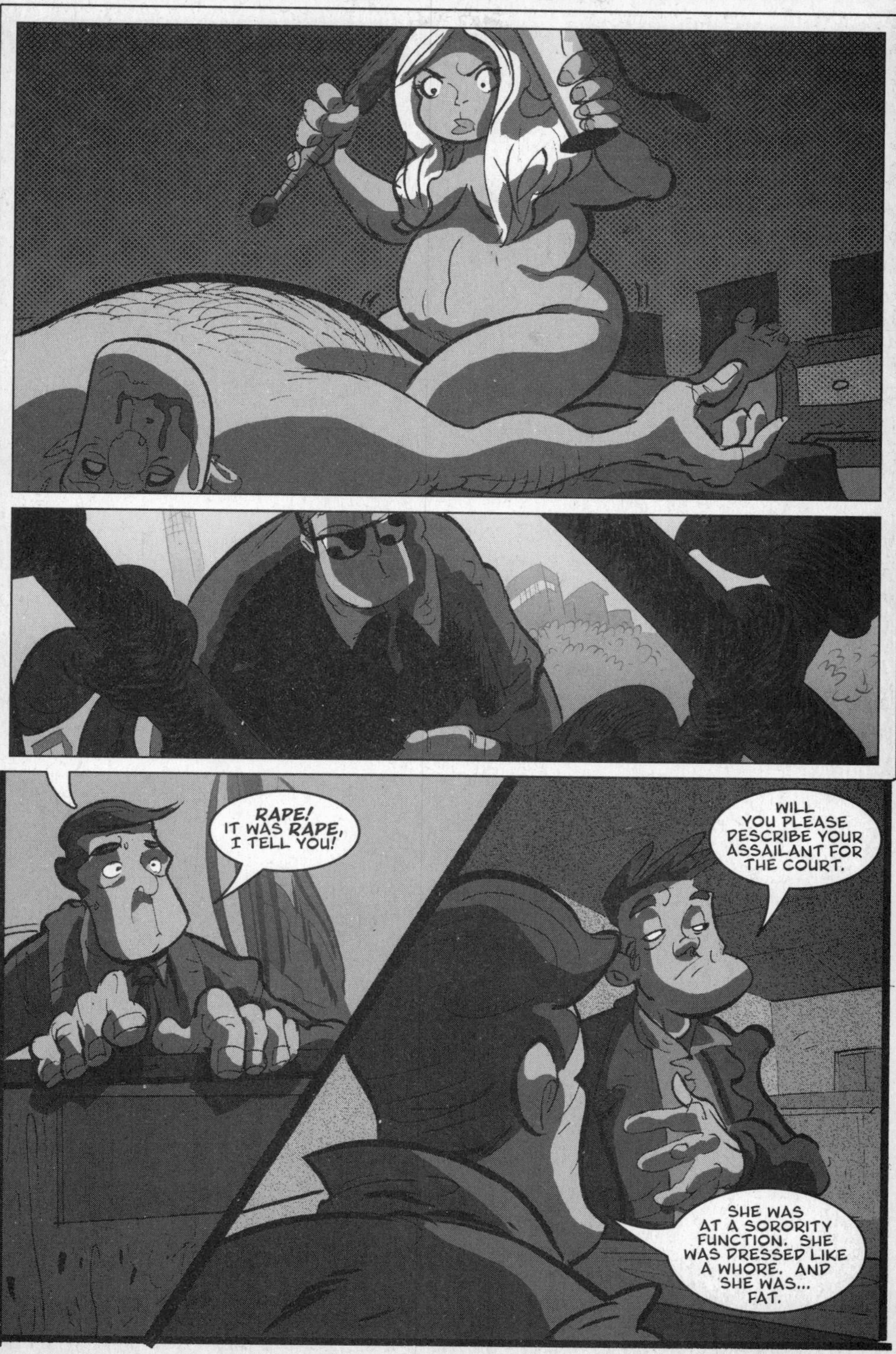
RAPE! IT WAS RAPE, I TELL YOU!
WILL YOU PLEASE DESCRIBE YOUR ASSAILANT FOR THE COURT.
SHE WAS AT A SORORITY FUNCTION. SHE WAS DRESSED LIKE A WHORE. AND SHE WAS... FAT.

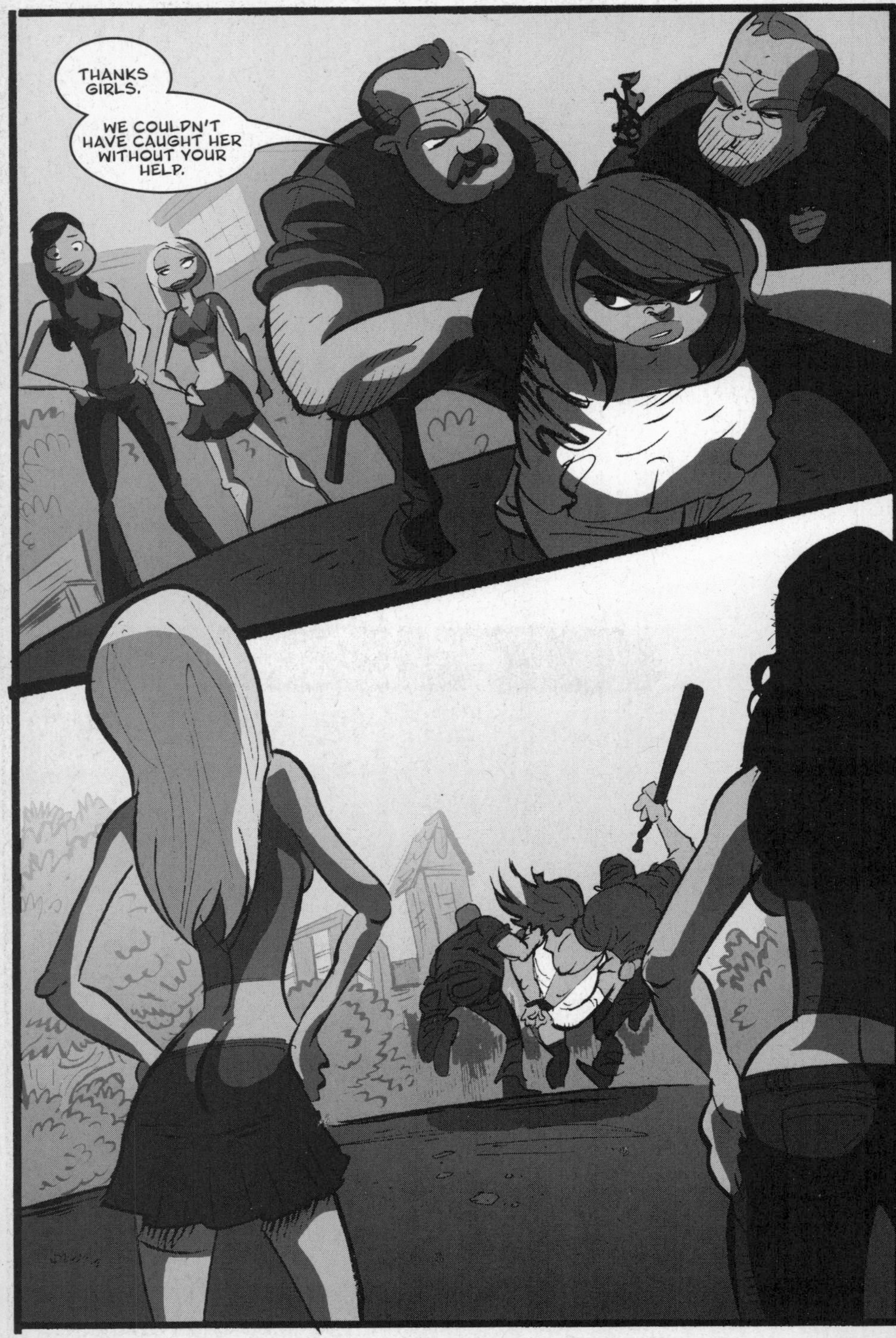
THANKS GIRLS.
WE COULDN'T HAVE CAUGHT HER WITHOUT YOUR HELP.